D0908726

THE HOLY BUREAUCRAT

The Holy Bureaucrat

Eudes Rigaud and Religious Reform in Thirteenth-Century Normandy

Adam J. Davis

Cornell University Press
Ithaca and London

First published 2006 by Cornell University Press

Printed in the United States of America

Library of Congress Cataloging-in-Publication Data

Davis, Adam Jeffrey, 1973–
   The holy bureaucrat : Eudes Rigaud and religious reform in
thirteenth-century Normandy / Adam Jeffrey Davis.
      p. cm.
   Includes bibliographical references and index.
   ISBN-13: 978-0-8014-4474-6 (cloth : alk. paper)
   ISBN-10: 0-8014-4474-8 (cloth : alk. paper)
   1. Odo Rigaldus, Archbishop of Rouen, d. 1275.
2. Bishops—France—Normandy—Biography.
3. Franciscans—France—Normandy—Biography.
4. Normandy (France)—Church history.   I. Title.
BX4705.R54D35 2006
282.092—dc22
[B]
                                                                  2006006527

Cornell University Press strives to use environmentally
responsible suppliers and materials to the fullest extent
possible in the publishing of its books. Such materials include
vegetable-based, low-VOC inks and acid-free papers that are
recycled, totally chlorine-free, or partly composed of
nonwood fibers. For further information, visit our website at
www.cornellpress.cornell.edu.

Cloth printing   10 9 8 7 6 5 4 3 2 1

For Alexandra

Contents

Acknowledgments

It is a pleasure to be able to thank those who have helped make this book possible. My greatest intellectual debt is to my teachers. A course with Jaroslav Pelikan that I took as an undergraduate first sparked my interest in medieval history. In graduate school, over lunches at the Institute for Advanced Study, Giles Constable helped me think in new ways about medieval religious life. Drawing on his own experience of writing the biography of a much more famous bishop, Peter Brown helped me frame difficult conceptual issues. Anthony Grafton gave careful readings of my drafts and wisely encouraged me to broaden my horizons by considering parallel examples outside France and in different historical periods. Most of all, I owe an immeasurable debt of gratitude to my adviser, William Chester Jordan, who has been exceptionally generous over the years in the many ways he has provided instruction and guidance. His own example as a scholar has served as an inspiration.

Research has been generously supported by the Department of History at Princeton University, the Chateaubriand Foundation, and Denison University. Two of the chapters of this book appeared in earlier forms. Earlier versions of chapter 1 appeared in the *Revue Mabillon* 12 (2001) as "The Formation of a Thirteenth-Century Ecclesiastical Reformer: Eudes Rigaud and the Franciscan *Studium* in Paris" and, under a similar title, in *Medieval Education*, ed. Ronald B. Begley and Joseph W. Koterski, S.J. (New York: Fordham University Press, 2005). An earlier version of chapter 7 was published in the *Journal of Ecclesiastical History* 56, no. 3 (2005), as "A Thirteenth-Century Franciscan Money Manager: Archbishop Eudes Rigaud of Rouen, 1248–1275."

I wish to thank the courteous and helpful librarians and archivists at the Bibliothèque Nationale de France, the Institut de Recherche et d'Histoire des Textes in Orléans and Paris, the Archives de la Seine-Maritime in Rouen, the municipal library of Arras, Princeton University's Firestone Library, the Princeton Theological Seminary's Speer Library, Yale University's Sterling Memorial Library, Columbia University's Butler Library, the New York Public Library, the Library of Congress, the Ohio State University's Thomson Library, and Denison University's Doane Library.

This book benefited from the input of my fellow graduate students in medieval history at Princeton. I also wish to thank several colleagues at other institutions: Nicole Bériou, Marielle Lamy, Alain Boureau, Katherine Jansen, and Paul Freedman. I owe a special debt of gratitude to the anonymous readers for Cornell University Press for reviewing the manuscript so thoroughly and expertly. I'm also grateful to John Ackerman, director of the Press, for his encouragement.

At Denison University, I am fortunate to be surrounded by wonderfully supportive colleagues. Meghan Vesper helped with the preparation of the bibliography. I also offer warm thanks to a number of close friends, now in different parts of the country, who have patiently watched this book come to fruition: Reinier Leushuis, Samuel and Elizabeth Dyson, Richard Bennett, Deborah Peikes, and Arnold Franklin.

Finally, I wish to thank my family, and in particular, my parents, Toni and David Davis, for their unfailing love and moral encouragement. For many years, my father has shared with me the joys of historical study, and it was especially meaningful to be completing this book at the same time he was finishing a book. I could never have written this book without the loving support of my wife, Alexandra Schimmer. I have often relied on her wise counsel and expert editorial skills. She has lived with the "holy bureaucrat" for a long time and joined me in retracing some of the archbishop's travels to abbeys and churches in the hinterlands of Normandy. This book is for her.

Abbreviations

AD   Archives départementales (followed by département name)

AFH   *Archivum Franciscanum Historicum*

BEC   *Bibliothèque de l'École des Chartes*

BM   Bibliothèque municipale (followed by city)

BnF   Bibliothèque Nationale de France, Paris, Département des manuscrits (lat.: manuscrits latins)

CN   *Cartulaire normand de Philippe-Auguste, Louis VIII, Saint-Louis, et Philippe le Hardi.* Edited by Léopold Delisle. Caen, 1882; reprint, Geneva: Mégariotis, 1978.

CR   *Concilia Rotomagensis provinciae.* 2 vols. Edited by Guillaume Bessin. Rouen: Franciscum Vaultier, 1717.

GC   *Gallia Christiana in provincias ecclesiasticas distributa.* 16 vols. Paris: Ex Typographia Regia, 1715–1865.

HF   *Recueil des historiens des Gaules et de la France.* 24 vols. Edited by M. Bouquet and others. Paris: Aux dépens des librairies, 1738–1904.

LTC   *Layettes du trésor des chartes.* 5 vols. Edited by A. Teulet, J. de Laborde, E. Berger, and H. F. Delaborde. Paris: H. Plon, 1863–1909.

PL   *Patrologia cursus completus . . . Series latina.* 221 vols. Edited by Jacques-Paul Migne. Paris, 1844–64.

RER   *The Register of Eudes of Rouen.* Translated by Sydney M. Brown. Edited by Jeremiah O'Sullivan. New York: Columbia University Press, 1964.

RLS   *Repertorium der Lateinischen Sermones des Mittelalters für die Zeit von 1150–1350.* 11 vols. Edited by J.-B. Schneyer. Münster-Westfalen: Aschendorffsche Verlagsbuchhandlung, 1969–90.

RV   *Regestrum visitationum Archiepiscopi Rothomagensis.* Edited by Th. Bonnin. Rouen: A. Le Brument, 1852.

Editorial Note

Medieval monies are given in *livres tournois* (l.t. or l.) unless *livres parisis* (l.p.) is indicated. The internal rate of exchange during the thirteenth century was 4 *livres parisis* for every 5 *livres tournois*. 1 *livre* (l.) was worth 20 *sous* (s.), and 1 *sous* was worth 12 *denarios* (den.).

Eudes Rigaud's *Register* used the medieval Paris calendar, which marked a new year at Easter rather than January 1. All dates in this book, however, are in modern standard dating, with January 1 marking the start of a new year.

Where no edition of an English translation is cited in a note, the translation is my own. I have provided references to both the Latin edition of Eudes's *Register* (*RV*) and the English translation (*RER*), except for the sections of the Latin edition that did not appear in the translated edition.

THE HOLY BUREAUCRAT

Introduction

Its small and relatively compact size was essential for an itinerant archbishop. Measuring six by nine inches, the size of a fairly small book, it was not difficult to carry. Except for the last few folios, which are charred, and an occasional hole, it is in remarkably good condition for a document seven hundred and fifty years old.[1] At 387 folios (774 pages), it is by no means short, but it has a long and detailed story to tell. From August 1248 through December 1269, it records the daily activities of Eudes Rigaud, the first Franciscan archbishop of Rouen. The archbishop's *Register* paints a vivid picture of day-to-day ecclesiastical life in thirteenth-century Normandy from the perspective of an administrator in search of problems needing correction.[2] Reading the *Register*, we eavesdrop on the archbishop's hundreds of visitations to monasteries, nunneries, houses of regular canons, hospitals, cathedral chapters, and country parishes. We follow the archbishop as he finds clerics who are unchaste, who gamble, and who get drunk; we hear about monasteries that are financially mismanaged; we meet parish priests who still have to be taught how to conjugate simple Latin verbs; we learn of priests who do not attend their local church councils; and there are even the exceptional reports of two monks thought to have had sexual relations with each other.

The *Register* is not a self-conscious document. Its author seems to have had no desire to project a particular image of himself or his times. He intended it solely for his own use and that of subsequent archbishops of Rouen. The *Register* functioned as both a calendar and an archive. While inspecting a monastery, for example, Eudes could turn to his *Register* to review his previous visitations. Had he collected a procuration fee at his last visitation? Had he warned the abbot about the need to impose greater moral discipline? In many ways, the *Register* functioned like the notes of a modern physician. Just as doctors' notes follow patients' medical histories, the *Register* tracked the spiritual and financial health of religious establishments. At the top of each folio appeared the year, week, and diocese under visitation. For quick and easy reference, headings in the margins provided the names of places visited and the procuration fees collected (*summa procurationis*). During subsequent visitations of the same religious house, if the archbishop encountered any resistance to his collection of a procuration, he could turn to his *Register* for a record of exactly how much he had collected during previous visitations. Eudes was an assiduous collector of procurations, and they represented a major source of revenue. In a typical year, he collected over 200 *livres tournois* in procurations from monastic houses. Thus it was extremely useful to have a record of every procuration collected, and in cases where he collected no procuration, a note indicated that he had paid for his own expenses (*cum nostris expensis*). Eudes's lists of the procurations he collected resembled the roll lists found in royal and municipal receipt rolls beginning in the early thirteenth century.[3]

In addition to recording the past, the *Register* served as a kind of working calendar. Places that the archbishop intended to visit were entered next to the appropriate dates. If the archbishop's secretary later found that not enough space had been left for a particular date, he used arrows and carets to squeeze additional information into the margins and corners.[4] At times, too much space was allotted for a particular day, and a large blank space was left.[5] When the archbishop changed his plans, his secretary had to cross out scheduled trips and move them to different dates.[6] Perhaps at the archbishop's insistence, the *Register* was constantly being amended and updated. Errors in page numbering and dating were crossed out and corrected.[7] In a section dealing with the crimes of priests (*diffamationes*), several priests' records were crossed out and replaced by simple explanations in the margins: "he resigned," "he was incarcerated," "he was deprived [of his benefice]." It was almost as though Eudes excised these priests' existence from the record. When the archbishop admitted men to orders, his secretary created a chart with four columns, one with the names of those ordained as acolytes, one for those promoted as subdeacons, one for deacons, and one for priests. Eudes could thus keep careful track of who had been admitted to which orders and when. Letters from the king or the pope, statutes from Eudes's provincial councils, the financial receipts of monastic houses, the French text of the peace treaty of 1259 between England and France (which Eudes helped broker)—all these were copied into the *Register*. At times, incoming documents, written in an urgent cursive, were directly inserted into the *Register* rather than copied, and some outgoing documents were copied in a more formal cursive. Papal bulls copied into the *Register* were sometimes even accompanied by short synopses in the margins, indicating an expectation that future readers would rapidly flip

The first folio of Archbishop Eudes Rigaud's *Register*, BnF ms. lat. 1245 through the pages.[8] Although much of the *Register* is written in a professional, business hand, indicative of the training and experience of the archbishop's secretaries, in general, little attention was paid to appearance: the layout of the pages is fairly cramped, and the script is not what one would consider book hand. For twenty-one years, day in and day out, the *Register* traveled wherever the archbishop did, and in it, he recorded, reviewed, and revised a vast amount of information.

Keeping an episcopal register was perhaps a natural outgrowth of Eudes's university training in theology. His university lectures at Paris on the *Sentences* of Peter Lombard, the standard theological textbook, had required him to digest and compartmentalize enormous quantities of information. By the time Eudes ascended to the archiepiscopal see in 1248, he was used to applying systematic, Aristotelian logic to philosophical and theological issues. It may have been the habit of organizing information in coherent ways that led him to keep a detailed record of his episcopal activities.

Eudes's *Register* also illustrates a new administrative mentality and confidence in the written record among some churchmen in the thirteenth century. Eudes used written tools such as his *Register* and a polyptych (a kind of census book with information on the population of every parish in the Rouen archdiocese) not only to strengthen his authority and that of his office but to hold others accountable for their conduct. Just as monks in twelfth-century France began to manage their patrimony in new ways, especially by keeping more explicit written instruments that permitted them to manage their lands more effectively and hold others accountable, so too did bishops begin to use written records of administration, not only for fiscal and juridical purposes but also to monitor and discipline moral-religious behavior, whether in the context of an inquisition bent on destroying heresy or a bishop trying to keep the everyday abuses found in his diocese in check.[9] An episcopal register like Eudes's was a disciplinary tool that was both descriptive and prescriptive, permitting the archbishop (and his successors) to trace change over time, to compare what was real and what was ideal. In this connection, it is worth noting that the Franciscans and Dominicans took a leading role in using written records in new ways, cataloging library collections, indexing the subjects covered in the writings of the church fathers, and creating the first alphabetical biblical concordances.[10] Moreover, it was not just that the friars had a reputation for piety, making them attractive candidates to serve as inquisitors, *enquêteurs* (investigators), university masters, and bishops; they were also known for being smart, efficient, practical, and conscientious.

The archbishop's *Register* thus reflected larger historical developments in thirteenth-century ecclesiastical administration. In many parts of Europe, this was a period that witnessed the growth of more sophisticated local ecclesiastical government, part of what one French historian has called "une révolution pastorale."[11] It was only in the late twelfth and early thirteenth centuries that bishops and archbishops began keeping registers.[12] In addition, from Pisa to Trier to Canterbury, thirteenth-century bishops and archbishops conducted systematic visitations of religious houses, examined candidates for clerical ordination, and held regular diocesan synods, which had been made obligatory by the sixth canon of the Fourth Lateran Council of 1215.[13] In dioceses across Europe, the thirteenth century saw a remarkable increase in the volume of *acta* (administrative documents) coming out of episcopal chanceries.[14] In Rouen, an archiepiscopal *familia*, or entourage, made up of loyal archdeacons, deans, canons, and friars, accompanied the archbishop and served as his associates. Eudes's traveling staff also included secretaries, a confessor, and personal physicians, the latter needed to treat the archbishop's chronic rheumatism. In judicial and financial matters, the archbishop was represented by an "official" (*officialis*), often a former member of his *familia*, who was generally stationed at the cathedral in Rouen.[15] Local ecclesiastical bureaucracies in the thirteenth century such as the one at Rouen paralleled, albeit on a much smaller scale, developments in papal and French royal administration, where officials made chanceries more active, extended their jurisdiction, created new administrative offices, and instituted new systems of accountability and better mechanisms for collecting revenue.[16]

Although the ecclesiastical administration of Rouen during the thirteenth century was fairly representative of developments in other dioceses in northern France, no thirteenth-century episcopal register quite compares with Eudes's in its length or detail.[17] As Benoît-Michel Tock notes, the kinds of administrative documents emanating from a medieval episcopal chancery could reflect aspects of the bishop's personality.[18] And though a wide range of types of documents emanated from bishops' chanceries, as Michael Clanchy observes, episcopal registers are the "best measure of the rate of episcopal record-making because they are summaries of other documents, deliberately made for future references."[19] In the *Register*'s pages we feel the Franciscan archbishop's unflagging discipline, his desire for meticulous organization, and his obsession with accurate and systematic record keeping and data collection, all characteristics associated with Max Weber's "Protestant ethic." As Robert Brentano comments, "Record sources are notoriously unsatisfactory aids to the delineation of character; but occasionally . . . they tell so exactly what a man did that they intimate, at least, what he was."[20] Eudes's *Register* provides a window into the life of a thirteenth-century archbishop, informing us what a medieval archbishop did, what he cared most about, and what he struggled against. In the archbishop's *Register*, in other words, we observe ecclesiastical reform in action, including how it was implemented and how it was contested.

Making historical sense of an episcopal register involves certain perils, above all the temptation to draw hasty conclusions about the state of the medieval clergy based on a bishop's private record of the problems he found among its members. The archbishop's *Register*, one must remember, is virtually silent about the many clerics who behaved well. Indeed, several scholars have compared episcopal registers to police blotters, pointing out that a study of a society based solely on police blotters would present a highly warped picture.[21] "Cases of priestly ignorance, when recorded in detail in bishops' registers," one historian rightly argues, "indicate not that priests were generally ignorant but that reformers were requiring higher standards."[22] Yet early studies of Eudes Rigaud's *Register*, such as an article published in 1846 by the prolific and erudite French scholar Léopold Delisle, used the *Register* to illustrate the abuses committed by the medieval Norman clergy.[23] In the early twentieth century, the British historian G. G. Coulton embraced Eudes's *Register* as proof that the medieval church was steeped in immorality, decay, and scandal. Coulton, who viewed himself as defending "the moderate Anglican position," was deeply disturbed by what he regarded as some modern Catholics' romanticization of the medieval past.[24] Any rational modern person who knew something about the Middle Ages, Coulton maintained, would not dream of being transported back to that cruel and nasty world.[25] Assuring his readers that his scholarly works were "written entirely from orthodox pre-Reformation sources" and were therefore objective and historical, Coulton celebrated Eudes Rigaud as a proto-reformer who battled a church that was as corrupt in 1250 as it was alleged to be in 1500. Coulton exploited Eudes's *Register* in a narrow, polemical, and misleading way. Far more balanced and scholarly was Pierre Andrieu-Guitrancourt's 1938 monograph, but it too focused primarily on what the *Register* revealed about monastic and parish life in the thirteenth century.[26] Surprisingly few other studies have since appeared.[27] Until now, there has been no effort to study the Franciscan's career as a whole—his years at the university, his ties to the mendicant orders, and his involvement in secular politics—with all the insights it provides into ecclesiastical reform and the interplay between the university, the church, and the state in thirteenth-century France.

The present book is interested above all in the man behind the *Register*, in connecting the Eudes of the *Register* with the Eudes who was a Franciscan preacher, university theologian, judge, financial manager, and royal councillor. It is a rare and fortunate occurrence when a wide range of sources—from university sermons, to theological disputed questions, to synodal sermons, to financial records, to judicial records—exists, documenting such different facets of an individual from the thirteenth century. Eudes's career spanned the three major centers of power in the thirteenth century: the *studium* (center of intellectual power), the *sacerdotium* (center of sacral power), and the *regnum* (center of lay power).[28] He was also among the first generation of both Franciscan university theologians and Franciscans to become bishops. His career thus provides a window into the complex relationship between thirteenth-century institutional power and evangelical devotion, in the guise, in his case, of Franciscan piety. The career of Eudes Rigaud illuminates how the church functioned in an age of reform and how at times it compromised and adapted its principles.

Did Eudes (along with the other early Franciscan bishops) compromise the values of the Franciscan order by accepting a powerful church office? According to the Franciscan chronicler Salimbene de Adam, when Eudes was traveling to Rome with a retinue of some eighty horsemen, and an Italian bishop offered to pay his expenses, Eudes declined, acknowledging that he could live in splendor on only half his income.[29] From a close reading of Eudes's *Register*, one might also reasonably conclude that the archbishop was a fussy and oppressive disciplinarian who admonished illiterate priests, meddled in the affairs of his suffragans, and exacted steep procuration fees even from some of the most impoverished priories and abbeys he visited.

Yet while Eudes was surely authoritarian, he was also a tireless reformer. Williell Thomson, who has studied the careers of thirteenth-century Franciscan bishops as a whole, argues that unlike Eudes, the typical thirteenth-century friar-bishop was rather lazy, perhaps conducting a visitation, endowing a chapel, or mediating in a dispute only once or twice every decade: "the onerous business of visitation, with all its concomitant unpleasantness, he would shun, trusting his archdeacon to see that the churches, priories and other physical establishments within his jurisdiction ran on an even keel."[30] Eudes, in contrast, did not shirk his duties, nor was he afraid to get his hands dirty in the messy business of personally correcting abuses in the hinterlands of Normandy. He showed an unusual concern for the plight of the sick and the poor, conducting frequent visitations to hospitals and leprosaria. According to Salimbene, every time Eudes was to eat a particular dish, he made sure that two large silver serving bowls of the same food were presented to the poor.[31] Bernard of Bessa, who served as secretary to Bonaventure, commented that Eudes Rigaud, though distinguished by the family he was born into, was even more distinguished for his morals and was "the most famous preacher."[32] Drawing attention to the Franciscan's humility, Bernard added that Eudes's "life and learning were such that before being in holy orders, he was dragged and forced to the *curia*, and he shined so excellently in the administration of his church, that his example as bishop was highly esteemed."[33] Eudes's alleged reluctance to accept the archiepiscopal dignity may of course merely have been a Franciscan trope invoked by Bernard to excuse Eudes's acceptance of a high church office.[34] Yet even the historian R. W. Southern, who viewed Eudes as something of a grandee, acknowledged that Eudes was "a model archbishop in the most peaceful and best adjusted society of western Europe." Of the Norman church under Eudes's administration, Southern wrote: "This is the secular medieval church at its modest best. Disturbed by no serious dissensions, moderate in action, orderly in procedure, every part fitly conjoined to every other; no heretics, no desperate disorders, no impossible standards of behaviour. Church life did not long nor often appear in this peaceful passivity. It is usual to find currents more violent than the gentle ripples which disturbed the placid surface of Odo's administration."[35]

Both in the way he conducted his own life and in the way he governed the faithful in Normandy, Eudes Rigaud embodied the thirteenth-century "discipline of the minute." While medieval monks and nuns lived according to a particularly demanding set of rules, they were not the only ones expected to exhibit *disciplina Christiana*. The secular clergy were also trained to conduct themselves in a prescribed manner, as were lay Christians. As the Catholic liturgy made plain, there were important parallels between the spiritual and moral discipline needed to win the battle against Satan and the military discipline that armies had used for centuries to defeat their adversaries. The word *disciplina* had several connotations during the Middle Ages.[36] It could refer, as it did in the Rule of Saint Benedict, to a specific form of punishment, including corporal punishment. It could also denote the authority that a superior, such as a bishop, exercised over his subordinates. But the Middle Ages inherited the classical meaning of *disciplina* as teaching or instruction as well. In contrast to *doctrina*, *disciplina* tended to refer more to the moral (as opposed to purely intellectual) side of education, to the rules and prescriptions for leading a moral life. It was precisely this type of education, with its orientation toward pastoral activism, that characterized instruction at the Franciscan *studium generale* at Paris, where Eudes Rigaud had taught.

When Eudes arrived on the scene in Rouen, he was accustomed to being surrounded by highly educated university students. Graduates of the university knew their theology and their Bible, they knew how to preach good sermons, and they certainly knew their Latin. Eudes came to Rouen with a clear notion of how the clergy ought to conduct itself. This included everything from how a cleric should behave in public, to how he should dress, how he should chant, and how well he should know the liturgy. In other words, the Franciscan archbishop had a certain moral-religious aesthetic about the way things ought to be. As his *Register* illustrates, however, Eudes's values collided sharply with the realities he sometimes found. In some sense, then, this book is about the collision between the world as it was and the world as Eudes Rigaud thought it ought to be.

This book is also a study of how the archbishop sought to transform the world he found. What could Eudes do about the abbot known in his community to be a sloth, or the priest who was a slob? How did he deal with the nun who was addicted to sex with her community's gardener? Was there anything that could be done about the parishioner whose terrifying seizures disrupted the celebration of the mass? Eudes believed that a certain Christian bodily discipline and a discipline in the way things were allowed to appear were just as vital as moral discipline. Appearances, after all, could make a difference in the way people conducted themselves. When a priest rode into town with his outer gown open, he created the potential for scandal by blurring the lines that distinguished the clergy from the laity. Dressed more like a layman, the priest might feel free to act like a layman, frequenting taverns, playing games of chance, and becoming involved in a sexual relationship. Laypeople around him might also act differently toward him. Other priests might begin taking greater license in their own dress and conduct. What began as the relatively minor issue of a priest's open gown could have a ripple effect, disrupting order within the church and town. The archbishop thus strictly enforced the prohibition against priests wearing their gowns open.

In some ways, Eudes's style of governance was similar to the "broken windows" philosophy that guided the New York City Police Department's "revolution" during the 1990s, when it was argued that the police's neglect of minor offenses, such as graffiti, littering, public urination, and the playing of loud boom boxes on the subways, created the appearance of lawlessness and invariably led to more serious offenses. If a window were broken on a city street, it needed to be fixed before New Yorkers began thinking that "anything goes." By personally inspecting hundreds of churches and monasteries, by using archdeacons and deans as his eyes and ears, and by keeping meticulous records of the information he and his clerical agents gathered, Eudes worked to locate the Norman church's "broken windows" and fix them promptly. He worried, for instance, about whether a church in Rouen used the liturgy customary in Paris instead of the preferred liturgy of Rouen. Whichever liturgy was used, he insisted, had to be chanted with proper intonation and with every syllable clearly enunciated. The archbishop questioned clerical candidates on their knowledge of whether the Latin verb *patere* had a supine. Altar cloths in Norman churches had to be clean and unwrinkled if priests wished to avoid the archbishop's displeasure. Eudes expected his own secretary to be able to tell him at a moment's notice the precise number of parishioners in any given parish, using a recently begun census book that contained information about each of the more than one thousand parishes in the archdiocese. Centuries of the highly regulated and regimented monastic tradition had left their imprint on both the church and its laws. From dress to food, from language to liturgy, salvation, it was believed, depended in large part on Christian discipline.

Although there are very few known cases where Eudes combated heresy, his meticulous collection of data and his rigorous examination of the clergy during his visitations of parishes and monasteries had parallels in the techniques that had been used a few decades earlier against the Albigensian heresy in the great inquisition in the south of France, a project largely executed by members of the mendicant orders. Eudes's visitations also bore certain similarities to the visitations of the *enquêteurs* appointed by the French king, Louis IX (Saint Louis), to clean up the alleged corruption of royal officials in the provinces. Franciscans and Dominicans were also over-represented in this undertaking, and it is possible that before his election as archbishop Eudes worked for a short time as one of the king's *enquêteurs*. As archbishop, Eudes made his own attempt at creating such a system, appointing investigators whose job it was to observe and report back on the work of other investigators. In creating a more complex and sophisticated ecclesiastical bureaucracy, which included a system of surveillance, data collection, and mechanisms for correction and reform, the medieval church resembled contemporary developments in French royal administration.[37]

But the church's bureaucratization did not represent a movement toward secularization. The avowed aim of the church was, as it always had been, securing the salvation of souls, and this awesome aspiration required at the very minimum that the clergy be well trained and their conduct be regularly supervised and corrected. The constantly repeated rituals of *correctio*—the archbishop's almost daily visitation and inspection of the clergy, his instructions on what needed correction, his secretary's transcriptions of the newest information into the episcopal register, and his assigning other church officials the responsibility of following up on the corrections he had made—these rituals were themselves manifestations of the archbishop's own discipline and religious devotion.

Was there a connection between Eudes's university background and his commitment to ecclesiastical reform? Many of the better-known thirteenth-century episcopal reformers, such as Robert Grosseteste, John Pecham, Stephen Langton, Guillaume d'Auvergne, and Boniface of Savoy, received university educations.[38] University graduates not only possessed an impressive knowledge of the Bible, theology, and canon law but often were also skilled preachers, since preaching was a standard part of the university curriculum. In addition, Eudes clearly had an interest in questions of moral philosophy while at the university. In both his theological writings and his sermons, he gave serious thought to the problems of sin, free will, the relationship between divine grace and human merit, and the degree to which ignorance lessens a person's culpability. He was particularly fascinated by the nexus between ideas and actions, between knowing and doing. It seems to have been at the university, in other words, that Eudes first began considering humans' capacity for reform. As regent master of the Franciscan *studium*, he was essentially dean of students and therefore dealt on an almost daily basis with questions about discipline, reform, and the avoidance of sin (and not merely as academic subjects). Although it is impossible to establish a clear cause-and-effect relationship, the university no doubt planted some of the seeds for Eudes's later episcopal reforms.

As I have noted, Eudes's episcopal career had certain parallels in the reforms of French royal administration. The Franciscan archbishop was involved in royal administration in a number of capacities, acting as a judge in the Norman Exchequer, holding a seat in the Parlement of Paris, and serving as councillor to Louis IX. Eudes apparently first became involved in secular politics after Louis IX returned from crusade in 1254. By that time, the Franciscan had been archbishop for six years and had already shown himself to be a reformer. There is no reason to think, in other words, that the impetus for episcopal reform came from the king. But the two men clearly had common values and enjoyed each other's company. Both men loved charity, both showed an interest in helping hospitals and mendicant convents, both favored a hands-on approach to government, and both appointed special investigators (*inquisitores, enquêteurs*) to monitor local problems and complaints. Although both men recognized the possible corrupting influences of power, they also believed that power, properly used, could be put to holy ends.

Did the bureaucratization of the church, however, come at a cost? Could administrative strategies used by the state be applied with equal success by the church? Even on a local level, it was extremely difficult for a large centralized institution, such as the medieval Roman Catholic Church, to exert control over something as complex and intangible as the spirituality and moral behavior of human beings. Let us now see why this was so.

1

The Formation of a Reformer at the Franciscan *Studium* in Paris

In his 1957 book *Les intellectuels au moyen âge,* Jacques Le Goff suggested that the thirteenth-century intellectual was in danger of completely removing himself from the larger medieval society. According to Le Goff, the scholastic's language—Latin—and his abstract and technical ideas distanced him from the masses of laymen, their problems and their psychology. "Attached to abstract and eternal truths, the scholastic risked losing contact with history, with what was contingent, moving, evolving. . . . One of the great pitfalls of the scholastic intellectuals was that of forming an intellectual technocracy."[1] That Le Goff's critique of medieval intellectuals is jarring to us today is testimony to how much our knowledge of the medieval university has expanded during the past forty years, in part because of the work of social and cultural historians like Le Goff himself. We know much more now about exchanges between the medieval university and larger society and about how the medieval university functioned as a society and culture in its own right. The experience of studying and teaching at a medieval university involved a great deal more than the production of technical commentaries on the *Sentences* of Peter Lombard. Nicole Bériou and David d'Avray, for instance, have studied how model sermon collections, produced at the University of Paris, were disseminated around Europe and then preached (albeit in somewhat different form) to laymen and women.[2] Michèle Mulchahey has shown that the primary responsibility of Dominican university masters was training teachers for the order's provincial *scholae*, where most Dominican preachers and confessors received their education and training.[3] We are beginning to learn more, in short, about the university's impact outside its walls.[4]

There is still much more work to be done, however, particularly in exploring how the university served as a training ground for talented ecclesiastical and secular administrators.[5] During the thirteenth century, members of the new, mendicant, evangelical orders—the Franciscans and Dominicans—entered universities in large numbers. The mendicant *studia* attached to a university such as Paris trained students, most of whom, after graduating, dispersed into the provinces and growing urban centers as preachers and confessors, as well as teachers in provincial *studia.* A few student friars remained at the university, rising through the ranks to become distinguished university masters. Of these masters, 25 percent left the university for high ecclesiastical position, such as bishop, archbishop, cardinal, and pope.[6]

This was the trajectory followed by Eudes Rigaud, Franciscan regent master at the University of Paris, who was elected archbishop of Rouen and consecrated by Innocent IV in Lyon in March 1248. During his tenure as archbishop, Eudes became a close friend and councillor to the king of France, Louis IX. He held a seat in the Parlement of Paris, served as a master or judge at the royal court of the Exchequer in Normandy, and was instrumental in negotiating a peace treaty in 1259 between the kings of England and France, ending more than fifty years of war. From the detailed episcopal register he kept over a twenty-one-year period, we know that Eudes was an extraordinarily hardworking and meticulous episcopal administrator and reformer. Before being elected archbishop, however, Eudes had a distinguished career in theology at the Franciscan *studium* in Paris. The scholarly attention that has been paid to Eudes's career has focused on either his university career or his administrative career, reflecting the modern divide between intellectual and social historians. Yet one must ask whether teaching theology in a university and working as an ecclesiastical administrator were absolutely distinct careers. How did a career as a university theologian prepare someone for a career as an ecclesiastical administrator?

Not much is known about Eudes Rigaud's university career. There is no edition of his commentary on Lombard's *Sentences,* and few of his other theological works have been published.[7] Although there have been some recent studies of Eudes's philosophy and more speculative theology based on his unpublished *Sentences* commentary,[8] there remains a need to illuminate the continuities and discontinuities between Eudes's university and episcopal careers.

Several unpublished manuscripts of sermons Eudes preached at the University of Paris in the mid-1240s, shortly before he was elected archbishop, present a fuller picture of his university career.[9] In the sermons, we hear not only Eudes the teacher but also Eudes the rhetorician, using various strategies to persuade his students of the value of leading an evangelical, mendicant life. Rather than invoke Aristotelian philosophy, as he did in his lectures on theology, he calls on biblical-moral themes, applying them to practical problems. In short, the sermons are less about theological and philosophical speculation than about the moral values and simple wisdom with which a friar was expected to live. As archbishop, Eudes would largely devote himself to the task of reforming the practices and lives of the Norman clergy. Already as a master at the university, however, he fulfilled a pastoral role, preaching the religious life to students.

Some of Eudes's formal theological writings, particularly his publicly "disputed questions" (*quaestiones disputatae*), also call for serious examination, especially in light of their relevance to his later administrative career.[10] As Leonardo Sileo notes, Eudes's *quaestiones disputatae* sometimes grew out of his lectures on Lombard's *Sententiae*.[11] In the *quaestiones*, Eudes displays a deep interest in human free will, the relationship between divine grace and human merit, and the degree to which ignorance lessens a person's culpability. What the Franciscan believed was possible in terms of humans' capacity for reform could certainly affect the way he would later approach his administrative duties as archbishop, although his attitudes toward these questions might also change over time. As one might expect, Eudes's theological writings are different in tone and purpose from his university sermons, which tended to evolve from his lectures on the Bible. The formal theological works are generally philosophical and abstract, and the language is technical. Moreover, several of Eudes's *quaestiones disputatae* could be characterized as examples of speculative theology, having little or nothing to do with ecclesiastical reform. In his disputed *De ideis*, for instance, Eudes took up the question of whether there are a plurality of divine ideas, each corresponding to the multitude of God's different creatures, or whether there is only one, single divine idea.[12] Eudes's theological writings and sermons reveal that like many university masters of the time, the Franciscan was ambidextrous, equally capable and interested in moral theology as in speculative theology, logic, and metaphysics.

The University Curriculum

Before beginning his specialized studies in theology, Eudes probably spent about seven years during the 1230s in the Faculty of Arts at the University of Paris. It was likely during these years that he received his training in philosophy.[13] Increasing numbers of Aristotelian texts were translated into Latin during the 1240s, including direct translations from the Greek.[14] Yet, as it happened, there was little in the way of Aristotelian controversy during Eudes's time at the university. He arrived on the scene after the bans on Aristotle's *libri naturales*, which occurred in 1210 and 1215. By the 1230s, the forbidden books on natural philosophy apparently were again being read, since they were quoted by such masters of theology as Guillaume d'Auxerre, Philip the Chancellor, and Guillaume d'Auvergne.[15] And by the time the Aristotelian debates reignited during the 1250s, Eudes had left the university.

Even so, during his years at the university there was ambivalence about the "new" Greco-Arab philosophy and the blurring of lines between theology and the secular sciences. Although Eudes showed a willingness to use the "new logic," he viewed himself as doing so in the service of theology. In this respect, Eudes was no different from his teacher, Jean de la Rochelle, who had also maintained that philosophy and the secular sciences could aid understanding of not only theology but the Bible.[16] Eudes did not hesitate to cite Aristotle, if only to sometimes argue against his position. Above all, Eudes was representative of a second generation of Franciscan theologians, fascinated by questions surrounding human morals but willing to go beyond some of their mendicant teachers' reliance on the Bible and Augustine. Rather than base his conception of theology purely on the model of Aristotelian science or purely on the model of the Bible, Eudes viewed theology as a wisdom and unique science that incorporated both sources.[17] Eudes and his generation of theologians were eager to draw from a growing treasure chest of intellectual traditions—what one historian has termed "eclectic Aristotelianism," a mix of Aristotle, Neoplatonism, and Augustinianism.[18]

We do not know precisely when Eudes took the Franciscan habit, but it is likely that he did so after arriving at the university. The *Chronicle of the Twenty-Four Generals* refers to Eudes as a member of the order at the time Elias was minister general, from 1232 until 1239.[19] In taking the Franciscan vows, he may have been following the example of his teacher, Alexander of Hales, who had entered the Franciscan order in 1236.[20] At that time, Alexander was about fifty years old and had already established himself as one of the most distinguished secular masters of theology at the university. His decision to take the Franciscan habit not only gave new intellectual credibility to the Franciscan order but also came as a blow to the secular masters, who were upset at losing one of their chairs. In 1238, Alexander, with the help of the bishop of Paris, Guillaume d'Auvergne, secured a second chair of theology for the Franciscan *studium*. Jean de la Rochelle was thus recognized as co-regent of the *studium*.[21] As more secular masters followed Alexander's example in taking the religious habit, the Franciscan convent in Paris, previously only loosely affiliated with the university, became a central player in its intellectual life.[22]

On entering the faculty of theology, Eudes would have spent two years as a "biblical bachelor," lecturing on the complete Bible and biblical glosses. Beginning in about 1240, he started his tenure as a "sententiary bachelor," lecturing on the *Sentences* of Peter Lombard.[23] He would have been one of the first Franciscan students (if not the first) to lecture on the *Sentences* as part of his theological training. The only Parisian university masters before him to write commentaries on the *Sentences* were Alexander of Hales, who had written a commentary as a secular master in the 1220s, and Hugues de Saint-Cher, who had written one in the 1230s. It was only in the early 1240s, however, when Eudes was lecturing, that the *Sentences* became the standard university theological textbook.[24] To lecture on the *Sentences* meant synthesizing the entire university theological curriculum in an organized and coherent form; finding creative ways to reconcile the hundreds of scriptural, patristic, and medieval *auctoritates'* conflicting positions on the major points of theology; and raising new questions of one's own by building on existing theological foundations.[25] Eudes's commentary on the first three books of the *Sentences* seems to have met with success. There are at least fifteen extant manuscripts, showing that it was widely diffused.[26] Although the commentary reflects the influence of his teachers, Alexander of Hales and Jean de la Rochelle, it also manifests a certain intellectual independence. Odon Lottin argues that three of the greatest thirteenth-century theologians—Albertus Magnus, Bonaventure, and Thomas Aquinas—not only read Eudes's commentary on the *Sentences* but drew heavily from it in their own work, particularly with regard to the nature of free will.[27]

In 1241, when Eudes had not yet lectured much beyond book 2 of the *Sentences*, a Franciscan chapter of diffinitors requested that each province appoint a committee of learned brethren to draft a report on the Franciscan Rule of 1223.[28] Eudes was chosen to represent France, along with his mentors, Alexander of Hales, Jean de la Rochelle, and Robert de la Bassée. Thus, while still a sententiary bachelor, Eudes had already emerged as a promising leader among the second generation of Franciscan theologians. In submitting an *expositio*, or commentary, on the rule, the four Parisian masters acted contrary to Saint Francis's desire that the rule never be glossed.[29] In their preface to the *expositio*, however, the four masters made it clear that they did not view themselves as in any way revising the rule.[30] They felt that there was a need, however, to make some clarifications about the constitution of the order in the aftermath of the damaging generalate of Brother Elias (1232–39).[31] In addition to addressing constitutional issues, the *expositio* confronted some of the unsettled questions raised by the Rule of 1223. Even Pope Gregory IX, who claimed to have helped Francis with the composition of the rule and reminded the brethren of Francis's wish that the rule never be glossed, admitted in the bull *Quo elongati*, published on September 28, 1230, that the rule contained "certain things doubtful and obscure and certain things difficult to understand."[32] The four masters clarified, for instance, the rule's precept that all brothers were to wear "poor clothes" (*vestimentis vilibus*), arguing that by "poor" the rule meant the "value" (*pretium*) and "appearance" (*colore*) of clothes according to the judgment of the people of a particular region.[33] In other words, the same tunic might be permissible for friars to wear in one place, if the inhabitants of that region considered the tunic poor, but impermissible for friars in another region, where the tunic conveyed no such meaning. The four masters also supported Gregory IX's judgment in *Quo elongati* that there was a necessary distinction between the possession and use of property.[34] The brethren were permitted to make use of houses, furniture, and books, but such items remained the possessions of the donors, who loaned them for the brethren's use. Eudes's contribution to the *expositio* demonstrates that as early as 1242, he was confronting the problem of maintaining the "perfect" poverty of his order by translating Franciscan ideals from theory into practice.

On February 3, 1245, Jean de la Rochelle died, and Eudes Rigaud replaced him as regent master.[35] Only six months later, Alexander of Hales died. Until his death, Alexander had continued to occupy a second Franciscan regent-master chair. However, the provincial-general of the order, John of Parma, renounced the second Franciscan chair, wishing to conciliate the secular masters, who were increasingly distressed by what they viewed as the mendicants' encroachment on their rights.[36] Eudes was suddenly thrust into the position of being at the head of the Franciscan *studium* in Paris. His ascendancy was so rapid that he apparently did not even have time to finish his formal theological training. As far as we know, he never commented on book 4 of the *Sentences* and did not quite finish the commentary to book 3.[37] As regent master, Eudes continued his theological work. He authored a number of publicly "disputed questions" (which were initially public performances, later copied down in an expanded form) and contributed to Alexander of Hales's *Summa*, a cooperative venture begun while Alexander was still alive and carried on posthumously by Alexander's disciples. The *Summa* was meant to serve as a systematic theological encyclopedia for students. Yet above all, as the contemporary Franciscan chronicler Salimbene de Adam reported, Eudes became known as "one of the finest scholars in the world . . . exceedingly adept in disputation and a very pleasing preacher."[38]

As his "disputed questions" and sermons demonstrate, the Franciscan master held a pragmatic view of the theological enterprise. He argued that theological knowledge is virtuous only to the extent to which it leads humans to morally virtuous action.[39] This understanding of the purpose of theology, and education more generally, corresponded with the way the Franciscan *studium* viewed its own mission. For mendicants in the *studium*, the study of theology was not just an academic exercise but also part of their spiritual and pastoral training. The great majority of them left the university after receiving their license to teach, returning to the provinces as preachers, confessors, and teachers. Even among those few who stayed on as university masters, many eventually left the university to do pastoral work. Thus the Franciscan *studium* not only played its part in defining church doctrine but also educated many prelates who would be the programmatic vanguard of the church. Eudes Rigaud's own career reflects how a university master could reach the highest ranks of the ecclesiastical hierarchy, thereby having a direct impact on hundreds of individual parish churches and monasteries.

A few years after Eudes had left the university, the Dominican Thomas Aquinas was asked in a university quodlibetal debate whether it would not be preferable for him to give up teaching theology so as to be able to work directly to save souls.[40] In response, Thomas affirmed the superiority of the university master over the parish priest, comparing the theologian to an architect and the ordinary priest to a manual laborer. An architect, he pointed out, is paid more than a manual laborer because the laborer merely carries out the architect's instruction. Bishops, he argued, are architects like university masters, since they teach priests how to save souls. Above all, both university masters and bishops are superior to ordinary priests since they instruct others how to instruct, thereby reaching a larger number of people than the ordinary priest, who instructs individuals capable only of helping themselves. Although Thomas recognized that as a university master he was not addressing laymen directly, he assumed that his university lectures, sermons, and writings would ultimately reach the local parishes through various qualified intermediaries, such as friars, who had been trained by him at the university. Thus Thomas felt that even within the confines of the university, he was able to reach far greater numbers of Christians than any single parish priest or friar could do.

In the late twelfth century, the famous theologian at Notre Dame in Paris, Peter the Chanter, took a different view, one that reflected his desire that more of the clergy with the cure of souls be recruited from the schools. Echoing the rhetorical cadences of the book of Ecclesiastes, Peter argued that just as there was a time for discussion and a time for silence, so too was there both a time for discussion and debate in the schools and a time for preaching in churches. "Woe is the student," Peter said, "who wishes to die in devoting himself to discussion in the schools! The apprentices of whatever trade, don't they begin to work as soon as they know how to by themselves? The Lord invites us to preach when he says to the wife: 'Get up, hurry up, and come' etc. . . . that is: 'Get down from your contemplation so that you can win over others for me.' "[41] Peter and his circle in Paris believed (as many friars later would) that the principal responsibility of the church was to spread the Word. The mission of the cathedral schools, in teaching Scripture and theology, was to instruct students both how to live and how and what to preach.[42] A school of theology, in other words, was conceived of not as a place for a lifetime of learning and teaching but as a place for a short-term apprenticeship.[43]

It is quite probable that Peter the Chanter and his circle indirectly influenced the formation of Eudes Rigaud, who was studying at Paris about forty years after the Chanter's death. Eudes may even have used one of the preaching tools that Peter or one of his disciples prepared.[44] It was common, for instance, for Parisian preachers in the mid-thirteenth century to use Peter's *Verbum abbreviatum*, which was a moral treatise containing everything from scriptural passages, to *exempla*, to citations from classical authors. Peter arranged the *distinctiones* on biblical terms and words dealing with vices and virtues in alphabetical order, making it relatively easy for a preacher building a sermon on a particular biblical verse to quickly find relevant words and phrases.[45]

Although Peter the Chanter died more than fifteen years before the Fourth Lateran Council was held in 1215, some of his disciples played a role in shaping the council's canons. Indeed, in 1214, in preparation for the council, Innocent III appointed Peter's former student, Robert of Courson, as papal legate to France. Robert convened a number of local councils, including in Paris and Rouen. These local councils provided Robert with the opportunity to try out some of the reforms that he and other members of the Chanter's circle had developed before he presented them in Rome.[46] A number of the canons from these legatine councils were adopted by the Fourth Lateran Council, which would have a profound influence not only on Christian law and doctrine but on the way Eudes Rigaud and other prelates governed their churches. Moreover, the canons from both the Fourth Lateran Council and the Rouen council of 1214 served as the basis for many of the statutes of later Rouen councils and synods, including ones presided over by Eudes.[47] Some of the practical, moral issues that Eudes grappled with at the University of Paris, such as whether ignorance is an excuse for sin, surely also had an impact on his own conciliar legislation and his approach to administering his archdiocese.

The influence of the Chanter and his circle on Eudes is also apparent in the Franciscan master's interest in practical, moral theology. With his emphasis on preaching and ecclesiastical reform, the Chanter has been called "the John the Baptist" of the mendicants, a precursor of the friars.[48] In his *Summa de sacramentiis et de animae consiliis*, organized around the sacraments and recorded in the form of *quaestiones*, Peter addressed a wide range of practical problems in moral theology. He raised, for instance, the problem of clerics who failed to reside in their parishes, often because they held more than one benefice. The Chanter addressed what he deemed acceptable reasons for a priest's absence, such as being away from his parish due to academic studies. But Peter quickly added that it was unacceptable for a priest to use his studies merely as a way to save himself some money.[49] Quite often, Peter's *Summa* was an explication of canon law, such as his discussion of whether it was permissible for a layperson to withdraw from a Mass being celebrated by a fornicating priest and his treatment of how a priest should deal with an excommunicate entering his church while he was celebrating the Mass.[50] These were precisely the kinds of issues that prelates like Eudes

Rigaud faced. Far from living in an insulated academic world, Peter the Chanter confronted the realities of his time, tackling complex issues ranging from usury, to the celibacy of priests, to military service.[51] In a treatise on prayer, Peter devoted an entire section to the issue of prayer postures, using both text and illustrations to describe proper and improper body postures for prayer.[52] He complained that some priests were ashamed to appear in public in humble and reverent postures. According to the Chanter, it was due to sheer laziness that some Christians leaned against a wall while they prayed, while others used props such as kneelers so that their knees did not touch the hard, dirty floor.[53]

The Chanter also examined the question of whether a letter or syllable omitted from a prayer invalidated it. Even if someone properly enunciated every word and syllable of a prayer, Peter argued, it was essential for that person not only to understand the meaning of the prayer but to remember its content afterward; if someone could not remember the prayer that he had recited, he was obligated to repeat it. As we shall see, Eudes Rigaud showed particular concern as archbishop of Rouen with the problem of canons who did not enunciate clearly enough when they chanted the divine hours. As archbishop, Eudes also insisted that proper reverence always be paid to the real presence of Christ in the Eucharist, one of Peter the Chanter's principal concerns in his *Summa*.[54] In his criticism of secular bishops for not imitating more closely the lives of the apostles (a criticism the mendicants would later echo) and his discussion of what material things were necessary for a bishop's life (including whether it was licit for bishops to demand procurations from churches they visited but did not preach in), Peter seemed almost to anticipate the dilemmas that friar-bishops like Eudes would face (and that monastic bishops already faced).[55] Eudes was also heavily influenced by the Victorines' moral and allegorical reading of the Old Testament, as is evident in his frequent invocation of the Victorines as authorities, and he often cited the mystical theology of the Cistercian, Saint Bernard of Clairvaux. Yet with his interest in logic and speculative thought, Eudes differed from Bernard and the Victorines. It was rather Peter the Chanter and his circle, who combined an interest in logic and speculative theology with a commitment to pastoral theology and ethics, who most closely resembled Eudes's intellectual temperament.

Preaching the Religious Life

Partly owing to the influence of Peter the Chanter and his school, renewed attention was paid in the later twelfth century to preaching, both by bishops and priests and by university masters charged with the formation of clerics.[56] When the friars arrived at universities in the thirteenth century, they made preaching a central component of students' religious formation.[57] Sermons were normally preached on Sundays and feast days, and the audience included both secular and religious masters and students. The Franciscans and Dominicans often convened to hear sermons together. Although the sermons were typically scholastic in their organization and drew heavily on biblical and patristic sources, they appealed to their listeners' emotions as much as their reason. In this way, the sermons, often concerned with practical moral lessons, were quite different from formal theological lectures or publicly disputed *quaestiones*.[58] Indeed, university sermons sometimes served as models for sermons that would be preached outside the university to quite different audiences.[59] University preachers were eager to show off various rhetorical devices that they had learned from ancient texts on rhetoric by Aristotle and Cicero, as well as contemporary manuals on rhetoric being produced in the universities.

Because university sermons, including those by Eudes Rigaud, made such frequent reference to the Bible, the sermons themselves almost seemed to be the word of God (*sermones Dei*). Eudes used motifs and playful word associations as a way of linking a variety of biblical passages to his desired theme. In doing so, he may have had access to a preaching aid such as an alphabetized, biblical *distinctio* collection like Peter the Chanter's *Verbum abbreviatum*, mentioned above.[60] In his sermon on the theme of *consummatum est* (John 19:30), for example, Eudes referred to approximately twelve biblical passages containing the word *consummatio*,[61] elevating the authority of his sermon, and allowing him to claim that he was merely serving as God's mouthpiece. His sermon, in short, was the *sermo Dei*. At the same time, however, a preacher like Eudes could take on the dual role of speaking *for* God and *to* God. In the *prothema*, or introductory prayer, Eudes allied himself with his audience by speaking on its behalf: "Dearest ones, let us ask him who is the founder and perfecter of faith, that by that same mercy for which he who was born and suffered for us, he should give power to his declaration (*verbo*) so that his word (*sermo*) and that remarkable example may penetrate to our souls."[62]

University sermons were not only intended to persuade listeners, however; they also served to teach student audiences *how* to persuade. In addition to hearing masters preach dozens of sermons, students would preach themselves. Most theology students ultimately became preachers, whether as mendicants, bishops, or teachers in a *studium* or university. Sermons served to ensure that graduates left the university with eloquence as well as wisdom.

The primary function of the mendicant university sermon was to instill students with good judgment and steep them in the culture of the religious life, exemplified most dramatically in the lives of Christ and the apostles.[63] Eudes Rigaud's university sermons addressed the contemporary social preoccupation with material wealth, pride, and sex, all central concerns to members of the Franciscan order. But like other mendicant preachers of his time, Eudes translated these contemporary problems into the theological language and topos of the three major vices: *luxuria, avaritia,* and *superbia* (lust, avarice, and pride).[64] In the unusually long *prothema* of a sermon he preached on the feast of Saint Nicholas sometime in the mid-1240s, Eudes appears to have been recruiting either a group of novices who had yet to profess or secular students wavering about whether to enter one of the mendicant orders.[65] The feast of Saint Nicholas was the day the boy bishop was elected at Notre Dame and the chief feast for the young clergy. Choosing a subject that was particularly relevant to the feast being celebrated, the Franciscan master acknowledged that he was surely not the first preacher to appeal to the students to enter the religious life: "It has often been preached to you," he says, "that you should do penance, abandon the vanity of the world, and enter religion."[66] He reassured his audience that Christians of all ages could enter the religious orders, some entering during their youthful years, and others not entering until their later years of life (he might have had his own teacher, Alexander of Hales, in mind).[67] Moreover, it was never too late or too early to enter the religious life. Eudes acknowledged that one of the principal tactics he and his fellow mendicant preachers used to recruit new mendicants was to convey the "miseries, troubles, and worries of the world which harass lovers and possessors [of worldly things], which ought to recall us from the love of those things, rather even provoking us to condemn them."[68] If describing the destructive symptoms associated with a love of worldly things did not suffice, Eudes invoked the constructive examples of "Saints Jerome, Augustine, Nicholas, and Martin, the holy hermits and monks, all of whom preach to us a contempt of worldly things and recommend in words, deeds, and examples a life of religion which all of them confessed."[69]

Anticipating an objection that perhaps some seculars had already made, Eudes raised the question of the status of celebrated figures from the Hebrew Bible, such as Abraham, Moses, and Job: "We are not better [than they were]," he admits, "and yet they were rich in the world and they did not enter religion. Why therefore do we preach all day an order and poverty and such?"[70] As he explained it, the biblical patriarchs were excused from living a religious life of poverty because they lived before the life of Christ. They had not worshiped Christ, nor had they read the Gospels, nor heard of "the blessed poor" (Matt. 5:3), nor heard the Lord say, "If you wish to be perfect, go and sell all of your things" (Matt. 19:21).[71] Eudes believed that if Abraham, Moses, or Job had heard Christ's words, they would have willingly agreed with his counsel and entered a religious life of voluntary poverty, celibacy, and humility.[72] The Franciscan preacher ended the protheme of his sermon with a prayer to the Son of God that he and his university audience be helped to resist carnal pleasures and to endure the tribulations of the present life.[73]

Eudes could not apply his argument about the biblical patriarchs who lived before the time of Christ to Saint Nicholas, who was the patron saint of clerics. Yet as Eudes pointed out in his sermon, Nicholas "never was a monk, nor made a vow of religion, and was called upon by the Lord to remain as such for the preserving and governing of his people."[74] It was not simply that Nicholas had never entered a religious order; he was also of noble birth, as Eudes noted, and had inherited enormous riches from his parents. Nonetheless, the Franciscan preacher celebrated Nicholas as a paragon of the "blessed rich," maintaining that while the saint possessed temporal wealth, he "was more noble in his sanctity and in his conduct, which is truly nobility, nor did he put a stain on his honor."[75] Eudes thus broadened the meaning of "rich" (dives), arguing that Nicholas was rich not only in life but also in reputation and miracles. Most impressively, the saint had lived unstained by the spiritual sins of avarice, pride, and carnal lust.

What is most surprising about Eudes's sermon on Saint Nicholas was his admission that temporal wealth is not an inherently evil and corrupting force. The life of Nicholas proved that material wealth does not preclude someone from living a religious life, "rich" and "noble" in conduct. Eudes appealed to his audience: "Dearest ones, if we do not wish to be the blessed poor, at least let us be just as that blessed one who was rich, such that we may be without stain, just as he was."[76] In part, this may have been a rhetorical device appropriate for an audience that included students not committed to voluntary poverty. But Eudes was also not the only Franciscan theologian to draw a distinction between having riches and loving riches. His own teacher, Alexander of Hales, suggested that it was permissible for a layman to adorn his clothing according to the nobility of his person, the customs of his country, and the dignity of his profession, so long as his motivations were acceptable.[77] In other words, it was the pride and ambition so often associated with luxurious clothing that was sinful, not the clothes themselves. Bonaventure, echoing what his former master, Eudes Rigaud, had said about the Old Testament patriarchs, cited them as illustrations of the possibility that the rich could also be virtuous.[78] These conciliatory tones on the issue of wealth may have reflected the mid-thirteenth-century Franciscans' increasingly ambiguous relationship with the saeculum, or world. On the one hand, Franciscans were committed to working in the world: traveling, preaching, hearing confessions, and interacting daily with ordinary laymen. On the other hand, Franciscans lived according to an ascetic rule, which required them to renounce all property, live celibate lives, and show total obedience to the leaders of their order. Eudes may well have identified with Nicholas's sense of a divinely assigned role: working in the world and governing his people while also living a religious life. Later Eudes would have to harmonize his role as a Franciscan with his temporal and spiritual responsibilities as archbishop of Rouen.

Yet while he was still at the university, Eudes displayed a particular interest in the nexus between ideas and actions, preaching and practice. In a sermon preached on Good Friday, he used the commemoration of the Crucifixion to exhort his audience to a life of service and action. Pointing to the life of Christ, Eudes argued that for preaching to have any value, it must be accompanied by the preacher's own virtuous example.[79] Here, too, Eudes would have embraced Peter the Chanter's suggestion, drawing on the gloss on Paul's second epistle to Timothy, that the qualities required of all preachers and prelates were their life (*vita*), knowledge (*scientia*), and eloquence (*facundia*).[80] In the case of Christ, according to Eudes, the Crucifixion represented the consummate moment, echoed by Christ's final words, "It is finished" (*consummatum est,* John 19:30), when all words and actions were perfected and fulfilled.

Eudes discussed in concrete terms both the process by which someone commits a sin and practical ways the temptation to sin can be thwarted. Sinful action, he explained, begins with a mere idea or suggestion; it then moves on to a dangerously delightful tickling sensation; then the decision to sin; and finally the committing of the sin itself.[81] Yet the temptation to sin can be overcome, he argued, by surrounding oneself with wise and good men, around whom there is less chance that sinful ideas will arise in the first place; achieving a sense that one has enough (*consummatio sufficiencie*) and is not in need of anything more; and always persevering.[82] The problem of sinful temptations was particularly acute in a group of predominantly young male mendicants, who, though having taken a vow of voluntary poverty, obedience, humility, and chastity, were at the same time committed to living and preaching in cities and towns, where they would be surrounded by the temptations of sex, bustling commercial districts, drinking, and gambling. The students had already faced these kinds of temptations living in Paris, but they had been under the protective and watchful eyes of their mendicant masters.

What would happen, however, to a student friar when he left the university and served as a preacher and confessor in a province? Who would watch over him? As Eudes solemnly informed a group of students still at the university, "Dearest ones, those who are an example in evil to others are their parents in evil. Thus it is said in the Book of Wisdom: 'All who are born of iniquity are therefore witnesses of evil against their parents at their [parents'] interrogation."[83] What Eudes wished to stress above all was the responsibility that the student friars would bear when they left the university to fulfill pastoral functions. They would be the new representatives of the religious life. It was common for friars to cast contemporary prelates in a negative light, drawing attention to their indifference to their flocks, their dissolute lifestyles, and their careerism and desire for wealth.[84] Such exaggeratedly critical portraits of prelates served to instill an audience of friars with a sense of pastoral urgency while inspiring them to outdo their secular counterparts. Whether they were preaching the Gospel, disseminating doctrine, hearing laymen's confessions, or merely walking down a city street, the friars would always be in the public eye. Thus, if the Franciscans wished to guard the public's trust, they would have to remind themselves that the laymen they were serving were not only listening to their preached words but also scrutinizing their daily conduct. As Eudes told a group of friars, quoting Saint Bernard, "A good conscience is necessary before God, and a good example necessary before man."[85]

In his sermon discussions of how to live well, Eudes relied heavily on simple maxims from the wisdom literature of the Bible, often citing the Wisdom of Jesus the son of Sirach, the Wisdom of Solomon, and Proverbs. But he also made frequent references to Leviticus and showed great respect for the Mosaic law. In his sermon on the feast of Saint Nicholas, for instance, Eudes affirmed the contempt expressed in Jewish law for a stain in a house (domus), which Eudes took to mean one's family; one's dress (vestimento), which he understood as outward behavior; and one's oblations (oblationes), which he said were the deeds one offers to God.[86] Eudes identified with the ancient Israelite temple, its liturgy, and the priestly office. Perhaps he viewed his own Order of Friars Minor as the natural successor to Aaron the high priest and his sons. When, as archbishop, Eudes addressed the Norman clergy in a synodal sermon, he was explicit in saying that he and his clergy belonged to an elite class of priests, much like the high priests of the Israelite temple, chosen by God as his ministers. And as elite priests, the Franciscan would argue, they were expected to live according to special criteria, particularly with regard to their moral and bodily purity. As his university sermons demonstrate, however, Eudes was already deeply engaged while at the university, on the most practical level, with the question of what it means to live a religious life.

Eudes's deep-rooted interest in moral theology is reflected as well in his formal theological writings, where he first began working out a systematic philosophy of human nature and the possibility for human reform. Although he had confronted some of the philosophical problems related to moral theology in his commentary on the Sentences, the commentary had limited him to the curricular outline laid out by Peter Lombard in the twelfth century.[87] In Eudes's own "disputed questions," however, which were composed after his Sentences commentary, he found greater freedom to explore the questions that interested him most.[88] Again and again, he returned to the nature of human free will, the relationship between human merit and divine grace, and human ignorance as an avoidable cause of sin. Eudes was certainly not alone in displaying an interest in moral theology.

Earlier theologians, such as Hugh and Richard of Saint-Victor, Peter the Chanter, Stephen Langton and Philip the Chancellor, and contemporary ones, such as the Dominican Hugues de Saint-Cher, took a pragmatic approach to moral questions. Eudes's interest in moral theology was thus part of an ongoing inquiry among theologians into the ethical problems arising in everyday life.

Eudes asked probing questions about the nature of the theological enterprise itself.[89] He devoted an entire "disputed question" to "whether theology is a science." Although he believed that philosophy, metaphysics, and physics could be useful to theology, and drew on profane philosophic and scientific works in his own theological work, he also upheld theology's distinctiveness. Strictly speaking, theology is not a science, Eudes maintained, since theology requires illumination by faith and a science should be a *habitus* with its own independent certitude. On the other hand, theology could be considered superior to sciences that were based solely on human reason. Indeed, the fact that theology depended in part on the light of divine grace rendered its certitude superior to that of the other sciences. In this way, Eudes held that theology is a science, but a special kind of science, more powerful in its end (God), its method (invoking *auctoritas*), and its subject (God) than any of the profane sciences.[90] Theology is a unique science not only in producing faith in addition to understanding but also in requiring the grace of faith in the first place.[91] Perhaps most important, theology is unlike the purely speculative sciences in having *practical* ends. Eudes rejected the argument of some that both metaphysics and theology are partially speculative and partially practical. In the Franciscan's eyes, metaphysics are purely speculative and theology purely practical in their ends.[92] Not content to stop with the mere recognition of truth, theology leads to good and virtuous works. Eudes disagreed with Aristotle, who in the *Nicomachean Ethics* had said that "the receipt of knowledge has little or no value for one's salvation" (*acceptio scientiae parum vel nihil valet ad salutem*).[93] On the contrary, Eudes argued, "as much as anyone is a good theologian and preacher, unless he wishes that which he knows to be realized in actions, it profits him little or nothing."[94] In short, theological knowledge is virtuous only to the extent to which it leads humans to morally virtuous action.[95] One of the most significant legacies of Peter the Chanter was his new functional understanding of the theological enterprise, his argument that theology is not as valuable in its own right as in its application in the church, particularly in the domain of preaching.[96] The Chanter's legacy is visible in the mid-thirteenth century in Eudes and other theologians who viewed the process of theological study as only beginning with acquiring an understanding of the Word, to be followed by putting that understanding into practice in one's own life and conduct and then imparting that knowledge to others through preaching and teaching.[97]

Yet how does theological knowledge actually find expression in virtuous action? Do theologians, according to Eudes, necessarily lead more perfect lives because of their theological knowledge? Eudes always insisted that divine grace is necessary for humans to achieve merit. In the disputed question "On Grace," he skillfully navigated himself clear of the treacherous shoals of the Pelagian and Manichean positions, stressing the gift of grace as the source of every good human thought and action, at the same time maintaining the free will of man.[98] When Eudes was not dealing with the issue of grace directly, however, he asserted the necessity of grace for merit as a kind of required refrain, while carrying on the genuine business of distinguishing the merits of various human actions. In a "disputed question" on psalm singing (*de eo quod est psallere*), for instance, he asked: Is it good to say the hours out loud or better only to think them in one's mind? He responds by describing the benefits of saying the hours out loud: the likelihood of inspiring others, and the fact that by forcing oneself to enunciate every syllable, one is better able to concentrate on the meaning of the words and fight off the sluggishness of sleep.[99] Is it permitted to sing in praise of God with a capella polyphony and with the accompaniment of instruments? Eudes responds that it is acceptable to praise God using such devices but they should not be used in churches.[100] Does someone receive merit even when he chants without understanding? If someone has no understanding whatsoever of what he chants, says the Franciscan, then he receives no merit for his chanting. But if the person has even some general sense that what he is doing is in praise of God, then he does receive merit. Is it a sin to sing for one's own pleasure rather than in praise of God?[101] Eudes argues that it is not a sin to sing psalms to acquire intellectual pleasure, since this helps develop the faculty of the mind, but it is sinful to sing psalms for sensual pleasure.[102] Thus even while at the university, Eudes was concerned with the practical problems of chant, liturgy, and church life more generally. It is noteworthy that as archbishop, he repeatedly showed a special interest in chant and modulation, in one case even attempting to move the location of an episcopal consecration ceremony from the cathedral in Evreux to Lisieux, where he greatly preferred the canons' chant.[103] But in addition to displaying an interest in chant per se, Eudes also conveyed the importance of knowledge and education. If one knew how to chant properly, one would have a better chance of chanting meritoriously.

The nexus between knowing and doing also arose in Eudes's work on free will, where he drew particular attention to the role of reason in human action. Here Eudes seems to have been particularly influenced by Philip the Chancellor's theory of free action in the *Summa de bono*, a work that also influenced Albertus Magnus.[104] By "reason" (*ratio*), Eudes seems to have meant "human judgment" or "moral conscience." Reason's judgment is always morally correct, he argued, assuming it is properly instructed and is not mistaken for the will's sometimes overpowering passions. He defined free will as the will penetrated by reason (*voluntas vel deliberata sive consiliata*).[105] Reason and understanding allow humans to will deliberatively. Animals (and infant humans), in contrast, do not have the capacity to reason and therefore have wills more like instincts, governed by sensitive appetites.[106] Eudes assumed that animals have no moral sense and no sense of the past or the future. As beings endowed with reason, however, humans not only are able to make judgments but are able to make judgments about their judgments; they are able to give into their desires or will not to follow their desires; and they are able to think about the implications of their actions with respect to the past, present, and future.

Although Eudes emphasized the role of reason in humans' free will, he did not go so far as to equate reason with will. In short, he disagreed with the Socratic position, which held that it is impossible to knowingly do wrong.[107] A bad act, Eudes argued, is not necessarily a reflection of an error or ignorance on the part of the intellect, since there are times when reason is shut down or overpowered by the passions of the will.[108] By definition, free will gives a person the freedom to act contrary to his rational judgment. The will, while penetrated by reason, always retains its autonomy (assuming there is no external coercion) in being able to move toward that which it wants.[109] As archbishop, Eudes would often confront situations in which Christians knowingly sinned. The fact that a monastery had a copy of its monastic rule and its monks knew the rule well did not mean that the rule would be heeded. That a religious house kept careful financial records did not always prevent reckless spending.

Nonetheless, Eudes viewed knowing what is morally right as the first step in doing what is morally right. Unlike most of his university contemporaries, he argued that unwilled, intellectual ignorance diminishes the voluntary nature of a sinful act and therefore the sinner's culpability.[110] There was no reason not to prevent this kind of unwilled ignorance through moral instruction. As archbishop, he insisted that every religious house have a copy of its financial records, its rule, and the statutes promulgated by Pope Gregory IX in 1235 for the reform of Benedictine monks. And the archbishop's own visitations, which usually included a sermon and an inspection of the spiritual and temporal state of the community (along with appropriate admonitions), served as a kind of instruction and moral monitoring of the community's conduct.

Although it was not unusual for thirteenth-century university graduates and masters to become prelates, there were significant differences in the job descriptions and skills required. A newly elected archbishop like Eudes, who had come from the university, would have had to do a certain amount of on-the-job learning. As a university master, Eudes rarely left Paris. Governing the large Norman province, on the other hand, required almost daily travel, more reminiscent of the life of an itinerant apostle. As archbishop, Eudes faced a constant barrage of decisions to make, responsibilities to delegate, sermons to preach, ceremonies to hold, correspondence to write, and charters to seal. An archbishop wielded power and authority (whether or not he chose to express it through his clothing and the symbolic objects he carried) which no university master did.

Yet the medieval intellectual did not live in an ethereal world of abstract scholastic commentaries, removed from the practical realities of the day. The thirteenth century witnessed a growing number of university masters who became bishops, archdeacons, canons, councillors, and ministers. In the case of English royal administration, one historian has suggested a correlation between the employment of former university masters and an improvement in political administration.[111]

Furthermore, an examination of Eudes's university career reveals that he was not even at that stage engaged in mere abstract scholastic commentaries. He viewed the theological enterprise as serving a pragmatic and redemptive purpose. His sermons addressed the challenges of living a religious life and thus conveyed a tone of activism. Eudes appears to have taken his responsibility as a teacher seriously, showing concern not only with his students' theological knowledge but also with their moral conduct, both while at the university and once they were serving the larger church society. Eudes's interest in moral theology extended to his more speculative theology, where he assessed humans' capacity for reform. In his capacity as theologian and Franciscan, he stressed the important connection between thought and action, word and deed. This connection would be dramatized most vividly in his episcopal career. Yet already in his career at the university, he displayed a dual commitment to the moral and spiritual as well as the speculative and metaphysical.

2

Itinerant Archbishop, Itinerant *Familia*

Little can be said with any certainty about Eudes Rigaud's social origins, but it is possible that he was the son of Adam and Adeline Rigaud, who are recorded in 1209 as ceding a mill and land at La Louverie to the abbey of Saint-Germain-des-Prés for a sum of thirty *livres tournois*.[1] In 1230, there is a record of an Adam Rigaud, a knight from Courquetaine, selling all that he possessed at Villeneuve-Saint-Georges to the abbey of Saint-Germain.[2] Whatever the case, contemporary chroniclers clearly believed that Eudes came from a noble and illustrious family, and from what is known of Eudes's siblings and nephews, the family does seem to have been part of the *petite noblesse* in the Île-de-France and to have wielded considerable influence.[3]

For seventeen years of Eudes's archiepiscopate, his brother Adam, also a Franciscan, was a regular member of his *familia*. Several of Eudes's other blood relatives appear from time to time in the *Register*, although not as part of the episcopal *familia*. The archbishop had at least one other family member who was a religious, a sister, named Marie, who was abbess of the Paraclete, the convent known for its founder, Abelard, and first abbess, Heloise. Eudes visited Marie at the Paraclete on several occasions, consecrating her as abbess during his visit in June 1249.[4] In addition, Eudes had at least two other sisters, whose names do not appear in the records but whose sons do. One sister had a son named Adam de Verneuil (de Vernolio), a *magister* and Rouen canon beginning in 1263 and mentioned as dean of the Rouen chapter in 1299.[5] The other sister's son was Amaury de Muzy, an esquire, whom Eudes visited in 1261 at the nephew's manor in Normandy at Motelle-sous-Muzy (Eure).[6] Eudes also maintained ties with a brother, Pierre Rigaud, a knight, who possessed a fief at Courquetaine, in the region of Brie-Comte-Robert, about 25 kilometers southeast of Paris, quite possibly the town where Eudes grew up.[7] Eudes returned to Courquetaine several times to see this brother.[8] In 1263, Eudes went to Paris to celebrate a certain Pierre Rigaud's marriage to Nazarea, the daughter of a road surveyor from Auxerre.[9] It is not known whether this Pierre Rigaud was Eudes's brother or another nephew, the latter more likely, given the date.[10] Another nephew mentioned in the *Register*, Adam Rigaud, was a doctor in theology who, like Eudes's nephew Adam de Verneuil, was a canon in the Rouen chapter in the 1260s; he may have been the son of Eudes's brother Pierre. It was Eudes who conferred prebends on his two nephews.[11]

Eudes Rigaud was no stranger to Rouen when he arrived on Easter Day, April 19, 1248, after having been consecrated archbishop by Pope Innocent IV in Lyon. In 1246, while regent master of the Franciscan *studium* in Paris, Eudes had been sent to Rouen by the Franciscan order to be guardian of the Franciscan convent of Saint-Marc, which only that year had been founded by the then archbishop of Rouen, Eudes Clément.[12] Although Eudes surely spent most of the period from 1246 to 1247 in Paris, he would have made important contacts in Rouen as well. Little can be said for certain about the events leading up to his election to the archiepiscopate, but there appears to have been nothing unusual about it.[13] According to the seventeenth-century Franciscan chronicler Luke Wadding, it was through Eudes's role at the Rouen convent that his outstanding virtues became known to the chapter and he was elected archbishop.[14] A dubious but much repeated story suggests that the canons of the Rouen cathedral, unable to agree on whom they should elect, decided that the first cleric to enter the Rouen cathedral to pray would be their new archbishop. According to this story, Eudes was on his way to the convent of Saint-Marc early the next morning when he stopped by the cathedral to pray, thereby unknowingly electing himself the next archbishop.[15] The implication of this claim of miraculous election was that it was Eudes's piety or divine fate that got him elected rather than the personal involvement of the king or pope. Claims of miraculous elections were still occurring in the thirteenth century, as in the case of Saint Guillaume de Donjeon, the Cistercian abbot at Challis elected to the see at Bourges in 1200.[16]

Pope Innocent IV, who had made Parisian theologians cardinals and had taken up long-term residence at Lyon, may also have been directly involved in Eudes Rigaud's selection for the Norman see (if so, the pope probably worked in tandem with the French king). A chronicle from the Rouen abbey of Sainte-Catherine-du-Mont suggests that after the death of Archbishop Eudes Clément in 1247, the canons from the Rouen cathedral elected a certain Magister Odo, a canon from Saint-Denis, but that his election was quashed by other Rouen canons.[17] According to the chronicle, the pope then stepped in and provided the Rouen canons with Eudes Rigaud. There is reason to doubt the accuracy of this chronicle, however, since its author confused the disputed episcopal election in Rouen of 1245, in which there were two candidates named Odo from Saint-Denis, with the election of 1247.[18] According to the medieval Franciscan chronicler Salimbene de Adam, it was not the pope but the French king who was directly responsible for Eudes's election to the archiepiscopate.[19] French kings Louis VII and Philip Augustus had worked out a compromise whereby the king and cathedral chapter would try to find candidates who were agreeable to both parties. It was standard procedure for a cathedral chapter to formally ask the king's permission to proceed with an episcopal election, and for a province as politically important to the French king as Normandy, there is every reason to think that the king might have recommended a candidate to the Rouen canons.[20] Because the crown enjoyed regalian rights in Rouen (during episcopal vacancies, the king had a customary right to estates, income, and patronage belonging to the bishopric), the king could withhold the regalia from a newly elected archbishop of whom he did not approve.[21] There were also surely political advantages for the Norman church to choose an archbishop with royal influence. Eudes Rigaud's predecessor, Eudes Clément, not only had been abbot of Saint-Denis but had earlier been archdeacon of Paris, dean of the enormous royal monastery of Saint-Martin of Tours, royal clerk, and even a substitute president of the Court of the Exchequer.[22] Eudes Rigaud clearly had royal influence during his career as archbishop, but it is not known when he first developed a personal relationship with the French king, although it is likely that the king, with his close ties to the Franciscans in Paris, would at the very least have heard of the prominent Franciscan preacher and theologian at the university and would have been partial to him.

When Eudes Rigaud first entered Rouen in 1248 as the newly elected archbishop, the city had approximately 40,000 people and was the largest in the French kingdom after Paris.[23] Although Rouen, like many European cities, expanded during the thirteenth century, it still would have had a largely rural feel to it. Residential neighborhoods were interspersed with gardens, orchards, fields, and vineyards. Along the Renelle River, tanners worked busily. Drapers, dyers, and fullers were located at the eastern end of the city.[24] The area just to the west of the cathedral (where the public entered) was occupied by a cemetery but also a walled atrium in which canons leased shops and houses and cultivated gardens.[25] In 1248, many of the city's buildings were new or recently rebuilt; a massive fire in 1200 and another in 1211 had destroyed large portions of the city, including much of the cathedral, numerous parish churches, the abbeys of Saint-Ouen and Saint-Lô, and dozens of houses, most of these buildings made of wood.[26] But on the feast of Saint Lawrence (August 10) 1248, only a few months after Eudes's arrival in the city, another major fire broke out, this time beginning near the gate of Beauvais. The fire destroyed the entire abbey of Saint-Ouen (not far from the cathedral) and severely damaged the nunnery of Saint-Amand, the churches of Saint-Lawrence and Saint-Gildard, and many of the city's other structures.[27] Although Eudes was not in Rouen during the conflagration, he returned to the city on August 14 and, curiously, made no mention of the fire in his *Register*.[28] The frequent outbreaks of fire not only caused many monastic houses to plunge into debt but also disrupted religious life in a variety of ways. [29] For instance, Eudes often noted the disruptive presence of workmen in churches and abbeys damaged by fires.[30]

In many ways, ducal Normandy had been the linchpin for the Angevin empire. Not only did Angevin kings spend a great deal of time in Normandy, but any travel from England to Anjou or Aquitaine usually involved travel through western Normandy.[31] Although Philip Augustus's conquest of Normandy in 1204 lessened ties between Normandy and England, Rouen continued to dominate trade between England and Paris. For instance, large quantities of wine from the Île de France and Burgundy were shipped via the Seine to England and the North Sea rim more generally.[32] Except for a few periods when the wine traffic was slowed, wine made up almost half of all traffic that passed through the port of Rouen.[33] Various other products, including cheese and pork, flowed from England into Normandy via the Seine and Oise rivers. Rouen also controlled a large share of trade with Ireland. Now that Normandy was part of the French kingdom, it had even closer ties to the Paris basin, although there was fierce competition between Parisian and Rouennais merchants for control of the Seine. Large quantities of fish and salt were transported by boat from Normandy to Paris.[34] Some of the most important trade into and out of Capetian France passed through Rouen.

Although the archbishop was not the lord of the city (Rouen, once a ducal city, was now a royal one), he was the lord of the large towns of Dieppe and Louviers, the vast plateau of Aliermont, and the rich lands of Fresne in the Norman Vexin.[35] The diocese of Rouen was sprawling, containing some fourteen hundred parishes, twenty-eight deaneries, and six archdeaconries. Eudes was also determined to exercise his jurisdiction as metropolitan over the province's other six dioceses: Evreux, Bayeux, Lisieux, Sées, Avranches, and Coutances. The boundaries of the ecclesiastical province were nearly coterminal with the relatively well defined borders of the duchy, which, in Upper Normandy, had been protected by an almost continuous string of rivers, including the Bresle, Epte, Eure, and Avre. Like the duchy, the ecclesiastical province extended southeast to Pontoise, only about 25 kilometers from Paris. Upper Normandy, with its excellent agricultural land and rich beech forests in the valleys of the Seine and the Eure and their tributaries, contained most of the dioceses of Rouen and Evreux. Lower Normandy, which more or less contained the other five dioceses, was more varied, with hilly, rich pasturelands as well as a band of Jurassic limestone (which runs from the Bessin through Caen down to the Perche),

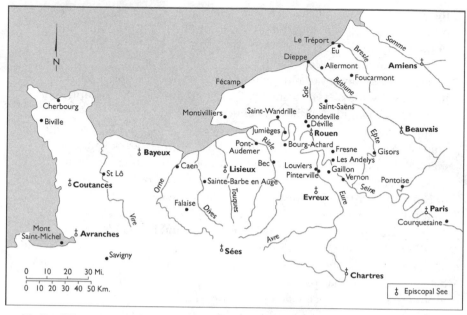

Medieval Normandy and Its Neighbors: The World of Eudes Rigaud

known for its valuable stone quarries and metal deposits, and the Amorican massif, a region of hilly, wooded countryside with sandstone and granite.[36] If the archbishop wished to travel from Rouen to the great abbey of Mont-Saint-Michel in the southwest corner of the diocese of Avranches, or, for that matter, the abbey of Cherbourg in the northwest of the province, he would have to travel some 230 kilometers. From either of these abbeys to the abbey of le Tréport in the northeast corner of the diocese of Rouen was well over 300 kilometers.

Thus it is not surprising that during his twenty-six and a half years as archbishop of Rouen, Eudes Rigaud traveled a great deal. It has been calculated that between 1248 and 1269 (the years covered by his episcopal register), he traveled 86,611 kilometers (54,131 miles), averaging 4,028.4 kilometers (2,517.7 miles) each year.[37] Wherever he went, the archbishop was surrounded by his *familia*, or entourage, much like a medieval king. It consisted of various associates (*socii*), fellow Franciscans (*fratres*), secretaries (*clerici*), and servants (*servientes*). At times he was also joined by at least one physician (*fisicus*), who was on hand to treat his rheumatism. Just how large was the archbishop's *familia*? It is difficult to say precisely; witness lists found in the archbishop's *Register* often indicate that there were many present in addition to those named (*et multis aliis*). Yet because lists of witnesses for episcopal *acta* generally name attesters in order of rank, it is unlikely that a simple priest would be listed and not an archdeacon or official who was also present.[38] In other words, the members of an episcopal *familia* who tended not to be named in witness lists were probably lower-ranking members such as household servants. Thus, although the lists of attesters do not provide a complete picture of the size of an episcopal *familia*, they likely identify its higher-ranking members.

In general, the archbishop's travelers seem to have numbered around twenty, including servants, who rarely appear in witness lists and were probably not considered part of the *familia*.[39] Franciscan chronicler and contemporary Salimbene de Adam reported seeing Eudes Rigaud in Italy, traveling with "eighty mounted attendants and a proper household."[40] It is unlikely that Eudes would have had this number with him during his regular travels in Normandy, especially given the Third and Fourth Lateran Councils' prescriptions limiting the number of horses or other mounts in an archbishop's entourage to forty or fifty.[41] The small and often poverty-stricken Norman priories where Eudes and his entourage stayed during visitations could not have accommodated or afforded such a large entourage. On the long journey to Rome in 1254, however, Eudes probably traveled with an unusually large group, including several of his suffragans and their staffs (the archbishop's adversaries and, thus, the reason for traveling to Rome to appear before the pope).[42]

Many of the members of Eudes's *familia* were canons from the Rouen cathedral.[43] It was certainly not unusual for canons to be involved in diocesan administration. The cathedral chapter had its origins in the bishop's *familia* and had emerged as a separate body only in the eleventh century.[44] But there continued to be close ties between the chapter and the bishop's household during the thirteenth century.[45] Eudes not only invited a few of his favorite canons from the Rouen chapter to be part of his *familia* but also rewarded loyal clerics who had already spent time in his service to vacant canonries in the cathedral. Several of the canons of the Rouen chapter, in other words, were or had been members of the archbishop's or his predecessors' *familia*. Having canons from the Rouen chapter in his household permitted the archbishop to fulfill his canonical obligation to consult with his chapter before making decisions, and the Rouen chapter may well have felt less threatened by the archbishop's power, knowing that its voice was heard through representatives who served in the archbishop's household.[46] Another attraction of the Rouen chapter was that it contained some talented and experienced administrators, a number of whom had been employed (or would later be employed) by the papal curia.[47] Around 81 percent of the Rouen canons carried the title *magister* (an unusually high percentage), indicating that they had been university trained.[48] During

Eudes's archiepiscopate, the chapter at Rouen, made up of somewhere between forty and fifty canons, included a half dozen papal chaplains, a cardinal chaplain, and a papal notary (to say nothing of two future cardinals and a future pope).[49] An organized and effective archiepiscopal administration simply would not have been possible without a talented team of associates, archdeacons, deans, secretaries, servants, and officials on whom the archbishop could rely.

One of the other advantages of having beneficed canons in his *familia* was that Eudes did not have to worry about their incomes.[50] The pope customarily permitted nonresidence for canons in the episcopal entourage, and in 1250 Eudes received papal confirmation of this custom. Specifically, Innocent IV granted Eudes the privilege of having three canons from the Rouen cathedral and three canons from Les Andelys accompany him wherever his episcopal business took him. The real significance of this grant was that the beneficed canons in Eudes's *familia* could enjoy the revenues from their benefices as if they were residing in their chapters.[51]

The canons served the archbishop in several capacities. Some bore specific titles and roles, such as Guillaume de Flavacourt (Guillelmus de Flavacuria), who served as Eudes's official, the archbishop's vicar in all juridical matters in the diocese, from 1263 to 1265. Another canon, Richard de Sap, served as the archbishop's personal secretary. In most cases, however, the canons who were part of the archbishop's retinue filled nonspecific roles and are called *socii*, or associates, in the *Register*. We find these *socii* as witnesses during juridical proceedings and as agents carrying out specific missions assigned to them by the archbishop. Several of Eudes's *socii* were highly educated. Etienne de Lorris, for instance, who served as Eudes's official, was a doctor of canon law, having been trained at Paris. Jean de Neuilly-en-Thelle (Johannes de Noentolio) was a doctor of theology and civil law. As a former university master, Eudes may have felt especially comfortable working with other university-trained churchmen. Eudes promoted many of the canons in his *familia* to administrative positions within the diocese, such as the archidiaconate, and several of the canons eventually advanced to even higher offices.[52] Guillaume de Flavacourt, who started as a simple canon in the Rouen cathedral, became the archbishop's official for three years and was appointed by Eudes archdeacon of the Petit-Caux, a position he filled for twelve years. He later succeeded Eudes as archbishop of Rouen. Jean de Neuilly-en-Thelle, another Rouennais canon, began serving in the archbishop's household in 1257. Seven years later, Eudes appointed him archdeacon of the Petit-Caux, then archdeacon of the Grand-Caux, and finally archdeacon of Rouen. In 1270–71, as archdeacon of Rouen, Jean served as the archbishop's vicar, managing the archbishopric while Eudes was on crusade.[53] The rise of the Rouen canon Simon de Brie (more often referred to as Simon de Meinpiciaco, since he was born in the castle at Montpensier in the province of Touraine) is most impressive of all. First appearing in Eudes's household in 1249, Simon acted as the archbishop's official as well as the archdeacon of the French Vexin from 1250 to 1252. He was later appointed archdeacon of Eu and archdeacon of Rouen. But this prelate, who began his career as a canon in the archbishop's *familia*, is best known for his later career, as a cardinal, papal legate, and then Pope Martin IV.[54]

We do not know how Eudes went about choosing canons to serve in his *familia*. Once he saw them perform within his household, however, he was able to identify those who showed the greatest promise. The *familia*, in short, provided a testing ground for administrative talent. But Eudes also used the *familia* as a way of grooming the kinds of leaders he wanted as archdeacons, officials, and treasurers. Perhaps most important, the archbishop could build trust and loyalty among those who would serve in the diocesan administration. When Jean de Neuilly-en-Thelle was appointed archdeacon of the Petit-Caux, for example, he had already spent seven years in Eudes's household. Jean's name appears in the *Register*'s folios more than fifty times before his archidiaconal appointment in 1264, and surely this figure represents just a fraction of the time he spent with the archbishop. Jean's appointment to the archidiaconate was a reward for his years of loyal service, and this loyalty, Eudes hoped, would not evaporate. Whereas in some dioceses archdeacons enjoyed increasing autonomy from their bishops, at times even challenging the bishop's authority, in Rouen, under Eudes's archiepiscopate, archdeacons remained the archbishop's vicars— his allies and not his rivals.[55] In this sense, the archdeacons never fully ceased being part of Eudes's household. They continued to accompany him on his visitations, to act as his deputies, and to serve as witnesses in legal proceedings. On January 21, 1250, for instance, while Eudes visited the cathedral chapter of Lisieux, the archdeacon of the French Vexin, Guillaume de Saâne, acted as the archbishop's vicar, visiting the Benedictine nunnery of Lisieux.[56] What was Guillaume doing visiting an abbey of nuns in Lisieux, far away from his own archdeaconry in the southeast corner of the Rouen diocese? Guillaume and other archdeacons like him continued to perform many of the same functions that they had as members of the archbishop's *familia*.[57]

It is certainly true that archdeacons conducted their own archidiaconal visitations and convened regular synods.[58] But here, too, the *Register* reveals how surprisingly well informed the archbishop was of local conditions and the activities of his archdeacons. He regularly attended, for instance, the synods of the greater archdeaconry of Rouen and the archdeaconry of the French Vexin.[59] And when an archdeacon such as Simon, the archdeacon of Eu, accepted the resignations of several priests, he was careful to do so on the authority of the archbishop.[60] Even Eudes's language, above all his frequent references in the *Register* to an archdeacon as "my archdeacon" (*meus archdiaconus*), conveyed his understanding of the archdeacon as an extension of his *familia*.[61] The archdeacons, moreover, continued to function as the *oculi episcopi*, "the eyes of the bishop."

It has already been suggested that Eudes tended to choose archdeacons who had served in his *familia* and whom he knew to be effective and loyal. But he also rarely allowed an archdeacon to remain in a particular archdeaconry for long. It was the archbishop's practice to shift his personnel frequently among archdeaconries and offices (archdeacon, official, treasurer, secretary). Several archdeacons served in three different archdeaconries during Eudes's archiepiscopate (Etienne de Sens, Jean de Neuilly-en-Thelle, and Simon de Montpensier). What accounts for this shuffling of personnel? In some cases a change in personnel was made simply in response to a vacancy due to a death or resignation. In other cases, Eudes appears to have decided to move a particularly effective archdeacon to an archdeaconry that had been plagued by problems. But the archbishop may also have continually relocated his personnel to avoid having resident administrators form intimate ties with the communities they governed and thereby become complacent or corrupt. By rotating his personnel, Eudes sought to preserve their integrity, ensure that they remained fresh, and remind them, if they needed any reminding, that he was actively overseeing everything they did. Eudes's practice of making frequent personnel shifts within his administration had parallels in French royal administration. Kings such as Louis IX and Philip IV shuffled their *baillis* and *sénéchaux* around the kingdom (and paid them extremely well) to ensure that they remained loyal to the crown and did not become fixtures in local politics. [62]

Eudes also used his visitations of archdeaconries as a way of both reinforcing his own influence and strengthening the authority of archdeacons. By having an archdeacon accompany him on his visitation of the archdeaconry, Eudes could instruct the archdeacon on the proper way to conduct a visitation, since the archdeacon was expected to conduct his own. The archbishop demonstrated the kinds of questions the archdeacon should ask when he examined a group of parish priests, the kinds of corrections he should make, and how he should record his findings and injunctions. The archdeacon would also be able to follow up on specific problems that Eudes discovered and tried to correct. Surely part of Eudes's inspection of a particular archdeaconry also consisted of determining whether the archdeacon had been performing his job well. There are few traces in the *Register*, however, of any reprimands of archdeacons. On the contrary, many of Eudes's visitations seem more like opportunities for the archbishop to mop up problems already uncovered by the archdeacon but still unresolved.[63] In this sense, Eudes's visitations were a way of supporting archdeacons and showing parish priests that the archdeacon had the archbishop's clout behind him. The archdeacon was also able to provide the archbishop with an insider's view of the state of religious life in the archdeaconry, something the archbishop undoubtedly found helpful. Without the archdeacon by his side during a visitation, the archbishop might have been far less successful in uncovering information. Moreover, an archdeacon who was conscientious in performing his duties may not have feared the archbishop's visitations or resented him as an oppressive outsider but rather welcomed him and his help, in much the way that when the modern French president or prime minister passes through a provincial French town, local notables clamor to be photographed with him.

Whereas Eudes's archdeacons appear to have traveled with him frequently, his *officialis* remained in Rouen with his own court, the consistory court, along with a sizable staff of notaries and clerics.[64] The official was, along with the archdeacon, the archbishop's chief legal officer, responsible for both adjudicative and nonadjudicative jurisdiction.[65] The position was most likely created in response to both the huge increase in the production of episcopal chanceries and the increase in the volume of cases appearing before bishops and archbishops in the late twelfth and early thirteenth centuries.[66] The large production of *acta* coming out of the official's consistory court in the thirteenth century (dealing with arbitration, spoliation of church property, wills, contracts, sales, gifts, exchanges, and the authentication of other *acta*) suggests that the creation of consistory courts relieved bishops of much of their administrative duties. Indeed, it is questionable whether an archbishop like Eudes would have been able to conduct as many pastoral visitations had he not had an official in Rouen carrying out much of the daily juridical and financial business.

The archbishop of Rouen's official was somewhat unusual in the prestige and power he was accorded. Unlike in many other dioceses, in Rouen there were no archidiaconal *officiales*, nor were there capitular or decanal *officiales*.[67] The semi-exclusive power of the archbishop's official probably resulted in the curtailment of the archdeacons' power, particularly the archdeacon of Rouen. Whereas archdeacons in many dioceses had their own justice, which was, in practice at least, somewhat distinct from the bishop's court, in Rouen the archdeacons traveled with the archbishop and served as his minister or vicar, while the archbishop's *officialis* presided over his consistory court at Rouen.[68] Furthermore, the metropolitan *officialis* had appellate jurisdiction over the six other episcopal *officiales* in the province. The official was rarely found without the title of *magister*, and his seal performed most of the notarial work for the archbishop. Several formularies from the thirteenth-century *officialité* of Rouen have survived. Although these skeletal letters are usually without any names or dates, they provide a sense of the kinds of cases and appeals the archbishop's official was accustomed to hearing and the kinds of documents that the consistory court regularly produced.[69]

It is difficult to know just how much coordination there was between the archbishop of Rouen and his official. They presumably saw a good deal of each other when Eudes was in Rouen. But it was perhaps Eudes's frequent absences from Rouen that made it especially important for his official to remain there. When assigning a defamed priest or abbot to appear before the archiepiscopal court in Rouen on a particular day, Eudes specified that the accused should "appear before us at Rouen or in the vicinity, if we should be there, or before our official if it should happen that we were away."[70] Although the archbishop was rarely certain where he would be on a particular date, he could rely on his official being in Rouen to oversee the consistory court. The court's business generally took place in one of three halls (referred to in the *Register* as "the smaller chamber," "the middle chamber," and "the larger chamber") that were part of the episcopal manor house in Rouen.[71] Presiding over the archbishop's court, the official heard cases involving defamed clerics, abbots who were in contempt for failing to appear at synods, priests who did not reside in their churches, and the like. The official also served as peacemaker, in one instance drawing up an ordinance to settle a dispute between a priest and a manager over who had administrative rights in the Hôtel-Dieu of Gournay.[72] But the Rouen official seems to have been most occupied by the archbishopric's finances. Almost every charter of sale, donation, and exchange involving the archbishopric was overseen by the archbishop's official. The parties involved in such transactions normally appeared before the official in Rouen. Again, it is difficult to determine to what extent the archbishop was personally involved in these transactions. What seems clear is that the consistory court, though symbolically attached to the archbishop's *familia*, often functioned as a separate physical body, stationed in Rouen and having its own chancery and seal.

Information was central to Eudes's ability to govern, and most of the information on which he relied was collected and organized by his personal secretaries, referred to in the *Register* as *nostri clerici*. As the *Register* makes clear, the *clerici* were a fixed presence in the archbishop's *familia*, traveling with him on all official business. Given the archbishop's frequent travel, the chancery had to be a portable one. During his first eight or nine years as archbishop, Eudes normally had two secretaries with him: Evrard and Morel. By 1259, both had left the *familia* and had been replaced by Jean de Morgneval, who stayed on as Eudes's principal secretary until 1269, when he became a beneficed canon in the Rouen cathedral.[73] Most of the charters that came out of Eudes's chancery were copied in typical thirteenth-century, Anglo-Norman documentary script (*cursiva anglicana*), suggesting that Eudes's scribes were well educated.[74] In addition to drafting charters and letters, the secretaries were charged with keeping the *Register*. This responsibility involved recording everything from the minutes at councils and synods, to word-for-word transcripts of the archbishop's examinations of candidates for the priesthood, to the details of what the archbishop found and ordered corrected during his visitations of religious houses.

The secretaries were more than mere stenographers; they were also great organizers of data. This role is illustrated most dramatically in the polyptych begun under Archbishop Pierre de Colmieu (1236–44) and corrected and elaborated by Eudes's secretaries. The polyptych listed every parish in the Rouen diocese, giving for each one the name of the patron, the annual income from the benefice, the number of parishioners, the name of the rector, and the name of the archbishop who invested him.[75] The *clerici* also assisted the archbishop in other ways. They were used as official witnesses in juridical proceedings. The *clericus* Jean de Morgneval appears to have been one of the archbishop's most trusted associates, on several occasions serving as his deputy. When Eudes was unable to attend the synod at Rouen, he nonetheless learned what transpired, thanks to Jean's careful note taking.[76] Twelve different names appear in the *Register* under the title *clericus*, and the original manuscript of the *Register*, which traveled with the archbishop, plainly shows changes in hands. Despite the variations in script, however, there is a remarkable uniformity to the *Register*'s 389 folios. Moving from year to year and from hand to hand, we find the same matters recorded, the same language employed, and few changes in the physical format. A single archbishop saw to it that the information was recorded and organized as he desired.

A distinctive feature of Eudes's entourage was the presence of several Franciscans. Indeed, one of Eudes's first acts as archbishop was to request permission from the pope to have Franciscans in his *familia*. In October 1249, Pope Innocent IV granted the request, authorizing Eudes to have four Franciscans (*fratres*) in his episcopal entourage. The pope also allowed the *fratres* to ride on horseback and wear shoes, both of which would otherwise have been prohibited by the Franciscan rule.[77] Although there is no mention of the *fratres* in the *Register* until December 1248, well over a year after Eudes began keeping his *Register*, from this point on, there were always two or three Franciscans listed as regular members of the household.[78]

It was fairly common for thirteenth-century bishops to have members of the regular clergy in their households. Robert Grosseteste, the secular bishop of Lincoln, for example, traveled with several Franciscans and Dominicans.[79] Having regular clergy in an episcopal entourage helped counter the impression that the episcopal visitation of a monastery was mercenary.[80] Yet as far as I can tell, that is not why Eudes, himself a pious Franciscan, wished to have several Franciscan brothers in his company. He probably believed that with Franciscans by his side, he could maintain his close ties with the order and preserve the Franciscan values he cherished. Attempting to serve as archbishop while observing the Franciscan rule invariably posed challenges. We know from the *Register*, for instance, that as archbishop, Eudes wore pontificals (even while celebrating Mass in the Franciscan convent at Rouen), thus compromising the prescription in the rule to always wear the Franciscan habit. Yet by having several Franciscans in his entourage who were committed to observing the rule, he guarded against the danger of gradually slipping into the life of a secular prelate. His Franciscan companions were there to remind him of his obligations as a humble, pious, and obedient imitator of the evangelical life.

It should be noted that Eudes never once had a Dominican in his entourage, and it is possible that like many Franciscans of the time, he felt a sense of rivalry with the Dominicans. Salimbene, however, specifically commented that Eudes "loved the Order of Preachers, as well as his own Order of the Friars Minor, and he was very generous to them both."[81] The archbishop's *Register* indicates that the Franciscan archbishop periodically visited the Dominican convent in Rouen, where he not only at times celebrated Mass and preached but ate with the brothers. Indeed, perhaps so as to appear impartial, Eudes seems to have taken care to visit the Dominican house at Rouen a day or two before he visited with the Franciscans. Still, it is difficult to imagine that Eudes would have been evenhanded in his treatment of the two orders, and the *Register* bears this out, showing that the Franciscan prelate visited Franciscan convents almost five times as often as Dominican convents.[82]

Beginning in August 1252, one of the Franciscans in Eudes's *familia* was Adam Rigaud, the archbishop's own brother.[83] Adam remained part of his brother's household until his death in August 1269. During these seventeen years, he appears in the *Register* almost seventy times, more times than anyone except Jean de Morgneval, the archbishop's secretary. It is rare for the *Register* to list those in the archbishop's presence and not mention Adam; the two brothers appear to have been together almost always. When Eudes had a special investigation to carry out or was unable to perform his normal responsibilities because of illness, he turned to his brother Adam. In September 1258, for instance, while afflicted with stomach pains (*dolore stomachi*), Eudes sent Adam to the priory of Saint-Laurent-en-Lyon to conduct a visitation in his stead. Adam preached a sermon just as his brother would have done, calculated the number of resident Augustinian canons (fifteen), indicated the number who were priests (one), recorded the canons' total debt (300 *livres*), and determined that the canons had sufficient provisions (*estauramenta*) to last the year.[84] In other cases, Eudes delegated tasks to Adam and a trusted canon or archdeacon, such as Richard de Sap or Jean de Neuilly-en-Thelle.[85] These deputies were said to act "in our place" (*loco nostro*), with the archbishop's *familia* accompanying them and the *clerici* recording entries in the *Register* just as they did for the archbishop. Although Adam had no official title, he was given enormous power. Acting as his brother's representative, he even had the authority to absolve a sentence of excommunication imposed by the Rouen official. Given Eudes's closeness to his brother, the *Register*'s matter-of-fact tone in reporting Adam's death is all the more jarring: "On this day, brother Adam died. At Rouen, in the house of the friars minor, we buried the body of the said brother, with the Lord's help, and we spent the night in our manor house."[86]

Eudes's travel was frequently interrupted by his battle with rheumatism, probably made more troublesome by the damp and rainy Norman climate. The archbishop tried as much as possible not to let his ailments affect his pastoral duties. In 1268, on October 4, the feast of Saint Francis, "with God's grace, although weak and infirm, we celebrated High Mass in pontificals at the Rouen cathedral and had the entire chapter at our manor for the feast day."[87] On some enormously important occasions, however, Eudes simply was unable to press on. In 1269, on the feast of Saint Denis, Eudes was staying at the abbey of Saint-Denis with the king, the papal legate, and many of France's greatest prelates. It was only a few weeks before they would leave on crusade. But Eudes was so afflicted by his rheumatism that he was unable to attend Mass.[88]

In June and July 1251, Eudes did not leave his manor house at Déville for five weeks because of illness. Illness again immobilized him for five weeks in 1252–53. It became so bad that he could not celebrate Christmas in Rouen, remaining bedridden at his manor house in Aliermont. In 1259, severe pain in his legs caused him to miss Easter celebrations in Rouen. A week later, he received an urgent letter from King Louis, "asking us to hasten to him at Fontainebleau without delay as soon as we should see his letter, for he was seriously ill." Eudes took the king's letter seriously: "Ignoring the severity of our own infirmity, we made haste and spent that night at Genainville, where we received another special messenger bringing us a letter from the king urging us not to proceed further, for that, with God's grace, he felt better and was growing stronger."[89] Eudes was surely relieved at this news, not least because of his own need for convalescence. After two days, however, he received a third letter, informing him that the king was again ill and might be dying. "Having read this, we immediately took our way to him, though not without great travail, hastening along with the aid of horses and a wagon."[90] Despite the fact that Eudes was not well enough to ride on horseback and had to be carried by wagon, he made extraordinary time, covering the 122 kilometers between Genainville and Fontainebleau in only two days. When he arrived at the king's bedside, he found Louis greatly improved. Under the strain of rushing to the king, however, Eudes's own health took a turn for the worse: ". . . at St. Cloud, where we were so seriously attacked by fever and rheumatism that we were compelled to stop and go to bed, for we could not proceed any further."[91] The archbishop remained incapacitated for 105 days. A few months later, on January 15, 1260, Eudes received news of the death of King Louis's eldest son, Louis. The king sent the archbishop a letter expressing his enormous grief over the loss and asking for Eudes's prayers and those of all religious and conventual houses in Normandy. The archbishop immediately set out to console the king. After a day's journey, however, "our old rheumatism attacked us once again and we were unable to proceed further, and were compelled to take to our bed."[92] It was several days before Eudes was able to resume his journey to the king.

Eudes and his entourage generally traveled by horse, and rarely by water, except when by necessity they crossed the Seine.[93] The procurations in kind that the archbishop collected during visitations included forage for horses (*foraginem pro equis*) and bedding for horses and servants.[94] And the archbishop's concern about getting the grain that was owed to him probably reflected his constant need for oats, for, among other things, feeding his horses. An entourage of about twenty men, including secretaries, canons, *fratres*, physicians, servants, and horses, would have required a heavy load of equipment and supplies. When Eudes was again called to the ailing king in October 1260, he left most of his *familia* and burdensome equipment (*hernesium*) behind so he could travel more quickly. We can presume that this equipment and supplies would have included food, cooking utensils, salt, oats and hay for horses, the archbishop's pontifical robes, and scribal materials.

Inclement weather had little impact on the travel of the archiepiscopal entourage.[95] Normandy was ravaged by floods and heavy rains in 1255, 1257, and 1258, but there is not a single reference to these events in the *Register*; Eudes traveled the usual distances during these years and made the same number of visitations. Aside from an occasional remark about an extraordinary lightning storm, the only reference to weather in the entire *Register* comes during Eudes's journey to Rome. Just before crossing the Alps during the fiercest winter months of 1254, the archbishop and his entourage were stranded for three days at Salins because of heavy snow.[96]

For the most part, the travel routes Eudes used during his long journeys were quite conventional for the time, and he showed a propensity for traveling by horse alongside rivers.[97] On his journey to Rome, for instance, he followed the Seine from Troyes to Dijon (before reaching Troyes, he had taken detours in order to visit his sister at the Paraclete and his brother at Courquetaine) and then traveled southeast to Lausanne and around Lake Geneva. He then followed the Rhone from Sion up to Brig. Climbing higher into the Swiss Alps, he used the Simplon Pass to cross over into Domodossola, Italy, and made his way along the Toce Valley, near Lake Maggiore to Milan, where he spent two days, most likely meeting with Leo de Valvassori da Perego, the Franciscan archbishop of Milan, with whom he had much in common.[98] From Milan, Eudes chose to head southeast for the Adriatic coast, making his way to Rimini via Mantua, Ferrara, and Bologna.

In Mantua, he was hosted by Bishop Martino of Parma, who, according to Salimbene, was a great drinker and a generous host, providing lavish banquets for his guests.[99] The bishop of Mantua insisted on sending his steward ahead to make arrangements and pay for the entourage's journey to Bologna. But Eudes refused the bishop's offer, saying that he and his household could live in splendor on only half his income. It was at this point that Salimbene noted that Eudes was traveling with a retinue mounted on some eighty horses. Assuming that Salimbene's story was accurate, one can only wonder whether Eudes was bragging about his income, not wishing to be outdone by the generous Italian bishop.[100] Or was Eudes rather expressing humility in saying that he would be content (perhaps more content) if he had a much smaller income? As if to try to counter the impression that the Franciscan archbishop was proud of his archbishopric's wealth, Salimbene quickly added that at Eudes's next stop, in Ferrara, the archbishop dined with four Franciscans and, as was his custom, gave half the food that was served to him to the poor.[101] The three days Eudes spent in Bologna are perhaps indicative of his desire to see various prelates and *magistri* at the renowned university.

On his way to Rome from Rimini, Eudes made sure that he stopped for four days at Assisi, a place that would have had great meaning for him as a Franciscan. Furthermore, the bishop of Assisi was a fellow Franciscan, Niccolò da Calvi.[102] On March 11, Eudes and his entourage reached Rome, and on the following day, he recorded in his *Register*, "We went to the Lateran and kissed the foot of the Lord Pope." Eudes spent the entire month of May back in Assisi, awaiting the papal decision on the matter of his dispute with his suffragans, the reason for his journey. After almost four months, the papal decision was handed down, and a week later, Eudes and his entourage set out on the long journey home. This time he chose a more direct route, traveling the western side of the peninsula to Siena, Pisa, Genoa, and then Turin. It was certainly easier crossing the Alps in early August than in early February, and Eudes and his entourage used the Mont Cénis Pass, descended into Chambery, and traveled on to Lyon and then to Paris and Rouen, where they were received in a procession, having been gone for 252 days.[103]

In terms of Eudes's travel, however, what is most striking in the *Register* is what Oscar Darlington calls "the regularity, the consistency, and the prodigious extent" of the archbishop's travels: 86,611 kilometers over twenty-one years, some months averaging as much as 881 kilometers; and an average of 18–23 kilometers per day, every year between 1248 and 1269.[104] By 1269, the year he left on crusade (and the *Register* stopped being recorded), Eudes would have been between sixty-five and seventy years old. His rheumatism continued to plague him. But in the years leading up to 1269, he continued to cover the same distances and conduct the same number of visitations as before.

Not all of Eudes's travel, however, involved official ecclesiastical business, visiting parishes and religious houses. At times, he traveled to see friends and cultivate relationships with important lay patrons. After receiving a procuration at the Cistercian abbey of le Valasse, for instance, he would sometimes spend a night or two at the nearby castle of Guillaume, the chamberlain of Tancarville, whose ancestors (hereditary chamberlains) had been major monastic benefactors and had founded the abbey of Saint-Georges de Boscherville. On one such visit to Tancarville, Eudes dedicated the new chapel in Guillaume's castle. When the Norman aristocrat died just before Easter in 1269, Eudes performed the funeral ceremony at the abbey of Boscherville, where the Tancarville family was buried. Eudes then took Guillaume's heart to Rouen to be buried in the chancel of the Franciscan convent, perhaps something Guillaume had included in his will under the inspiration of the Franciscan archbishop.[105]

Although as an administrator Eudes appears to have prized efficiency and organization, as a traveler he did not always take the quickest or most direct routes. Rather, there were times when he went out of his way in order to visit the shrine of Saint Julien (significantly, the patron saint of travelers), with its history of miracles, or kiss the relics at Notre-Dame-le-Puy, or celebrate Mass on the altar at the shrine of Saint-Gilles-du-Gard in Provence, one of the most famous pilgrimage sites in Europe.[106] In July 1261, Eudes accompanied the bishop of Auxerre by foot on a pilgrimage from Paris to the shrine at Chartres.[107] On a pilgrimage to the church of Saint-Hildevert at Gournay in 1263, Eudes heard Mass and kissed the relics and then switched to his administrative role, conducting a formal visitation of the canons of the church.[108]

Reading the *Register*, one has the impression that the Franciscan led as itinerant a life as the apostles he wished to imitate, twice crossing the Channel to England, crossing the Alps on his way to and from Rome, three times traveling to Lyon (twice to see the pope and once to attend the Second Council of Lyon), going on several long pilgrimages, and traveling to North Africa on crusade. Within Normandy, he conducted well over one thousand visitations at more than two hundred different abbeys, priories, chapters, hospitals, and parish churches. Whether he was conducting visitations, dedicating new churches, blessing abbots, consecrating bishops, conferring holy orders, visiting shrines of saints, or attending the Parlement in Paris, he was almost always traveling.

In spite of all his travel, however, Eudes managed to spend a little over half his nights in one of eleven manor houses belonging to the archbishopric, in Déville, Paris, Rouen, Fresne, Aliermont, Pinterville, Pontoise,

Gaillon, Louviers, Andelys, and Saint-Matthieu. His favorite stopping place appears to have been Déville, located on a plateau just 3.5 kilometers northwest of Rouen. He spent a total of 958 nights in Déville in the years covered by the *Register,* compared with 722 nights in his Rouen palace.[109] All told, he spent the night in or near Rouen about 20 percent of the time. Returning from a long journey to the south or east of Rouen, Eudes still tended to go the extra distance up the steep slope to his house in Déville rather than spend the night below in Rouen. It is odd, perhaps, that a Franciscan preferred rural solitude to urban cacophony, although Saint Francis also had a penchant for the rural solitude of the hermitage outside the town of Assisi. It may be that the luxury-averse archbishop preferred the half-timbered house at Déville precisely because it was a humbler edifice than the much larger and more formal stone palace at Rouen, which had three different sized rooms or floors (*camerae*) where synods were held and priests were ordained, as well as a hall (*aula*), a kitchen, a gallery (*logia*), an ambulatory, a prison, and a chapel that measured 8 by 16 meters (somewhat smaller than the episcopal chapels in Reims and Lisieux).[110] Yet the manor house at Déville does not appear to have been all that modest. It also had a hall where Eudes conducted official business; the residence was large enough to accommodate the king of France and other bishops; and like the manor house at Rouen, it had a private chapel (*capella*), perhaps in a separate building, to which the archbishop could withdraw for contemplation and prayer.[111] The manor house at Fresne was one of the archbishop's more modest rural residences, essentially consisting of a large barn (46 by 11.5 meters) with a tile roof. The property included cowsheds, pigsties, sheepfolds, and a dovecote, as well as a private chapel and a prison.[112] The archbishop also showed a predilection for this manor house, which he visited at least once a month from 1249 to 1269, except for somewhat more sporadic visits from 1250 to 1253.[113]

More than 10 percent of Eudes's nights (832) were spent at his archiepiscopal residence in Paris, located on the rue du Paon, near the convent of the friars minor.[114] Having a house in Paris was extremely useful, especially given the frequency of Eudes's visits there. As he became more involved in royal administration and began sitting in the king's Parlement, his trips to Paris became even more frequent. While some of his manor houses, such as the one in Aliermont, had belonged to the archbishopric for several generations, others, such as the ones in Pinterville, Gaillon, Pontoise, and Les Andelys, were purchased or built during his own episcopate.[115] That all the newly purchased residences (and all the previously owned residences except Déville and Aliermont) were southeast of Rouen was no coincidence; they made strategic stopping places on the archbishop's most heavily trafficked route, the Seine valley, which connected Rouen and Paris.

Eudes's manor houses were more than simply places to spend the night. Various kinds of ecclesiastical and secular business occurred in these residences. The manor house at Aliermont, an imposing fortress that he visited at least 150 times, was conveniently located near the valuable town of Dieppe, where Eudes was viscount and collected an annual rent of 1,100 *livres tournois*. That the archbishop conducted secular business at his house in Aliermont is clear from numerous charters of sale involving burghers from Dieppe.[116] While serving both as convenient stopovers and centers of spiritual and temporal administration, the archbishop's manor houses were also symbols of the dignity and honor of the archiepiscopal office, and Eudes frequently used his residences to entertain the king and queen, the masters of the Court of the Exchequer, the papal legate, and visiting bishops and archbishops from as far away as Tyre.[117] It appears, however, that his rural residences were somewhat unusual in their modest surroundings, lacking symbols of luxury and status, such as ponds and game parks, that were commonly found around other episcopal residences, including those in the other Norman dioceses.[118]

3

A Metropolitan's Contested Jurisdiction

Although the concept of ecclesiastical reform was extremely popular during the high Middle Ages, its implementation frequently provoked conflict. In addition to tensions between those who sought to carry out reforms and those who resisted being reformed, various jurisdictional conflicts arose among reformers themselves. During the archiepiscopate of Eudes Rigaud, such conflicts arose between the archbishop and his suffragan bishops regarding the archbishop's jurisdictional rights as metropolitan outside his archdiocese. Did the archbishop have an unrestricted right to visit the parishes and religious houses in his province? Did he have the right to hear appeals against the sentences of archdeacons outside his archdiocese, thereby bypassing the suffragan bishop as the judge of first instance? From the perspective of the parties involved, these questions were much more than petty quarrels or turf battles. The suffragan bishops accused the archbishop of abusing his power and violating custom and law. The archbishop, however, argued that he was preserving public order and acting both in accordance with custom and in the best interests of the church. Contributing to this conflict was the fact that in the mid-thirteenth century, the Norman church was run by a group of talented and zealous administrators who were determined to carry out what they considered their religious duties. Neither Eudes Rigaud nor his suffragan bishops were willing to concede the project of reform (with its concomitant authority). Ambiguities about the legal definition and parameters of the office of metropolitan only served to fuel the potential for conflict over diocesan jurisdiction.

During the Middle Ages, the power of the metropolitan, or chief bishop of an ecclesiastical province, varied widely according to time and place. There was a good deal of confusion about the meaning of the terms *metropolitan, archbishop, primate,* and *patriarch.*[1] At certain times during the earlier history of the church, the title of metropolitan was honorific and did not confer any juridical authority beyond that of a normal bishop. Drawing on Isidore of Seville and others, Gratian distinguished between an archbishop, who was a papal delegate and whose jurisdiction was vicarial, and a metropolitan, who held an established seat as the ordinary head of the provincial episcopacy. By the thirteenth century, however, the distinction between an archbishop and metropolitan was nominal, and the two terms were increasingly used interchangeably.[2] In the West, metropolitans first began exercising extrajuridical powers in relation to bishops during the Carolingian period. In the wake of the so-called False Decretals in the mid-ninth century and then the Gregorian reforms in the eleventh century, metropolitans lost much of their jurisdiction to bishops and the pope. By the thirteenth century, however, metropolitans were again exercising greater episcopal jurisdiction within their ecclesiastical provinces.[3] Yet the canonical parameters of a metropolitan's jurisdiction remained unclear.

The jurisdictional status of a metropolitan was particularly difficult to define because a metropolitan was a bishop and at the same time something more. His jurisdiction fell somewhere between that of the pope and that of the bishops of his province. The metropolitan was the ordinary of his archdiocese, meaning that he was the officer with original jurisdiction in his own right. What was less clear, however, was his juridical authority in the other dioceses of his province. If each bishop had full jurisdiction in his own diocese, how could the archbishop also have jurisdiction? What was the meaning of "with the plenitude of power" (*potestatis plenitudo*)? The early-thirteenth-century canonist Raymond de Peñafort argued that a metropolitan possessed a kind of quasi-universality of jurisdiction within the various dioceses of his province. Raymond compared the metropolitan's jurisdiction in his province with the pope's universal jurisdiction. The pope's universal jurisdiction was expressed in the pallium, an insignia of episcopal power, which the pope could wear "always and everywhere" (*semper et ubique*). Yet if a metropolitan possessed this kind of universal jurisdiction within his own province, as Raymond suggested, why did he have the right to wear a pallium only within his own archdiocese? Why did the metropolitan not have the right to wear the pallium in the other dioceses of the province? Whereas Raymond asserted a metropolitan's jurisdiction within his province, other canonists insisted on safeguarding the jurisdictional autonomy of the suffragan bishops as the ordinaries of their respective dioceses. Although a metropolitan confirmed a suffragan bishop's election, received an oath of fealty from the bishop-elect, and consecrated the new bishop, this did not then mean that the metropolitan had full jurisdiction within the bishop's diocese.[4] When Eudes Rigaud asked Pope Innocent IV for the privilege to wear the archiepiscopal pallium in all the dioceses of the Norman province, for instance, the pope granted the archbishop's request, but with the condition that the archbishop first receive the consent of each respective diocesan.[5]

Many of the unresolved questions about a metropolitan's jurisdiction were being raised about episcopal jurisdiction more generally.[6] The question of the source of episcopal jurisdiction was at the center of an intense struggle between mendicant and secular theologians at the University of Paris during the 1250s. The seculars argued that a bishop's power was derived directly from God whereas the mendicants argued that a bishop's power was derived from the pope. This question also applied to a metropolitan's power. Was a metropolitan essentially a papal delegate for his province? During the thirteenth century, the pope increasingly confirmed a metropolitan's election and performed the consecration ceremony, but at times it was rather the suffragan bishops who performed these roles. There are even some cases of a metropolitan's cathedral chapter consecrating the archbishop-elect.

Even if a bishop or archbishop derived his power from the pope, however, this did not mean that the pope could exercise his authority through his delegate arbitrarily. Even among canonists who supported the notion of a papal monarchy with universal jurisdiction, there was a sense that the pope's absolute and universal power had limits, as Kenneth Pennington notes: "After building a formidable theory of papal monarchy, the canonists did not conclude that the pope's supreme sovereignty reduced the bishops to officers whose authority was simply delegated by the pope or derived from him. The bishops had rights that the pope should safeguard. Christ had established the 'status ecclesiae' in which the bishops occupied an important place, and even the pope could not destroy it."[7] This renewed emphasis during the thirteenth century on the "rigid hierarchy of inviolable jurisdictions" also applied to a metropolitan's limited power with respect to his suffragan bishops.[8] As we shall see, the metropolitan's authority as the episcopal superior of his province did not mean that he could simply usurp his suffragans' rights as the ordinaries of their respective dioceses. Although thirteenth-century popes were generally supportive of the pastoral work of metropolitans, they did not approve of metropolitans who infringed on their suffragans' rights. An aggressive archbishop not only created discord within his province but also threatened to diminish the pope's own power and influence within the province.

Based on Eudes Rigaud's episcopal *Register*, we know that the Norman archbishop had frequent interactions with the six bishops of his province. Eudes confirmed the elections of bishops-elect, received oaths of obedience, and performed the consecration ceremonies in the presence of the other bishops. He also convened and presided over at least nine provincial councils during his twenty-six years as archbishop, roughly 10 percent of all provincial councils known to have been held in France during the thir-

teenth century.[9] In calling for a provincial council, the archbishop of
Rouen customarily asked the bishop of Bayeux to summon the other suffragan bishops, abbots, archdeacons, deans, and collegiate bodies outside the
archdiocese to appear in Rouen on a particular date. The bishop of Bayeux
was the senior bishop of the province (after the archbishop), and in this capacity he summoned the other bishops to provincial councils and formally
opened the council with the reading of a letter. The hierarchy within the
Norman episcopate was reflected in the seating arrangement at provincial
councils: the archbishop sat in the middle, flanked on his right, in descending rank, by the bishops of Bayeux, Evreux, and Lisieux, and on his left by
the bishops of Avranches, Sées, and Coutances.[10]

Although the archbishop presided over the council, he was required by
law to consult his suffragans. It is difficult to determine from the *Register* to
what extent Eudes sought his suffragans' counsel. When describing the
provincial councils in his *Register*, Eudes often used the phrases "with their
requisite advice," "by common consent of our brothers," and "the council
having been celebrated harmoniously."[11] In one case, Eudes claimed to have
consulted his suffragans about the question of a resumed provincial visitation. He then went further, however, making a bold declaration about his
unconditional right to visit the dioceses of his province. His declaration provoked a long and bitter dispute. In other words, even though he had sought
his suffragans' advice on the visitation issue, he clearly did not heed it.

Aside from this notable example, however, most of the provincial councils appear to have been celebrated without much conflict. In the first
place, the councils were as much about religious ritual as about the internal
politics of the ecclesiastical province. The councils began with the celebration of the Mass, followed by the chanting of the *Veni creator spiritus*, the
litany, the Lord's Prayer, and various other prayers customarily recited at the
beginning of synods. Second, the archbishop and suffragan bishops faced
many of the same problems in disciplining the clergy of their respective
dioceses. A provincial council was less an adversarial confrontation between
metropolitan and suffragan bishops than an opportunity to work together
to reform the morals of the clergy. The council facilitated greater coordination in the episcopal leadership of the province, including improved coher-
ence between the statutes from diocesan synods and those from general
councils.

Provincial councils and consecration ceremonies were not the only occasions on which the archbishop saw his diocesans. Eudes dined with the
diocesans at various times and spent nights as a guest in their manor
houses.[12] In the course of his travels outside the archdiocese, the archbishop and his entourage would have been far better accommodated in a
bishop's manor house than in many of the cramped religious houses they
visited. Eudes seems to have had generally friendly relations with the Nor-

man diocesans. In 1255, for instance, he made a special trip to visit the bishop of Evreux, who was lying ill at Brosville.[13] In several cases, the Norman archbishop mediated conflicts between a suffragan bishop and his cathedral chapter.[14] If the diocesans had not considered the archbishop trustworthy, they presumably would not have agreed to have him serve as mediator. Eudes also occasionally asked one of the diocesans to fill in for him when he was ill or otherwise occupied. Once when he was to celebrate High Mass at the Franciscan convent, for instance, Eudes had the bishops of Saint-Malo and Avranches celebrate Mass at the Rouen cathedral in his stead.[15] The bishops of Evreux, Lisieux, and Sées also substituted for the archbishop at various times by performing holy orders in the Rouen diocese.[16] Although Eudes does not seem to have delegated much authority, he allowed the Norman diocesans to help him with his sacramental duties in the archdiocese when he was temporarily incapacitated. If he had seriously viewed his diocesans' aspirations as a threat to his own power, he would have been reluctant to invite them into the archdiocese to perform duties within his own jurisdiction.

Eudes's presence in a suffragan's diocese, however, posed at least a symbolic threat to the suffragan, not least because the archbishop entered uninvited and with the intention of investigating the state of ecclesiastical affairs, the results of which reflected on the diocesan's own performance. Although no diocesan wanted the archbishop to meddle in his diocese, there was always some degree of coordination between the visiting archbishop and the diocesan. When Eudes decided to visit a diocese, for instance, he first notified the diocesan.[17] The bishop sometimes accompanied the archbishop during his visitations of the diocese.[18] When the bishop was present, Eudes referred the problems he found to the diocesan directly.[19] But even when the bishop was not present, Eudes referred some of the problems he found to the bishop's attention. During a tour of Evreux, for example, the archbishop jotted down reminders in his *Register* about matters he wished to take up with the bishop: "We must speak to the bishop about this monk who goes alone to celebrate Mass at the château at Ivry, also about Brother Peter le Cordelier and Simon of Paris, both monks of Ivry."[20] A few days later, Eudes noted that he wished to speak with the bishop about the need to have two novices from the priory of Saint-Sulpice, near Laigle, returned to the abbey, and to have Brother John Chicaut, "a sower of discord," removed altogether.[21] Why did Eudes, who generally appeared so eager to involve himself in the details of disciplining the clergy, leave certain problems to the diocesans? It is most likely that he simply did not have time to take care of every problem he encountered. As he himself explained in his *Register*, on finding the female convent of Almenèches in a state of disarray, "since we could not spare the time to break our journey and undertake a reformation of their state, which they needed, we told the bishop to consult and treat with the abbess and, after studying the ordinance which G. [Bishop Geoffrey de Maiet, 1240–58] of good memory, former bishop of Sées, had drawn up for them as a way of life, to issue such orders as he should deem both useful and becoming for the monastery and favorable to the salvation of the nuns."[22]

Even the problems Eudes had time to correct needed continued monitoring by the local bishop. It was therefore essential for Eudes to relay to the local bishop what he found and did during his own visitations. Eudes's *Register* permitted him and future archbishops to review a particular religious community's history in light of past visitations, and it is quite possible that the *acta* from the archbishop's visitations were copied into the diocesan's records. In a few cases, Eudes heard of corrections a diocesan had already made during a previous visitation.[23] In theory, the archbishop's visitations were carried out merely to assess what a diocesan or archdeacon had already accomplished. But in practice, the archbishop seems to have had to repeat what a previous visitor had allegedly completed or to correct additional problems not found earlier.

A diocesan was particularly sensitive to the archbishop's visitation of the cathedral chapter. Since the cathedral was generally where the diocesan lived, and in most cases the diocesan had direct cure of the chapter's canons, the state of the cathedral chapter reflected directly on the bishop. When Eudes visited the cathedral chapter of Sées on July 16, 1250, he was appalled by the problems he found and ordered the bishop "to correct all of these excesses, and to see that your reformation program is carried out, so that you may not deserve censure for greater negligence."[24] In addition to holding the diocesan responsible for the state of the cathedral chapter, Eudes made a separate visitation of the bishop, in which he investigated the bishop's performance of his duties by questioning the canons. The *Register* describes, for instance, how Eudes went about "visiting" the bishop of Evreux on May 15, 1250:

> In the evening we sent word to the chapter of Evreux and to all the canons who were in the city and physically able to attend to appear before us in our chambers. When they had appeared we inquired of them in what manner the bishop conducted himself both in his church and in his episcopate, or diocese; how he exercised his pontifical office; his manner of conferring benefices; his general conduct and way of life; and such other things as we thought fitting. They replied that he performed his duties well and conducted himself worthily in everything.[25]

It is easy to imagine how the archbishop's visitation of a suffragan's diocese could have been perceived as a threat to the suffragan's authority.

On January 22, 1252, Eudes Rigaud presided over his first provincial council since being consecrated archbishop in March 1248. The council was attended by the six Norman diocesans and the proctors of five of the cathedral chapters (the proctor from the chapter of Evreux was absent). It was at this first provincial council that the archbishop of Rouen made a declaration that provoked four years of bitter dispute with his suffragans. Eudes addressed the question of whether he had the right to resume an interrupted provincial visitation: "We stated unequivocally that we may proceed to visit our province when and where it may seem best to us."[26] At the time of this provincial council, Eudes had already completed a visitation of all seven dioceses in the ecclesiastical province of Normandy. He was no doubt planning a second provincial visitation (although as it would happen, he would not visit a diocese outside Rouen for another two years). Before embarking on this second round of provincial visitations, however, Eudes made this emphatic declaration about his freedom to visit when and where he wished.

In making this declaration at his first provincial council, Eudes was likely testing the waters. He was no doubt aware, as his suffragans would later remind him, that the notion that he could make official visitations when and where he wished was in clear opposition to Pope Innocent IV's Constitution of Reims of 1246 (*Romana Ecclesia*), in which the pope had laid out specific conditions under which the archbishop might visit his province.[27] According to Innocent's decree, an archbishop could visit his province only after he had visited all the other religious houses (*omnia loca ecclesiastica*) of his own diocese.[28] If the archbishop's visitation of a diocese (outside his own diocese) was interrupted, he would have to visit the entire province before resuming his visitation of the original diocese. And once the archbishop had visited all the dioceses in his province, he would have to consult with the suffragans about where to visit next. These stipulations were meant to curb abuses, such as an archbishop's visiting only wealthy religious houses where he could collect the largest procurations, a loud and frequent complaint among churchmen. Various popes and councils tried to stem this particular abuse by limiting the size of episcopal entourages, since the procurations that bishops collected during their visitations, whether in money or in kind, were supposed to be based, at least in part, on the number of mouths that needed to be fed in their entourage.[29] In *Romana Ecclesia*, Innocent IV prohibited the archbishop from asking religious houses for money (or accepting any kind of gift) unless to reimburse the archbishop and his entourage for the "moderate" food expenses they incurred during their visitation.[30] Since limiting the size of episcopal entourages was not always effective in easing the financial burden episcopal visitations placed on religious houses, in 1336 Benedict XII fixed at 140 *sous tournois*, or 7 l., the amount that a bishop could demand as procuration at a monastic house with a population of twelve or more monastics.[31] Many decades earlier, however, Eudes Rigaud had regularly collected procurations of more than 11 or 12 l., even at priories with populations of only two to four monks.[32] Although he occasionally remitted a portion of a procuration because of a monastery's poverty, the size and wealth of a monastic house seem to have mattered little to him.[33]

In 1250, in response to Eudes's requests, Pope Innocent IV granted the archbishop two privileges related to special visitational rights in his province. The first permitted Eudes to resume a visitation of a suffragan's diocese if an earlier visitation had been interrupted by a summons from the king or queen of France, the Roman court, or papal legate.[34] The other privilege gave Eudes the right to visit his province after visiting only the "famous places" (*loca famosa*) of his archdiocese.[35] The archbishop had argued that it was impractical for him to be required to visit "all the ecclesiastical places" in the archdiocese before embarking on a visitation of the province, as the pope had stipulated in *Romana Ecclesia*, given the large number of small, remote religious houses in the Rouen diocese. Although these two papal privileges extended Eudes's ability to exercise provincial visitations, they were nonetheless quite narrow in scope and by no means gave him free rein to visit his province as he saw fit.

Eudes's assertion of his right of free provincial visitation appears all the bolder when one considers that just two months before his provincial council, the twelve diocesans from the province of Canterbury had filed an appeal with the pope against what they charged was their archbishop's unlawful visitation and collection of procurations in the diocese of London. The dispute was actually a rehashing of an unsettled dispute from 1239 over "whether a metropolitan is able to visit the monasteries of his suffragans, even when the bishops are not negligent" (*utrum metropolitanus visitare possit monasteria suffraganeorum, ubi episcopi non sunt negligentes*).[36] The pope ultimately ruled in favor of Archbishop Boniface of Canterbury, but this papal decree did not appear until May 1252, four months after Eudes made his assertive statement at his provincial council.[37] Thus in January 1252, when Eudes held his first provincial council, it was still unclear whether an archbishop had a legal right to visit a suffragan's diocese when there was no evidence of negligence on the part of the suffragan. Whereas the archbishop of Canterbury was merely trying to argue that there need not be a negligent bishop for him to have the right to visit a diocese outside his own, the archbishop of Rouen was making the much more aggressive claim that he could visit wherever and whenever he wanted.

Less than two months after holding his provincial council, Eudes received a short letter from the bishop of Bayeux and the five other suffragans, informing him that they had appointed a proctor to lay out their complaints against him. The proctor presented the letter to Eudes, accompanied by the bishops of Bayeux, Sées, Lisieux, and Coutances. The suffragans' letter accused Eudes, his officials, and his agents of committing "injuries" (*grava-mina*) against them, their churches, and their subjects. They called the archbishop's actions a violation of justice and contrary to the spirit of the Constitution of Reims.[38]

The suffragans' appeal to the pope was based on two central objections. First, they objected to the archbishop's assertion that he could repeat a visitation of his province whenever he wished, pointing out that "by old and approved custom" the archbishop of Rouen had been obliged to wait three years before repeating a provincial visitation.[39] Second, the suffragans complained that the archbishop and his officials had been hearing appeals of the sentences of archdeacons and their officials, absolving the appellants by throwing out sentences of excommunication, suspension, and interdiction and all the while profiting from pecuniary amends they collected from the appellants.[40] They also accused the archbishop and his officials of punishing those subjects of theirs, such as archdeacons and rural deans, who refused to testify or execute the archbishop's orders.[41] Most important, they argued that their authority and jurisdiction as the judges of first instance had been bypassed by the archbishop and his officials. The suffragans were determined to preserve their diocesan authority and jurisdictional independence against what they perceived as the unlawful claims of an aggressive archbishop.

The Norman suffragans had good reason for believing that they would receive papal support for their two central complaints. First, in *Romana Ecclesia*, it seemed the pope had taken a clear position against an archbishop's presumption that he could visit his province when he so desired. Second, the suffragans were no doubt aware (as was the archbishop) of a dispute that took place in 1236 between the bishop of Sées and the archbishop of Rouen over the archbishop's right to hear appeals from the subjects of the bishop of Sées. The dispute had ended in an arbitrated compromise, ratified by the chapters of Sées and Rouen, and was intended to have permanent application. The judgment was that neither the archbishop nor his officials were to receive appeals from archdeacons or rural deans by bypassing a bishop (*praetermisso episcopo*). Although the judgment allowed the archbishop to hear "simple complaints" (*querimonias simplices*), it stipulated that the archbishop could hear such complaints only as long as he was in the diocese in which the complaint originated. Once he left the diocese, the case would automatically be turned over to the bishop.[42]

Romana Ecclesia had also addressed the issue of an archbishop and his official bypassing the jurisdiction of a suffragan bishop by hearing appeals against the sentences of archdeacons and deans in the suffragan's diocese. Here, too, the pope had plainly tried to protect the jurisdiction of the diocesan as the judge of first instance. Archbishops were forbidden from having an official and permanent archiepiscopal tribunal in each diocese of the province. They were to respect the jurisdiction of a diocesan as the judge of first instance within the diocese.[43] Both *Romana Ecclesia* and the arbitrated judgment of 1236 in Normandy confirmed a bishop's original jurisdiction in his diocese. Both decisions carried the message that the metropolitan held original jurisdiction in his own diocese alone.

The constant refrain heard from the Norman suffragans in 1252 was that Eudes Rigaud had claimed rights that no previous Norman archbishop had dared claim (*licet nullus predecessorum ipsius archiepiscopi hec fecerit*).[44] With respect to whether he could visit his province only once every three years, Eudes dismissed the custom that the suffragans invoked, saying "in this case we do not believe that that custom has a place."[45] Nevertheless, Eudes appears to have withdrawn his earlier declaration of an unrestricted right to visit his province, telling the pontiff that he never had suggested that he could visit the province before the time determined in *Romana Ecclesia.*[46] Standing before the pontiff, Eudes suddenly showed a new respect for the rules governing a metropolitan's provincial visitation as laid out in *Romana Ecclesia.* Responding to the question of whether he could hear appeals from the subjects of his suffragans, Eudes's position was that he had acted in accordance with "old and approved custom" (*de longa et observata consuetudine*), consonant with law and reason. At the same time, however, Eudes portrayed himself as willing to admit wrongdoing if in fact wrongdoing could be proved. He claimed to have offered the suffragans the "proper remedy" for any injuries he or his officials had committed but said that when the suffragans had been confronted directly with their own articles of grievances, not one of them claimed to have been aggrieved by all the articles.[47] There were clearly falsehoods, according to the archbishop, in the suffragans' claims of what he and his officials had done.

It is difficult to know just how involved Eudes and his officials had been in hearing the appeals of the suffragans' subjects. Did the archbishop have an official and permanent archiepiscopal tribunal in every diocese? Eudes's *Register* never once mentions one of his own officials hearing an appeal in a suffragan's diocese, nor have I found any such record in the archives. Eudes's arguments as summarized in the pope's bull, however, suggest that he was not merely defending his right to hear appeals in the abstract. He argued, for instance, that there had been appeals against the sentences of archdeacons and their officials to the archiepiscopal court "by old and approved custom," both in Normandy and in other French provinces. He justified his taking of pecuniary amends in appeal cases, arguing that this was standard procedure and that the suffragan bishops did the same.[48] He also defended his practice of hearing an appeal even before the diocesan had handed down a sentence, arguing that in this way his court could determine whether a case was reasonable and just, avoiding a scenario in which an appellant might go forty days under an unjust sentence of excommunication.[49] Above all, Eudes argued that he was justified in hearing appeals without regard to procedure or the nature of the case, in order to protect the suffragans' subjects from the evil (*malitia*) of the suffragans' officials, who were known to seize appellants' possessions. In other words, although Eudes knew that some would accuse him of abuse of power, he believed he acted responsibly in using his office to preserve the public order.[50]

The suffragans appear to have been particularly frustrated by what they perceived as Eudes's dismissive response to their complaints. The archbishop did not seem to take them or their appeal to the pontiff seriously. In a letter the suffragans sent to Eudes in December 1253, they even commented that they were unsure whether he had studied their complaints and proposed that both parties provide each other with copies of their respective arguments and objections.[51] They also made clear that if Eudes refused to disclose his arguments, they too would withhold theirs. The suffragans seem to have wanted to negotiate with the archbishop in good faith, but only if he would meet them halfway.

Although the suffragans were suspicious of their archbishop, it is clear from Eudes's *Register* that he was making at least some effort to conciliate them. The *Register* records two meetings, one in 1252 and one in 1253, in which Eudes tried to reach an agreement with his suffragans.[52] There is no indication of who instigated these meetings, nor do we know what transpired or whether any progress was made; nevertheless, neither meeting could have been wholly successful since the dispute continued. What seems clear, however, is that Eudes Rigaud invested enormous time and energy trying to win his dispute with his suffragans (in spite of the archbishop's curious letter to the pontiff in 1251, which appeared so perfunctory and dismissive). The archbishop cared enough about the principles at stake in the dispute to travel all the way to Rome, crossing the Alps (in spite of his painful rheumatism) in the dead of winter of 1254, all to defend his case before the pope.[53] In addition, Eudes met with his suffragans on ten separate occasions between his first provincial council in January 1252 and his second provincial council in September 1257, when he confirmed his right to visit his province where and when he saw fit. Every one of those ten meetings was occupied with the dispute. Not a single provincial council was called during the five years of the conflict, and Eudes did not visit any of his suffragans' dioceses again before the pontiff handed down his decision.

Although the conflict appears to have been sparked by Eudes's declaration of his unrestricted right of provincial visitation, the pope's judgment of 1254 devoted only one short line to the matter, and the accord of 1256 between the archbishop and his suffragans did not even mention the question. Dismissing the suffragans' invocation of a Norman custom restricting the metropolitan to one provincial visitation every three years, the pontiff upheld the laws pertaining to provincial visitation as laid out in *Romana Ecclesia*.[54] This judgment certainly represented a defeat for the suffragans. Yet *Romana Ecclesia* hardly supported Eudes's original claim of an unrestricted right to visit his province, stipulating, for instance, that a metropolitan could visit his province for a second time only with the written consent of his suffragans.[55] It appears all the stranger, then, that Eudes understood the pontiff's decision as a confirmation of his unrestricted right of visitation. When, in 1257, Eudes convened his second provincial council (having already sealed a peace treaty with his suffragans), he made the symbolic gesture of having his suffragans confirm his right to visit his province whenever and wherever he wished.[56] In over two decades as archbishop, however, Eudes never exercised his right to visit a diocese more often than once every three years. He had won a battle for the sake of principle and not practice.

Ultimately, however, Eudes's dispute with his suffragans centered much more on the archiepiscopal court's juridical authority in the suffragans' dioceses than on the archiepiscopal right to visit his province. The prominence of this issue is reflected in both the papal bull of 1254 and the peace treaty between the archbishop and his suffragans, ratified at Pont-Audemer on June 24, 1256. In the simplest terms, the pope did not accept Eudes's claim of a custom that allowed him to bypass his suffragan bishops (*omissis suffraganeis*) in hearing appeals against the sentences of archdeacons and their officials. The pope conceded that the archbishop had the right to hear appeals from those excommunicated by the suffragan bishops themselves, since in such a case the archbishop was the judge of first instance. But the pope did not want the archbishop to usurp the jurisdiction of his suffragan bishops. If, the pope warned, the archbishop were permitted to absolve provisionally (*absolvere ad cautelam*) all those under the authority of the suffragans, then "all those who have been excommunicated will plan to appeal to him [the archbishop] so that they will likewise be absolved by him, and thus the authority and liberty of the Norman Church, with regard to coercing the excommunicates in their persons and goods, will be destroyed wholly in respect to the suffragans."[57] The pope conceded that in a case in which there was suspicion surrounding a bishop or his official, the archbishop had a responsibility to intervene and take over, but such a case was the exception and not the rule.

The Pont-Audemer compromise of 1256 was reached between the archbishop and bishops of Bayeux, Lisieux, and Coutances.[58] A separate charter from Richard Laneus, bishop of Avranches, indicates that he, too, approved of the accord.[59] The bishops of Evreux and Sées are mysteriously absent from all records of the Pont-Audemer accord, even though they were part of the original complaint. Based on a group of charters, however, it is clear that the bishops who were involved in the Pont-Audemer accord, including Eudes himself, ratified the agreement with the consent of their respective deans and cathedral chapters. One charter attests that the official of Bayeux convened all beneficed ecclesiastics of his diocese and asked for and received their verbal consent to the compromise with the archbishop. The same official did not seek consent from the abbots and conventual priors, but he felt assured that they would not have objected to the accord.[60] Thus the agreement ratified at Pont-Audemer represented a wide consensus within the province. As part of the accord, Eudes renounced the right to receive appeals by bypassing the suffragan bishops (*omissis mediis*).

The accord contained two other provisions that do not seem to have been part of the original dispute. The first dealt with the implementation of the archbishop's or his official's injunctions in the suffragans' dioceses.[61] Rural deans, parish priests, and nonconventual priors were to be held to archiepiscopal injunctions, whereas abbots, conventual priors, canons, and persons belonging to a cathedral church were considered exempt, except in cases of common law. The second provision addressed the appearance of witnesses from the suffragans' dioceses in appeals to the archiepiscopal court.[62] Witnesses were normally permitted to testify in their own cities or dioceses (abbots and priors were allowed to testify in their convents), but in certain cases, such as heresy, simony, and homicide, witnesses were forced to appear in Rouen. The accord granted the archbishop's officials the power to punish a subject of the suffragans who refused to carry out the officials' injunctions. But the officials were also to swear an oath to the archbishop (or cathedral chapter if the archiepiscopal see was vacant) that they would punish advisedly (*de ne punir qu'à bon escient*). The suffragan bishops were invited to be present for this swearing ceremony. The treaty of Pont-Audemer thus sought to set clear limits on the juridical power of the archiepiscopal official in the suffragans' dioceses. Above all, the suffragan bishops were to remain the ordinaries of their respective dioceses, and although they were forced to recognize the archbishop as their superior, they would not have to contend with a permanent archiepiscopal presence in their dioceses.[63]

The issues involved in Eudes's dispute with his suffragans were hardly new. They had been raised before, both in Normandy and in other provinces, most notably in the contest between Archbishop Juhel of Reims and his suffragans less than ten years before. Nor did these questions come to an end with the resolution of Eudes's dispute with his suffragans in 1254. The Norman conflict was replayed in almost identical fashion in the 1280s in a dispute involving the archbishop of Canterbury, John Pecham, and his suffragans. Once again, the complaint was that the archbishop's officials were hearing appeals from the subjects of suffragan bishops, bypassing the bishops as judges of first instance.[64]

The repeated conflicts during the thirteenth century between metropolitans and their suffragans arose out of an environment of heightened sensitivity to the question of episcopal jurisdiction. This was particularly evident in a carefully managed province like Normandy, where the episcopacy took its pastoral responsibilities unusually seriously. In such an environment, seemingly trivial matters were politically charged. The Norman archbishop moved delicately to avoid giving the impression of encroaching on another bishop's jurisdiction. In July 1267, while Eudes was in Paris, he confirmed the election of the bishop of Lisieux. Before proceeding with the electoral confirmation, however, Eudes deferred to the ordinary of the diocese, asking the bishop of Paris for permission to confirm the bishop of Lisieux's election. Although Eudes was not performing an act affecting the Paris diocese, he was obliged to consult the bishop of Paris simply because he was in the bishop's diocese.[65]

In an earlier instance, Eudes was less suspecting of the possible implications of his actions. In January 1251, he summoned his suffragan bishops to Rouen for the consecration of the bishop-elect of Coutances. The bishop-elect appealed, however, saying he wished to have the ceremony in Coutances itself. Eudes, who always showed a special affinity for chant, rejected the idea of Coutances on the grounds that the canons in Coutances did not customarily chant.[66] Eudes proposed moving the ceremony to Evreux, perhaps thinking that the bishop-elect of Coutances had particular objections to Rouen. The bishop of Bayeux then entered the argument, saying that holding the consecration in Evreux would be prejudicial to his bishopric, which was next in dignity to Rouen. The canons of Rouen joined the fray, arguing that it was customary for all consecrations of Norman diocesans to take place in Rouen. In the end, Eudes moved the consecration to Rouen but made it clear that "we did not harken to them [the Rouen canons], nor did we postpone the consecration because of their allegation or supplication. But, because we did not wish to do anything which would seem to injure the rights of the church of Bayeux, we postponed the consecration to the following Sunday, and we gave a letter to the bishop of Bayeux the same Saturday, ordering him to summon our suffragans to attend the said consecration at Rouen."[67]

What accounts for this heightened sensitivity to the boundaries of episcopal jurisdiction during the thirteenth century? Some jurisdictional conflicts appear to have resulted from tension between local custom and canon law, which was undergoing rapid change. In Eudes's dispute with his suffragans, both sides invoked "custom" as a justification for their position. The suffragans cited a custom limiting the archbishop to one provincial visitation every three years. The archbishop argued that it was customary for a metropolitan to hear appeals from the suffragans' subjects. In both cases, the arguments relying on custom failed to persuade the pontiff. These arguments showed a continuing respect for local custom: one determined proper procedure by looking to the past for precedent. Yet the attempt to make canon law universal threatened the viability of these customs, which varied according to region. Although Innocent IV's judgment in *Romana Ecclesia* was inserted into the *Liber Sextus*, becoming universal law, Eudes Rigaud may still have felt that Norman custom made Normandy different from Reims. As it turned out, Innocent's decretal on the Norman case was also inserted in the *Liber Sextus*, right beside *Romana Ecclesia*, and yet the same issues arose in Canterbury about twenty-five years later.

Contests over the boundaries of episcopal jurisdiction were also a natural product of a general increase in local, ecclesiastical administration. It was only during the thirteenth century that bishops began performing systematic episcopal visitations and holding regular provincial councils.[68] In other words, the growth of centralized papal power did not suppress the power and influence of local ecclesiastical power, as some historians have suggested.[69] Rather, the Fourth Lateran Council and frequent papal exhortations about the need for pastoral reform, as well as the influence of reform-minded schoolmen such as Peter the Chanter and his circle, helped stimulate local ecclesiastical administration.[70] This flurry of administrative activity, while requiring a great deal of coordination among different members of the ecclesiastical hierarchy, also provoked complex power struggles, as prelates of all ranks, from rural deans to metropolitans, sought to exercise the power of their offices.

A rise in the power of archdeacons during the thirteenth century appears to have indirectly precipitated tension between metropolitans and suffragan bishops. As archdeacons exercised increasingly broad supervisory and disciplinary powers over the clergy of their archdiaconates, carrying out regular episcopal visitations, overseeing the state of the church's buildings and other possessions, and hearing a wide range of cases in their courts (courts that were independent of the bishops' courts), what nonsacramental responsibilities were left to the diocesans? Did an increase in the administrative activity of archdeacons undermine the jurisdiction of bishops? This seems to have been the fear of Raoul de Grosparmi (Rodolphe de Chevrières), bishop of Evreux, who in 1268 promulgated an ordinance on the jurisdiction of his archdeacons.[71] The ordinance addressed the collection of procurations during episcopal visitations and tried to ensure that archdeacons did not abuse their power by performing visitations too frequently or collecting excessive procurations. Archdeacons were instructed to refer the more serious cases and problems they encountered to the bishop. In many ways, the bishop's ordinance echoed the concerns several popes had earlier voiced about bishops' own visitations. Diligent archdeacons could serve as valuable instruments of the bishop's own power so long as they did not over assert their power and render the diocesan irrelevant. The bishop of Evreux reminded his archdeacons that they were his subordinates, accountable to him, and that as bishop, he would still involve himself in the administration of each archdeaconry.

A metropolitan such as Eudes Rigaud complicated matters for the Norman bishops, however, by giving such prominent attention to archdeacons. Eudes not only relied heavily on archdeacons in the administration of his own archdiocese but used them while visiting the other dioceses of the province. When he really needed to know what was going on in a particular locale, he turned to the archdeacon for help, not the bishop. He also made archdeacons the official investigators (*inquisitores*) of the province, responsible for overseeing what was being done to reform morals and correct abuses, an office that resembled the *enquêteurs* King Louis IX appointed to reform local secular administration.[72] The archdeacons who served as investigators reported to the archbishop and his suffragans at each provincial council. And then there was the issue of the archdeacons' courts. If, as in earlier periods, archdeacons had not presided over a court, bishops would always have been the judges of first instance within the diocese. But the growing role of archdeacons threatened to overshadow the bishops, who found themselves awkwardly sandwiched between the metropolitan above and the archdeacons below.

Such jurisdictional conflicts, though exacerbated by general trends such as tensions between local custom and canon law, and the increase in local ecclesiastical administrative activity, often arose because of the actions and words of charismatic prelates, such as Boniface of Savoy, John Pecham (both of whom were archbishop of Canterbury), and Eudes Rigaud. It may not be entirely fair to place the Norman archbishop in the company of the two archbishops of Canterbury, both of whom seemed entirely incapable of getting along with others. In contrast, Eudes had excellent relationships with both the king of France and the various pontiffs he dealt with. Unlike Pecham, Eudes did not let his Franciscan identity hinder his relationship with secular bishops. He had friendly relations with French bishops outside his province and relatively good relations with his own suffragan bishops, despite their one major dispute. At the same time, though, Eudes was an unusually assertive prelate, willing to test the limits of his legal jurisdiction for the sake of what he considered his divinely ordained pastoral responsibility. Two hundred years later, another zealous archbishop of Rouen, Louis of Luxembourg (1437–43), turned to Eudes Rigaud's career as a model. Louis even had portions of Eudes's *Register* copied so he could invoke the actions of the famous Franciscan as precedents in his own disputes with the Rouen chapter over his rights and privileges.[73]

4

Fixing Broken Windows

Episcopal Visitation and the Mechanisms
for Monastic Reform

Benedictine monasticism flourished in Normandy during the high Middle Ages. Some of the most distinguished Norman monasteries, such as Mont-Saint-Michel, Saint-Ouen-de-Rouen, Montivilliers, Saint-Wandrille, and Jumièges, were pre-Viking foundations, some founded as early as the seventh century. Although religious life in the province was disrupted during the late ninth and early tenth centuries, when churches and abbeys were attacked by Vikings (and Franks) and many monasteries were evacuated, there seems to have been more continuity between Neustrian (pre-Viking) monasticism and Norman monasticism than previously thought.[1] During the eleventh century, Norman monasticism experienced a great revival. Monasteries were restored and reformed, and many new monastic houses were established. This revival contributed to the process of Norman state building, as dukes and local aristocrats played a leading role in founding and patronizing monastic houses.[2] Several Norman monasteries, such as Bec and Fécamp, were intellectual centers that produced some of the most eminent churchmen of the day. By the middle of the twelfth century, under the influence of the new reformist ideals, religious life in Normandy became more diverse, as larger numbers of Cluniac, Cistercian, Augustinian, and Premonstratensian foundations were established.[3]

The movement of regular canons (who were quasi-monastic in that they generally adopted a common life and followed a rule, in contrast to secular canons) was particularly strong in Normandy. Indeed, by the end of the twelfth century, there were more houses of regular canons than even Cistercians (including the congregation of Savigny) in Normandy, despite the fact that the Cistercian order included female convents whereas the communities of regular canons were all male.[4] In 1131, the cathedral chapter of Sées was regularized and placed under the protection of the canons of

Saint-Victor in Paris. In the eyes of twelfth-century bishops, the regular canons were a valuable tool in their efforts to reform the clergy. Compared with the Benedictines, whom many bishops viewed as corrupt and undisciplined, the canons were loyal allies of a reformist papacy and episcopate. Indeed, bishops succeeded in converting some Benedictine abbeys into communities of regular canons, thereby reorganizing the regular clergy under a different model.[5] It was the regular canons' pastoral function, particularly their service in parish churches, that made them, in Mathieu Arnoux's words, "a precious instrument in the hands of episcopal authority."[6] Augustinian canons increasingly helped the secular clergy in the management of the pastoral ministry, whether by naming vicars to individual parishes or serving as vicars themselves.

Eudes Rigaud's *Register* shows that a large number of Norman regular canons lived outside their canonries while serving parishes. In some cases, as many canons lived outside their community's house as inside, a testament to the canons' substantial involvement in parish life.[7] Admittedly, this arrangement threatened the canons' communal life and their ability to maintain their religious vows and discipline, particularly when they lived quite a distance from their mother house.[8] These canons often lived in priory-rectories, small dependencies of two or three canons, where they sought to lead the lives of regulars while serving one or more parish churches.[9] It was also not uncommon for regular canons engaged in parish work to live alone, and this kind of autonomy raised special concerns within both the order and the episcopate.[10] The canons' pastoral functions also meant that laymen and women were frequently present in the canonries, a problem that Eudes sought to correct.[11] One might expect the Franciscan archbishop to have had a particularly favorable view of the regular canons, since like him, they viewed the *vita apostolica* as involving living according to a rule (which, like the Franciscan Rule, placed special emphasis on poverty), while at the same time engaging in pastoral work, serving parish churches, preaching, and managing hospitals and leprosaries.[12] Yet during the course of his almost two hundred visitations to more than thirty different communities of regular canons, the archbishop found many of the same spiritual and temporal problems as among the other kinds of regular clergy.[13] Eudes Rigaud's *Register* is a remarkable source on the great variety in forms of monastic life (including the quasi-monastic life of regular canons) in thirteenth-century Normandy, from the number of monastics who lived in the typical Norman abbey or priory, to the wealth of these houses, to how religious discipline was imposed.

The great Fourth Lateran Council, convened by Pope Innocent III in 1215, is generally considered by modern historians as the culmination of the religious reforms of "the long twelfth century." The council's decision to prohibit the creation of new religious orders signaled the close of a long period of religious renewal and reform. At the same time, the council helped launch a new program of monastic and pastoral reform. The success of the council's reforms depended on how they were implemented on a local level, as Paul Pixton persuasively argues: "Crucial to the implementation of Innocent III's reform program was an episcopacy which could be inspired, cajoled or threatened into fulfilling their roles as 'watchmen on the tower,' recognizing the spiritual enemies of their respective churches and taking the necessary steps in the eradication of such problems."[14] One suspects that Eudes Rigaud was precisely the kind of "watchman on the tower" that Innocent III would have embraced. But Eudes was unusual in being among the first wave of friars to be recruited for the episcopacy. As David Knowles puts it, "The new orders of friars inaugurated a wholly original ideal and type of organization in the religious life, and the establishment at the Fourth Lateran Council of a code of disciplinary decrees gave a legal basis for a system of ecclesiastical administration different in method from all that had gone before."[15] As the first Franciscan archbishop of Rouen, Eudes Rigaud exemplified both the coming of the friars and their role in implementing the reforms of Pope Innocent III and the Fourth Lateran Council.

Innocent III's sense of an urgent need for Benedictine reform may have stemmed from his own visits to the monasteries of Santa Scolastica and Monte Cassino, where he reported finding a wide range of abuses: decadence, sexual activity, poor monastic leadership, inadequate hospitality, the presence of hunting dogs and birds, monks who did not eat and sleep communally, and violations of the rules for silence.[16] The Cistercian order, which held regular provincial chapter meetings and appointed order visitors to conduct visitations of Cistercian houses, served as a model of monastic organization that stood in sharp contrast to the decentralized Benedictine order. Innocent III and subsequent popes attempted to borrow from the Cistercian model (and the model of diocesanal synods) to introduce similar instruments of reform for the Benedictines.[17] Canon 12 of the Fourth Lateran Council established general chapters of the Benedictine order for each ecclesiastical province (including abbots and conventual priors). The provincial chapters were instructed to meet once every three years and refer extreme cases, such as the deposition of an abbot, to the diocesan or pope.[18] Canon 12 also directed each provincial chapter to appoint Benedictine visitors, who would conduct visitations of the province's Benedictine houses. There is little documentary evidence, however, to show how often these capitular visitations were conducted; it may be telling that not a single set of injunctions has survived from Benedictine capitular visitations during the period 1215–1350.[19]

The real instrument for the reform of Benedictine monasticism came not from within the order but from the episcopacy. Canon 12 of the Fourth Lateran Council reaffirmed the responsibility of archbishops and bishops to supervise and correct monastic discipline by holding regular synods and conducting visitations of monastic houses. The notion that monasteries were subject to episcopal control was not a new one; as early as the late sixth century, Pope Gregory the Great had affirmed a bishop's right to visit and discipline the monks of his diocese.[20] Gratian and other twelfth-century canon lawyers maintained the rights of bishops to supervise and correct monastic discipline, although there was some question about whether a bishop could give orders without first getting the abbot's permission.[21] By the thirteenth century, however, spurred by the Fourth Lateran Council and other conciliar and papal legislation, it was increasingly common for bishops, archbishops, and even papal legates to conduct regular, systematic visitations of monasteries.[22] Monastic houses were also required to turn to the diocesan for permission to elect their monastic superiors; following the election, the monastery needed the bishop to confirm the election; and finally, the monastic superior had to swear an oath of fidelity to the bishop. Abbots were also required to participate in diocesan synods. [23]

Even before the archiepiscopate of Eudes Rigaud, provincial councils and episcopal visitations were being conducted, making the ecclesiastical province of Normandy unusual in its administrative activity.[24] At the Council of Rouen of 1214, the cardinal legate Robert of Courson ordered his suffragans to see to it that monasteries were properly closed, that women were kept out of male houses, that monks did not live alone, that a proper number of monastics was maintained, and that nuns were provided with able and decent confessors.[25] Subsequent Rouen councils published additional legislation that reaffirmed and expanded the episcopacy's responsibility in directing monastic reform.[26] In 1222, the archbishop of Rouen, Thibaud d'Amiens, conducted visitations of Saint-Ouen-de-Rouen, Corneville, and Bourg-Achard.[27] In 1235, Pope Gregory IX published statutes "on the reformation of the monks of the order of Saint Benedict." These statutes, which in 1237 were sent to the Benedictine abbots of Normandy and other provinces, served as a kind of gloss on the Benedictine Rule, responding to issues that commonly arose in monasteries but that were not specifically addressed in the rule. Every Norman house was expected to have a copy of the statutes (including one in French if some monastics did not have sufficient Latin) and periodically have them read aloud. The statutes also provided a practical guide for episcopal visitors, who could use them as a checklist while inquiring into the state of a monastic house. With a copy of the statutes inserted into his *Register*, Eudes Rigaud had them with him wherever he went.[28] To his consternation, some monasteries, such as Saint-Martin-de-Troarn, Jumièges, and Saint-Ouen-de-Rouen, were able to obtain papal dispensations freeing them from the obligation to observe the statutes, since their own monastic rule was considered sufficiently rigid and difficult to observe.[29]

Monastic Resistance and Claims of Exemption

Although the episcopacy generally received papal support for its jurisdictional claims over Benedictine and Augustinian houses, it was denied jurisdiction over an increasing number of monastic houses, including those belonging to the orders of Cluny, Cîteaux, and Prémontré, as well as the Norman abbey of Fécamp and the nunnery of Montivilliers, all of which enjoyed the privilege of exemption from episcopal control and owed their allegiance directly to the pope.[30] But what did a claim of exemption from episcopal control mean in actual practice? Although technically exempt from episcopal visitation, Cistercian, Cluniac, and Premonstratensian monasteries (as well as La-Roche-Guyon, a priory dependent on the exempt abbey of Fécamp) nonetheless received Eudes and his *familia* as guests and were obliged to pay the appropriate procuration. At female Cistercian houses, Eudes consistently conducted full visitations without any apparent resistance, although curiously, he received no procuration.[31] The archbishop continued to consecrate abbots and abbesses, even in cases of exempt houses; he preached and celebrated Mass in exempt houses; and he dedicated churches there.[32] The abbey of Marmoutier (in the province of Tours), which had initially adhered to Cluny (legally it was not a member of the Cluniac order and its abbot was elected freely), had hundreds of priories in France and England. These priories claimed to be exempt from episcopal control through their earlier affiliation with Cluny, leading to struggles between bishops and dependent priories all over France and England.[33] Eudes consistently collected procurations from priories dependent on Marmoutier, and despite their claims of exemption from episcopal visitation, he tried and sometimes succeeded in visiting their houses, such as when he arrived only four days after the arrival and installation of a still naive prior who perhaps did not know enough to protest.[34] Even when Eudes was unable to conduct a formal visitation of a priory dependent on Marmoutier, he nonetheless warned the monks "to live as uprightly as they could, since in the event of crime we can deal with them."[35]

At other exempt houses he tried to visit, Eudes faced opposition when he made aggressive jurisdictional claims, claims that only served to reinforce the view some monastics had of bishops' pretensions. That an archbishop happened to be a Franciscan did not change the fact that he was a powerful prelate who might turn out to be like the others, namely, a greedy collector of procurations, a usurper of rights, an oppressor of churches under monastic patronage, and a harsh disciplinarian who was unmoved by a monastic house's long-standing customs.[36] At Saint-Martin-de-Bellême, a priory of the exempt abbey of Marmoutier, Eudes not only collected a procuration but demanded an additional procuration for a chapel in the château of Bellême. The monks refused to pay this second procuration, however, and appealed to Rome, saying that the demand was undue and unaccustomed. Yet on the following day, instead of retreating from his claim, the archbishop asserted a new claim, attempting to conduct a full visitation of the "exempt" house. Not surprisingly, the monks refused to answer any of the archbishop's questions, saying "that they had an abbot and a prior from whom they received correction if there were anything to be corrected there."[37] Eudes ordered them to produce evidence of their privilege of exemption within one month's time. Nothing more is said about the priory in the *Register* until five years later, when Eudes again tried without success to visit the priory and collect a procuration. This time, he argued that he had the right to two procurations because, as he had learned, the bishop of Sées had collected two procurations.[38] But the archbishop never did win the right to conduct a visitation of the priory.[39]

Monastic claims of exemption had been one of the favorite complaints of the twelfth-century theologian Peter the Chanter, who addressed the problem in his *Verbum abbreviatum*. Indeed, in a story that was repeated by Gerald of Wales, Peter claimed that when Abbot Suger of Saint-Denis was lying on his deathbed, he summoned the bishop of Paris and promised obedience to him, saying it was the devil who had been responsible for obtaining the abbey's exemption from episcopal control.[40] Eudes had surely heard discussion of the problem of monastic exemption while he was at the university in Paris. Then, as archbishop, he experienced firsthand how the many monastic houses that claimed privileges of exemption could impede his efforts at monastic reform. Eudes was familiar with the humiliation of having a priory's gates slammed shut in his face; monks had literally turned their backs on him as he tried to ask them questions.[41] By conducting monastic visitations, he believed he was merely exercising the canonical duties of his office. Rather than resist his visitations, the monastics should have been receptive, he thought; he was their doctor bringing them their medicine, or their shepherd lovingly tending them, his sheep. Eudes would have agreed with the way Robert Grosseteste, bishop of Lincoln, articulated the problem: "For, even though exempt [Religious] fornicate, even outside the precincts of their monasteries, or commit adultery or any other enormous and diabolical offences, the bishops or other pastors can do nothing against the devils which wholly possess such folk, or against their spiritual sicknesses; but the shepherds see their sheep strangled by such ravening wolves, yet their mouths are so closed by the privileges of these exempt Religious that they may not even cry a little aloud to save them."[42] Addressing the notion that exemption from episcopal control represented a type of freedom, Grosseteste wrote the dean and chapter of Lincoln: "Not to be visited, not to be corrected, not to be reformed cannot possibly be called liberty, because these negations or privations are bad, and all liberty is good."[43]

Like Grosseteste, Eudes refused to concede defeat each time a monastery claimed a privilege of exemption, particularly since the papacy had shown a willingness to support episcopal visitation of non-exempt houses, even if that meant threatening disobedient houses with ecclesiastical censure.[44] The prior of Gisors, a priory dependent on the exempt abbey of Marmoutier, evaded the archbishop for almost ten years.[45] When Eudes arrived there on July 17, 1249, he found the doors locked and was denied entry.[46] The archbishop appealed to the pope, who issued a bull ordering the official of Paris to excommunicate Pierre, the prior of Gisors, for his refusal to pay the procuration owed to the archbishop and for his failure to appear on the assigned dates to explain his actions.[47] The archbishop's right to collect a procuration at Gisors was thus confirmed, but Eudes pushed his claims further, insisting on the right to conduct a visitation of the "exempt" priory, despite the fact that the papal bull had made no mention of such a right.[48] In 1257, the matter was placed in the hands of arbiters, who decided that the priory was indeed exempt from the archbishop's visitation but must pay the procuration of 112 sol. p.[49]

A monastic house that was exempt from episcopal control was subject to direct papal control. Thus when Eudes attempted to exert control over an exempt house, he encroached not only on the house's privilege but on the papacy's jurisdiction. The wealthy nunnery of Montivilliers had been exempt from episcopal control since 1035, and its privilege of exemption had been confirmed by Innocent III in 1203.[50] One of the nunnery's privileges was that although its abbess could be inspected by an episcopal visitor, the other nuns were immune. During his first six appearances at the nunnery, over a six-year period, Eudes seems to have respected this privilege, questioning the abbess only. But on December 11, 1257, he began giving orders to the community at large.[51] By his next visitation, a little more than two years later, Eudes declared his intention of making "a complete visitation, both in head and in members, as our office requires of us."[52] It is unclear what changes had occurred to make the archbishop suddenly think he had such a right.[53] Protesting loudly, the nuns adamantly refused to allow Eudes to inspect their community, supporting their arguments by citing charters, custom, and privilege. The dispute continued the following year at the archbishop's next visitation. At first, the nuns refused the archbishop the right to interrogate anyone other than the abbess, but they eventually submitted to his will, and thereafter, he conducted full visitations. In this contest with popes and tradition, Eudes was sometimes able to extend the boundaries of his jurisdiction simply by being assertive.

Some monastic houses tried to resist episcopal visitors by more crafty means. Especially in the case of small priories, Eudes was often unable to learn much during a visitation if the prior was absent. Indeed, Eudes sometimes canceled visitations on account of the absence of the monastic superior.[54] Priors who did not wish to answer the archbishop's questions could "happen" to be away on business during the archbishop's visitations. Arriving at the priory of Saint-Pierre in 1266, for instance, Eudes was not happy to learn that the prior and one other monk (out of a total of five resident monks) were away, even though (or precisely because) they had been informed of the archbishop's impending visit.[55] In July 1250, the monks of Sainte-Gauburge, a Norman priory whose monks were from Saint-Denis, made certain that their prior was conveniently summoned to the mother abbey just before the archbishop's announced visitation.[56] To learn about monastic conduct, a visitor like Eudes was dependent on the system of mutual accusation, whereby members of a monastic community openly accused and corrected one another in chapter. This custom not only ensured regular accountability within monasteries but also made it easier for a visitor to learn what had been happening. There are almost one hundred references in the *Register* to houses of regulars that did not practice mutual accusation.[57] When Eudes found that monastics were not accusing one another in chapter, he reminded them that "he who does not accuse his companion of an offense shall incur the same penalty as the perpetrator would merit."[58] That monastics could conspire to keep silent about something was always a danger, and some visitors made a practice of asking monastics directly whether their superior had forbidden them to reveal things in need of correction.[59] Like many political institutions in future centuries, extending to twentieth-century Chinese communist communes, the church was experimenting and wrestling with fundamental questions of privacy, morality, and power.

By relying primarily on episcopal documents for information about episcopal visitation of monasteries, we hear little about how the monastics viewed the visitations by bishops and archbishops. Monastic documents rarely yield much additional information. C. R. Cheney suggests that "in the eyes of the regulars the episcopal visitor remained always an outsider to be outwitted, whose intrusion should be curtailed as much as possible."[60] Matthew Paris, a thirteenth-century English chronicler and Benedictine monk, illustrates how a highly partisan monk viewed the relationship between an episcopal visitor and monastic visitands. Matthew described the bishop of Lincoln's 1251 visitation of the Ramsey abbey as "an act of tyranny: he [the bishop] broke open their coffers like a burglar, and trod to pieces the cups ornamented with circles and supported on feet of silver, which, if he had acted wisely, he could have given to the poor entire. What is unfit to be mentioned, he also went to the house of religious females, and caused their breasts to be squeezed, to try, like a physician, if there was any debauchery practiced amongst them."[61]

It is not at all clear, however, that Eudes Rigaud's visitations were always so resented by monastic communities. In several cases, his visitation was actually solicited by a monastic superior in need of the archbishop's help. On May 13, 1267, for instance, Eudes visited the abbey at Corneville (a house of Augustinian canons) at the abbot's request, even though it had been less than a year since his last appearance. The abbot, who was embroiled in a dispute with a certain Brother Osbert and had been accused of various crimes, needed the archbishop's help to resolve matters and keep the abbey in order. In other cases, Eudes was welcomed by a monastic community that was unhappy with its superior. The abbey of Saint-Florent de Saumur in the diocese of Angers, an abbey known to be unusually protective of its privileges, referred to the local bishop as "the defender of this monastery," despite the bishop's complaints to the archbishop of Tours about the various scandals and abuses he found in the monasteries in his diocese.[62] Monastic communities did not necessarily view their diocesan as an enemy, especially if they perceived him as their protector or potential ally in their struggles with the secular authorities in a town, another monastic house, or even the monastery's own oppressive monastic leader.[63]

Conducting a Visitation

What was the protocol for one of Eudes's monastic visitations? Before conducting a visitation, he sometimes sent a house written notice of his intention.[64] The visitation itself could begin with an elaborate procession in which the archbishop was greeted outside the monastery by the abbot and monks. One of the monks carried an aspergillum, and all the monks knelt while the archbishop sprinkled them with holy water. The abbot then led the archbishop by the hand to the monastery, with the monks following behind singing the psalm "Hear, O Israel."[65] After entering the church, which had been specially decorated for the occasion, the archbishop preached a sermon.[66] Following the sermon, the archbishop and monks generally moved into the chapter room, where the formal visitation was conducted. At cathedral chapters, Eudes generally first interviewed the chapter as a whole and then interviewed certain individual canons separately and secretly (*iuximus ut in partem secederent, et sigillatim et secreto vocavimus*), perhaps under the theory that a canon might be willing to divulge certain things in private that he would not in front of his brethren.[67] It is not clear whether Eudes used this same approach in monastic houses. Although it might have been most effective to examine every monastic individually and then cross-examine certain individuals with the new information that had been learned during the first round of questioning (much like the process followed by modern police departments in questioning suspects), it is difficult to imagine how Eudes would have had the time to do so, especially at larger houses. His visitations must not have lasted much more than an hour or two, in view of the fact that he sometimes conducted several visitations in the course of one day, even when the houses he visited were fairly far apart.

Eudes sometimes used a standard set of visitation articles to begin his inquiry. Conducting his first visitation at the priory of Sacey, for instance, he asked the monks a series of preliminary questions about the state of their house: did they live in common? did they clothe themselves from the common resources of the house? did they hand in their old clothes when they received new ones? did the prior have the cure of their souls? were they all priests? did they all celebrate their masses? did they receive Communion and make confession with the recommended frequency? did they use feather beds or eat meat?[68] Such a general inquiry was used to determine whether any of the clergy was ill-famed (*infamatus*), having committed a transgression. The *detecta* were everything that the visitor learned from his inquiries, much like a doctor's notes on a patient's medical history and current symptoms. The *comperta* were summaries of the problems the archbishop found. This stage can be likened to a doctor's diagnosis of an illness. Finally, the archbishop issued a set of injunctions, or course of treatment, and wrote out the appropriate prescriptions. When Eudes found a monastic ill-famed, he generally issued a formal, verbal warning and recorded it in his *Register*. During subsequent visits, he paid close attention to whether his warnings had been heeded; repeated warnings generally led to disciplinary action, with the punishment becoming more severe the more times a warning had been repeated.[69]

But was the existence of *infamia* a presumption of guilt?[70] Some twelfth- and thirteenth-century canonists drew a distinction between the ill fame of a deed (*infamia facti*), which presupposed a notorious crime, and more general defamation of character (*infamatio*), which was only a condition of probable cause. Eudes rarely conducted formal investigations of monastics to determine the veracity of rumors, probably because he did not have time.[71] What generally interested him more than establishing a cleric's guilt or innocence was putting an end to public scandal.[72] Long, drawn-out investigations simply made a public scandal more public and more scandalous. Thus Eudes generally did not begin formal inquiries when he found a monk defamed of incontinence; he warned the monk, instructed the monastic superior to follow up on the problem, and moved on.[73] Finding a scandal surrounding a priest who worked at the nunnery of Bival, Eudes summarily dismissed him, although, as the archbishop admitted, "we did not find anything bad about him that could be proved."[74] *Infamatio* represented a problem in itself, whether or not the defamed cleric was actually guilty. In criminal cases involving secular clergy, Eudes showed greater interest in establishing the cleric's guilt or innocence, and he often required that the accused clear himself of suspicion by swearing a purgative oath or admit his guilt and swear that if he ever was found to be ill-famed again, he would voluntarily resign his benefice.[75] But in cases involving the life and manners of regular clergy, Eudes's objective was to restore order, discipline, and communal peace as quickly as possible. In the archbishop's eyes, the only way to curb monastic incontinence (and there was really very little that he could do) was to make sure that monastic superiors enforced the claustration of their monasteries as much as they could. Violations of the monastic rule were most likely to occur when lay friends, relatives, or workers were allowed to spend time inside a convent, or likewise, when monastics were permitted to leave their monastery unaccompanied. Paradoxically, Eudes's own visitations may have unearthed embarrassing revelations and scandals that would otherwise have remained quiet, private matters.[76] Yet according to the monastic ideal, there were not to be any private matters; the practice of mutual accusation in chapter held each monastic accountable to his brethren and revealed his every fault. Eudes also recognized that some monastics might use his visitations as a way of paying off personal grudges against their brethren.[77] There was a need, moreover, to distinguish serious accusations from frivolous grumblings and fabrications.

The disintegration of the common life in monastic houses was a problem that especially concerned the archbishop. He repeatedly found houses, such as the nunnery of Almenèches, where members no longer ate in the refectory as a body. Instead of sleeping in the communal dormitory, several of the nuns at Almenèches had their own rooms, where, in addition to sleeping, they ate their meals in cliques of twos and threes.[78] The monks at Saint-Martin-de-Pontoise were known to hold drinking parties in "Bernard's Room," the room of a particularly sociable monk.[79] There was little that Eudes could do to restore the common life other than remind monastics that they were forbidden to sleep outside the dormitory and to eat or drink outside the refectory, the infirmary, or the monastic superior's room (with his or her invitation). The breakdown in communal living was attributable to the fact that monastic superiors were not enforcing the rules and were not even observing the rules themselves. Eudes frequently reported finding monastic superiors who did not eat in the refectory, who were absent from the Divine Offices, and who took other liberties. It had become so common for monastic communities to observe periods of "recreations," when part of a community ate meat in a room other than the refectory (where meat eating was banned), that in 1249 the Benedictine Chapter legalized "recreations" and meat eating, so long as meat was eaten only near the infirmary, where it was permitted for those most weak. Prelates such as Eudes Rigaud and John Pecham opposed this ruling and continued to insist that Benedictine monks strictly adhere to their rule.[80] In this still worldly society, abbots were eating meals in their own rooms, either with monks they particularly favored or with guests from outside their monasteries. They were also eating meat and sumptuous foods denied to their communities, thereby provoking further resentment among their brethren. Again and again, Eudes faced the challenge of repairing relations between monastic communities and their superiors.[81]

Eudes also confronted other kinds of internal disputes within monastic houses. Finding two groups of nuns at the nunnery of Bival who were not on speaking terms, he ordered them to make up and symbolically kiss each other on the mouth. He also threatened them with excommunication should they ever mention the cause of their disagreement again.[82] At his next visitation, however, he found more "discord and quarrels," and this time tried using humiliation as a punishment, placing the trouble-making nuns on a cart, thereby stripping them of their dignity.[83] The archbishop sometimes had a particularly contentious monk or nun transferred to a different religious house.[84] In one case, he had an unruly monk taken to Rouen and incarcerated in the archiepiscopal prison.[85]

Eudes viewed personal property as the most common and natural source of monastic discord. At the nunnery of Saint-Aubin, for instance, he attributed the frequent quarrels among the nuns to the fact that several had their own hens and chickens, something he tried to correct: "We ordered them to feed all the hens and chickens together and to possess them in common. We ordered that such eggs as might be produced be served equally to the nuns."[86] Eudes's objection to personal property was not merely based on his sense that it caused divisions within monastic houses. Strictly prohibited by the monastic Rules of Saints Benedict and Augustine, personal property was also anathema to Franciscans. This may help explain why Eudes was so concerned about personal property, particularly in female monastic houses, where he exhorted abbesses and prioresses to conduct surprise inspections of their nuns' coffers to see if any personal property was being kept.[87] At the nunnery of Almenêches, he was unhappy to find that the nuns did not eat from common dishes but had their own plates; certain nuns owned their own copper kettles and necklaces and were served by their own maidservants; they slept in private dormitory rooms with locks.[88] The abbess of Bival gave each of her nuns twelve shillings a year for clothing and allowed them to keep any money that was left over.[89] Some of these cases represented blatant violations of the Benedictine Rule's prohibition of private ownership.

Eudes sought to hold the monastic houses under his jurisdiction to the strictest standards of religious life. He instructed monastic superiors to collect their communities' old habits when distributing new ones. He did not want monks drinking out of their own cups; all cups were to be held in common.[90] Nuns were not permitted to make alms bags (*elemosinarias*), fringes (*fresellas*), needle cases (*acuarias*), small pillows (*auriarias*), and the like, even if they intended to give them away.[91] Echoing the monastic reform statutes of Gregory IX, Eudes prohibited nuns from having anything fancy, such as knives with carved silver handles; metaled belts; or ornaments made of peach-colored cloth on the collars or cuffs of their pelisses.[92] In northern France during the middle of the thirteenth century, monks and nuns who spent time outside their cloisters were exposed to a bustling commercial world and an unprecedented diversity of material temptations.[93] The archbishop was especially concerned that the female religious not be enticed by furs, velvet, silks, linens, and gold and silver colors, which were increasingly available, to say nothing of the new kinds of haircuts.[94]

As a Franciscan, Eudes was committed to working in the world. Yet during his visitations of monasteries, he placed a high priority on preserving the barriers that separated the monastic cloister from the lay world. He ordered monastic superiors to be more strict in limiting their members' visits outside the convent.[95] In the archbishop's eyes, the dangers for a religious woman venturing beyond the protective walls of her cloister were even greater than for a religious man. The Franciscan archbishop of Canterbury, John Pecham, set strict limits for nuns' visits to the houses of their relatives: nuns were not permitted to visit their relatives for more than three days, and if a nun's parents were sick, she could stay with them for up to six days if she first received the bishop's permission.[96] Eudes also recognized that both monks and nuns would inevitably spend a certain amount of time outside the cloister, including their occasional visits to secular relatives, and so he insisted that any monastic wishing to travel first obtain permission from his or her superior and be accompanied outside the cloister by at least one other member of the religious community. The archbishop also stressed the importance of guarding the entrances of monasteries to keep laypeople out. At the same time, he understood that it was in monasteries' best interests to maintain good relations with their surrounding communities, on whom they depended for many things, including financial donations. Thus, at the priory of Saint-Lô-de-Rouen, he encouraged the porter to keep lay folk out of the cloister, only so far as he could do so "tactfully."[97] And at the nunnery of Bival, Eudes forbade the admission of any lay folk into the cloister, "except those whom it might be a scandal to keep out."[98]

Who were the laypeople Eudes was trying to keep out of cloisters? One category was the relatives of monastics. Eudes generally allowed these non-religious relatives to enter the religious houses of their kin, but he tried to keep the visits short and restricted the laypeople to certain spaces. He was displeased to find, for instance, that the mothers of the novices at the abbey of Bival had eaten with their sons in the infirmary and abbot's room. Eudes forbade the mothers from eating in any room other than the great common hall.[99] Friends and relatives of the nuns of Bondeville were prohibited from entering the cloister, dormitory, or refectory and were permitted to speak with the nuns only "in some public place, as for example the parlor."[100] The archbishop was particularly concerned about female relatives visiting male houses, and male relatives visiting female houses. Finding that the sister of the abbot of Aumale sometimes dined with her brother in the abbey, Eudes forbade the abbot from inviting his sister again, telling him to invite his brother-in-law instead.[101] Likewise, Eudes forbade the men of the village of Sigy from bringing their wives with them when they dined at the local priory.[102]

Lay servants and laborers who worked in monastic houses represented another problem.[103] Some of these servants were *conversi* (or *conversae*), who followed a modified and less strict version of the monastic rule. But again, what seems to have disturbed Eudes most was not so much the socializing of regular clergy and laypeople but rather the contacts between members of the opposite sex. Visiting the priory of Sainte-Radegonde, where the prior was absent, Eudes found only a single monk, Reginald, and a young woman, who was reportedly staying at the priory to prepare the monk's meals. Eudes ordered her to be removed at once.[104] At the priory of Ticheville, where there were two monks, Eudes also found two women, presumably maidservants. He drew particular attention in his *Register* to the fact that one of the women was "young" and the other was about thirty years old. He ordered the monks to send the two women away "and to get another or others who would not arouse suspicion," by which he probably meant older ones.[105] Much of Eudes's concern stemmed from a fear that monastics would develop sexual relationships. The archbishop's *Register* contains several references to monks defamed for violating the vow of chastity, as well as cases of nuns who became pregnant and gave birth in their convents.[106] A high incidence of fires in thirteenth-century Norman monasteries meant that laborers were frequently present, in addition to the servants who were employed on a more permanent basis. The presence of lay workmen, as Eudes discovered, made it virtually impossible for a cloister to be well guarded. It was relatively easy for a scandal to arise, such as the one at the abbey of Aumale, where it was rumored that a female nurse named Alice Telière was sleeping with the abbey's laborers.[107] Any observer at monastic gates saw an influx of lay relatives, servants, laborers, and even an occasional trader or apothecary.[108] In the diocese of Canterbury, some nunneries accepted laywomen as boarders in an effort to bring in additional income. The archbishop of Canterbury expressed concern about the threat lay boarders posed to religious discipline.

What also concerned the archbishop was laypeople's use of monastic churches (frequently the abbatial churches of Augustinian canons) for hearing Mass on Sundays and feast days.[109] Quite frequently, smaller Norman towns lacked their own parish churches and therefore relied on local monasteries for their pastoral needs.[110] This did not please the archbishop, and he encouraged such towns to build their own parish churches.[111] But in the meantime, he tried to find ways of allowing lay parishioners to use monastic churches without disturbing the *opus dei*. At the abbey of Eu, for instance, he encouraged the Augustinian canons to arrange for lay parishioners to reach the Eucharist without walking through the choir, which was to be reserved for the canons.[112] When holy relics were displayed on the high altar, the archbishop ordered that they be moved to a different vantage point so laypeople could see them and worship them without entering the choir.[113] He rejected one abbey's custom of involving laymen and women in a Sunday processional through the cloister.[114] Discovering that parishioners frequented the abbey of Corneville not only to hear masses but to strike two bells that belonged to the parish and were located in the abbey's tower, he instructed the canons to build a partition between their bells and the bells belonging to the parishioners, "so that the canons might sound their own bells more freely and be able to concentrate upon the divine cult with more quiet."[115]

During the thirteenth century, as the endowment of hospitals became an increasingly popular way of remitting one's sins and attaining salvation, churchmen and laymen founded a significant number of new hospitals and leprosaries.[116] The Benedictine Rule stipulated that each monastery have an infirmary, and the statutes of Gregory IX contained a clause prescribing that monks who were sick be provided with such foods, beds, helpers, and other necessities as their illnesses required.[117] Innocent III had also stressed the responsibility of the clergy, particularly bishops, in helping the sick and the impoverished. The pope himself had founded the hospital of Santo Spirito for the *miserabiles*, including the indigent, abandoned children, the sick, and widows.[118] The pastoral reforms initiated by Innocent III and Gregory IX gave further impetus for bishops and other clerics to care for the sick and the powerless. The general expansion of episcopal administration in the late twelfth and early thirteenth centuries extended to the interiors of hospitals and leprosaries.[119] A thirteenth-century anonymous pastoral manual written for the archdeacon of Paris included a chapter on how he should oversee leprosaries.[120]

Although Eudes's program of monastic reforms drew to a large extent on the statutes of Gregory IX aimed at reforming Benedictine monks, the archbishop's visitations also reflected his own personality and values as a Franciscan, as is evident in his sensitivity to the ill, poor, and aged in Normandy's hospitals and leprosaries. For Eudes, the hope of securing salvation lay not so much in the founding of new hospitals but rather in ensuring that the sick were properly cared for, both in monastic houses and in the more than one dozen hospitals and leprosaries he visited regularly.[121] Eudes's attention to illness may have stemmed from his own suffering from rheumatism, as well as the emphasis his religious order placed on caring for the infirm. Lepers had played a central role in the life story of Saint Francis. The archbishop may also have been inspired by the example of King Louis, who founded many hospitals (including one at Vernon) and whose own altruism toward the sick linked him with "the new apostles," the mendicants. Eudes's fellow Franciscan, Guibert de Tournai, preached several sermons either to lepers or on the subject of lepers. Guibert showed unusual compassion for lepers, suggesting that these unfortunates, precisely because they were shunned by society, were in a sense God's chosen people, selected to undergo the most difficult moral, physical, and social trials.[122] The Franciscans, it should be said, were not the only preachers who sometimes showed respect for lepers.[123] The regular canon Jacques de Vitry likewise suggested that lepers were signs of God's love (*signum dilectionis*) and compared lepers to monks in their patience and willingness to endure physical suffering and social isolation. According to Jacques, when sin manifested itself in physical sickness, as in leprosy, it could lead to penitence, conversion, and the attainment of a healthy soul.[124]

Again and again during his visitations of monastic houses, Eudes lent his voice on behalf of sick canons, monks, and nuns, telling monastic superiors to provide the sick with better food provisions, to build new and better infirmaries, and in general to pay the sick greater consideration and kindness.[125] Having one or two physicians in his own archiepiscopal entourage, Eudes wanted to make sure that religious houses also had access to physicians.[126] Here Eudes differed from some ecclesiastical authorities who expressed hostility toward physicians. Since bodily sickness was widely believed to be the result of spiritual disease, some churchmen maintained that physicians of the soul, that is, priests, were far better qualified to treat physical infirmities than physicians of the body.[127] Yet the archbishop was not so conservative (or cold-hearted) as to suggest that even the sickest monastics should be required to lead the strictest and most ascetic form of the religious life. Eudes displayed a certain practicality in ordering monastic superiors to be sensitive to the special needs of the sick, especially when they were weak after being bled. The abbey of Sainte-Catherine, which, according to the archbishop, was led by a "wrathful and bitter" abbot, did not even have an infirmary for the sick. Eudes found that the sick there were "wretchedly attended" and that the abbot forbade them from having anything but bread and water. "Nothing is given to the bled monks," the archbishop complained, "except in the measure that it is given to those who are not bled."[128]

Although he argued that the sick be granted special consideration in light of their infirmity, Eudes also went along with the ancient idea, reaffirmed in canon 22 of the Fourth Lateran Council and incorporated into diocesan legislation, that sickness was a form of divine punishment for sin and therefore required spiritual healing.[129] The Fourth Lateran Council stressed that precisely because physical infirmities were sometimes the results of sin, the sick were especially in need of physicians of the soul. The sick needed to be physically separated from the healthy as well as distinguished in some way by their dress. At the abbey of Saint-Wandrille, for instance, the archbishop was unhappy to find Reginald de Caudebec, thought to be a leper, wearing no distinguishing sign of his condition even though Eudes had earlier ordered him to do so.[130] The archbishop prohibited an epileptic regular canon from Saint-Laurent-en-Lyon from celebrating Mass, perhaps worried that an epileptic seizure might interrupt the ceremony.[131] Eudes once even punished a "healthy" nun by sending her to a leper house to do service for having "arranged" the fornication of another sister and then having attempted to perform an abortion on the pregnant nun by giving her certain herbs to drink.[132]

Despite these cases, the *Register* makes clear that Eudes was deeply committed to improving the religious lives of the sick and abject in Normandy's hospitals, leprosaries, and monastic infirmaries. He viewed this as a central part of his apostolic mission as archbishop. At the abbey of Saint-Ouen, as well as other monastic houses, he ordered that the Office of the Hours be read daily to the sick and that Mass be celebrated daily in the infirmary chapel. The Epistle and Gospel were to be read to anyone who was unable to come to Mass but wished to hear them.[133] He ordered the prior of one hospital to have sermons preached to the infirm more frequently than had been the custom.[134] The archbishop wished to ensure, in other words, that sickness would not preclude anyone from participating in the sacraments and liturgy of the church. If sickness was sometimes a form of divine punishment for sin, requiring spiritual healing, the sick were even more in need of physicians of the soul than physicians of the body.

Imposing discipline on hospitals and leprosaries was especially difficult, since the constituencies of these communities were diverse.[135] Mont-aux-Malades, a typical leprosary located on a hill above Rouen, was home to ten regular canons, five healthy lay brothers, sixteen healthy lay sisters, twelve male lepers, and seventeen female lepers.[136] Although some hospitals and leprosaries observed a monastic rule (usually a modified version of the Augustinian Rule) and required the sick to give up their property, others observed no rule at all.[137] Hospitals under ecclesiastical control often comprised a religious community living alongside laymen. Eudes tried to impose the religious life on the hospitals and leprosaries he visited, urging the brothers and sisters to bind themselves by vows of chastity, to live without possessing property, and to eat in common.[138] But the way hospitals were administered also complicated matters. Even if a hospital followed some form of monastic rule, the resident priest who had cure of the hospital's souls was not necessarily a professed brother. At the hospital of Chaumont, it was a parish priest rather than the resident priest who actually administered the sacraments and who held the cure of the hospital's souls (both patients and staff). The hospital's financial accounts were overseen by its resident priest along with the town's elected mayor.[139] As with running a monastic house or parish, the running of a hospital or leprosary involved a wide range of disciplinary, administrative, and spiritual issues, and power struggles between different lay and ecclesiastical authorities over control of a hospital or leprosary were not uncommon.[140]

Many thirteenth-century synodal statutes forbade lepers from entering towns or leaving their leprosaries without authorization. Even more so than nuns, lepers had a reputation for creating scandal and being undisciplined, and for this reason, there was a particular fear of lepers and leper houses among members of monastic houses, who tried to keep leprosaries from being built anywhere near their own houses.[141] This attitude helps explain why a reforming archbishop, with his strong desire to impose discipline and eradicate scandal, was particularly interested in the state of leprosaries. It is worth noting that Eudes seems never to have spent a single night at one of the hospitals or leprosaries he visited. Most likely, however, it was because they were too small to accommodate him and his entourage. He may also have avoided staying at hospitals because there were women there. He never once stayed overnight in a nunnery either. Finally, most of the hospitals and leprosaries he visited happened to be close to one of his own manor houses.

Although Eudes seems to have believed that lepers needed to be physically separated from the healthy population, he also expressed displeasure whenever he learned that the sick were being shunned. He was upset to find that when the nonresident brothers of the hospital of Gournay came to their hospital, they refused to spend the night there, preferring instead to sleep at the houses of burgesses. Eudes ordered the dean to compel the brothers to spend the night at the hospital whenever they were in town.[142] Hearing that various healthy travelers, including priests and sergeants of the king who guarded the forest of Lyon, were receiving hospitality (probably in the form of a procuration fee) from the hospital at Gournay even though they refused to sleep there, Eudes forbade the hospital from granting anything to anyone who was unwilling to sleep among the sick.[143] Perhaps most striking about Eudes's visitations of hospitals and leprosaries is their similarity to his visitations of conventional religious houses. Just as he did in the case of a great abbey, he inquired into the financial and material state of a hospital, investigated the moral discipline of its community, particularly its obedience to the monastic rule, and when necessary, drafted a detailed ordinance of correction and reform "as a permanent guide and reminder."[144]

Measuring Success

How much success did Eudes have in his efforts to reform the monastic communities of Normandy? The *Register* provides a wealth of statistics on

Norman monasticism, everything from the percentage of monastic houses that did not possess a copy of their rule, to the percentage that did not keep satisfactory financial accounts, to the number of houses in which Eudes found monastics defamed of incontinence. Since the total number of Eudes's visitations of monastic houses varied from year to year, it is necessary to calculate the number of certain infractions he recorded as a percentage of the number of monastic visitations for that year. During his first few years as archbishop, the frequency with which Eudes recorded almost every kind of infraction increased (except incontinence, which was mentioned slightly less frequently each year from 1248 to 1252), perhaps indicative of the archbishop's becoming more thorough and systematic with experience. In 1248, for instance, he records problems with the way a monastery kept its financial accounts (including not involving more members of the community) only 16 percent of the time, whereas in 1250 he mentions problems with financial accounting 43 percent of the time, more often than in any subsequent year. Confirming this trend is the fact that during Eudes's first year of visitations, he specifically comments on a monastery being in a satisfactory state 32 percent of the time, whereas during most of the 1250s, he calls a monastery satisfactory less than 10 percent of the time.

There is some evidence, however, that during the mid to later 1260s the state of monasteries was improving, at least in the archbishop's eyes.[145] During the later 1260s, Eudes records fewer cases of monastic incontinence, poor financial accounting, disobedience, violations of the rule of silence, and monastics leaving their convents. In 1266, for instance, there is only one accusation of monastic incontinence out of forty-three monastic visitations (2 percent), whereas in 1248, charges of incontinence are mentioned during 16 percent of the archbishop's twenty-five visitations. Further confirmation of this trend can be found in the increased frequency with which Eudes remarks during the 1260s that monasteries are in a satisfactory state. Whereas during the 1250s Eudes rarely comments that a monastery is satisfactory, in 1266 he uses a phrase such as "with God's grace we found them in good condition as to spirituals" (*spiritualia, per Dei gratiam, invenimus in bono statu*) to describe a monastic house 51 percent of the time.[146] Nor is there any evidence that Eudes was becoming less active or conscientious during these years. Indeed, the archbishop conducted his third largest number of monastic visitations in 1266 (the number of visitations in 1269 was not far behind) and showed that he was still perfectly capable of finding much wrong with a monastery.

Although the statistics provided by the *Register* suggest certain general trends, the findings also pose some interpretative problems.[147] Does the increased frequency of comments about the "satisfactory" state of monasteries (the archbishop's highest compliment) during the later 1260s truly reflect an improvement in the state of monasteries? Quite often, the comment about a monastery being in good or satisfactory condition followed a list of the problems needing correction. At Noyon-sur-Andelle, for instance, Eudes noted that the priory was in a satisfactory state *except* for the cellarer (one of only six resident monks), who was a drunk and such a disturbance to the community that Eudes ordered him removed.[148] At times Eudes commented on the satisfactory state of a monastery's spirituals only to contrast this with the miserable state of its temporals. At other visitations, Eudes did not explicitly label a monastery as being in a satisfactory state, and yet his own record of findings seems to indicate that it was in quite good shape. There are dangers, moreover, in concluding too much from the phrase *in bono statu*, which might in the end have merely been a new secretary's favorite formula for saying that everything else in a monastic house (besides the items mentioned) was in a satisfactory state.

Despite its staggering detail, the *Register* is not a comprehensive record of everything the archbishop found and did during his visitations. For example, the *Register* sometimes refers to an injunction the archbishop made at an earlier visitation, but an injunction of which there is no record in the *Register*. Furthermore, there is a danger in assuming that the injunctions recorded in the *Register* always reflected actual transgressions. Although for the most part, Eudes's injunctions to monasteries do not seem to have been formulaic (as some bishops' were) but rather reflected the actual problems he encountered, every injunction cannot be taken as evidence of a transgression, and Eudes's silence may reflect a moment of lethargy or overwork. At houses with a troubled history, Eudes may sometimes have issued injunctions as reminders, even when there was no evidence of a transgression.[149] Injunctions, moreover, could serve as deterrents just as they could serve to correct preexisting problems. As a result of his second visitation of the abbey of Saint-Ouen in Rouen, for instance, Eudes drew up a series of seventeen regulations for the abbey. Some of the injunctions are clearly in response to specific problems he found. Others appear to have been preemptive warnings based on problems he had found at other abbeys. Eudes ended the regulations with a threat that he hoped would serve to deter any future abuses: "Be it known that if we find anyone negligent or rebellious in these matters, we will deal with him in such a way that his punishment will be a source of terror to the rest."[150]

There is also the question of what Eudes considered problems. It is probably a mistake to assume that what concerned him remained constant during the more than twenty-one years he conducted visitations. It would only have been natural for him to have undergone some changes of his own. Why, for instance, was it only around 1262 that he began taking an interest in (or recording) the matter of pittances that monastic superiors owed their communities? The subject of pittances frequently arises in the *Register* after

1262 but not before. Had it simply not been an issue before 1262, or had it not been an issue to the archbishop? There is no way of knowing whether increases or decreases in the number of Eudes's injunctions reflected changing conditions in monasteries or changes in what mattered to him.

Perhaps the most important point missed by using statistics to gauge the archbishop's reforming success is that each monastic house Eudes visited had its own ups and downs during the twenty-one years covered by the *Register*. It is hardly as though every Norman house experienced steady or even gradual improvement (or decline) from 1248 until 1269. Many of the conditions in monastic houses were beyond the archbishop's control, especially since he was able to visit only once every year or two. As Eudes himself recognized, the spiritual and temporal state of a monastery was primarily shaped by the abbot or abbess who managed the house on a day-to-day basis.[151] And though Eudes took an interest in how monastic superiors administered their houses, he rarely went so far as to depose a monastic superior (even though he held this canonical power and certainly had occasion to exercise it). Nor did he often reject an elected candidate or try to install his own candidate as abbot or abbess. Finally, forces outside his control—the quality of harvests, destructive fires, inflation that eroded the value of monasteries' fixed income, the behavior of the monastics themselves, and the actions of monastic superiors—had the most impact on monastic houses.

Knowing that he could conduct a visitation of a monastic house only once every year or two, Eudes made every effort to institute mechanisms of reform that would continue to operate even in his absence. The *Register* itself served as a powerful disciplinary tool. By recording the date of every monastic visitation, the abuses he found, and the injunctions he issued to correct the abuses, the archbishop held monastics accountable not only to him but to future archbishops who might use the *Register*. It was much more difficult for a monastery to claim that it was exempt from episcopal visitation or the obligation to pay a procuration if there were written records of past episcopal visitations and procuration payments. The ritual of recording the disciplinary measures that had been imposed on monastic houses was itself a mechanism of reform, a way to preserve the past and ensure future accountability. Monasteries had begun using new kinds of written instruments during the twelfth century to manage their patrimonies in new and more aggressive ways. So too in the thirteenth century, episcopal administrative activity expanded as bishops and archbishops began keeping new written tools, such as visitation registers and polyptychs, that enabled them to hold the secular and regular clergy of their dioceses morally and religiously accountable. Bishops and archbishops believed that on the final day of reckoning, they would be held accountable for the conduct of the clergy for whom they were responsible.[152]

The archbishop's policies were most likely to be enforced if there was an effective monastic superior who was supported by other competent monastic officials such as kitcheners and porters.[153] Ideally, a community possessed copies of both its rule and the statutes of Gregory IX and had them read aloud periodically. Daily mutual correction ensured that monastics were in the practice of checking the conduct of their peers. At one abbey, Eudes instructed the abbot to appoint a custodian (*custodia*), whose duty it was to keep a lookout for the offenses of the brethren and accuse them accordingly.[154] Finally, there were the occasional visitations by the local archdeacon and dean, both of whom reported to the archbishop.

None of these measures, however, was a substitute for Eudes's own inspections. As the *Register* demonstrates, the archbishop showed tremendous perseverance in trying to correct problems that would not go away. At many of the monastic communities he visited, for instance, he found monastics eating meat in violation of the rule. There are some 393 references in the *Register* to monastics eating meat, roughly 40 percent of all infractions.[155] It was rare for monks or nuns to heed the archbishop's injunctions on the matter of eating meat even though such corrections merely followed the prohibitions contained in both the rules and the statutes of Gregory IX.[156] At times, Eudes backed down on the issue. The monks of Chaumont l'Aillerie, for instance, told him "that eating meat is not an essential of the Rule, and that the Lord Pope had granted them a dispensation from those things which are not an essential of the Rule; therefore we have permitted it for the present."[157] But although he occasionally left the matter of meat eating "to their conscience," Eudes generally refused to compromise and warned monks that they would be dealt with according to the punishments prescribed in Gregory IX's statutes.[158]

The frequency with which Eudes enjoined monks and nuns to cease eating meat reflects more, however, than his perseverance in the face of resistance. What is striking is that Eudes continued to be preoccupied with the problem of meat eating at the same time that he was confronting much larger and more serious problems of monastic discipline. Even if some monastics dismissed prohibitions against eating meat as unimportant, the issue was not a minor one for the literal-minded archbishop, devoted as he was to every word contained in the monastic rules and Gregorian statutes. For Eudes, the abstention from eating meat was an important and necessary component of the religious life, something that distinguished the regular clergy from the secular. Monastic discipline required that every precept contained in the rule be observed. Minor discipline violations that went uncorrected could quickly lead to more serious offenses. The path to holiness depended in part on a vigilant policeman and his mechanisms for the reform of monastic discipline.

Managing Monastic Temporalities

Eudes Rigaud believed there was an important connection between the moral discipline of a monastic community and the state of its temporalities. Admittedly, there was no absolute correlation between the two. As the archbishop's *Register* shows, some monasteries that were excellent in their spiritualities were poor in their temporalities.[159] Contemporary chroniclers sometimes suggested an inverse correlation: a monastery's poor temporalities were attributed to its abbot's disregard of finances in favor of spiritual matters, as if to suggest that the two were mutually exclusive. It is clear from his *Register,* however, that the Franciscan archbishop did not feel that business details were in any way beneath him; he was just as concerned with the material conditions (*status*) of the religious houses he visited as he was with the state of spiritual affairs. The reality was that even for something as spiritual and otherworldly as the *opus dei,* a certain amount of income was necessary. Although members of monasteries were committed to lives of voluntary poverty, the monasteries themselves were institutions with assets and economic interests.[160] The archbishop recognized that monasteries' survival was inexorably tied to the worldly realities of price and wage fluctuations. A monastery without an adequate supply of wine, for instance, could not celebrate the Eucharist with the recommended frequency. When liturgical objects such as chalices, were pawned, the celebration of Divine Offices suffered. A shortage of food provisions not only posed a problem for a community's religious members but also could lead to a decrease in almsgiving and hamper the community's ability to provide hospitality to guests.

Although it might at first appear ironic that a Franciscan archbishop, whose own religious order emphasized voluntary poverty, would have taken such an interest in the finances of religious houses, Eudes, like so many of his religious contemporaries, viewed monastic finances and the church fabric as a necessary means to an end. Furthermore, by the late thirteenth and early fourteenth centuries, the Franciscans had become, as Joel Kaye puts it, "among the most sensitive and understanding of economic observers."[161] Although it is not clear whether particular Franciscan theological positions, such as an emphasis on the freedom and primacy of the will, played a role in shaping the economic theories of thinkers such as Pierre Jean Olivi, Geraldus Odonis, and Duns Scotus, these Franciscans would take a leading role in exploring issues such as equalization in exchange. Thus, Eudes's concern with monastic finances, not uncommon among bishops, and his own business acumen were not unusual for a Franciscan.

Eudes's concern for monastic temporalities is most apparent in his frequent exhortation to monasteries to invest more in liturgical objects, books, and building repairs. When, in the course of a visitation, he found a priory with only one chalice, he did not hesitate to recommend that a second one be bought. Nor did he want a single chalice shared by a priory and parish church, since this meant that Mass could never be celebrated at the same time.[162] In one case, he even loaned a prior the six *livres* needed for a new chalice.[163] After hearing some monks at Saint-Wandrille's indicate that they celebrated Mass less frequently as a result of having only three altars, Eudes instructed them "to provide themselves with several altars and in sufficient quantity."[164] He also regarded it as absolutely essential that all monastic houses own a sufficient number of liturgical vestments, needed for performing Mass.[165]

Eudes also displayed an interest in the physical appearance of liturgical objects and vestments. The archbishop adhered to the Fourth Lateran Council's insistence (in canon 16) that church vestments be clean and suitable (*honesta, competentia*). He complained, as had the bishop of Paris, Eudes de Sully, about church ornaments that were dirty, insisting that altars always be covered by clean altar cloths.[166] At Saint-Mellon-de-Pontoise, he ordered "that the ornaments, the altar linen, and the old altar cloths be folded, preserved, repaired, and maintained in a cleaner and better condition than had been the practice."[167] Among the ordinances he drew up for the abbey of Saint-Ouen after his second visitation there in December 1249 were regulations governing the physical care of the Eucharist: "Since we found that the sacrosanct and venerable Blessed Sacrament which should be kept with all care and diligence and treated with reverence and honor according to the canons, was being improperly cared for, we will and decree that every effort be made to assure its proper care. Likewise, we will and decree that you remove the unsuitable and shameful altar ornaments, especially the corporals, in which the real Body of Christ is wrapped, and that each altar be furnished with clean and decent cloths."[168] The Franciscan archbishop was adamant that the real presence of Christ in the Eucharist be treated with the greatest reverence. He simply would not tolerate any sign of disrespect, whether in the form of a soiled or tattered altar cloth or a monastery in which the Eucharist was placed in a window, making it impossible for the monks to say their hours without turning their backs on the Holy Sacrament.[169]

It is clear from Eudes's sermons, discussed in chapter 1, that he saw an important connection between outward appearance and inner devotion. He used *munditia* to refer to moral and bodily purity as well as the cleanliness of priests' vestments (which signified the clergy's chastity). Drawing on the book of Leviticus, he suggested that the clergy of his own day, especially the regular clergy, were the natural successors to Aaron the high priest and his sons.[170] Although Eudes was a critic of luxury, he nonetheless drew a connection (which he explicitly attributed to Leviticus) between holiness and the appearance of material objects used in religious ritual. Explaining the need to keep churches, vessels, corporals, and vestments clean, the

Fourth Lateran Council declared, "For it seems too absurd to take no notice of squalor in sacred things when it is unbecoming even in profane things."[171]

Perhaps because of his own scholastic background, Eudes also paid particular attention to the books religious houses possessed.[172] Finding a priory in possession of only one missal, he ordered that more be procured.[173] Saint-Mellon de Pontoise, a chapter with about ten Augustinian canons, repeatedly received instructions to expand its collection of liturgical books. On March 6, 1256, Eudes found that the chapter had "only two graduals, two antiphonaries," and some deficient psalters.[174] At a subsequent visitation, he noted that Saint-Mellon did not have a copy of the Lives of the Saints, an ordinal, or even a Bible![175] He was also displeased to find that some of the canons there chanted the hours according to the usage of Rouen, but others chanted according to the usage of Paris. Suspecting that this discrepancy was the result of their not having an ordinal, he promised to give them one with the chant used in Rouen. In other cases, he instructed a monastery either to purchase a book it did not own or to have a copy made from an existing book.[176]

Eudes was also attentive to the condition of books, frequently ordering that they be rebound. Finding inaccuracies in a liturgical book, as he did with a passional belonging to the abbey of Eu, he ordered that it be corrected and improved.[177] He expected monasteries to maintain careful catalogs of their books so that they would know exactly what they owned. He told the prior of Beaulieu, for instance, "that he should have all books of the priory catalogued and checked over, and frequently displayed in chapter; that he should recall those which they had loaned."[178] When Eudes found that the Augustinian priory of Bourg-Achard had loaned the glossed epistles of Paul and the *Summa* of William of Auxerre to a priest, he ordered the prior to have them returned at once.[179]

The archbishop's commitment to improving the church fabric of monastic houses is nowhere more apparent than in his efforts to repair deteriorating monastic buildings. There are thirty-three references in the *Register* to monasteries, nunneries, and religious hospitals with substandard physical structures. In a number of cases, the situation was dire. Visiting the priory of Sainte-Gauburge on January 17, 1256, Eudes found the buildings in such need of re-roofing that he believed they were on the verge of collapse.[180] Likewise, at the hospital at Neufchâtel, he worried that the building might fall, crushing the sick lying in bed.[181] At the nunnery of Saint-Aubin, the roof of the main building was in such a state of disrepair that the nuns could hardly remain there when it rained.[182]

What is striking is not simply that the buildings of many Norman monasteries were in a ruinous state but that the archbishop was attuned to these problems and determined to correct them. He may have been inspired by the founder of his own order, Saint Francis of Assisi, who rebuilt several churches himself and showed a commitment to the proper maintenance of churches.[183] When Eudes visited the chapter of Saint-Mellon-de-Pontoise on December 11, 1264, and found continued problems with the roofing of the monastery, especially the bell tower, as well as defects with the altar cloths, rochets (ceremonial vestments), and books, he ordered his vicar, Simon de Brie (de Montpensier), "to sequestrate as much of the canons' property as would be sufficient to supply the church adequately with altar cloths, rochets, and such things, and to have the hall properly repaired and re-roofed, since it was badly and improperly roofed. Likewise, [we ordered] that our procuration be paid from the same source. We ordered the treasurer to have the monastery, and particularly the bell tower, properly re-roofed."[184] In another case, he ordered the dean and treasurer at Auffay to force parishioners to contribute 120 l. toward the rebuilding of the priory's church. The nave of the church was in such a bad state of repair that it was exposed to the weather and the faithful were not able to stand in it to hear the Divine Office.[185] The archbishop's *Register* reveals that he was as much a building inspector as a supervisor of monastic conduct. When he found insufficient lighting in a monastery, he ordered that lanterns be bought.[186] When the roof of a priory's bell tower had leaked so much that the timbers and vaults of its building were in danger of collapse, Eudes demanded that repairs be made.[187] What was at stake was nothing short of a monastic community's ability to function at the most basic level.

Eudes's frequent injunctions for monasteries to spend more on building repairs raise the question of how monasteries were able to afford such capital expenditures. How could he have expected monasteries to spend more on buildings, books, liturgical objects, almsgiving, and hospitality? The second half of the thirteenth century is often seen as the beginning of an economic decline for Benedictine monasticism.[188] In asking monasteries to make capital expenditures, was Eudes showing himself to be out of touch with the financial resources of Norman monastic houses? Or do Eudes's injunctions indicate that Norman Benedictine houses were not so badly off after all?

It is clear from the archbishop's *Register* that a central component of his visitations was learning as much as he could about a monastery's finances. He did not tell a monastery to spend large sums on building repairs, for instance, without first investigating its financial state. As part of his visitation of a religious house, he inquired closely into the community's sources of income (including collectible debts), investments, expenditures, and debts owed. All this information was recorded in his *Register* so he could compare his findings from different visitations.

Some of the abbeys he visited, such as Saint-Etienne de Caen and Saint-Martin de Troarn, were enormously wealthy, with annual revenues in excess of 3,000 l. Just around the corner from his cathedral in Rouen was the large abbey of Saint-Ouen, which had as many as sixty resident monks, several dependent priories, and possessions and rights in the city of Rouen and in more than fifty different rural domains.[189] Despite its large income, however, Saint-Ouen found itself continually plagued by debts during the 1250s.[190] After the destructive fire of 1248, the abbey had to bear the cost of rebuilding, but even so, in 1251 Eudes reported that the abbey owed only 73 l. 23 d. more than what it was owed.[191] However, the election in 1251 of a new abbot, Nicholas II de Beauvais, inaugurated a period of financial decline for the abbey. At the archbishop's next visitation, in January 1255 (after a surprisingly long absence, given that the abbey was only a few blocks from the cathedral), he found not only that the abbot was often absent from chapter, rarely ate in the refectory, and seldom arose for matins, but that the abbey's debt (over and above what it was owed) had increased from 73 l. to more than 2,333 l.[192] By 1256, the abbey's net debt had more than doubled to 5,565 l. (the gross debt was over 7,240 l.).[193] Contributing to the abbey's indebtedness may well have been the abbot's lengthy and costly legal campaign to win the privilege from Rome of being able to wear a miter.[194] In response to his desperate financial straits, the abbot seems to have tried to reduce the number of monks residing in Saint-Ouen's priories, thereby freeing up more of the abbey's income and keeping it away from the priories.[195] By 1266, Eudes learned more about the "carelessness or negligence of the abbot": he was known to be extravagant in food and wine, some of his nephews were living at the abbey's expense, and some of the abbey's administrators had tried to win the abbot's favor by presenting gifts to his sister. Hearing several seniors of the community say "that the house was seriously harmed by the abbot," Eudes ordered the community to nominate ten monks to consider with him how best to improve the management of the abbey's temporalities. Shortly thereafter, Abbot Nicholas resigned. The scale of Saint-Ouen's indebtedness was exceptional, for most religious houses Eudes visited owed relatively little.

For monastic finances to be managed properly, Eudes believed good financial accounts had to be kept. How could a monastery manage its finances without first knowing what its revenues, expenditures, and debts were? At practically every monastic house he visited, he enjoined the head of the monastery to conduct a general audit at least two or three times a year. In larger houses that used a system of obedientiaries, he ordered individual officials, such as kitcheners and infirmarians, to prepare accounts of their receipts and expenditures as frequently as every month.[196] In this regard, the archbishop was following the statutes of Gregory IX and Innocent IV.[197] From 1289 to 1302, the abbey of Saint-Ouen conducted a series of investigations of its possessions and rights, and the result was the massive *Livre des jurés*, a *censier*, or landbook, 315 folios long, which was added to over a period of many years. It was precisely this kind of meticulous survey of lands and rights that Eudes wanted monasteries to possess. But in certain respects, such an exhaustive *censier* would not have sufficed, because Eudes would have demanded a separate accounting book that provided him with the bottom line: what were the abbey's gross and net revenues and debts for that year? Though a *censier* could be helpful if a particular question arose about the value of a rent the abbey had purchased, it provided almost too much information. The length of the *censier* for Saint-Ouen illustrates just how enormously complex the management of finances at a large abbey could be.

One reason Eudes had such difficulty learning about the financial state of a large monastery was that there was rarely a central business office concerned with the collection and distribution of revenue.[198] For the archbishop to draw up a complete statement of a larger monastery's finances, he had to visit each individual obedientiary. The fragmented structure of larger monasteries not only presented an inconvenience for a visitor trying to learn about the overall financial state of the house but also revealed a growing problem in larger monasteries, namely, that no one was overseeing the *general* financial state of the house. A centralized monastic treasury, instituted during the thirteenth century and favored by the papacy, did little to alleviate the problem. The treasury was responsible for receiving unassigned revenue for the general business of the house, such as building repairs. Early thirteenth-century papal legates insisted that every abbey have such a centralized treasury and that audits be conducted regularly. Instead of serving as an office through which the activities of all obedientiaries could be monitored, however, the treasury often became merely another obedientiary.[199]

In theory, the abbot, as monastic superior, was charged with managing the general finances of his house, but some abbots showed little interest in business affairs. And even when the head of a monastery did take an active role in managing finances, the obedientiary system (whereby a monastery was divided into separate offices, each one run by a different officer who in many cases had total control over his office's income) could make it difficult for him to exert much control. The incomes assigned to individual monastic offices, which supplied most of the daily needs of the monastery, were independent of the monastic superior's control.[200] As R. H. Snape observes, "The overlapping of duties, the muddling together in one account of all sorts of disconnected items, the lack of any one account which would show roughly at any period of the year the gross receipts and expenditure of the whole establishment must have made it a task of singular difficulty for the most willing of abbots to keep track of the business affairs of the house."[201]

From Eudes's perspective, good record keeping was the critical first step in putting a monastery's finances in order. The archbishop insisted that each monastery keep a register for the accounts of the establishment as a whole, as well as individual registers for separate offices within the monastery. The financial registers facilitated the archbishop's visitations by making the financial states of monasteries more readily accessible. From his *Register*, it is clear that Eudes was familiar with the frustrating experience of attempting to conduct a visitation of a house that had not kept any financial records and therefore knew little or nothing about the state of its temporalities. At the Augustinian priory of Beaulieu, for example, he noted that "no one knows anything about the financial state of the house."[202] This statement was not entirely accurate, since Eudes had received some information, albeit conflicting, about the priory's debts and had also learned that the priory's annual income was 450 l. But Eudes was dissatisfied with the priory's accounting, complaining that the prior's accounts were incomplete because they failed to record sources of income. In this case, Eudes wanted more than the bottom line; he wanted something more like a detailed *censier* that would give him greater confidence in the numbers the prior had in his account book. For the archbishop, detailed, written, financial accounts were a first and necessary step in ensuring accountability.

Knowing that monastic superiors, who generally controlled finances, sometimes made unwise business decisions, Eudes encouraged monastic houses to elect several members of their communities to oversee their superiors' casting of accounts. At the female priory of Villarceaux, for instance, he ordered the community to elect a nun to oversee the prioress's management of finances. The prioress was prohibited from spending anything without the knowledge of this nun, who represented the interests of the community.[203] In cases where Eudes had grave doubts about the competence of a monastic superior, he asked the local bailiff to render the monastery's accounts in the presence of the monastic superior and several representatives of the community. Finding temporal mismanagement at the abbey of Saint-Martin-de-Pontoise, where the abbot had taken so little interest in sales and provisions that a grain steward had been able to steal grain without being detected, Eudes directed the abbot to call "a prudent man, a cleric or a secular priest, whose aid and counsel he should use in handling the temporal affairs of his abbey."[204] Additionally, Eudes instructed his vicar at Pontoise to be present for the monthly audits of the abbey's receipts and expenditures, to be conducted "in the presence of the entire community." Three copies of the accounts were to be made: one for the abbot, one for Eudes's vicar, and one for the community.[205] Having multiple copies lessened the dangers of a copy becoming lost. The archbishop's larger goal, not only at houses where he found temporal mismanagement, such as Villarceaux and Saint-Martin-de-Pontoise, but also at houses with sound finances, was democratizing the process by which financial accounts were computed.[206] Finances were too important to be left to the sole control of a monastic head or individual officers. It was quite common in the thirteenth century for popes and bishops to restrict the power of abbots by requiring them to seek the consent of their communities before proceeding with significant actions, such as alienating large pieces of property.[207] By involving more members of the monastic community, particularly the elders (*seniores*) or sounder brothers (*saniores*), and having financial accounts periodically read aloud to the community at large, Eudes believed there would be a greater sense of accountability and less chance of financial mismanagement.

Eudes's supervision of monastic finances was characterized by pragmatism. When an abbot reassured him that his abbey would be receiving payment on a large debt that it was owed, Eudes was not immediately satisfied. He wanted to know whether the debt was a "good debt" or a "bad debt," in other words, whether the debt was collectible.[208] Uncollectible debts were always a problem, especially in Normandy, where many monasteries depended on revenues from properties they held in England. Norman monasteries had first suffered during the Anglo-French wars, when King John seized the Normans' English lands and forbade the export of revenues, costing some large Norman houses one-fifth their income.[209] As part of their revenues, these Norman monasteries were accustomed to receiving from England both payments in coin (often carried by merchants) and certain English food supplies and other resources. A number of Norman monasteries, for instance, owned sheep in England.[210] King John's next move was to force Norman monks to pay large fines to regain their custody and privileges over their English properties.[211] Norman monks with property in England found themselves at the mercy of English kings, who used everything from interdicts to abbatial vacancies as opportunities to seize English lands belonging to Norman monasteries.[212] In the 1240s, the Norman monks' "foreign allegiance" was cited by Henry III as further justification for seizing Norman monasteries' English properties.[213] Various Norman abbots and abbesses were forced to come to England to pay the king homage for their English lands.[214] The English king had seized the English properties and revenues belonging to the archbishopric of Rouen during the vacancy that preceded Eudes's consecration, and in order to receive the arrears of the archiepiscopal revenues from the time of his consecration, Eudes had had to travel to England to pay homage to the king.

During the Barons' War (1263–67) and the constitutional crisis that led up to it, monastic revenues from English priories were intermittent at best. At his visitation of the priory of Envermeu, on February 22, 1258, Eudes learned that of the fifty marks the Norman priory received annually from its English properties, only eighteen marks had been received that year, five marks the preceding year, and no English revenues whatsoever the previous four years.[215] English revenue made up over 10 percent of the priory's annual income. At the priory of Neufmarché, the situation was even graver. Half the priory's revenue normally came from England, but in 1264, the priory had gone several years without receiving any of its English revenues.[216] The priory had become impoverished and had been forced to reduce the number of its monks. The abbey of Saint-Wandrille was also heavily dependent on its English revenues, receiving an income from overseas of 4,000 l.[217] On September 2, 1255, Eudes noted that "the house would be in good condition as far as its finances are concerned if it could collect the money which is due from England."[218]

Eudes also inquired into the state of monasteries' provisions. He asked whether a monastery had a surplus of provisions that could be sold at high market prices, one way some monasteries were able to pay off sizable debts. Did the monastery have sufficient wheat, oats, and wine to last the year? Having to buy provisions could represent a major expenditure, pushing a monastery into unproductive debt. In the spring of 1260, the priory of Beaulieu, which was already 500 l. in debt, was found to have an insufficient supply of provisions for its own use to last until the summer harvest, meaning that the priory would have to spend an additional 100 l. for wheat and oats.[219] A shortage of provisions was a recurring problem for this priory, as it was for many Norman monasteries.

According to the *Register*, one of the most common shortages in Norman monasteries in the thirteenth century was wine, which, in addition to being drunk with meals, was needed for the celebration of the Mass.[220] Although the land in Normandy was (and is) ill-suited for viniculture, many medieval Norman monasteries were willing to pay large sums for relatively poor wine-growing land simply to avoid the prohibitively high costs of buying wine.[221] It is clear from Eudes's *Register*, however, that monasteries engaged in viniculture often experienced problems with their harvests. The priory of Noyon-sur-Andelle, for example, regularly put aside 100 l., or one-fifth its total income, toward improving its vineyards.[222] Visiting Beaulieu on February 18, 1255, Eudes found that the priory lacked both meat and wine. The priory's vineyards had been burned after the previous harvest, and the archbishop wished to make sure that an outstanding debt of 100 l. owed to the priory and due by August would be received in time for the priory to purchase the supplies it would need to replant its vineyard.[223] By asking monasteries about the state of their provisions, Eudes encouraged them to plan ahead and think about whether they might need extra capital for purchasing food. It was not always easy, of course, to plan ahead, especially for something as unforeseen as a bad harvest. And even if a monastery was aware that its supply of wheat would not last the year, the mere awareness did not solve the shortage. At the same time, however, Eudes recognized that monastic poverty was sometimes a function of overinvestment, of a monastery's simply not having enough (or any) liquid capital for emergency expenditures. This was something that the archbishop believed could be remedied, at least partially, through better financial accounting and planning.

As Cheney notes, "the financial statistics are the least comprehensible and the least trustworthy" aspect of Eudes's *Register*.[224] While a tantalizing source for the modern historian interested in thirteenth-century monastic finances, the *Register* also presents real interpretative difficulties. Both Cheney and Snape used the *Register* to study the relationship between monastic debt and revenue relative to time, the size of monasteries, and the type of monasteries (whether of monks, nuns, or regular canons).[225] They calculated monastic debt by subtracting what was owed to a monastery from what the monastery owed. When a monastery owed less than it was owed, the debt was understood to be zero. By studying debt relative to revenue, Cheney and Snape believed they could draw conclusions about the financial health of the Norman monasteries Eudes visited.[226] But Eudes does not appear to have used Cheney and Snape's model of "debt as a fraction of revenue" as a criterion for determining the health of monastic economies. The archbishop did not consistently record monastic revenues (that is, ordinary incomes), and he made virtually no references to monasteries' ordinary expenditures (which may explain why Cheney and Snape ignore the subject of ordinary expenditures altogether).[227]

What interested the archbishop was the relationship between a monastery's extraordinary debentures (or what it owed, *domus debet*) and extraordinary income (or what it was owed, *debentur domui*). Above all, Eudes wanted to know whether a monastery was carrying a surplus or deficit with respect to its extraordinary debentures and incomes. It is not made clear what these extraordinary debentures and incomes included or what their relationship was to ordinary receipts and expenditures. There may well have been some overlap, and yet some instances seem to indicate that the two were understood as separate categories.[228] Take, for example, the financial statement for the abbey of Saint-Victor-en-Caux from September 1258, which was copied into the archiepiscopal register:

> Value of grain was: one hundred fifteen muids, that is to say, thirty muids of mixed grain, twenty-five muids of barley, and sixty muids of oats.
>
> Consumption of grain was: for milling, thirty-eight muids; for brewing, twenty-eight muids; for the prebendaries, thirty muids; in pensions, two muids; in seed, eight muids; by sale, nine muids of oats.
>
> The value of the money was: four hundred fifty pounds, and one hundred pounds from England: total, five hundred fifty pounds.
>
> The total of monetary expense for the kitchen, for wine, for build-

ings, for the shoeing of horse, for the clothing and shoes of the monks, for servants' wages, for Abbot William's pension, for the forty pounds for the royal tithe, for purchase of land: six hundred four pounds and fifteen shillings. Therefore the expenses have exceeded the assets by fifty-four pounds, fifteen shillings.

Such is the state of the house: one hundred twenty pounds in grain and money is owed to the house and the house owes one hundred forty-four pounds.[229]

This statement permits a good picture of the abbey's assets, expenditures, and revenues and was the kind of general account Eudes expected monastic houses to maintain. We can see in this account how the abbey's ordinary assets and expenditures (there is a deficit of 54 l. 15 s.) were distinguished from its extraordinary income and debentures (there is a deficit of 24 l.).[230]

The archbishop was most concerned about monasteries that were carrying deficits (whose extraordinary debentures exceeded their extraordinary incomes). In 1259, the abbey of Aumale owed 12 l., most of it at interest, and by the following year, the abbey's debts had grown to 550 l., most of which was owed to Lombards at interest.[231] About 25 percent of the enormous debts owed by the abbey of Saint-Ouen (which averaged around 5,000 l.) was owed at interest.[232] Debt, even interest debt, was not always a bad thing, and much of the monastic debt in the thirteenth century was productive. A monastery might take out a low-interest loan in order to build a bridge, which would then bring in large revenue from tolls. But during his visitations, Eudes probably did not consider whether the monastic debts he encountered were productive debts or consumption debts.[233] He was interested, above all, in seeing that a monastery's extraordinary debentures did not exceed its extraordinary income.

When Eudes found a monastery running a deficit, he encouraged the house to find ways to pay off its debts. For example, at the Augustinian abbey of Eu, which possessed a charter giving the community the right to sell and acquire property freely, Eudes encouraged the canons to pay off their debts by selling a portion of their woodlands. The sale brought in tremendous revenue and effectively erased the abbey's debts. Before the sale, in February 1263, the community had been running a deficit of 1,300 l., but after the sale, in September 1264, the community was running a surplus of 220 l.[234] A few years later, however, the abbey was again running a sizable deficit, in part because of costs associated with building a manor house.[235] Within a year, an additional sale of land and woodlands had turned the abbey's deficit of 474 l. into a surplus of 500 l.[236] Thus monastic debts could fluctuate rapidly.

At the same time that he was encouraging the abbey of Eu to pay off its debts by alienating portions of its property, Eudes was looking for new investment opportunities for the abbey. In the entry for February 3, 1263, in which he reported the abbey's worst deficit to date (1,300 l.), Eudes also commented on the money the abbey of Eu had received from bequests: "we ordered that it be used to purchase leases or that it be put in reserve in some common chest until something appropriate is offered for sale."[237] Historians have argued that monastic poverty was sometimes a function of overinvestment.[238] By tying up too much capital, a monastery left little liquid capital for unexpected but necessary capital expenditures, such as legal expenses or costly building campaigns. Yet the fact that abbeys such as Eu could buy rents as long-term investments even while paying off debts reflects the sound fundamentals of the general Norman monastic economy.

There was, of course, the problem of inflation, which was especially burdensome to monastic houses whose incomes were heavily dependent on fixed rents.[239] But as we have seen, many Norman monasteries were able to take advantage of high market prices by selling their surpluses of wood, grain, or wine. As the value of old rents was eroded by inflation, monasteries sold their rents and reinvested the capital, sometimes in the form of new and more productive rents.[240] Monasteries also continued to receive bequests and other gifts from laypeople, the values of which tended to increase with inflation. Other sources of monastic revenue (from, for instance, the patronage of churches, collection of tithes, exhibition of relics, and collection of tolls) also increased with inflation. Eudes found that the nunnery of Bondeville was able to raise some liquid capital by farming out a tithe it owned. Although the tithe normally brought in 40 l. each year, the nunnery, in need of 80 l. worth of building repairs, was willing to farm out the tithe for 75 l. for a period of three years.[241]

Although Eudes is generally preoccupied in his *Register* with problems in need of correction, it is striking how frequently he reports that the finances of a particular religious house are *good*: Saint-Wandrille, Jumièges, Saint-Sauveur, Mont-Saint-Michel, Montomorel, Valmont, Saint-Georges-de-Boscherville, Saint-Evroul, Saint-Pierre-de-Pontoise, and Sainte-Catherine-du-Mont all had satisfactory finances.[242] Norman monasteries would not have been able to invest substantial capital (as the *Register* indicates they were) in repairing existing buildings and erecting new buildings if they had been facing serious financial difficulties. They certainly were not able to make these kinds of capital investments in the first half of the fourteenth century when famine and economic depression struck northern Europe.[243]

And then there was the issue of monastic population. According to thirteenth-century canon law, every religious house and cathedral chapter had a statutory number of resident clerics based on its financial resources. When a monastery was facing economic pressures, one of the simplest ways to cope was to reduce the number of resident monastics. This response clearly was happening in Normandy. At the priory of Beaumont-le-Roger in the dio-

cese of Evreux, for instance, Eudes found five monks when there should have
been twelve, "but because of the new buildings which they are constructing
the number has been lessened."[244] At Notre-Dame-de-Pré, where a damaging
fire had resulted in additional financial burdens, the number of monks had
been reduced from twenty-four to eighteen.[245] The priory of Saint-Martin-la-
Garenne, suffering from a deficiency of goods and repeated bad vine harvests, sent two of its five monks to its mother abbey of Bec.[246] The number of
monks at the priory of Saint-Laurent-en-Cornecervine increased as a consequence of the financial problems of its mother abbey, which tried to cut costs
by sending more of its own resident monks to its daughter priories.[247] Although Eudes does not appear to have ordered any of these reductions in monastic numbers, he also does not seem to have opposed them, merely noting
the change in his *Register.*

In the case of other monastic houses, however, Eudes actually called for
an increase in monastic numbers to their former levels. That the monastic
numbers had decreased may have been indicative of an earlier period of
economic pressure or of problems in recruitment of new monks. But as
long as a monastery was not extraordinarily burdened financially, the archbishop insisted that it maintain its statutory number. Visiting the abbey of
Saint-Taurin on May 2, 1258, Eudes found only twenty resident monks, as
opposed to the twenty-eight he had found at his last visitation three years
before. Six of the abbey's monks, he learned, had died. The abbey's finances were strong: the monks had sufficient provisions to last until the
new harvest, and they had no debts. Eudes did not hesitate to recommend
that the abbey add several monks.[248] At the provincial council held at Pont-
Audemer in September 1257, Eudes and the Norman clergy passed a canon
stating, "We decree that the certain number of religious shall be re-
established in those abbeys and priories whose resources have not been di-
minished, unless some delay be granted by the express permission of a superior, and for reasonable causes."[249] The fact that Eudes so frequently
exhorted the monastic communities he visited to increase their numbers is
further evidence of his belief in the overall health of the monastic economy.

Nevertheless, Eudes also confronted monastic houses with serious financial problems. The houses of Augustinian canons, which could be quite
heavily populated, tended to be poorer than Benedictine male houses. Although the Augustinian priory of Sainte-Barbe-en-Auge had roughly
seventy-one canons (including those in its daughter houses), its annual revenue was only 2,000 l.; the Augustinian abbey of Vœu in Cherbourg had
forty-five canons and a revenue of less than 1,000 l.; the Augustinian priory
of Sausseuse had thirty canons and a revenue of only 400 l. In contrast, the
Benedictine abbey of Jumièges had forty-eight monks and a revenue of
3,300 l., and Mont-Saint-Michel had forty monks and a revenue of 5,000 l.[250]
Norman nunneries, which tended to be even larger in population than Au-

gustinian or male Benedictine houses, were even more strikingly underendowed relative to male houses.[251] In contrast to his exhortations to male houses to increase their numbers, Eudes adamantly forbade nunneries to veil new nuns or accept new girls, arguing that nunneries simply did not have the financial resources to support larger numbers.[252] Yet Eudes found that despite his orders to the contrary, some nunneries accepted new nuns to be veiled. To his great consternation, he found that the female priory of Saint-Saëns had promised to receive and veil four of the nuns' nieces, provided the archbishop gave his consent. Each of the nieces had letters from the community promising that she would be veiled. Describing Eudes's reaction to the nunnery's concession, the *Register* provides a rare glimpse of the archbishop's temper and frustration: "We, in full chapter, broke and tore to pieces these letters, being highly annoyed at a concession of this kind. Once again we expressly forbade them to receive or veil anyone without our special permission."[253]

Why would nunneries, already overpopulated and stretched beyond their financial capacities, have been so eager to veil new nuns? In the case of Saint-Saëns, it was probably the desire of certain nuns to help their nieces. Often, however, a community's willingness to receive novices stemmed from the financial incentives of entry dowries, which could take the form of land, money, or rights. The young girls whom nunneries were accepting tended to be "noble girls" (*domicelles*) whose families could offer substantial entry dowries with their daughters. Various ecclesiastical councils (including canon 64 of the Fourth Lateran Council) and papal decretals prohibited monastic houses from demanding these simoniacal "gifts" on the pretext of monastic poverty.[254] At the synod convened in Rouen in 1214, the papal legate Robert of Courson included a statute prohibiting monasteries from demanding food, clothing, or money from recruits. Monasteries were also told that they could not reject a monastic candidate simply because he or she did not offer a gift.[255]

Yet it was often in the poorest nunneries that entry dowries appeared most appealing and continued to be received despite legal prohibitions to the contrary.[256] Admittedly, the nunneries were not always frank with the archbishop about their reasons for wishing to recruit new nuns. The fifteen nuns of Saint-Saëns begged the archbishop for permission to receive and veil five additional nuns "so that their number might be twenty, in order to advance the divine cult."[257] Their request was promptly denied, and at the same visitation, Eudes ordered that two young girls who had been staying at the priory, the daughter of the châtelain of Bellencombre and the elder daughter of the lord of Manières, be sent back home. The Franciscan archbishop did not like the idea of nunneries accepting noble girls as a moneymaking venture, something he viewed as simony and greed, plain and simple.[258] Despite the archbishop's repeated orders to the nuns of Saint-

Aubin that they not receive any new nuns, the priory bestowed the veil on the daughter of Lord Robert Malvoisin. When Eudes asked the nuns why they had ignored his instructions, they replied that "urgent necessity and poverty" had compelled them and that the father of the girl had endowed them with an annual income of one hundred *sous*.[259] From a purely economic standpoint, a regular source of income such as this one would have been attractive to the impoverished priory and would have offset the cost of accepting a new nun. From a moral standpoint, however, a regular and guaranteed source of income was even more objectionable than a one-time gift. After ordering that the new nun be removed from the priory and sent back to her father, Eudes imposed a penance on the nuns and their prioress.

In addition to limiting the monastic numbers in houses that were financially burdened, Eudes tried various other ways of reducing expenditures. As noted earlier, the abbey of Saint-Ouen-de-Rouen was mired in substantial debts, primarily stemming from a costly legal battle with Eudes himself over the abbot's claim of his right to wear pontificals.[260] Observing that the abbey was "grievously burdened by pensions," Eudes forbade it to grant further pensions without papal authority or the permission of a superior.[261]

A second way for the abbey to cut expenditures was to stop supporting the abbot's relatives and guests. The abbot of Saint-Ouen reportedly used the abbey's provisions to support his sister, brother-in-law, and guests, placing an added burden on the abbey's already strained finances.[262] The abbot of Mont-Saint-Michel had allegedly contributed to the abbey's debt by giving several of his nieces dowries and financially supporting one of his nephews at the University of Paris, even giving him a most beautiful copy (*pulcherrimum*) of the multivolume *Corpus legum*.[263] The archbishop also found cases of a prior using priory revenues to support his relatives at schools in Paris. In addition to being concerned about the financial impact of nepotism, Eudes was troubled by the way nonmonastic relatives disrupted the discipline of a monastic community. Even the appearance of nepotism on the part of a monastic superior could engender feelings of distrust between the superior and his or her community.

Another means of cutting monastic expenditure was to limit the number of servants employed. In the average thirteenth-century English monastery, monks made up only about one-third of the population, often being outnumbered by servants.[264] In addition to being financial burdens, servants were frequently found to lead dissolute lives and disrupt the spiritual discipline of religious houses. In a number of cases, particularly at nunneries, Eudes ordered that servants be dismissed.

The procurations that archbishops, bishops, archdeacons, and abbots (in the case of priories) collected during visitations were also financially onerous, particularly for small and poor monastic houses, since procuration amounts were based not on the size or income of a house but on the cost of provisions needed to support the visitor and his *familia* during their stay.[265] Procurations were most often paid in money, but they were also sometimes paid in kind (cooking utensils, cups, drink, straw for men and beasts, and wood) or a combination of the two. Some monastic houses tried to avoid paying procurations altogether by arguing that they were exempt. Although the archbishop showed little sympathy for such claims of exemption, he also recognized how financially straining procurations could be for the poorest houses. Visiting the priory of Gasny, Eudes observed that the abbot of Saint-Ouen (the mother abbey) "goes there too often and so impoverishes the priories."[266] But this did not stop the archbishop from collecting his own procuration during each of his eighteen visitations of the priory (at times, he collected as much as 8 l.).[267] At monastic houses that he considered truly impoverished, Eudes generously remitted the procuration owed to him. In such cases, however, he insisted that the community draft a letter confirming his legal right to collect a procuration. He did not want his generosity to serve as a legal precedent that could later be used to deprive his office of its rights.

Judging from the extraordinary number of visitations he conducted— over one thousand visitations at more than one hundred fifty of Normandy's religious houses—one can only conclude that Eudes Rigaud felt a strong sense of duty to reform monastic life. The nature of his visitations corroborates that he was a strict and strenuous enforcer of monastic reforms. Like some other contemporary prelates, Eudes believed that ecclesiastical reform required the reestablishment of full episcopal jurisdiction, and as a result of his efforts to exercise what he regarded as his full jurisdiction, Eudes was surely viewed by some in monastic houses as an overzealous and combative archbishop who encroached on others' time-tested rights and privileges. In a society that was fiercely protective of customary practice, an abbot accustomed to having an episcopal visitor might nonetheless protest loudly if a visiting bishop deviated from past practice by asking for two meals during his stay rather than the customary one meal or requested a bed when none of his predecessors had ever required one.[268] It is quite understandable that monastic houses, many of which were financially pressed as it was, resented such episcopal visitations, since they posed a genuine financial burden (even if the bishop did not demand a second meal for his entourage of fifteen or twenty men). Furthermore, few monastic communities enjoyed being subject to the scrutiny and possible reprimand of an episcopal visitor. Although in theory all Benedictine monks lived in the same way, the reality was that the affairs of each house were managed slightly differently. Perhaps a monastery kept careful track of its finances, for example, but did not record its written accounts precisely the way the archbishop wished.

Eudes did not look kindly on variations in religious life. He believed that monastic life required a literal observance of monastic rules and papal reform statutes, constant monitoring, and organization. As his own *Register* demonstrates, he viewed meticulous data collection and record keeping as a necessary mechanism for religious reform. But in addition to his attention to detail, he showed a broad vision of the church's mission and standards in his handling of all aspects of the institutional bureaucracy of monasticism, from finances and obligations to a common-sense application of rules. In his own career as scholar and administrator, he combined an interest in and commitment to advancing theological knowledge with a practical and patient exercise of day-to-day administrative authority, dealing in a pragmatic way with the sins and frailties of human nature among Normandy's religious. Eudes was precisely the "watchman on the tower" envisioned by Innocent III and the Fourth Lateran Council.

5

Shepherding the Shepherds

*The Challenges of Supervising
Normandy's Secular Clergy*

Eudes's *Register* suggests that he did not have much direct contact with ordinary, lay parishioners. Aside from some residents of the city of Rouen who would have heard him preach in the cathedral, most laymen and women in the diocese probably had little familiarity with the archbishop. During his visitations of the parish clergy, Eudes did not question the laypeople about the conduct of their priests or about their own lives. This was in contrast to at least one thirteenth-century archdeacon, who took an active interest in parishioners during his visitations of individual parishes.[1] Eudes reached the laypeople of his province indirectly, however, through the parish priests who interacted with parishioners on a daily basis and were charged with the salvation of their souls. Acting as the archbishop's representative in their respective parishes, the clergy performed five of the seven sacraments: baptism, the Eucharist, penance, marriage, and extreme unction. Only the sacraments of confirmation and holy orders were reserved for the archbishop. The parish clergy included not only rectors and vicars but also large numbers of chaplains, who were not beneficed but were hired for wages by rectors and vicars.[2] It was these chaplains, vicars, and rectors who served as the pastoral workforce of the medieval church. And it was the archbishop who supervised them, first ordaining them as priests, then instituting them with their benefices, monitoring the way they conducted themselves in their benefices, and working with them in councils and synods.

Celebrating the sacrament of holy orders presented Eudes with his first opportunity to ensure that the right kind of men were ordained and admitted to service in the church. A candidate could be disqualified for failing to meet certain canonical requirements relating to his birth, age, learning, and character.[3] In theory, each candidate for the higher orders was also expected to show a "title," or statement of affiliation with a parish. The title was meant to ensure that each ordinand was economically self-sufficient and had a home in which to exercise his ministry. But the titles tended to be formalities; often a letter attesting to a candidate's good reputation sufficed.

Eudes presided over sixty-one ordination ceremonies during the twenty-one years covered by the *Register*. For nineteen of these ceremonies, the *Register* provides the names of 2,012 ordinands, including not only secular clerics but Augustinian and Premonstratensian canons and Benedictine, Cluniac, and Cistercian monks.[4] The large number of clerics ordained at a ceremony (often well over one hundred) would have made it difficult for the archbishop to screen candidates individually beforehand, so Eudes may have left the preordination scrutinies to his archdeacons.[5] Yet it is also evident that the archbishop took a personal interest in who was ordained. Eudes performed ordination ceremonies three or four times a year in a variety of locations in his diocese: parish churches, abbeys, the chapter at Les Andelys, the Franciscan and Dominican convents in Rouen, the royal chapel at Pont-de-l'Arche, and the private chapel of Eudes's archiepiscopal manor in Rouen. He included charts in his *Register* that listed the names of every cleric he ordained. The names were arranged in columns according to clerical order. Eudes's secretary updated these lists regularly, crossing out the names of clerics who had resigned, died, or been deprived of their benefices, indicating in the marginalia *resignuit, mortuus est, privatus est,* or *incarceratus est et de maleficiis convictus.*[6] When he admitted a subdeacon or deacon to a benefice, Eudes required him to swear an oath that he would be ordained to the priesthood within a specified period of time or risk losing the benefice. The ordination lists permitted Eudes to see whether these clerics were advancing as they promised.

The patron (or patrons) of a church controlled the church's buildings, lands, and revenues, including the tithe collected from the parish. In addition, the patron usually held the right of presentation, that is, the right to appoint a church's rector or priest. The person whom the patron appointed was not automatically instituted but required the approval of the ecclesiastical ordinary, normally the bishop or archbishop. Still, with the initial right to appoint the curate, the patron's power was vast. The Gregorian reformers of the eleventh and twelfth centuries had attacked the notion that a layman could hold the right to present a candidate for an ecclesiastical benefice, arguing that it violated the freedom of the church. Nevertheless, the practice persisted long after the formal end of the investiture struggle by the Concordat of Worms in 1122.

During the twelfth and thirteenth centuries, a higher percentage of churches were under lay patronage in Normandy than in any other French province.[7] Whereas lay patronage made up 35 percent of all patronage in Normandy, it represented only 2 percent of all patronage in the diocese of

Rennes, 4 percent in Chartres and Saint-Malo, and 5 percent in Le Mans.[8] Little of the lay patronage in Normandy was royal; most of the lay patrons were local lords, few of whom had patronage over more than one church.[9] Bishops and cathedral chapters were particularly underrepresented as patrons. Whereas episcopal patronage made up only 6 or 7 percent of all patronage in the archdiocese of Rouen, it made up 72 percent of all patronage in the diocese of Dol, 62 percent in Saint-Malo, 35 percent in Rennes, 25 percent in Beauvais, 22 percent in Tours, and 16 percent in Amiens.[10] This was not only because of the high incidence of lay patronage but also because 83 percent of Normandy's ecclesiastical patronage was in the hands of monastic houses, including the houses of Augustinian canons and even Cistercians.[11] Monks and regular canons tended to regard their patronage of parish churches as though it were ordinary property. Although the church preferred that ecclesiastics rather than laymen collected parish tithes, even then the tithes by no means always served their original purpose. A monastery or college that collected a tithe might well come to view it as an additional source of revenue rather than as a way to support the parish poor or aid in the administration of the diocese.[12] It was for this reason that Eudes drew up a synodal statute reaffirming that all ecclesiastics (including abbots and priors) who received major tithes in parish churches had to use the full value of the tithe "to restore the fabric, books, and ornaments" of the parish.[13]

There were financial consequences to all these arrangements. As Henri Dubois shows, the average Norman priest's revenue was actually higher when his benefice was under lay patronage than it was under ecclesiastical patronage. In 88 percent of the cases, lay patrons did not touch the revenues of their benefices, whereas when the patrons were ecclesiastics, only 17 percent left all the revenues to the rectors. Lay patrons, Dubois concludes, were less in need of revenue than ecclesiastical patrons. Patronage, he argues, was attractive to laymen not for money but for power and control over the appointment of clerics. Norman monastic houses, however, profited financially from having patronage of churches. And Norman bishops and cathedral chapters, which were underrepresented as patrons, missed out on what could have been an additional source of income.[14]

The real consequence of the fact that over one-third of all patrons in Normandy were laymen, however, was that the Norman church had less control over the choice of persons holding benefices. Already in the twelfth century, popes such as Innocent II and Alexander III singled out "the many evils" that polluted the Norman province. They were appalled, for instance, to hear that Norman bishops were not only exempting lay patrons from episcopal control but granting them the authority that archdeacons normally possessed.[15] Did the large amount of lay patronage in Normandy have a deleterious impact on the quality of its secular clergy? Was there anything that an archbishop like Eudes Rigaud could do to rectify the situation? In addressing these questions, we are fortunate to have a polyptych, or census book, for the diocese of Rouen, begun by Eudes's predecessor, Archbishop Pierre de Colmieu (1236–44), and updated and expanded by Eudes and his successor, Guillaume de Flavacourt.[16] The polyptych lists almost every parish in the diocese of Rouen (arranged by archdeaconry and deanery) and gives its number of parishioners, the value of its benefice, the name of its patron, the name of the current rector, and the archbishop (or vicar) who instituted the rector.[17] Using the polyptych, one can determine the identities of most of the patrons who presented rectors later ill-famed for various crimes (mostly incontinence). A section of the *Register* entitled *Diffamationes* includes both letters of resignation from priests and letters promising resignation should the priest be found ill-famed of the same crime again.[18] Interestingly, there is no evidence that priests presented by lay patrons were any more likely to get into trouble than those presented by ecclesiastical patrons. Indeed, 45 percent of the ill-famed priests were presented by lay patrons, almost exactly the total percentage of lay patronage in Normandy, and 24 percent of the ill-famed priests were presented by monastic patrons. A significant number of the ill-famed priests (20 percent) were rectors of churches in which the patronage was shared, whether between a layman and an ecclesiastic, between laymen, or between ecclesiastics. The archbishop shared patronage in several of these churches. Although it was fairly rare for the archbishop to have been the sole patron of a church with an ill-famed rector (it occurred only about 7 percent of the time), we must remember that the archbishop of Rouen had patronage of only 6 or 7 percent of the churches in his archdiocese.[19]

Between the 1230s or 1240s, when the polyptych starts, and the end of the century, when it stops, there appears to have been little change in patronage. It is rare to find an ecclesiastic holding patronage over a church that was previously held by a layman, although such a pattern was a common trend in large parts of Europe during the twelfth century.[20] Although there appears to have been little change in Norman patronage during the thirteenth century, Eudes took an active interest in who was being appointed and by whom.[21] Indeed, the issue of patronage was Eudes's paramount concern in the polyptych, where the name of each parish's patron was always recorded, even when the number of parishioners or value of a benefice was not. One reason for the archbishop's interest was his fierce protection of his own patronage over some 139 churches and chapels.[22] When, in 1252, his right of patronage was challenged by Gautier d'Atre, a knight, Eudes did not back down.[23] Nor did he yield when his right of patronage was challenged by the king. Just before Eudes was elected archbishop, a conflict erupted between the king and Eudes Clément, then archbishop, over the church of Vaterville. In the end, the two parties agreed to share patronage of the church, a common practice.[24] But when the church became vacant again in 1250, the dispute re-ignited, this time between Eudes Rigaud and the king's mother, Blanche of Castille, who was acting as regent while her son was on crusade. The archbishop and the queen decided to assign the right of presentation to the abbot of Foucarmont, a Cistercian abbey; whatever candidate he presented would then have to be approved by both the archbishop and the king.[25] This arrangement was only a temporary one, however, and Eudes eventually lost all patronage of the church to the king in the assize of Neufchâtel.[26]

The archbishop also cared about patronage because in order to institute a cleric to a benefice, he needed to know that the advowson, or right to present a candidate, in fact belonged to the patron making the presentation.[27] If a church benefice became vacant while the right of advowson was contested, for instance, Eudes refused to accept a cleric presented by either side. And once a church had stood vacant for a period of six months or more without its patron presenting a candidate, Eudes could take advantage of his right of devolution, that is, his right as ordinary to assume presentation.[28] The primary purpose of this right was to ensure that no church remained without a curate for too long. When the prior of Beaulieu, who ordinarily served as patron of the parish church of Haye-Routot, failed to present a candidate for the vacant church within the statutory period, Eudes presented his own candidate, Almauricus.[29] In the long term, this did not extend the ordinary's right of patronage, since the next time there was a vacancy in the church, the right of presentation reverted to the original patron.[30] But in the short term, using the right of devolution meant that Eudes was able to install his own candidate rather than accept a patron's choice.

Patrons who lost their right of presentation to the archbishop were quick to accuse him of using delay tactics. A knight by the name of Guillaume l'Orcher, for instance, filed an appeal against Eudes on September 12, 1248. Claiming to hold the right of patronage of a church at Varangeville, Guillaume said he had canonically presented to the archbishop a person qualified by character and knowledge to hold the church within the time specified by law. Yet according to Guillaume, Eudes had, "without reasonable cause, brought on one futile delay after another, with the intention of allowing the time to run out" so that he could confer the church, with its "fat and teeming income," on whomsoever he pleased.[31] The abbot of Saint-Josse-sur-Mer (in the diocese of Amiens) made a similar charge against the archbishop. Asserting that he was the true patron of the vacant church of Mesnil-David, the abbot accused the archbishop of using dilatory tactics so the statutory period would lapse and the right of presentation would devolve onto him.[32] From the perspective of a monastery with patronage of some parish churches, the ideal bishop or archbishop was one who confirmed the monastery's patronage of churches even when its title was weak, granting the monastery almost complete jurisdiction over its parish churches, including the freedom to hire and fire the clergy. As both monastic and lay patrons learned, Eudes was anything but the liberal archbishop they had hoped for. With relatively little parish patronage of his own, the archbishop looked for any opportunity to exercise additional jurisdiction over parish churches, whether the patrons were lay or ecclesiastical.

There were other ways the archbishop could exert control over the appointment of curates. As part of his right of institution, Eudes could personally inspect every candidate presented to him for a benefice and refuse to admit anyone he found to be unlettered or otherwise unsuitable.[33] Only males above the age of twenty-five, of legitimate birth, who lived a suitable lifestyle, who were ordained priests (or would be ordained within a year), and who were not already entitled to a benefice were eligible to exercise a parish ministry.[34] Eudes rejected the presentation of a priest named Thomas for the church of Saint-Médard-près-Beauvais on the grounds that Thomas's eyesight was not good enough for him to read or carry out the sacramental duties.[35] The archbishop was even willing to reject candidates presented to him by the king if he found them "too deficient in letters to have cure of souls."[36]

Eudes's examinations of candidates usually consisted of testing their knowledge of Latin and their ability to chant. Transcripts of the exams that Eudes's secretary copied into the *Register* record the precise questions he asked and the answers the candidates gave. In the case of Guillaume de Vardes, presented for the church at Ancourt, for example, Eudes grilled the candidate's Latin, making him translate each word from a passage from the legends of the Purification from Latin into French.[37] The passage was rather simple, and Guillaume easily translated each individual word or phrase: "*illa*, that one; *salus*, salvation; *generata*, engendered; *de Virgine Maria*, of the Virgin Mary; *hoc est*, that is; *die*, the day; *quadragesimo*, of the period of forty days; *Maria*, O thou Mary; *genetrice*, mother; *hodie*, today; *ab ipsa*, from her; *deportata*, carried; *ad templum*, to the temple; *ipsius*, of him; *ut ipse*, that he; *redemptor noster*, our father; *sit*, may be; *presentatus*, presented; *sic*, in such a manner; *cum substancia nostre carnis*, in the substance of our flesh; *etiam*, but; *adimplet*, he fills; *ipsam*, her." But when Eudes asked Guillaume to summarize the meaning of the passage in French, he had more difficulty. Lastly, Guillaume was instructed to conjugate verbs and decline nouns from the passage, which he did.[38] It is not known whether the archbishop instituted Guillaume to the benefice; nevertheless, by examining him, Eudes limited the power of the patron (in this case, the abbot of Fécamp) and tried to ensure that only competent curates were installed. Some bishops examined clerics presented to them for benefices on their morals and their knowledge of theology, but the *Register* makes it appear as though Eudes cared most about clerics' knowledge of Latin and their ability to chant.

In some cases, Eudes refused to institute candidates on the grounds that they were incompetent. On March 16, 1260, for example, Eudes examined a certain Nicholas, called Quesnel, who had been presented for the church at Vinemerville.[39] The archbishop chose to examine Nicholas's Latin using the first lines of the book of Genesis. Nicholas was able to decline most nouns, but he made occasional mistakes, such as not being certain whether the accusative plural of *deus* was *deos* or *dos*. He conjugated the verb *fero, fers* accurately until he got to the supine, which he omitted, saying he did not believe there was one. Conjugating the verb *fiere* ("to become"), he confused it with *facere* ("to make") and *esse* ("to be"), and when asked whether *fiat* has a passive, he correctly replied that it did not but became confused as to why, saying that it was because of the verb's neuter gender. It is clear that Nicholas knew some Latin, but he frequently confused his conjugations and declensions and made mistakes typical of a fledgling Latin student. The final straw, however, was that Nicholas refused to sing for the archbishop, saying that he knew nothing about chant. As we have seen, Eudes cared deeply about chant.[40] He had devoted an entire *quaestio disputata* at the University of Paris to the subject, and as archbishop, he frequently reprimanded monks and nuns on their failure to chant adequately. He once even moved an episcopal consecration ceremony because he preferred the canons' chant in one cathedral over another. Presented with a candidate for a benefice who admitted knowing nothing about chant and yet who, as rector, would be expected to celebrate Mass and chant the liturgy, Eudes immediately refused to admit the candidate, saying he had found him to be "completely deficient in letters, that is, he knew neither how to read competently nor to understand, nor was he willing to chant."[41] Nicholas threatened to file an appeal to the pope, arguing that he had been presented for the vacant church at Vinemerville by its true patron and that this should suffice for his institution. But the archbishop would not budge.

From the *Register*, it is clear that Eudes rejected a number of candidates on grounds of illiteracy, but it is not known what percentage was rejected of the total number of candidates he examined.[42] Given Eudes's university background, however, it is quite possible that he had higher standards than other contemporary bishops in judging the literacy level of clerics presented for vacant churches.[43] But how many well-educated clerics were there to choose from? The archbishop could not have been as selective as he probably would have liked. It was rare for someone already ordained a priest to have the opportunity for continuing education. How, after all, could a priest finance a university education? There was also the problem of how a priest could study at a university while maintaining residence in his parish. The Fourth Lateran Council had tried to ensure that bishops instructed candidates for the priesthood in the sacraments and divine services *before* they were ordained. But bishops did not have time to serve as private Latin tutors to every person who wished to become a priest.

Guillaume de Saâne, treasurer of Rouen and a permanent fixture in Eudes's *familia*, tried to rectify the problem by establishing a school of theological study in Paris for secular students from the diocese of Rouen.[44] Beginning in 1253 and continuing until his death almost thirty years later, Guillaume spearheaded an effort to raise funds for buildings, books, and other resources needed to support twelve students of theology and twelve students of liberal arts.[45] It was his intention, Guillaume wrote in 1280, "to diligently provide for and sustain only suitable, poor, hardworking students."[46] He insisted that all the students speak to each other in Latin, at least while they were at home.[47] If any of them was a troublemaker, he would stop receiving a stipend, because, as Guillaume put it, "we do not intend to support evil ones, or irritable ones, or ribald ones, or gamblers, or any who attend taverns and the houses of harlots, but good and true students, through whom it will be possible to provide for the welfare of the church and souls."[48] Perhaps from his own experience in the archbishop's *familia*, Guillaume understood that Rouen's secular clergy were not properly educated. The school he established in Paris was certainly a constructive first step, but with the resources to support only twenty-four students, it simply could not go far enough in educating the clergy of a diocese the size of Rouen, with more than fourteen hundred parishes.

Eudes's control over parish priests did not end when he invested them with their benefices. The archbishop continued to monitor the parish clergy through periodic visitations, just as he did with the regular clergy. Recognizing that it would be impossible for him to visit every parish individually, however, given the hundreds of parishes in the province, Eudes visited each deanery individually, summoning the parish clergy to a large and centrally located church where he interrogated and inspected them.[49] Even visiting the individual deaneries represented a major undertaking: the diocese of Rouen alone contained twenty-eight deaneries, and the province as a whole contained well over one hundred. Between January and July 1249, however, Eudes visited seventeen of his diocese's twenty-eight deaneries. He seems to have been determined to inspect as many of Rouen's secular clergy as possible within his first year in office so he could identify the problems most in need of attention.

Yet during the next nineteen years combined, Eudes never visited as many parish clergy from different deaneries as he did in 1249. For many of the deaneries in the Rouen diocese, the archbishop's visitation in 1249 was the first and only one he would conduct, and no deanery received him more than three times over a period of twenty-one years[50]—unlike the monastic houses, many of which received the archbishop on an almost annual basis. A papal privilege of 1250 indicates that the pope recognized the impracticality of a law stipulating that an archbishop had to visit all the churches of his own diocese before proceeding to visit the churches and monastic houses in the rest of his province. The pontiff granted Eudes's request that he be permitted to visit his province after visiting only the abbeys, priories, and other "famous places" of his own diocese.[51] After Eudes received this privilege, the great majority of the visitations he conducted were of monastic houses. This was not because the parish clergy were without problems but rather because the archbishop knew that his archdeacons were conducting their own visitations of the parishes. Eudes made frequent references in his *Register* to reforms that visiting archdeacons had already made. That archdeacons were closely monitoring the parish clergy and issuing their own warnings and corrections meant that the archbishop's visitations could be more of a follow-up to ensure that none of the corrected clergy had relapsed.

But Eudes also exerted control over the secular clergy in contexts other than personal visitation. In addition to choosing who was ordained to holy orders and who was instituted to benefices, he worked regularly with the clergy in synods and councils, preaching sermons to instill appropriate pastoral duties and values and promulgating statutes that bound them to certain rules. Finally, he conducted legal proceedings against defamed priests, not only suspending and excommunicating them but sometimes stripping them of their benefices.

A wide range of issues interested the archbishop during his visitations of secular clergy, but few were more important to him than clerical dress.[52] In 1187, Pope Gregory VIII prohibited clerics from wearing colorful or otherwise luxurious clothes and mandated that all clerics wear their gowns closed. These same decrees were republished in various councils, including the Parisian statutes of Eudes de Sully, the synod of Angers (often referred to as "the synod of the West"), and canon 16 of the Fourth Lateran Council, which required that priests' gowns be closed, without sleeves, and of a certain length.[53] Once again, Eudes proved himself a loyal and literal enforcer of the council's canons.[54] Again and again during his visitations, he warned priests not to go out in public without a closed, long gown (*cappa clausa*); the clerical clothes could not be embroidered or made of luxurious materials like silk; priests were not permitted to wear headdresses (*cufa*); and all priests holding benefices or the care of souls had to be tonsured. Deans were instructed by the archbishop to impose a fine of five *sous* on any priest wearing a gown that was too short (*tabardo*).[55]

Eudes himself (at least before he became archbishop) was committed to wearing the Franciscan habit, although it is not known whether he continued to do so even after becoming archbishop.[56] In his sermons, Eudes stressed the connection between a person's physical appearance and his moral conduct, suggesting that when one's dress conveyed modesty, purity, and holiness, one's behavior was more likely to reflect those same attributes.[57] During his visitations of the secular clergy, Eudes continued to draw a connection between a priest's appearance and his conduct. At the deanery of Longueville, for instance, right after ordering the priests "to refrain from shameful, scurrilous and unseemly words, especially before lay folk," he ordered those who did not have closed gowns to buy them before mid-Lent.[58] What seems to have mattered most to Eudes was ensuring that the secular clergy were physically distinguished from the laypeople they served.[59] He did not want priests uttering unseemly words around lay folk; wearing short, open gowns (*tabardo*) or head coverings (*cufa*); or carrying weapons (*arma*) while walking around town where they could be seen. Around the year 1200, the dean of the chapter of Troyes described the lower clergy as "different from the people by their habit, not by their spirit, by their appearance, not by reality."[60] This was also the central point of a wonderfully descriptive fourteenth-century constitution on clerical attire by Archbishop John Stratford. Although written in a different context from Eudes's thirteenth-century world, the constitution shows that clerical dress became an even more important issue as some clerics further blurred the lines separating the appearance of laymen and clerics:

> The external costume often shows the internal character and condition of persons; and although the behavior of clerks ought to be an example and pattern of lay people, yet the abuses of clerks, which have prevailed more than usual in these days, in tonsure, clothing, horse trappings, and other things, have created an abominable scandal among the people, because persons holding ecclesiastical dignities, rectories, honourable prebends, and benefices with cure of souls, even men in Holy Orders, scorn to wear the tonsure, which is the crown of the kingdom of heaven and of perfection, and distinguish themselves by hair spreading to their shoulders in an effeminate manner, and walk about clad in a military rather than a clerical dress, with an outer habit very short and tight-fitting, but excessively wide, with long sleeves which do not touch the elbow; their hair curled and perfumed, their hoods with lappets of wonderful length; with long beards, rings on their fingers, and girded belts studded with precious stones of wonderful size, their purses enamelled and gilt with various devices, and knives openly hanging at them like swords, their boots of red and green peaked and cut in many ways; with housings to their saddles, and horns hanging from their necks; their capes and cloaks so furred, in rash disregard of the canons, that there appears little or no distinction between clergymen and laymen; whereby they render

themselves unworthy through their demerits of the privilege of their order and profession.[61]

Living in the world and interacting closely with their parishioners, it was essential for the secular clergy to remember who they were and to be aware that what was suitable for the rest of society was not necessarily suitable for them. Their distinctive clerical dress served as an outward reminder not only for them but for the laypeople around them.

But as Eudes discovered, some parish priests who wore the proper clerical dress nevertheless engaged in illegal activities. Some frequented taverns, where they got drunk and sometimes brawled.[62] The priest of Guilmerville was even known to lose his clothes in taverns.[63] In the deanery of Envermeu, ten out of the deanery's thirty-five parish priests were cited in the *Register* for intoxication, and in the deanery of Bures, three out of the deanery's sixteen priests were defamed of the same crime.[64] Often the same priests defamed of drunkenness were defamed of sexual licentiousness and other crimes. But Eudes appears to have done little about inebriated clerics other than to warn them that if they were caught again, they would be severely punished.[65] Although according to canon law, a cleric could be suspended from his office or benefice if found publicly drunk, there is no record of Eudes carrying out such a punishment.[66]

Eudes found at least one priest publicly known for divination.[67] Gautier, the priest of the church at Bray-sous-Budemont, who admitted having sexual relations with numerous women, including a prostitute, and of committing usury and other "shady transactions," denied the allegation that he had constructed a wax figure for purposes of witchcraft.[68] In depriving Gautier of his church, Eudes referred only to the priest's "crime of incontinence," making no reference to the witchcraft accusation, perhaps because he had not found it to be credible. More than witchcraft or superstition, Eudes had to contend with clerics who played popular games of chance, which Eudes de Sully, the bishop of Paris, had earlier banned in his own synodal statutes.[69]

Clerics who engaged in commerce for personal gain were another problem. Priests were found buying such commodities as wine, hemp, horses, and rams in order to resell them at higher prices.[70] One priest took advantage of an especially bad harvest by selling grain at the highest possible price.[71] In a synodal statute published at Pont-Audemer in 1267, Eudes prohibited this kind of activity, especially what he called "dishonest trade," by which he may have meant simony, the selling of sacraments. Although condemned by canonical legislation, the collection of rents for performing the sacraments was a common practice among priests, who depended on it as part of their revenue.[72] Visiting the deanery of Envermeu, Eudes found that the priest of Saint-Laurent-le-Petit was publicly known for selling the sacraments.[73] The priest of the church at Cuverville sold the holy oils he used for baptism and extreme unction.[74] One priest was accused of charging thirteen pence for every churching ceremony he performed, and another was defamed of exacting fees for blessing marriages.[75]

These were isolated problems compared with the nonresidence of the parish clergy, which in Eudes's eyes was one of the biggest problems afflicting the church. A priest's failure to reside in his benefice often stemmed from pluralism, or the holding of more than one benefice with cure of souls. How did a priest with the cure of souls in eight different parishes expect to be able to administer and reside in all eight parishes at the same time? This was the argument of various councils, including the Third and Fourth Lateran Councils, both of which prohibited pluralism.[76] Bishops and archbishops were supposed to inspect any candidate presented to them for a curial benefice to ensure that he did not already hold a benefice. But although the church was opposed to pluralism in theory, the papacy was known for granting indulgences that permitted candidates to hold more than one curial benefice. The church's official position on nonresidence had also begun to soften, first in 1215 with the Fourth Lateran Council's admission of nonresidence for canons and then in 1245 with the First Council of Lyon, which authorized ecclesiastical ordinaries to free priests from the obligations of residence when there was reasonable cause.[77] Holders of multiple benefices were already in the practice of hiring vicars to reside in their parishes, preside at mass, and celebrate the sacraments in their stead. These vicars were paid with revenues from benefices, although they were often paid significantly less than the rectors were and they were not necessarily as qualified, never having been presented to the ecclesiastical ordinary for admission.

From the very beginning of his archiepiscopate, Eudes showed that he was genuinely concerned about the problem of clerical nonresidence. It is clear from papal letters addressed to him in 1249 and 1250 that Eudes had complained to the pope about papal indulgences that freed rectors in Rouen from their obligation to make personal residence in their parishes. The pope gave his most vigorous support to Eudes's request, confirming the archbishop's legal authority to compel the rectors of his diocese to make personal residence in their parishes, and annulling any possible letters from the past or future granting the privilege of nonresidence to the holder of a prebend.[78] Future popes, however, continued the practice of granting indulgences on the issue of nonresidence. In 1255, Pope Alexander IV granted Master Jean de Putot, rector of Saint-George's church in the diocese of Rouen, the privilege to leave his parish and attend school for five years while enjoying the full revenues from his church as though he were in personal residence. The papal privilege freed John from the oath he had sworn concerning the taking of successive orders and making personal residence. And most important, the pope declared that "should the Apostolic See ever grant to the local diocesan the right to compel personal residence by the parish rectors of his diocese, despite indulgences of this kind, we, by apostolic authority, make an exception in your case. Therefore, no one shall be permitted to infringe this our charter of concession, nor shall anyone presume to do so."[79] The important principle of residency was thus sometimes in conflict with the equally desirable principle of a better-educated clergy, the latter a need that Gregory IX had recognized in creating a provision that clerics be given a leave of five years for schooling.

In addition to confronting the pope with the problem of nonresidence, Eudes attacked individual cases of nonresident rectors in his diocese. In a synod of deans held in 1254, the archbishop ordered the deans of his diocese to seize the churches of all persons not making personal residence: "We enjoined them [the deans] to seize the churches of those who, without reason, handed their churches over to a vicar for a month or two, and then went wandering about the country, to return to their churches later and stay a week and hand them over again [to a vicar]. These we do not judge to be keeping residence."[80] For example, on finding that the rector at Rupefort had disregarded his oath, failing both to present himself for holy orders and to make personal residence in his church, Eudes imposed a fine of 50 l. In a few cases, the archbishop deprived a nonresident rector of his benefice, although this measure was normally taken only after the rector had been warned and had refused to reform his ways.[81]

The most common reason for depriving a rector of his benefice was concubinage. Making clerical celibacy the normal practice rather than merely an elusive ideal had been one of the central campaigns of the Gregorian reformers, and during the late twelfth and early thirteenth centuries, canonists, theologians (especially Peter the Chanter and his circle), and ecclesiastical administrators revived interest in how the rule of clerical celibacy could be enforced.[82] Some churchmen voiced doubts about whether the requirement of clerical celibacy was practical, particularly the much debated question of whether subdeacons were bound to celibacy.[83] As some pointed out, current law and practice with respect to clerical celibacy differed from what had been early Christian practice and law. Furthermore, some advanced the argument that there was a much better chance of clerics actually respecting the law if it were reasonable, and this in their eyes meant reducing the requirements of clerical celibacy. Although those who were discontent with the laws of clerical celibacy were not successful in their attempts to reduce the laws, they were correct in recognizing the problems the church faced in enforcing the laws. The church used a variety of formal and informal mechanisms for enforcing the rules of sexual behavior, from gentle persuasion in sermons to actions brought by courts to penalize offenders. Until the early thirteenth century, however, it was difficult for clerics to be convicted of sexual offenses. According to the *ordo iuris* as laid out in Gratian's *Decretum,* the proof of any criminal accusation required the sworn testimony of two credible witnesses of the crime, with the proof being "clearer than the mid-day light."[84] Although priests were frequently publicly rumored to have concubines, it was rare for there to be two credible witnesses to a priest's incontinence, since the criminal act itself was usually not seen. In addition to this high standard of proof, potential accusers feared the significant penalties they could face if they failed to prove their accusations.

Changes in the laws of evidence and system of proof in the early thirteenth century, however, made it easier for the church to prosecute sex offenses.[85] Canon 8 of the Fourth Lateran Council (which ratified Innocent III's earlier decretals) allowed someone to initiate a criminal action anonymously *per denunciationem.* Since no public accusation was required, a complainant did not have to face the liabilities that failed accusers had before. Also as a result of the council, in cases where there was common belief (*fama*) that a law had been broken, an ecclesiastical judge could proceed *per inquisitionem* to initiate an inquiry on his own authority. Common belief about a priest's incontinence was itself circumstantial evidence that there was probable cause for an action against the priest. This meant that an archbishop like Eudes Rigaud no longer needed an accuser, let alone witnesses, to initiate an action against a priest rumored to be incontinent. In a case referred to Innocent III by Bishop Eustace of Ely in 1199 dealing with clerics who lived openly with concubines, the pope went even further, ruling (in the decretal *Tua nos duxit*) that if a priest openly flaunted his relationship with a concubine and made no effort to hide it, an ecclesiastical judge could convict and sentence the "notorious" priest without further evidence. In a *per notorium* procedure, in other words, the perpetrator of a crime was not merely suspected but publicly known, and in such a case, notoriety constituted sufficient evidence for conviction.[86]

One of the functions of Eudes's pastoral visits of the parish clergy was to learn whether any of the priests were publicly known for incontinence. As a result of the developments in ecclesiastical criminal procedure just described, the archbishop in many ways had the upper hand in his dealings with priests defamed for incontinence. Visiting a deanery in his diocese, Eudes typically found that about 20 percent of the rectors were defamed of incontinence.[87] The first time a parish priest was found defamed, he usually received a formal warning from the archdeacon or archbishop. If the priest contested the accusation, the archbishop normally gave the priest a choice: either he could submit to the archbishop's judgment or, on the basis of the *fama,* the archbishop would initiate an *ex officio* investigation (*inquisitio*). If the investigation revealed that the priest had indeed had sexual relations while invested with his benefice, he would be deprived of his benefice. In the vast majority of cases, the defamed priest chose to submit to the archbishop's judgment rather than face an investigation. When a priest was de-famed of incontinence for the first time, Eudes generally made him prom-ise in writing that should he be ill-famed again, he would immediately re-sign his benefice without appeal.[88] These letters of submission allowed Eudes to avoid time-consuming investigations and lengthy trials. Further-more, by issuing warnings, Eudes gave defamed priests a second chance. This seems to have been Eudes's larger goal in the first place, namely, to teach and correct wayward priests rather than simply punish them.[89]

Yet with all the supposed power Eudes held, at times he was fairly lax in his dealings with priests known to be incontinent. During a visitation of the deanery of Longueville in 1249, for instance, he found that Girard, the priest at Martigny, was ill-famed of incontinence, nonresidence, and failing to attend the deanery kalends. Eight years later, in 1257, Girard was again ill-famed of incontinence with a concubine, and this time, Eudes had the priest sign a letter promising to resign his benefice if he relapsed. By 1261, Girard was again in trouble, this time for allegedly wounding a layman; the archbishop ordered a full investigation. In 1265, Girard was cited by the archdeacon for again being defamed of incontinence, the third time in twelve years. Girard denied the charge, but following an investigation by the archdeacon, Eudes ordered the accused to appear before the *officialis* and purge himself of the charge by bringing in seven priests who had to swear that they believed him. Although what became of Girard is not known, there is no record in either the ordination lists or the polyptych of a new priest being installed at Martigny.[90] Despite having the legal powers to do so, the archbishop does not seem to have been in any great hurry to deprive Girard of his benefice. Eudes sometimes stripped a priest of his benefice immediately on finding that the priest had relapsed in his sexual relation-ship despite his promise in a signed letter. Yet many of the letters of sub-mission that ill-famed priests signed provided them with the opportunity to purge themselves if they were found ill-famed again. In such cases, the priest would be forced to resign his benefice (or pay the archbishop a heavy fine) only if he failed to purge himself.[91] Canonical purgation, which de-rived from Germanic law, was a process whereby an accused was absolved if he could swear to his innocence on the Gospels and find a certain number of good men (usually five or seven, but sometimes as many as twelve) who knew him, were of his order, and would swear to his good reputation. The compurgators did not have to attest to the accused's innocence; they merely had to say that they took him at his word. If the accused was not able to swear an oath to his own innocence and find a sufficient number of com-purgators, his crime was considered demonstrated and he was condemned and sentenced.[92]

By the thirteenth century, chastity had come to represent perhaps the single most important boundary separating the clergy from the laity. It symbolized the clergy's moral superiority over the rest of society. It was thought that to approach the altar and celebrate the Eucharist, the ministers of the church had to be ritually pure, or chaste. In practice, many clerics with concubines continued to be presented to benefices, often under the condition that they immediately renounce their concubines. Parishioners were sometimes willing to ignore a rector who lived with his concubine (*focaria*), as long as he was discreet about the relationship. But it was not always so easy for a priest to be discreet about his sexual improprieties. When Eudes found that a father-priest had his children living with him, a scandalous arrangement that the Rouen synod of 1231 had explicitly prohibited, he ordered the priest to send the children away.[93] A thirteenth-century synod in Coutances banned the "shameful" practice of some illegitimate sons serving with their unchaste father-priests at the altar, where, the statute noted, the only begotten son of God was sacrificed for the salvation of mankind.[94] One priest arranged for his mistress to marry his servant, to allow the priest to have easier access to her.[95] In another case, Eudes encountered a dean accused of extortion. The dean had allegedly offered another priest forty *sous* if he would agree not to report his unchastity. The same dean was also defamed of agreeing to church two prostitutes in exchange for sex.[96] The archbishop made a note to himself in his *Register* about "finding the right time" to remove the dean. These colorful stories were clearly not representative of medieval parish priests, but they illustrate Eudes's deep concern with how the clergy were seen by the larger society.[97] The archbishop, who wished to maintain public order, sought to safeguard the clergy's reputation as the model of moral purity. If the church were going to win respect from the society it governed, it could not allow scandal to surround its leaders.

In confronting the problem of clerical concubinage, the archbishop received strong support from Pope Alexander IV, who in 1259 warned the archbishop and other prelates of Normandy about the need to crush clerical concubinage. Citing a verse from Isaiah (24:2), the pope argued that at a time when "the excessive corruption of the Christian people is witnessed from many regions in general," the people were crying out to priests for help, only to find that the priests were acting more and more like the people.[98] Priests were acting with far too much "liberty," "license," and "impunity," "relaxing their reins to the pleasure and lustings of their flesh." The pope wondered aloud at how priests could not blush at what they were doing. "Oh the pain" (*proh dolor*), he exclaimed at one point in the letter, lamenting that priests were living with concubines in open view of the people, thereby rejecting "the honor of clerical purity." Although the Norman archbishop might have interpreted the pope's letter as something of a rebuke, the archbishop's *Register* makes clear that Eudes shared the pope's desire for a quick and discreet resolution to any public scandal or appearance of wrongdoing involving a priest. One of Eudes's predecessors, Pierre de Colmieu, who had been concerned with similar matters, had issued a synodal statute prohibiting priests from inviting parishioners to banquets at their houses and accepting invitations from their parishioners lest a scandal might arise.[99] But Eudes's particular concern about clerical concubinage may also have stemmed from his identity as a Franciscan. Did Eudes hold the parish clergy to different standards than a secular archbishop would have?

It is risky to make generalizations about secular prelates versus religious prelates, or for that matter, university-educated prelates versus those who had not received a university education. Some secular bishops had episcopal careers that closely resembled Eudes Rigaud's. Federico Visconti, for example, who was archbishop of Pisa and an exact contemporary of Eudes's, had a university background, although he was not a friar. Yet the Italian archbishop was enormously conscientious and hardworking. Charged with overseeing an unusually large metropolitan province, Federico did not shy away from conducting frequent visitations, holding synods, and preaching. Like Eudes, Federico insisted that his clergy show unwavering loyalty to ecclesiastical authority and adhere to the strictest standards of moral conduct. Federico was one of many secular prelates who shared Eudes's values and pastoral practices.[100]

What role, if any, might a university education have played in shaping Federico's episcopal career?[101] Federico's learning is clearly evident in some of his sermons, where he displayed an impressive knowledge of the Bible (like Eudes, Federico was especially fond of the wisdom literature) and its commentators, and he also appeared well versed in law and science. He even structured some of his episcopal sermons in a question-and-answer format, much like the disputed questions (*questiones disputatae*) that were a standard part of the university curriculum.[102] But in addition to the style of his sermons, the substance of Federico Visconti's episcopal sermons provides a window into medieval theology in action, into how ideas worked out in the university were applied to contemporary moral and religious issues. Like Eudes (as discussed in chapter 1), Federico was profoundly aware that ignorance was sometimes a cause of sin.[103] As Federico explained in one of his sermons, ignorance might be the result not merely of a person's lack of intelligence but also of a person's weakness or laziness. Federico believed that the acquisition of knowledge and understanding required hard work. People could not expect knowledge to come to them effortlessly, from the grace of God, as it had during the time of the apostles.[104] Thus, laziness was not only a vice in itself but could cause ignorance, which in turn posed a whole host of moral dangers. After all, it was sheer ignorance that had led some in Federico's day to use the false reasoning that fornication is not a sin because sex is a necessary part of nature.[105] If they were to avoid misconduct, the clergy needed an understanding of what constituted proper conduct, and this required education. With a deep sense that he was responsible to God not only for his own actions but for those of his clerics, Federico took the obligation of educating his clergy very seriously.[106]

When it came to the conduct of their clergy, Federico and Eudes shared many of the concerns that had earlier been addressed in the Parisian synodal statutes of Eudes de Sully. Were the clergy tonsured and dressed in somber clothing with their capes closed? Did they concentrate intensely while reciting the offices and stand with the correct posture? Did they show charity in their personal interactions? Did they abstain from playing dice and carrying arms? Did they show the respect owed to the real presence of Christ in the Eucharist?[107] In short, did they lead holy lives? Both archbishops believed that if those charged with the care of souls misbehaved or were ignorant, the errors of their ways would inevitably spread like a cancer to the laity.

And no issue appears to have concerned Federico or Eudes more than the problem of the clergy's sexual activity. Federico's sermons were filled with discussions of fornication, adultery, sodomy, incest, prostitution, and birth control.[108] In his first synodal sermon after becoming archbishop, Federico said, "For there are few priests in my diocese, as I have learned, who do not have concubines."[109] The few who did not, Federico told his clerical audience, perhaps in a moment of caustic humor, were old priests, "and then it is not so much they who have abandoned sin, as sin which has abandoned them, as impotent."[110] It was even difficult to find senior clergy willing to censure those engaged in concubinage, according to the Italian archbishop, since the senior clergy so often had concubines of their own. In a rare admission of the "advantages" of clerical concubinage, Federico observed that sodomy was more common among clergy who did not have concubines or wives.[111] Was all clerical concubinage equally sinful, or should a moral distinction be drawn between public and private concubinage? In one sermon Federico argued, as Eudes Rigaud might have, that although private concubinage was hypocritical and wrong, it was better than cases of priests publicly known to have sexual relations with the wives of their parishioners.[112]

Admittedly, those in monastic and mendicant circles were especially sensitive to the rule of continence, since this was a central aspect of the religious life they had vowed to follow. Although Federico never became a friar, he maintained a close relationship with the mendicant orders throughout his life. As a young boy, he had heard Saint Francis preach in Bologna. As archbishop, Federico frequently stayed with Franciscans at their convents and praised their ability to combine the active and contemplative life, to balance daily prayer and preaching to laymen and women. The Pisan archbishop exhorted the faithful to give alms to the friars, whose prayers of intercession he believed to be especially efficacious because of their exemplary, evangelical lives. Rather than see the friars as a threat to the secular clergy as many secular prelates did, Federico viewed them as "the light of the world" and ideal partners in helping him carry out his pastoral duties.[113] In one of his sermons, he even described the friars as a brave militia pitted against "the world, the flesh, and the Devil."[114] Eudes used almost the same language in a sermon that he preached to students at the University of Paris, invoking a topos that was common in the twelfth and thirteenth centuries. Both archbishops viewed themselves as spiritual warriors who would defeat the enemy by teaching, correcting, and enforcing Christian discipline. In addition to their preaching, they would teach by example; they would fight luxury, avarice, and pride with chastity, charity, and humility.[115]

What a bishop found during the course of his visitations helped shape his view of what issues should be addressed in councils and synods. In a series of constitutions promulgated in Rouen between 1238 and 1244, for instance, Archbishop Pierre de Colmieu published a statute reaffirming secular clerics' obligation to wear a large crown with a large and round tonsure. The statute was quite explicit in saying that the archbishop had found many clerics delinquent in properly distinguishing themselves from laymen and that he had created the statute to correct this problem.[116] In another statute, Pierre enjoined priests to find a way to keep pigeons out of their church towers because of the damage the birds were doing to the church buildings and altars![117] But while the *detecta* and *comperta* found during visitations affected conciliar legislation, so too did conciliar legislation shape the kinds of questions a bishop (or archdeacon or dean) asked during his visitations, as well as the injunctions he issued and penances he imposed. Eudes was an assiduous enforcer not only of the canons of the Fourth Lateran Council but also of the statutes promulgated in his own provincial councils and diocesanal synods, many of which reaffirmed statutes from earlier diocesanal synods.[118] There was a good deal of interplay, in other words, between visitation and conciliar legislation, so much so that it is sometimes difficult to determine whether a set of statutes comes from a bishop's visitation or from a synod.[119]

It was only in the twelfth century that diocesanal synods began being held on a regular basis, and Rouen was unusual in having statutes come from not only diocesanal synods from an early date but also provincial councils from as early as 1096.[120] During the twelfth century, provincial councils and synods functioned primarily as ecclesiastical tribunals, where both clerical and lay delinquents were judged and conflicts were resolved. The creation of the official's consistory court in the late twelfth century, however, greatly reduced the number of cases heard during synods and councils, and as a result, the function of these assemblies became more legislative than juridical.[121] In addition, the Fourth Lateran Council gave new impetus to synodal activity by making the annual holding of diocesanal synods obligatory for the first time.[122]

No thirteenth-century French bishop or archbishop seems to have presided over more synods and councils than Eudes Rigaud.[123] It normally fell to the archdeacon to convene archidiaconal synods, but when an archdeaconry such as Rouen contained the episcopal or archiepiscopal see (in such a case it was called the "greater archdeaconry"), the archdeacon sometimes deferred the presidency of the archidiaconal synod to his superior, the bishop or archbishop.[124] During most of his archiepiscopate, Eudes held two annual synods for the archdeaconry of Rouen. These synods, which generally met in the Rouen cathedral twice a year, once in the fall and once in the spring, were made up of both secular clergy and nonexempt regular clergy from the greater archdeaconry. Whereas many bishops and archbishops would not have involved themselves in the local affairs of their archdeaconries (one modern analogy would be a president of a large university presiding over an academic department's monthly meetings), Eudes took an active interest in his archdeaconry, organizing at least twenty-eight archidiaconal synods in addition to synods for the parish priests of the diocese (the diocese included five other archdeaconries), synods for the deans of the diocese, and provincial councils.[125] He also presided over numerous synods for the archdeaconry of the French Vexin and the archdeaconry of Pontoise, and he even reminded deans to hold monthly synods in their deaneries.[126] According to the *Register*, Eudes presided over seventy-four synods and councils, a number that leaves out the synods we know he celebrated after he stopped keeping the *Register* (from 1269 until his death in 1275).[127] What all this activity reflects is the archbishop's hands-on, almost micromanagerial approach to governance.

The synodal statutes were the specific rules for the discipline of ecclesiastical officials and beneficed clergy, and the making of statutes was usually the principal business of a synod.[128] Yet by the time one of Eudes's synods was held, the statutes had probably already been drafted, and thus it was unlikely for the synod to hold any surprises.[129] To what extent did the Rouen statutes reflect the archbishop's own initiatives and concerns?[130] By law, Eudes was supposed to discuss any important matters in his proposed synodal statutes with his chapter and any proposed provincial statute with his suffragan bishops.[131] But who defined an important matter? And was the archbishop under any obligation to heed the advice that was given to him? Eudes recorded that at his first provincial council, he sought the advice of his suffragans on the question of resuming a provincial visitation—and it is clear from the long and bitter dispute that followed, that the archbishop acted against their will. The types of issues addressed in the synodal statutes seem to reflect what would have concerned the archbishop rather than the clergy assembled in the synod. On October 28, 1254, for instance, at a synod for the deans of the archdiocese of Rouen, a law was passed making it obligatory for deans to turn over to the archbishop any church that had stood without a curate for more than one month. Another law stipulated that the benefices of any church seized would automatically revert to the archbishop.[132] It is difficult to imagine the deans calling for the inclusion of such laws, laws that seem to reflect the personal interests of the archbishop. It is quite possible, however, that the deans sometimes suggested the inclusion of a particular law in response to a problem they were encountering in their deaneries.

Many of Eudes's synodal statutes copied or built on older canons. Indeed, the archbishop's conciliar activity is more remarkable for its frequency than for its substance. At most of his provincial councils, he reaffirmed a statute from the First Council of Lyon of 1245 that dealt with the collection of procurations by bishops and archbishops during visitations.[133] Many of the provincial statutes passed were also based on canons from the Fourth Lateran Council (some of which had been tried out by Robert of Courson at synods in Paris and Rouen in 1214) and the Norman provincial council of 1231 (which was deeply influenced by "the synod of the West," since Archbishop Maurice of Rouen had formerly been bishop of Le Mans), and Eudes repeated these statutes at each successive council, only occasionally adding one or two new ones.[134] There may be some significance to Eudes's choice of which statutes to incorporate into his own conciliar legislation. He adhered, for instance, to canon 16 of the Fourth Lateran Council, which banned the use by clerics of gilded or otherwise superfluously decorated saddles, reins, spurs, and pectoral crosses. As a Franciscan, Eudes might have been especially troubled by clerics consuming and displaying such signs of luxury, but the archbishop's statute was hardly original, and it trickled down from the Fourth Lateran Council into the conciliar legislation of many dioceses, where it was repeated year after year. Indeed, the statutes from Eudes's own provincial council at Pont-Audemer in 1257 would be repromulgated by his successor, Guillaume de Flavacourt, in a provincial council in 1279.[135] Originality, in short, does not seem to have been valued in the making of statutes. The desired end was rather the diffusion of pontifical decrees and canons from general councils into individual parishes.[136] Bishops and archdeacons ordered rural deans to have synodal statutes transcribed for parish priests, who were expected to carry their copies to synods, where the priests might even be quizzed on their knowledge of the statutes' contents.[137] Uniform accuracy in priests' copies of statutes seems to have been a particular concern of bishops. At the synods, priests could edit or make additions to existing statutes on their own copies. In 1245, the deans of Rouen were told that they had one month to correct their own copies of synodal statutes and to see to it that all priests' copies were corrected to accord with the original copy.[138]

But synods were not simply vehicles for bishops or archdeacons to impose reforms on the lower clergy; synods also gave parish priests the opportunity to inform their archdeacon or bishop of the problems they had encountered and thought needed correcting. Synods and councils were forums, in other words, for the transmission of information across deaneries, archdeaconries, and dioceses and between different levels within the ecclesiastical hierarchy.[139] As a result of his own visitations of deaneries, Eudes was unusually well informed about the state of the parish clergy. One can imagine that a synod served an especially important function for bishops who did not conduct visitations of their dioceses' parish clergy. Yet for Eudes, synods were also valuable in permitting him to enact legislation based on what he and his archdeacons had uncovered during their visitations. More so than the statutes from the Norman provincial councils, which tended to be formulaic and repeated from council to council year after year, the language from the diocesanal statutes suggests that they were intended to curb problems that Eudes had actually encountered. In 1267, for instance, he issued a set of constitutions for rural deans on the execution of citations and the publication of sentences of excommunication.[140] At the diocesanal synod in the fall of 1254, Eudes tried to prevent regular canons with the cure of souls from farming out their parishes; he also sought help from the deans in forcing those with the cure of souls who were not yet ordained to receive holy orders immediately or give up their benefices; finally, Eudes insisted that the deans keep better records on the property and income seized from vacant parishes which they were obliged to turn over to the archiepiscopal treasury.[141] Once promulgated, statutes became legally binding throughout the diocese.

Although the promulgation of statutes was the principal business of synods, it is often forgotten that these convocations involved elaborate liturgical rituals. Synods began with the celebration of the Mass, followed by the chanting of the *Veni creator spiritus*, the litany, the Lord's Prayer, and various other prayers, followed in turn by a sermon preached by the archbishop. Synodal sermons tended to highlight the pastoral duties incumbent on clerics, with frequent invocations of Scripture. As shown in the synodal sermons of Eudes Rigaud's near contemporary, Guiard de Laon, bishop of Cambrai (1238–48), the primary purpose of this type of sermon was clerical education.[142] In this sense, the synodal sermon was not that different from sermons preached at the university. Both Guiard and Eudes had ties to the university at Paris, and the synodal sermons of both men stressed the necessary balance between action and contemplation, the challenges of the pastoral ministry, and the value of the *imitatio Christi*. Synodal sermons sought to convey a positive image of the clergy's pastoral function, depicting the model cleric as one of the new apostles or as Christ himself. In addition, the sermons preached in synods counterbalanced the lists of terse, legal prohibitions contained in synodal statutes.

In 1976, Louis Duval-Arnould published three synodal sermons formerly attributed to Eudes's Franciscan teacher at the University of Paris, Jean de la Rochelle. But as Duval-Arnould shows, there is strong evidence to suggest that the sermons were preached not by Jean but by Eudes himself.[143] The three sermons bear a strong resemblance to the sermons Eudes preached at the University of Paris in the 1240s, discussed in chapter 1. Like the university sermons, the synodal sermons are replete with scholastic divisions. Structured almost like family-tree diagrams, they resemble summas more than conventional sermons. But this may reflect the bare-bones nature of the *reportationes* rather than the sermons as they were preached. As he did in his university sermons, Eudes showed a special affinity for the wisdom literature, especially the Wisdom of Jesus ben Sirach. He also frequently cited the examples of Aaron and his sons, drawing a connection between the high priests of the Israelite temple and those whom he viewed as their heirs, the Norman clergy.[144] Like God's earlier chosen ministers, the Norman clergy were expected to live according to special criteria, Eudes argued, particularly with regard to their moral and bodily purity.

The synodal sermon functioned as a kind of pep talk, but it was also something more. Eudes believed that synods were holy events because of the role that God played. Indeed, in one synodal sermon, Eudes explicitly identified his own ordination of the synod with God's giving of the Torah to Moses atop Mount Sinai, as recounted in Exodus 19. Just as God had given the law to Moses, so too had God given the pope—another Moses, as it were—the law of the sacerdotal statutes. Christ had said to the popes of the church, "He who hears you, hears me" (Luke 10: 16), and to some extent this applied to the pope's relationship with the archbishop, since Eudes acted as the papal representative in the Norman province.[145]

The Norman clergy, according to Eudes, were also prefigured in the Hebrew Bible through the image of the angels who descended and ascended Jacob's ladder. Like the angels, priests are mediators between the people and God, descending to bring divine sacraments to the people and ascending to offer gifts and sacrifices to God for the people's sins. The priestly office consists of three principal tasks: caring for the faithful by dispensing sacraments, teaching by preaching sermons, and correcting by hearing confession. Drawing on a long tradition (going back to the Gospels themselves) of likening the priestly office to other vocations, Eudes compared the priest to the doctor who cures, the shepherd who feeds, the farmer who cultivates, and the architect who builds. But as Duval-Arnould points out, Eudes made an original contribution in identifying a priest's penitential function with that of the *stabularius*, or innkeeper, in the parable about the Samaritan (Luke 10:30–35).[146] Following tradition, Eudes identified the Samaritan in the parable as Christ. What was new, however, was the identification of the innkeeper as the priest (*sacerdos*). The apostles had traditionally been cited as the representatives of the innkeeper, and beginning in the twelfth century, according to Duval-Arnould, the broad category of "prelates" began replacing the apostles. But Eudes went even further, elevating the rank-and-file priests he was addressing in the synod by identifying them with the innkeeper. Most important, the archbishop emphasized the priests' responsibility in performing the sacrament of penance, drawing an explicit connection between their penitential function and the innkeeper's having been paid by the Samaritan (Christ) to care for the wounded man.

As he plainly said in one of his sermons, Eudes considered his purpose in preaching to be "the instruction of those who are assembled in the synod."[147] Taking his theme from 1 Corinthians (4:2), "What is required here now of the stewards (*dispensatores*) is that one be found who is trustworthy," the archbishop discussed what it is that makes a priest trustworthy, comparing the trust a priest should show his parishioners with the trust a friend should show a friend, the trust a slave should show his master, and the trust a superior prelate should show his inferior subject.[148] Priests, he argued, are their parishioners' superiors, inferiors, and equals all at once. Like a good friend, the faithful priest shows perseverance; his fidelity is evident in his will, intention, and counsel; his actions and prayers serve as his parishioners' medicine and ointment; he suffers for God as Abraham and the other patriarchs did. Like a slave, the good priest guides his actions by fear, obedience, and a sense of a duty to guard, give, and serve. He upholds the dignity of his order through prayer; he gives pastoral care through solicitude; he spreads knowledge through the doctrine he preaches; he lends life through the example of his own conduct; and he contributes to church temporalities through generous almsgiving. Eudes also drew a distinction between the fidelity of the priestly office and of the person. The faithful person renounces his desires, displays gentle humility, and maintains chastity. The priestly office, when faithfully conducted, consists of acting as judge in hearing confession, serving as witness to the truths of Scripture in preaching sermons, and acting as legate in sending prayers to God on behalf of parishioners.[149]

These were priestly ideals, and as Eudes emphasized to the clergy attending the synod, not all priests were trustworthy, a theme often repeated in the sermons of thirteenth-century friars. Indeed, one wonders whether Eudes was tougher on the Norman clergy because he was accustomed to hearing his fellow friars use *exempla* in their sermons aimed at denouncing the state of the secular clergy. Preaching to the secular clergy at the synod, Eudes was not afraid to invoke this same approach: "Today this fidelity is found in few priests, because, if they receive the care [of souls], it is not with the intention of the love of Christ, but with the intention of any way of procuring some temporal gain."[150] Fidelity, Eudes noted, was especially important among priests, since they approached holy altars daily. "But alas, today it can be said about many priests what is said in Zephaniah 3:4 about the prophets: 'Her prophets are reckless, unfaithful men; her priests have polluted what is holy.' "[151] In theory, the clergy acted as the supreme *dispensatores*, distributing the church's temporal goods, preaching doctrine, and administering the sacraments. "But many [priests] today," Eudes exclaimed, "are not dispensers, but rather destroyers."[152] "Today on account of the examples of priests the church or parish is a kind of prostitute because since they are public fornicators, they do not dare judge or censure a single fornicator."[153] By contrasting the ideal priest with the typical priest of his day, Eudes posed a rhetorical challenge to those attending the synod: would any of them dare be one of the few faithful priests?

This challenge bore a greater sense of urgency in a synodal sermon that Eudes apparently preached in May 1250.[154] In an ominous tone, the archbishop referred to the current "tribulation of the church and the capture of soldiers on crusade" (*his diebus in tribulatione Ecclesiae et captivatione militum utra mare*), most likely a reference to the capture only a few weeks before of King Louis at Al-Mansurah. Was the crusade's sudden failure a sign of divine disapproval? Like the prophet Joel, who interpreted a catastrophic locust plague in Judah as a divine judgment, the Franciscan archbishop worried about the meaning of the French king's capture at the hands of the Muslims. Perhaps it was time for the Norman clergy to repeat the lamentation in Joel (2:17) while weeping: " 'Spare your people, O Lord, and do not make your heritage a mockery, a byword among the nations.' "[155] What if the other nations laughed at the church's tribulations and the French king's captivity, and asked, "Where is your God now?"

Eudes used the news of the king's capture to exhort the Norman clergy to take their priestly responsibilities more seriously. Quoting Ezekiel 3:18, he emphasized the responsibility that priests bore: "If I say to the wicked, 'You shall die in death,' and you will have given him no warning, nor have spoken to warn him from his wicked way, so that he might live, that wicked person shall die for his iniquity; but his blood I will require at your hand."[156] Echoing his exhortations as regent master at the University of Paris, Eudes continued to be concerned with the problem of clerical ignorance, reminding the priests at the Rouen synod about the dangers of priestly ignorance by quoting Jerome: "if a priest is ignorant of God's law, he does not deserve to be a priest of God."[157] He drew attention to the depravity of simony, the selling of sacraments. And to illustrate the hazards of assimilating to a foreign (or lay) culture, he pointed to the impious example of the high priest Jason in 2 Maccabees. Just as Jason assimilated to Greek culture, so too were the Norman clergy in danger of assimilating to lay culture in their dress, recreations, and relations with women.[158] Eudes contrasted a good priest like Phineas, the son of Eleazer (Numbers 25), who served God with zeal and purified the sins of the sons of Israel, with Eli in the book of Samuel, who failed to act after hearing that his sons were sleeping with women who came to the temple gate. Would the Norman clergy choose to be like a Phineas or an Eli, an Aaron or a Jason? As priestly persons, would they strengthen the weak, cure the sick, and bandage the wounded? Would they live lives of moral purity (*muniditae*) like the Levite priests or gluttonous, unchaste lives, approaching the altar each week to offer the Lord polluted bread?

6

An Ecclesiastical Administrator of Justice

In his roles as a master of the Norman Court of the Exchequer and a member of the Parlement of Paris, Eudes Rigaud was deeply involved in the administration of justice in both the Norman province and the French kingdom as a whole. The Franciscan archbishop was also invested with seigneurial rights in several areas of his province, including Pontoise, Gaillon, Dieppe, and Louviers. In these areas, he exercised high and low justice. But although Eudes was no stranger to the secular courts, his primary loyalty rested with the ecclesiastical courts of Normandy, over which he was the principal judge.

The archiepiscopal court, which was run on a day-to-day basis by the archbishop's official (*officialis*), heard all cases involving not only clerics but also other persons under the jurisdiction of the church, such as lay conversi, child oblates, canonesses, beguines, hermits, and brothers and sisters of hospitals.[1] There was debate among thirteenth-century canonists over the legal status of other groups, such as penitents, pilgrims, crusaders, widows, orphans, students, and the wives of clerics. Whether cases involving these groups fell within the jurisdiction of the ecclesiastical or secular courts depended largely on the custom of a particular region.[2] In Normandy, many of the customs established during the twelfth century survived the Capetian conquest of 1204. Private collections of customary law, referred to as the *Très ancien coutumier*, the first part of which was compiled around the time of the conquest (the second part was composed about twenty years later), and the *Summa de legibus*, the first version of which was composed in the 1250s, together demonstrate the extent to which twelfth-century customs first defined by Henry II and Thomas Becket, and later modified under Richard the Lionheart, were codified with some modifications in the thirteenth century when Normandy was under French rule.[3] At Caen in 1258, with Eudes sitting as one of the judges, the Norman Exchequer took up the question of jurisdiction over widows. Guillaume de Voisins, the *bailli* of Rouen, had been holding a certain Emma la Hardie in a royal prison for a debt she had admitted before the *vicomte*. The court found that the *bailli* did not have the right to pursue the case because Emma was a widow and widows were under the jurisdiction of the church.[4] This ruling confirmed twelfth-century Norman custom, as reflected in the *Très ancien coutumier*.[5] At the same session of the Exchequer, the court settled a dispute between the bishop and the *bailli* of Coutances over the *bailli*'s attempts to hear cases involving widows and crusaders.[6] Once again, the court sided with the church, ruling that both widows and crusaders fell within the jurisdiction of the ecclesiastical courts.

Disagreements also arose between lay and ecclesiastical courts over the types of cases each court could hear. Would the church retain its authority over cases involving marriage, legitimacy, and wills? What about cases involving arson, rape, and pillage—were they under the purview of ecclesiastical or secular courts? Often there were no simple answers to these questions. According to one Norman custom, for instance, dowries were under the jurisdiction of the church, but in one place the *Très ancien coutumier* stipulated that only movables that were part of a dowry or marriage portion (*maritagium*) were within the church's domain, whereas real property fell within the purview of the royal court.[7] Elsewhere, the *Très ancien coutumier* seemed to shift jurisdiction over dowries from ecclesiastical courts to lay courts, with the justification being that the ecclesiastical appellate system was too slow.[8] At the end of the twelfth century, the Norman clergy had tried to argue that all breaches of oaths and faith should be under the purview of ecclesiastical courts, a claim that if successful, would have shifted an enormous number of cases from lay to ecclesiastical courts, since most contracts involved the swearing of an oath or a pledge of *fides* guaranteeing the obligation contained in the contract. The clergy's claim, however, was not accepted, and in his inquest of 1205, Philip Augustus confirmed that breaches of pledges of faith and oaths involving lay fiefs or movables were not to be judged by ecclesiastics. The church had jurisdiction over breaches of pledges of faith or oaths only when they involved personages or issues over which the church already exercised jurisdiction, such as clerics, crusaders, testaments, and the movables that were part of dowries and marriage portions.[9]

As discussed in the previous chapter, there were frequent disputes over who had the right of advowson, that is, the right to present a candidate to the bishop to be instituted as the curate of a church.[10] According to Norman custom, whoever last presented a candidate for a church benefice (or his or her heir) was considered to possess the advowson. But when disputes over advowson arose, where would they be decided? Despite Pope Alexander III's assertion in 1179–80 that such cases were exclusively subject to the jurisdiction of ecclesiastical courts, the custom in Normandy was that advowson cases were tried in ducal courts, where a jury of twelve men was summoned to declare who last presented a candidate for a church.[11] After Philip Augustus confirmed this custom in his inquest of 1205, the Norman clergy, led by the archbishop of Rouen, appealed to him to reconsider, and in a compromise decision the king ruled that henceforth disputes over advowson would be decided by a panel composed of four priests chosen by the bishop and four knights chosen by the *bailli*.[12] By a majority vote, the panel would determine not only who possessed advowson but the proprietary question of the right of advowson.[13] If more than six months passed without a decision, however, the bishop could institute a candidate of his choosing, even though the right of advowson remained undetermined.[14] As previously discussed, Eudes Rigaud seized every opportunity presented to him to institute a candidate of his choosing when there was a protracted legal dispute over the right of advowson, and he was even accused of using delaying tactics in order to institute his own candidate rather than one presented to him by a patron. Furthermore, although the Norman polyptych indicates that most advowson disputes were adjudicated in lay courts, as was the custom, there were times when Eudes settled a dispute over who had the right of patronage himself, even when it involved two laymen.[15] In a dispute in which the archbishop and a squire both claimed to have the right of advowson, the two parties agreed to submit to arbitration. Yet all seven of the arbiters were canons, presumably more sympathetic to the archbishop's position, and two of them were even regular fixtures in the archbishop's *familia*.[16] What had happened to the seemingly more equitable custom whereby disputes over advowson were decided by a panel comprised of four priests chosen by the bishop and four knights chosen by the *bailli?* As a vigorous defender of the church's privileges, Eudes Rigaud was not afraid to challenge Norman custom and law.

During the late twelfth century, the Norman clergy's loyalty to the Anglo-Norman duke had weakened substantially. Under Richard, the Norman clergy increasingly complained that their financial burdens were too heavy, that they had been left defenseless against Capetian raiders and mercenaries, and that it was unjust for them to be tried in secular courts for "secular" crimes.[17] Although the Norman church began to win some concessions from the duke in the later twelfth century (partly as a result of the martyrdom of Thomas Becket), the prospect of being ruled under Philip Augustus increasingly appeared favorable to the clergy. Both before and immediately after the Norman conquest, Philip tried to win the favor of the Norman church by extending various ecclesiastical liberties, such as free canonical elections (without royal interference) and clerical immunity from royal justice (the *privilegium fori*). Philip even renounced the collection of regalia on vacant Norman royal sees.[18] Within several years after the Norman conquest, however, the king had less incentive to court the Norman church, and when the see of Rouen became vacant in 1209, he chose not to renounce the regalia.[19] The jurisdiction of ecclesiastical courts also appears to have slowly eroded, as Philip Augustus, Louis VIII, and Louis IX tried to return to a position closer to that staked out by Henry II in the Constitutions of Clarendon.[20]

Throughout his archiepiscopacy, Eudes Rigaud was vigilant in protecting the jurisdiction of the ecclesiastical courts from what he viewed as encroachments by the secular arm. In his defense of the clergy, Eudes fiercely guarded two long-standing principles: first, that because the clergy were considered sacred personages, any violence against a cleric would be regarded as a sacrilege (*privilegium canonis*); and second, that the clergy were exempt from secular courts and were under the exclusive jurisdiction of ecclesiastical courts (*privilegium fori*). The archbishop and his suffragans promulgated statutes at their provincial councils forbidding ecclesiastics to appeal to secular judges in cases pertaining to the church. The statutes also threatened to excommunicate any secular power that seized clerics "with greater violence than the resistance of the arrested one justifies," and *baillis* were threatened with excommunication for holding a cleric contrary to the orders of an ecclesiastical judge.[21] All these issues appear to have been problems from the beginning of Eudes's archiepiscopate. Even during his first year as archbishop, he complained to Pope Innocent IV about clerics and ecclesiastics from the diocese of Rouen being dragged into secular courts in cases involving their ecclesiastical or personal actions. In response, the pope prohibited barons, *baillis*, nobles, and others with temporal jurisdiction in the Rouen diocese from hearing cases involving the ecclesiastical or personal actions of clerics. Any secular authority that violated this rule was to be excommunicated and have its lands placed under interdict.[22]

In addition to protecting the jurisdiction of the ecclesiastical courts, the archbishop responded to specific incidents that he believed violated the church's liberties. On learning in July of 1252, for instance, that prisoners whom he believed were under ecclesiastical jurisdiction were being held in a royal prison, Eudes demanded that the *bailli* of Caux deliver them to the archiepiscopal prison at Rouen.[23] When the *bailli* refused, Eudes appealed to Jean de Limoges, the papal penitentiary, who had the pope appeal to the queen of France (regent during the crusade). She conceded that the *bailli* would have to surrender the prisoners to the ecclesiastical authorities.[24] All this conformed to twelfth-century practice, as is evident in a constitution delivered by King Richard in 1190 to the archbishop of Rouen and the other bishops of Normandy and incorporated in the *Très ancien coutumier* (and confirmed in Philip Augustus's inquest of 1205, which looked into the rights of Henry II and Richard over the Norman clergy).[25] In the constitution, King Richard ordered that clerics and priests captured and incarcerated for serious crimes be immediately returned to their bishop if the bishop so requested.

In August 1256, it came to Eudes's attention that the king's castellan of Vaudreuil had recently seized two squires in the king's preserves but that the squires had been able to escape and flee to Louviers, a town over which the archbishop had full seigneurial control. The king's castellan had followed the squires to Louviers, captured them there, and carried them back to the prison at Vaudreuil. Eudes immediately appealed to the king, arguing that the castellan's actions were prejudicial to him as lord of the town. Yielding to the archbishop's appeal, the king ordered the *bailli* of Rouen to return the squires to Louviers, where they were transferred by church officials to the archiepiscopal prison in Rouen. Eudes released the men as soon as they pledged to stand trial in the ecclesiastical court should charges ever be brought against them.[26] What these examples demonstrate is the lengths to which Eudes would go to safeguard his seigneurial rights. As we have seen in earlier chapters, the archbishop showed a similar desire to preserve the authority of his office in his contests with his suffragans and the regular clergy of the province.

Perhaps it was to be expected that in a province with unusually diligent ecclesiastical and royal administrators, there would be conflicts between secular and ecclesiastical courts. In 1258, the *bailli* of Rouen arrested a robber in a house that had been given to the chapter of Rouen. Because the house, like all dependencies of the chapter, had the right to protect criminals seeking refuge, the criminal, who was already condemned to hang, was instead taken back to the house where the *bailli* had found him and placed in the hands of the church.[27] In October 1261, a similar event occurred when a man accused of homicide was arrested by sergeants of the mayor on the place de la Calende, near la Madeleine (in the French Vexin). Because this property was under the jurisdiction of Etienne de Sens, archdeacon of the French Vexin, the criminal, whom the *bailli* had already condemned to die, was turned over to the archdeacon, who had him placed in an ecclesiastical prison and ultimately deported from France.[28] According to both the *Très ancien coutumier* and the *Summa de legibus* (the latter treatise first compiled right around the time of these events), although a layperson could seek asylum from royal justice on ecclesiastical property, he could remain there only up to eight days before being forced either to submit to royal justice or to abjure the land.[29] With secular authorities vigorously enforcing the law, the Norman church had to be careful about protecting its rightful jurisdiction.

Eudes Rigaud's jurisdiction also included certain types of cases touching laymen.[30] Crimes related to marriage, for instance, were under his authority. On January 22, 1265, Geoffroi de Cuverville, a knight who was repeatedly defamed of adultery, appeared before the archbishop and pledged under forfeiture of 20 l.t. that he would not renew his relationship with the woman with whom he had committed adultery. As public penance, Geoffroi vowed to go on pilgrimage to the shrine of Saint-Gilles-du-Gard in the extreme south of France along the Rhone before the coming feast of the Assumption of the Blessed Mary.[31] Gautier de Courcelles, a knight, had to pay a fine to the archbishop for having contracted a marriage without first publishing the banns, the public announcement of his intention to marry, which would have allowed a priest to conduct a prenuptial investigation of the bride and groom's freedom to marry.[32]

Any time a layman committed violence against church property, he became subject to ecclesiastical jurisdiction. It was not uncommon for Eudes to prosecute laymen caught hunting illegally in one of the church's preserves.[33] A knight named Raoul de Boscregnoult, for instance, hunted in Eudes's preserves and stole hunting equipment from the archbishop's men, beating them up in the process. Eudes made Raoul pledge that he would make whatever amends the archbishop might require of him.[34] In another case, André de St-Léonard, a ne'er-do-well but a member of one of the most powerful families in Rouen, admitted to leading an armed group of bandits to the archbishop's mill by the Rue-du-Bocq bridge, where he and his men stole grain and flour.[35] By committing violence against a cleric or an ecclesiastic, a layman violated the *privilegium canonis* and was automatically excommunicated. When the accused then came to the archbishop (only the pope or his representative could absolve in such cases, and Eudes acted as the papal representative) to ask for absolution, the excommunicate pledged to perform whatever penalty was laid upon him and offered a certain amount of money as surety, along with one or more individuals who became legally liable for the debt if unpaid.[36] After being excommunicated for laying violent hands on Hugues, a canon from Sausseuse, for instance, Guy, son of Guillaume called "Potel," submitted to Eudes's judgment under pain of 100 l.p. and the archbishop absolved him.[37] With two knights standing as surety, Richard de Espeigniaco, who had been excommunicated for burning the "cottage of a leper from Erquenciaco" (*bordellum leprosi de Erquenciaco*), gave his pledge to make whatever amends might be required of him, and the archbishop absolved him.[38] As he did with wayward secular clerics, Eudes favored having criminals make written promises that they would submit voluntarily to his judgment rather than face what could be lengthy investigations and trials. In order to resolve a conflict between two individuals, Eudes sometimes had them make a formal truce by promising *fides*. For example, he had Pierre Leboucher (Carnifex), a troublesome parishioner of Mucegros, pledge under penalty of 20 l.t. and swear on the

Holy Gospels that he would not cause any harm to Girard, the parish priest, and that he would prevent any potential harm to the priest that he knew of from a third party.[39]

No doubt, as diligent and effective judges and enforcers of the law, Norman *baillis* sometimes extended their authority beyond permissible bounds.[40] But the *baillis* also had to contend with criminals who found various ways (such as taking the cross after committing a crime) to claim exemption from secular jurisdiction and escape the severity of royal justice.[41] Even the church recognized that ecclesiastical privileges were sometimes abused. Questions arose about whether married clerics and those who illegally engaged in trade should lose their clerical privileges, such as their exemption from paying tolls and tallages.[42] In 1259, in response to a complaint from King Louis IX, Pope Alexander IV sent bulls to all French archbishops, bishops, and other prelates, ordering them not to prevent the king or secular lords of justice from taking legal action against lay crusaders or bigamous, widowed, or married clergy charged with serious crimes, meaning crimes that could result in capital punishment (*vindicatam sanguinis*).[43]

Eudes Rigaud was at times willing to concede powers to the secular courts. Troubled that some clerics used their privileged status merely to escape arrest and punishment by secular authorities, the archbishop and his suffragans published a statute at the Norman provincial council held at Pont-Audemer in 1267: "If after warnings have been issued, any clerics remain in apostasy with regard to tonsure and ecclesiastical habit and involve themselves in unusually barbarous acts, and it happens that for their excesses they are captured by secular judges, having been caught in crimes, we will not instruct them to be freed through ecclesiastical censures."[44] In the eyes of the archbishop, the *baillis* were not always the enemy of the church. The *baillis* made frequent financial gifts to the Norman church, and above all, the church relied on them to enforce the law.[45] Before criminous clerics could be tried in ecclesiastical courts, they first had to be arrested by the *baillis* or their agents.[46] The *baillis* were also needed to force excommunicates to seek absolution from the church, as Joseph Strayer describes: "The Church's chief weapon, excommunication, was useless in many cases unless the secular authorities forced the excommunicate to seek reconciliation."[47] Representing the other French prelates, Bishop Guy of Auxerre asked King Louis to command his *prévots* and *baillis* to seize and force all those who had remained excommunicated for at least one year and one day to have themselves absolved. The king refused, arguing that the excommunicate might have been falsely accused by the clergy.[48] Thus the church did not always have an easy time getting the *baillis* to act on its behalf.

Yet there were some cases in which the church relied on the power of secular officials to do what it itself could not. On April 18, 1266, for instance, in a public square in Rouen thronged with clergy and Rouennais citizens, Eudes condemned a Jew who twice had converted to Christianity and twice relapsed to Judaism as an apostate and a heretic.[49] The archbishop then turned the Jew over to the *bailli*, who had him burned to death.[50] Although technically the church could not issue a death sentence, by handing an apostate or heretic over to secular authorities, the church made its wishes clearly known. Despite their turf battles, the ecclesiastical and secular branches of justice shared many aims and could work in tandem to see that those aims were achieved.

The church also recognized that it was relatively powerless without the physical protection of royal or municipal authorities. In the spring of 1251, bands of shepherds in Flanders and northern France set out for what their leaders announced would be a crusade to help the French king in his struggles against the Muslims.[51] As the movement grew, the shepherds were joined by various other kinds of laborers, including urban artisans. By early June, in need of a scapegoat for the king's failed military campaigns in Egypt, bands of Pastoureaux in such cities as Paris, Orléans, and Rouen began to attack lay and ecclesiastical barons, whom they blamed for staying behind in France while the king fought in the East. Jews were also targeted.

On June 12 and 13, 1251, while Eudes Rigaud was holding his diocesanal synod, the Pastoureaux overran the city of Rouen. The archbishop and his clergy were forced from the Rouen cathedral and apparently sought refuge in a hall in the archiepiscopal manor house.[52] The thirteenth-century English chronicler Matthew Paris described the dangerously armed Pastoureaux as especially hostile to mendicants, who were considered "vagrants and hypocrites," and bishops and their officials, whom they hated for being "money-hunters, and affluent in all kinds of enjoyments."[53] As both a Franciscan and an archbishop, Eudes would have been a natural target for the Pastoureaux. According to Matthew's chronicle, the Pastoureaux received support from city residents who shared a contempt for the clergy. Although it is not known whether any Rouennais citizens joined the Pastoureaux in their attacks on the clergy, it is significant that on the day after the violence, the mayor and other municipal leaders appeared before the archbishop and other assembled clergy to beg for absolution. Were they seeking absolution for their failure to maintain peace in the city? Or had one or two of the municipal leaders given support to the Pastoureaux? The chronicles do not provide many clues. But according to Eudes's *Register*, on the day following the absolution of the mayor and other municipal leaders, the city administrators dined with the clergy at the synod of the deans, indicative of an effort at mending ties.

Tensions between the church and the city did not disappear, particularly when some municipal leaders demanded that the archbishop release a certain Thibaud du Chatel, a cleric and crusader suspected of committing homicide during the Pastoureaux uprising. Eudes had been holding Thibaud in the archiepiscopal prison in Rouen for several months. Being a cleric (and a crusader), Thibaud was clearly subject to the ecclesiastical court. But he also belonged to one of the most powerful families in the commune of Rouen, and municipal leaders, some of whom were relatives, were intent on getting him released from prison by invoking various communal privileges.[54] Eudes ultimately turned Thibaud over to city leaders but made them promise under oath that they would return him to the archbishop on the day after Easter, or on the archbishop's request, under pain of forfeiting 1,000 l.t. In the meantime, Eudes planned to conduct a formal inquiry into the homicide so he could deliver a final judgment. Thibaud had essentially been released on bail but was by no means free from the archbishop's authority.

Private penance was introduced by twelfth-century university theologians and established at the Fourth Lateran Council in the famous canon *Omnis utriusque sexus*, which mandated private, annual confession for all laymen and women.[55] Eudes embraced the new Parisian theology of secret contrition and private confession, showing a genuine concern that both the regular and secular clergy confess with the required frequency, in one case even ordering a prior to see to it that an incarcerated monk continue to confess weekly.[56] The archbishop was concerned about various aspects of confession, from the quality of confessors to whether a priest could confess to a neighboring priest when no penitentiary was available.[57] However, the relatively new practice of private penance did not replace public penance.[58] For one thing, *Omnis utriusque sexus* was never intended to challenge the imposition of public penance for public sins such as heresy. For public sins, Eudes continued to rely on the older rituals of public penance and humiliation as satisfactory punishment.

The archbishop imposed several forms of public penance. For solemn public penance, he followed an ancient ritual of expelling lay penitents from his cathedral on Ash Wednesday. On Maundy Thursday, immediately after matins, he preached a sermon in his cathedral. He then visited the monastic churches of Sainte-Catherine, Saint-Ouen, Saint-Amand, and Saint-Lô-de-Rouen and granted absolutions to the monastic penitents. Then he returned to the cathedral, where the lay penitents who had been expelled at the beginning of Lent were readmitted in a procession. Eudes preached a sermon, absolved the penitents, and blessed the holy chrism.[59] These penitents had committed sins that were considered "public" or scandalous, although little can be known for certain about the sinners or their sins, since the archbishop did not record such information in his *Register*.

Public processions and pilgrimages were two of Eudes's favorite forms of nonsolemn public penance.[60] There are over a dozen cases in the *Register* of the archbishop forcing penitents, both lay and clerical, to go on pilgrimages. One incontinent priest was sentenced to make a pilgrimage to Saint-Gilles-du-Gard and Saint-Amadour near the Dordogne valley.[61] A priest who had committed adultery with a parishioner was required to make a pilgrimage to Rome.[62] A squire who had committed an act of violence against a monk was freed from excommunication on the condition that he make a pilgrimage to the Holy Land.[63] These pilgrims were supposed to go on their pilgrimages barefoot, fasting all the while, except on Sundays and feast days. They were recognizable by their distinctive pilgrims' dress, and they sometimes had a cross sewn on their tunics.[64]

One case illustrates particularly well how the archbishop employed public penance in his administration of justice. Sometime in 1247, soon after the death of Eudes Clément, Eudes Rigaud's archiepiscopal predecessor, a group of men from the commune of Gamaches attacked and looted the archiepiscopal manor house at Aliermont. In addition, a man was killed and a nearby church pillaged. One of the ringleaders was Gautier Charue, a vassal of the Count of Dreux, who was excommunicated for his involvement in the affair. On September 24, 1248, Gautier sought and received absolution from the new archbishop, pledging fifty silver marks and submitting to Eudes's judgment. That judgment was handed down on January 21, 1249, following an inquest. At his manor house at Aliermont, the site of the crime, Eudes sentenced Gautier to pay damages in the amount of 1,200 l., 4 s., and 1 d.t. This extraordinary sum, much greater than the typical noble's annual revenue, was to be paid to the archbishop's servants at Aliermont before Easter. In addition, Gautier was forced to pay 30 l.t. to the woman whose son was killed, 30 l. to the priest at Saint-Aubin for damages done to his church, and 100 s. to a certain Nicholas, for the diverse injuries he suffered. Since there were many other claims for damages that had not yet been investigated, Eudes made Gautier pay an additional 100 l.t., with which new claims could be settled. Any money that remained could be used at the archbishop's discretion.

In addition to the fines, Gautier was ordered to make twelve solemn or Sunday processions, accompanied by eleven prominent men from Gamaches. Although the eleven men were not directly involved in the attack on the manor house, they represented the commune of Gamaches, which was implicated in the attack. As Mary Mansfield puts it, "the point was to shame and discredit the important men of Gamaches in front of their neighbors and, indeed, throughout the province."[65] The twelve men (symbolic in being the number of Christ's apostles) had to perform twelve humiliating processions with bared heads and feet, clad only in haircloth shirts and linen trunk hoses. Each carried a wand in his hands and received discipline from a priest after completing the procession. The people who gathered to watch the processions were informed of the crimes that had been committed. The twelve penitents were required to make separate processions to the cathedrals of Rouen, Evreux, Lisieux, Beauvais, and Amiens; three processions to the church at Aliermont, walking with bare feet all the way from the manorial limits to the church; and processions to the churches of Saint-Aubin, Saint-Vaast, Dreux, and Gamaches.[66] It was no accident that the processions were to take place in the communities where the crimes had occurred and where the penitents lived: each penitent was reconciled with his neighbor at the same time he was reconciled with the church and with God.[67] The processions also served as a lesson to the populace at large. After such a disruptive attack, there was a need to restore social order. Eudes viewed the public humiliation of penitents as a way of restoring order and solidifying his authority. By mocking and scorning a procession of penitents, the public reaffirmed its support for the ecclesiastical authorities that maintained order and enforced the law.

As humiliating as public penance was for sinners, it was much to be preferred to the punitive justice imposed by royal courts, which sentenced criminals not only to fines and forfeitures but mutilation and in some cases execution. Ecclesiastical courts were known for being merciful. The annual Norman custom that was part of the feast of Saint Romain helped popularize this notion of the church. Legend had it that in the seventh century, the bishop of Rouen, Saint Romain, had miraculously freed Rouen from a tormenting dragon. In honor of the bishop's deed, the king had accorded the church of Rouen the right to free an imprisoned murderer each year.[68] The first records of the elaborate ritual of Saint Romain date from 1210. In the week before Ascension, a group of delegates from the Rouen cathedral chapter visited each of Rouen's prisons, where they interrogated the prisoners and asked them to confess and indicate full contrition. The canons then returned to chapter with various prisoners' written confessions and discussed, debated, and lobbied one another until they had settled on a prisoner to release. On Ascension Day (le Jour du Prisonnier), the chosen prisoner was transferred from the secular guards to the canons and taken to the place de la Haute Vielle Tour, where he recited the *confiteor* and prayers of repentance. He was then given a decorated reliquary of Saint Romain, which he lifted over his head three times as a sign of deliverance. Joined by the clergy from local churches and monasteries, students from local schools, merchants, guildsmen, and musicians, the prisoner was paraded through the city wearing a new robe and holding a lit candle. At the front of the procession was a large statue of the dragon slain by Saint Romain. The whole city lined the streets shouting, "Noel, Noel, Noel." What this custom demonstrated was not only the fluidity of the lines separating civic and religious authority but the different ways those authorities conceived of justice.

For the church, public confession and procession could suffice for a murderer's absolution.

Yet as we have seen, Eudes was a tough enforcer of the law. He used a variety of legal procedures, from purgation to inquests and trials, and imposed a wide range of penances, including stiff fines, imprisonment of both laypeople and clerics, the suspension and deprivation of clerical benefices, and penitential processions and pilgrimages.[69] Eudes did not hesitate to turn a relapsed Jew or a heretic over to the *bailli* to be burned to death. A criminal facing trial in thirteenth-century Rouen likely would have been terrified by the prospect of coming before the Franciscan archbishop.

Consider what happened to Thomas the Miller of Dieppe. Thomas was accused in connection with the death of Gilbert de Sauqueville. A witness had testified that Thomas was directly responsible for Gilbert's death, and a long period of adjudication had ensued involving Thomas and the victim's brother, Guillaume de Sauqueville, in countercharges. Both parties finally agreed to submit to arbitration and chose Archbishop Eudes Rigaud. After conducting an investigation into the case, Eudes summoned the disputants to the upper hall of his manor house at Aliermont and delivered his decision:

> To satisfy the accusers and to appease their hearts, the aforementioned Thomas shall, on a solemn occasion and in the house of William of Sauqueville in Dieppe, if he permits it, or otherwise in the church of St. James in that town, present sixty worthy men—twenty priests, twenty knights, and twenty in holy orders, to swear with him that he did not, out of malice or intrigue or hatred for the dead man, do that which led to his death, and that what had happened was not and had never been any burden on his conscience; and we personally are of the opinion that they can fittingly and properly take this oath.[70]

The aim of having sixty worthy men swear to Thomas's innocence was the satisfaction of the victim's brother.

But the archbishop's belief in Thomas's innocence did not mean that he was prepared to absolve the miller without restitution. Indeed, Eudes ordered Thomas to conduct pilgrimages to the shrines of Santiago de Compostella in Spain and Saint-Gilles du Gard in Provence. In addition, Thomas was forced to pay for two thousand masses to be said for the soul of the deceased and for four foot soldiers to go on crusade with the next company, both of which represented considerable expenses.[71] Even if Thomas was not guilty of murder, his actions had created a scandal in the town of Dieppe. It was to appease Thomas's accusers and restore social order that Eudes imposed such a heavy penance. The administration of justice was as much about eradicating scandal and restoring order as it was about judging the truth in human actions.

But Eudes was also intent on getting to the truth, and careful investigation sometimes revealed that a person charged with a crime was not the one who was guilty. On May 12, 1256, Eudes summoned Pierre de Gamaches, a knight who was under suspicion for beating one of the archbishop's messengers.[72] Eudes had Pierre swear an oath to abide by his decision up to the amount of one hundred *livres*. But three months later, when Eudes questioned Pierre's brother, Matthieu, and stepson, Renaud, he discovered that Pierre was in fact innocent. Matthieu and Renaud confessed to striking Eudes's messenger

> with two rods on the head, shoulders, and arms, and throwing him to the ground. Asked whether they knew he was a messenger of the archbishop of Rouen, they said that they neither knew it nor believed it, but that they had harassed him because a woman had told them that he was a messenger bringing a citation against Pierre. Asked whether they had acted at the command or desire of the said knight, they said, "No"; indeed, they believed that they had displeased him, since he had run after them, and not being able to catch up with them, he cried when they were beating the messenger: "You are doing me an injury."[73]

Pierre's name was immediately cleared, and Matthieu and Renaud were ordered to make penitential processions on three Sundays in bare feet, clad only in shirts and trunk hoses. Failure to make the processions would result in a fine of 20 l.

The archbishop's evenhandedness may explain why Eudes was frequently asked to serve as an arbiter in disputes. In 1256, he served as an arbiter in resolving major conflicts between seculars and Dominicans at the University of Paris, disagreements that had been exacerbated by Guillaume de Saint-Amour.[74] In the same year, he was appointed papal judge delegate to investigate a bitter dispute over the rights to the relics of Saint Éloi (Eligius), the seventh-century bishop of Noyon, a conflict that pitted the bishop and chapter of Noyon against the abbey of Saint-Éloi and had been going on for twenty-four years.[75] A three-judge commission—the abbot of Saint-Denis, the chancellor of Paris, and the archdeacon of Beauvais—had been appointed by the pope in 1252 to settle the dispute, but the trial had subsequently been invalidated. A new three-judge commission was appointed, but this one also ended in failure, in part because the judges were so busy with other matters that they appointed subdelegates to do most of the work, and these subdelegates then appointed decretists, assessors, and other experts. Finally, in 1256, the pope appointed Eudes Rigaud as sole judge to settle the matter. Both the cathedral chapter of Noyon and the abbey approved of Eudes's selection. For his part, the archbishop was adamant that no subdelegates be appointed. From June 1256 until August 1258, Eudes visited Noyon seven times, spending a total of twenty-one days interrogating sixty witnesses and recording their testimony. The archbishop studied chronicles and liturgical books that dealt with the saint and the miracles associated with him. He pored over other written documents found in the reliquary. He closely examined the bones: two bones from the tibia, ribs, an arm bone, portions of a head, and some dust. Despite the fact that five years earlier the bishop of Soissons had organized a ritual opening of the cathedral reliquary, in August 1258 Eudes did the same, and this time King Louis IX attended the ceremony. After a lengthy investigation, the case ended in a compromise. Although the dean and chapter were ordered to pay all the monastery's legal expenses, Eudes ordered both parties to honor the relics they already possessed as authentic and not attempt to disturb those held by the other side for a period of ten years.[76]

While visiting the cathedral of Chartres in 1260, Eudes acted as a mediator in a disputed episcopal election.[77] By the time the archbishop left Chartres a few days later, some canons who had previously opposed the candidacy of Pierre de Mincy had agreed to join the majority in unanimously electing him. Harmony had once again been achieved. In 1262, the pope appointed Eudes judge in a long-standing struggle between the bishops of Brittany and the Breton count Jean Leroux.[78] That same year, Eudes was appointed mediator in a dispute between the king and the archbishop of Reims involving custody of the abbey of Saint-Remi in Reims.[79]

Given his own high standards of moral conduct as a friar, it is perhaps not surprising that Eudes Rigaud was a strict judge of human behavior. Yet the archbishop also seems to have enjoyed a reputation for being fair and judicious and was often called on to serve as a mediator in thorny disputes. In these situations, he showed himself to be skilled at resolving the most difficult conflicts and restoring peace. As will be discussed later, it was this trait, combined with his reputation for piety, that rendered Eudes and his counsel so valuable to the king of France.

7

A Franciscan Money Manager

The Archbishop's Two Bodies?

Although Franciscans first began holding episcopal offices only a short time after the death of Saint Francis in 1226, there was still something startling in the mid-thirteenth century about the notion of a friar minor serving as a bishop or archbishop.[1] How could a minor remain true to his religious order while discharging the functions of a *maior* in the secular church? The bishop or archbishop was charged with overseeing diocesan temporalities, which meant buying, selling, and leasing church property and collecting quitrents and other rents, tithes, visitation procurations, and seigneurial fees, including the fees due from litigation in ecclesiastical courts. In addition to his own direct involvement with finances, the archbishop was responsible for settling legal disputes that came before his court, many of which involved money. Handling money was an inescapable part of the archbishop's office.

Yet poverty was *the* distinctive mark of the Order of Friars Minor. The Franciscan rule seemed to be quite clear in prohibiting brothers from handling money or involving themselves in financial transactions. Chapter 7 of the first Rule of Saint Francis of 1221 (*regula non bullata*) appeared to ban the friars from assuming any responsibility that required them to administer money: "All the brothers, in whatever place they stay with others for serving or working, are not to be chief stewards, or cellarers; nor should they be in charge of the house in which they serve . . . but they should be little ones and subject to all who are in the same house."[2] It was not just the personal use of money that was prohibited but the handling of money in the interest of others. Chapter 8 of the rule stated:

No brother, no matter where he is or where he may go, should in any way accept, or cause to be accepted, money or coins, neither for clothes, for books, nor as wages for any kind of work, under any circumstances whatever, unless obviously necessary for sick brothers; for we should not grant nor accord greater usefulness to money or coins than we do to stones. And in no way are brothers to receive or cause to be received, or seek or cause to be sought, money for almshouses, nor coins for any house or place; and they should not go with any person who seeks money for the benefit of such places.[3]

Despite the rule's injunction, Franciscans involved themselves with money in a variety of capacities. Indeed, in 1266, the city of Perugia, which for some time had been employing Franciscans in its municipal government, turned to a Franciscan for expert advice on financial affairs![4] That some of the most talented economic theorists of the late thirteenth and early fourteenth centuries were Franciscans has led some scholars to question whether Franciscans were exceptional in their business acumen.[5]

Opposition to Franciscans serving in the episcopate predated the emergence of the Spirituals. In his *Second Life of Saint Francis*, written in 1247 (right around the time Eudes Rigaud was elected archbishop), Thomas of Celano suggested that some Franciscans were abandoning their status as *minores* by serving as court chaplains and bishops. According to Thomas, Cardinal Hugolino (the cardinal protector of the Franciscan order and later Pope Gregory IX) had once suggested to Saint Francis and Saint Dominic that friars be appointed bishops since the friars were considered outstanding in their learning, their conduct, and their poverty. Yet both Dominic and Francis flatly rejected the idea. Francis reportedly replied to the cardinal:

Lord, my brothers are called *minors* so that they will not presume to become greater. Their vocation teaches them to remain in a lowly station and to follow the footsteps of the humble Christ, so that in the end they may be exalted above the rest in the sight of the saints. If you want them to bear fruit for the church of God, hold them and preserve them in the station to which they have been called, and bring them back to a lowly station, even if they are unwilling. I pray you, therefore, Father, that you by no means permit them to rise to any prelacy, lest they become prouder rather than poorer and grow arrogant toward the rest.[6]

Even if this scene was largely constructed by Thomas, it reveals early ambivalence and even opposition from within the Franciscan order to friars serving in the episcopate.

The Franciscan chronicler Salimbene de Adam recounted the story of Rainaldo of Arezzo, who, after being elected bishop of Rieti, failed to persuade Pope Innocent IV to permit him to renounce his title.[7] But in addition to his own discomfort with the office, Rainaldo later faced opposition from within the order. While he was visiting the Franciscan convent in Genoa, a certain Stephen Anglicus preached a sermon in which he publicly rebuked Rainaldo for having accepted the episcopal dignity. In what must have been a humiliating experience for the Franciscan bishop, Stephen recalled how the previous night the friars had genuflected before Rainaldo while serving him dishes at the table. Episcopal office, in other words, had the potential to puff up what had once been a humble friar into a proud dignitary. As an elderly Cistercian monk who had voluntarily renounced the bishopric of Turin to retire to a monastery told Rainaldo, "I marvel that a wise man like you should have allowed himself to become so foolishly entrapped as to become a bishop, especially since you were in the noblest of orders, the Order of the Blessed Francis, the Order of the Minorites, the Order of supreme perfection. . . . It seems to me that you have erred greatly, almost to the point of apostasy, for, although you were in a state of perfection in the contemplative life, you have now regressed to the active life."[8] Despite the best efforts of Salimbene, the cardinals, and the pope to persuade Rainaldo of the value of his pastoral work in the diocese, the Franciscan resigned from his bishopric.[9]

The inherent tensions in the promotion of friars to bishoprics paralleled, albeit with some notable differences, the long history of service of various kinds of monks and members of religious orders as bishops.[10] Adam of Eynsham's *Vita* of the twelfth-century Carthusian Saint Hugh of Lincoln, for instance, explored the dilemmas it was thought a pious and humble monk would face if promoted to the episcopate.[11] The challenges thirteenth-century friar-bishops confronted in reconciling the monastic ideal with the worldly demands of a prelate's life were not new.

Yet some prominent Franciscan leaders appeared to embody the possibility of leading a humble life even while holding powerful office. The minister general, John of Parma, was later praised by the Spiritual Franciscan leader, Angelo Clareno, for wearing a tunic and habit of vile cloth (*de vili panno*), for never using a donkey, horse, or chariot for transport, and for traveling with at most two companions.[12] Indeed, the minister general appeared so humble and unworthy that he rarely received a greeting from those who passed him by. According to Angelo, John was "a man of ardent spirit and perfect observance," a true man of God.[13]

During the 1250s and 1260s, there was less internal criticism in the Franciscan order as the friars found their ministry increasingly under attack from the secular clergy and secular masters at the university.[14] In this period, Franciscans tended to unite in defending their order's usefulness to the church. The Franciscan archbishop of Canterbury, John Pecham, for instance, argued that at a time when sins seemed more and more prevalent, friars were needed in episcopal offices more than ever. In an indirect but stinging critique of secular prelates, Pecham added that Franciscan bishops would improve the church's moral reputation since they (unlike the secular clergy) had made vows of chastity and poverty.[15] While acknowledging the difficulties of balancing the religious life with one's episcopal duties, Pecham maintained that it was possible and necessary for friar-bishops such as himself to continue to strictly observe the Franciscan rule.[16] Pierre Jean Olivi echoed Pecham's sentiments. Seeking to refute those who suggested that a friar-bishop could be excused from some of his vows, Olivi argued, as Bonaventure had, that a Franciscan bishop remained bound to his vow of poverty. Olivi even went so far as to suggest that a Franciscan bishop's obligation to *usus pauper*, the restricted use of goods, was "in a way greater than before" he was bishop.[17] Olivi held out the hope that one day all bishops, both secular and religious, would live according to strict Franciscan poverty. Once this day arrived, the church would be able to spend its financial resources on the poor, and bishops would be able to devote themselves entirely to prayer, preaching, administering the sacraments, and living lives of evangelical perfection.

During the later thirteenth and fourteenth centuries, the papacy viewed the friars as some of the most competent, capable, and loyal ecclesiastical administrators.[18] Was the manner of life of friar-bishops different from that of their secular counterparts? How did friar-bishops manage the finances of their dioceses? These questions have been at least partially addressed with reference to the episcopal career of John Pecham, who was known in his day as a defender of the strictest poverty.[19] Pecham reportedly fasted for seven forty-day periods a year and continued to observe the rule's precepts on fasting as archbishop.[20] His observance of the rule was stricter than that of many friars. Before becoming archbishop, he served as the Franciscan provincial minister of England, and in his first year in office, he chose to travel to the general chapter meeting at Padua on foot rather than by donkey, despite the fact that many friars claimed that riding donkeys did not violate the statute forbidding them to ride (*equitare*).[21] In good Franciscan spirit, Pecham resisted accepting the archiepiscopal dignity.[22] When disputes arose in the archdiocese between friars and monks or friars and the secular clergy, Pecham "was not above taking unfair advantage of his position as archbishop in his effort to protect the Franciscans."[23]

Pecham's efforts to observe the Franciscan Rule as archbishop, however, were met with a number of obstacles. Above all, he was plagued by chronic indebtedness. Even before being installed in his see, Pecham was forced to borrow a staggering sum of 4,000 marks (roughly £2,666 sterling, the annual income of a wealthy bishopric) from the Riccardi banking company of Lucca to cover the cost of his consecration ceremony at Rome and his journey to Canterbury.[24] Despite his promise to repay the loan later that year, Pecham was unable to repay any of it and was forced to seek further loans. Pecham complained to the pope, "I do not have a single grain from anywhere to keep myself, my household, or my horses to the end of this year and the next."[25] In addition to feeling great shame at the prospect of having to borrow so much money, Pecham faced the terrifying threat of excommunication if he failed to repay his debt to the Lucca merchants in a timely fashion. He wrote to the bishop of Tusculum, "I would rather die than bear so great an injury."[26] Living in a state of indebtedness appears to have been particularly painful for a Franciscan, and it is clear that Pecham had regrets about ever accepting the archiepiscopal dignity: "Before I entered upon this pontifical state, I lived in peace, in the bosom of the church, and now, translated to this episcopal height, I am cast down with misery. . . . If I had thought that a curse so unexpected, so dreadful would follow the apostolic grace, all men living today would not have dragged me to undertake the burden of the church of Canterbury."[27]

How did Eudes Rigaud reconcile his episcopal duties with the vows he had taken as a Franciscan? More specifically, how did Eudes manage the temporalities of his archdiocese? As archbishop, Eudes maintained close ties to his order. The *Register* mentions forty-two visits the archbishop made to Franciscan convents (compared with nine visits to Dominican houses), principally those in Rouen, Déville, Pontoise, and Paris, where he ate with the friars, celebrated Mass, preached, and sometimes held councils and celebrated ordinations. According to the *reportatio* of a sermon Bonaventure preached (probably on Christmas Day, 1258), Eudes heard his famous former student, recently elected minister general of the Franciscan order, preach at the Franciscan convent in Rouen.[28] Interestingly, in his record of his visit to the Franciscan nuns of Longchamp in 1265, Eudes refers to the nuns as "our sisters" (*sororum nostrarum*), perhaps indicative of his special attachment to Franciscan nuns.[29] Eudes also always had several Franciscans at his side in his episcopal *familia*. On at least one occasion, he returned as archbishop to the Franciscan *studium* in Paris to preach a sermon. But in many aspects of his daily life, Eudes differed little from the typical secular bishop. He traveled by horse rather than by foot, was accompanied by an entourage of about twenty men, and wore episcopal vestments instead of a friar's habit.[30] Like Pecham, Eudes cared a great deal about the financial state of the religious houses he visited. As we have observed, he instructed the heads of houses to keep regular financial accounts and share them with their communities. During his visitation of a religious house, Eudes inquired into the community's income (including collectible debts), investments, expenditures, and debts owed. Above all, Eudes warned religious communities to be vigilant about not falling into debt. Although he generally encouraged monastic houses to invest more in liturgical objects, books, and building repairs, he also recommended ways of cutting expenditures for houses that were already financially burdened. At several poor nunneries, for example, he forbade the sisters from veiling new nuns or accepting new girls.[31]

Although it is impossible to reconstruct anything like a complete picture of Eudes's administration of his archbishopric's temporalities, a good deal of information may be gleaned about his financial dealings from single charters and an episcopal cartulary contained in the French departmental archives.[32] In the thirteenth and fourteenth centuries, the archbishopric of Rouen's average annual net revenue (subject to the tenth owed the papacy) was approximately 12,000 l.t., making it the wealthiest diocese in the French kingdom.[33] Eudes Rigaud played a decisive role in augmenting the temporalities of the Rouen church, so much so that one French historian argues that it was Eudes who was largely responsible for establishing the shape of the archbishopric's dominion, which remained fairly constant until the French Revolution.[34] The impressive assets of the Norman archbishopric under Eudes included seigneurial rights in a number of towns (including Dieppe, Louviers, and Gaillon), almost a dozen manor houses, urban properties, arable lands, mills, forests, and ponds. In addition, the archbishopric collected tithes, censuses, annual rents, revenues from dependent parishes during vacancies, and procurations from his visitations.

What is significant about Eudes Rigaud's archiepiscopate is not merely that a Franciscan archbishop managed such a heavily endowed diocese but that he worked aggressively to expand the archbishopric's assets even further, including making the significant acquisitions of Gaillon, Pinterville, Humesnil, and Alizay. In order to make these kinds of investments, Eudes needed large amounts of liquid capital. In October 1249, only a little more than a year after assuming office, Eudes borrowed 1,090 l.t. (£272 sterling) from a group of Italian merchants at the papal curia in Lyon.[35] The archbishop claimed that the loan was "both for certain affairs of his own and for the necessary services of his church which had to be accomplished and usefully set forth in the Roman court."[36] The loan's size seems to indicate that it was intended to cover more than just the expenses for the archiepiscopal *familia*'s trip to Lyon.[37] Given the fact that during the episcopal vacancy of 1247–48, the archbishopric had functioned on only the 70 l.t. from the regalia the French king had returned, it is not surprising that in 1249 the new archbishop needed to raise capital.[38] Eudes's loan did not carry any interest, but the loan contract contained a clause that was common in the Middle Ages, stipulating that if the archbishop was late in repaying the loan, he would pay damages of 10 percent on the unreturned principal.[39] In November 1250, during a month-long stay at the papal court in Lyon, Eudes again borrowed money, this time 1,300 l.t., from a certain Boniface Bonisegnoris, a merchant from Sens.[40]

The archbishop regularly employed other means of raising capital, such as leasing his seigneurial rights over certain towns. In 1251, for instance, he surrendered his lordship over the town of Dieppe for a period of two years to Robert de Torsac, a bourgeois of the town, for the considerable sum of 3,740 l.t., to be paid annually.[41] Two years later, Eudes leased Dieppe for another two years at the same price, this time to Gilbert de Torsac and Michel "the miller" (Molendinarius).[42] During this same period, Eudes leased a number of other towns over which he was lord.[43] As part of these lease contracts, Eudes usually retained certain rights, such as having at least partial jurisdiction over capital crimes and full jurisdiction over crimes involving usury. The lessees, meanwhile, promised to be good custodians of the town and not diminish the archbishop's rights in any way.

With a few exceptions, there is not much evidence that the archbishop alienated property as a means of raising short-term capital. However, there were other means of raising income. Eudes received several gifts for the Rouennais church, in the form of both land and rents, though most were fairly small in value. In 1258, for instance, he received the following rent donations from certain citizens of Déville: an annual rent of four *sous* and twelve capons from Robert le Foulon; another rent of four *sous* and twelve capons from Lucia Furguet and her son; a rent of four *sous* and one capon from Nicholas "the butcher" (Carnifex), and so on.[44] In 1268, Pierre de Montigny and his wife, Nicole, from the parish of Douvrendel, gave the archbishop three homesteads and buildings in their parish as a gift for their souls and those of their ancestors. The homesteads yielded annual rents of 100 *sous tournois*, 30 s., and 8 s. Some donations of rents were more sizable. In January 1263, Emmeline de Humesnil freely gave to the archbishop and his successors an annual rent of 55 l.t. that she possessed as part of her dowry.[45] It is not always easy to distinguish gifts from sales, since some gifts were not given freely. In 1258, for example, the same Pierre de Montigny and Nicole gave the archbishop, "for the love of God," three rural homesteads and yards at Douvrend, a tenement in Dieppe, and an annual rent worth 6 l., 18 s.t., on a marsh in Dieppe, but the archbishop was required to pay the couple a lifetime rent of 65 l.t. per year.[46] For the church, the profitability of the couple's gift depended in part on how many more years they lived.

What did the Franciscan archbishop do with the revenues he collected from donations, sales, and leases? He appears to have had sufficient liquid capital to make numerous new investments, most of them rather small, whether purchasing part of a garden at Alizay for 7 l.t. or acquiring a piece of a vineyard at Gaillon for 9 *livres parisis* or a house in the parish of Saint-Rémi in Dieppe for 14 l.t.[47] Eudes showed a particular interest in purchasing urban properties, stemming perhaps from his desire to reinforce and consolidate the archbishopric's dominance over certain towns, such as Dieppe and Louviers.[48] The charters of acquisition frequently indicate that property bought by the archbishop adjoined property already owned by the archbishopric.[49] The archbishop may have been motivated to make certain investments based on his own *familia*'s needs. Why, for instance, did he rent a pond at Martinville for 45 l.t. per year or rent a mill at Angreville for 25 l.t. per year?[50] Perhaps the fish caught in the Martinville pond were to be consumed by the archbishop and his *familia*. Eudes probably rented the pond and mill with the hope that he would earn more money from what the properties produced than he would expend on the rents. It may be significant that in 1261, the year he rented both the mill and the pond, wheat prices were at their highest point in Normandy in decades. Whereas a hectoliter of wheat had on average cost 37 *denarios tournois* in 1260, it cost 100 den.t. in 1261.[51] The archbishop may even have hoped to produce enough wheat to sell it at the current high prices.

Some of the archbishop's investments were significantly larger. In 1260, Pierre de Meulent, the king's butler (*scancius*), and his wife, Ligarde, sold Eudes everything they owned in the town of Pinterville (near Louviers), including land, rights, and revenues, for the large sum of 3,200 l.t., an amount that exceeded the gross revenues of some thirteenth-century French bishoprics.[52] Only two years later, Eudes was able to make an even larger investment, agreeing to give King Louis all his mills and ponds in Rouen, four of his mills in Déville, and 4,000 l.t. in exchange for the king's castle and town at Gaillon, the tower and town of Noes, and the towns of Douvrendel and Humesnil.[53] As the charter for this exchange makes clear, the archbishopric acquired a wide range of new rights and revenues. By becoming the lord of these towns, Eudes became the patron of the prebends at Gaillon and Douvrendel. He acquired arable lands, gardens, vineyards, meadows, woods, and warrens as well as capons, hens, geese, and sheep. Various kinds of dues, rents, and services were owed to him, including rents in wheat, oats, and wine, the tribute of the *terragium* (land rent), the service of carting and stacking, precarial (revocable) grants and the labor services of wheeled plows, the right of the *banvin* (wine sales monopoly during vintage), feudal aid, and the service of peasants and vassals. The archbishop even acquired a fishing net that the king's men had used in the waters of Sainte-Marie de Garenne. Although these newly acquired lands and rights would presumably raise significant income for the archbishopric, it is remarkable that Eudes had the capital (4,000 l.t.) to make such an enormous investment, particularly in light of a capital investment almost as large (3,200 l.t.) just two years earlier. The scale of Eudes's investments is most vividly illustrated by comparing his investments with those of his archiepiscopal predecessors and successors. Between 1197 and 1247, the archbishops of Rouen spent a total of only about 400 l.t. to purchase property and new sources of revenue (the largest purchase was 230 l.t. to acquire three mills).[54] Whereas Eudes invested about 10,000 l.t. (or 375 l.t. per year) on the purchase of properties and new revenues, his successors from 1275 to 1309 invested on average only about 87 l.t. each year.[55] Eudes outspent his successors by more than four to one.

Real estate made up the bulk (about two-thirds) of Eudes's acquisitions, but another substantial category of investments (about one-fifth) came in the form of perpetual rents.[56] In 1253, for instance, Eudes bought a perpetual annual rent of 13 muids (312 mines) of wheat from Jean de Solio of Senlis for 520 l.p. (roughly 650 l.t.).[57] Most of the rents Eudes purchased were from laymen and women, but in December 1266, he paid the abbess and nuns of Gomérifontaine 142 l. 10 s.t. for a series of rents in money and kind on lands of the Vexin, including 39 mines of wheat.[58] Most of the rents Eudes purchased were significantly smaller (almost all were less than 100 s.t.) and were rents in money rather than in kind (although some were a combination of money and kind). I found archival records of forty-four perpetual rents purchased by the archbishop between 1248 and 1275 (see appendix), surely only a fraction of the rents he purchased, but they give a sense of his investment practices. All the rents are perpetual, meaning that they are associated with a house or piece of land rather than with the person of the seller (and his or her lifetime).[59] If the rent were for some reason not paid, the archbishop could in theory seize the property on which the rent was based.

The perpetual rents the archbishop purchased seem to reflect a need on the part of some owners of urban properties for short-term liquid capital.[60] The archbishop, in contrast, seems to have had liquid capital at his disposal and was interested in making investments for long-term growth. Of course, the prospect of high inflation posed a problem for the buyer of rents, since it could quickly erode their value. The average rate of return on the archbishop's forty-four rents was 11.5 percent, only slightly higher than the average rate of return of 10 percent for the rents purchased by the cathedral chapter of Rouen for roughly the same period.[61] Real rates of return on perpetual rents can be extremely difficult to calculate since the purchase or sale of rents was often a means of concealing usury, repaying loans already contracted, or making new loans to the leasee. Charters that document rent purchases sometimes record only part of a series of transactions. Furthermore, it is often difficult to ascertain the value and characteristics of a particular rent, especially when there were multiple rents on a single piece of property. Thus it is not clear why in 1249 Eudes purchased a rent on property in Dieppe from the cleric Guillaume de Fécamp at a rate of return of 3 percent, whereas in 1253 the archbishop purchased another rent from the same cleric at a rate of return of 12.5 percent. Nor is it easy to explain Eudes's purchase of a rent of four *sous* from the Guillebelain sisters (who received the rent from Guillaume le Barrier on a *masura* along the cemetery in Saint-Rémi, Dieppe) for 20 *sous*, in other words, at the unusually high rate of return of 20 percent.[62] Was this sale of a rent to the archbishop perhaps an act of charity on the part of the two sisters? If this were the case, the charter would probably indicate that the two sisters had sold the rent as alms. No such language appears, and it is more likely that the terms of the sale point to the sisters' need for short-term capital. Eudes may even have charged the sisters a higher rate of return because they were unable to pro-

vide sufficient security.[63] One can imagine how in such cases the archbishop (and, of course, monasteries were active purchasers of rents as well)
might have been viewed as serving the function of a moneylender. Seen another way, however, the archbishop was helping those in need of immediate
cash while also securing the future financial health of the church.

Although Eudes was an active purchaser of perpetual rents, he rarely
sold such rents. In one unusual instance, Eudes purchased a house at Louviers on behalf of the archbishopric in 1261 by agreeing to pay an annual
rent of 8 l. 13 s.t.[64] The rent in this instance may have appeared less objectionable to the archbishop because it was owed to the Rouen chapter rather
than to a layperson. In general, however, Eudes appears to have desired to
be free of perpetual obligations. Indeed, in 1253 he repurchased for 350 l.t.
an annual rent of 25 l.t. that he had sold to Nicolas de Hotot, illustrating his
willingness to expend a large sum so as to release the archbishopric from a
perpetual financial burden.[65] Assuming a constant monetary value, it would
have been fourteen years before the archbishopric would have broken even
on the repurchase of this rent. Eudes clearly not only had access to significant liquid capital but also managed his see's temporalities with a view to
the long term.

Were the Franciscan archbishop's investment practices morally or even
legally problematic? Was there perhaps a moral difference, in the archbishop's eyes, between selling and buying a perpetual rent? A perpetual
rent was clearly different from an interest-bearing loan in that the buyer of
the rent could not demand reimbursement of the principal,[66] though he
could admittedly recover the paid principal by accruing income from the
annual rents. But this was no different from someone buying a piece of
land and earning income on the land so that the principal was eventually
recovered and net profits earned. The thirteenth-century canon lawyer
Hostiensis argued that a perpetual rent was licit so long as it was not a loan
at interest and did not exceed the just price. Giles of Rome also defended
perpetual rents, saying that because the rents were assigned on a piece of
land or property, money was not the means and object of the operation. Perpetual rents, he argued, were more like sales than loans.[67] When the rents
were understood in this way, Eudes's purchase of rents was no different
from his investments in landed property. Even Pierre Jean Olivi, who was
later condemned for his views on Franciscan poverty, maintained that rent
contracts were sales rather than loans and therefore not usurious. Olivi argued that the total sum from rent payments could justly exceed the purchase price for the rent since the cash from a rent's sale was more highly valued and secure at the time of the sale than the future right to collect a
periodic rent.[68]

At least one thirteenth-century theologian, however, took a different
view. Henry of Ghent condemned perpetual money rents, arguing that they

were in fact disguised loans and therefore usurious. According to Henry, the buyer of such a rent (the lender) was assured of financial gain or interest beyond the principal loaned. A money rent was illicit, he maintained, because although the rent was associated with landed property, nothing was actually sold except the obligation of discharging the pledge.[69] With rent contracts, in other words, money was an *extremum*, or end, rather than a medium of exchange.[70] There was also the issue of the "just price." Even Hostiensis and Pope Innocent IV had earlier admitted that perpetual rents were legal so long as they did not exceed the "just price."[71] Giles of Lessines maintained that a rent contract was a disguised loan and unjust in cases in which the seller of the rent was poor and in desperate need of cash but the buyer of the rent was wealthy. The rent seller's need, according to Giles, in essence coerced him into entering into an unwise contract.[72] During the fourteenth and fifteenth centuries, perpetual rents increasingly became credit operations (precisely as Henry of Ghent had feared). Instead of lending money at interest, investors purchased rents at high rates of return. In the fifteenth century, the papacy finally found it necessary to fix a "just price," or maximum rate of return, of 10 percent on rents.[73]

Were not perpetual rents antithetical to the spirit of the Franciscan order? Did Eudes Rigaud exploit the short-term financial needs of townspeople for the church's long-term gain? As Duncan Nimmo has argued, perhaps the cardinal feature of Saint Francis's poverty was the insecurity that marked his day-to-day existence.[74] Francis's message to the brethren was that they should think only about today, never giving thought to tomorrow or the next day. In this way, a friar should never seek or receive any reliable source of income. Indeed, in the bull *Exiit qui seminat*, promulgated on August 14, 1279 (a few years after Eudes's death), Pope Nicholas III decreed that it was permissible for convent procurators to sell property and receive a lump sum of money but it was not permissible for them to receive a permanent and assured flow of cash by accepting property that carried with it a rent.[75] As we have seen, not only did Eudes Rigaud buy numerous properties that carried rents (such as ponds, mills, and seigneurial rights over towns), but he also purchased rents directly, ensuring an ongoing flow of cash.

In making these investments, Eudes was acting as archbishop on behalf of the archdiocese. Admittedly, it would have been another thing had a Franciscan convent made the types of investments that Eudes did. But should a diocese suffer the loss of its ecclesiastical temporalities simply because its diocesan was a friar who took no interest in financial matters? Voluntary poverty (both individual and communal) was an ideal for the friars minor, but few popes would have looked kindly on a diocese that was financially mismanaged (or unmanaged), let alone declared itself to be voluntarily poor! Responsible bishops were charged, among other things, with overseeing the growth of ecclesiastical temporalities. Indeed, in the promises he made to the pope at his archiepiscopal consecration, Eudes vowed to work faithfully to protect the property of the Rouen church.[76] Eudes's investments were not made on behalf of the Franciscan order, nor certainly on his own behalf. As secular prelates so often pointed out in their conflicts with the friars, a distinction needed to be made between a prelate's office and his person. The reality was that substantial ecclesiastical revenue was necessary for bishops and archbishops to fulfill their charitable responsibilities toward the poor, to say nothing of their other pastoral obligations. In managing his see's temporalities, Eudes was imitating the Gospel's injunction to be "a wise and faithful steward."[77]

Although Bonaventure, who had studied with Eudes at the University of Paris, held a strict interpretation of Franciscan poverty, he was nonetheless a staunch defender of the church's right to possess and own property, and in the *Apologia pauperum*, he argued that this right derived from divine law.[78] Private property, according to Bonaventure, emerged only after the Fall and was thus a reminder of human sinfulness. Although voluntary poverty represented the most perfect, evangelical way of life, Bonaventure conceded that private property was necessary for peace and order in the earthly world.[79] Money, he maintained, was sinful only when it functioned as an end in itself. It was not sinful, however, when used to support the needy and indigent, as ecclesiastical revenues were. In the seventh chapter of his *Apologia pauperum*, Bonaventure argued that there was nothing unperfect about Christ having a purse. Rather, as Augustine had earlier pointed out, Christ's purse was the first instance of ecclesiastical finances. The purse of Christ, moreover, served as a paradigm for what ecclesiastical administrators did and had always done, namely, raise revenues for the maintenance of the church's ministers and for relieving the needs of the poor.[80]

In his visitations of monastic houses and in the legislation he passed, Eudes expressed his belief in the religious obligation of prelates to be wise and efficient stewards of the church's temporalities. Careful financial accounts needed to be kept so that revenues, expenditures, and debts could be monitored and appropriate actions taken. Eudes showed a genuine concern for the financial health of monastic houses even while admonishing any monk or nun who showed a desire for luxury. He drew an important distinction, in other words, between the ideal of voluntary poverty and real, involuntary poverty that threatened to disrupt the life of the church. It is perhaps not surprising that an archbishop who conducted such scrupulous visitations of his clergy and kept such detailed records of his activities would administer the temporalities of his see with the same zeal and thoroughness.

John Pecham appears to have displayed greater ambivalence about finances than Eudes Rigaud, perhaps in part because he was plagued by debt during so much of his episcopal career. But neither Pecham nor Eudes was so revolted by the subject of temporalities that he appointed someone else to oversee his archbishopric's finances.[81] Indeed, what is striking is the degree to which both Franciscan archbishops immersed themselves in the details of not only their own archbishopric's finances but the finances of parishes and religious houses in their respective archdioceses. Both men recognized that supporting and advancing the spiritual life of the church required financial resources. They likely would not have become archbishops if they had not acknowledged the need for financial support of church government. Their Franciscan ideals, moreover, in no way lessened the seriousness with which they took their responsibility to administer the church's finances. In the end, it may have been their Franciscan ethos and commitment to reform that propelled them to invest so aggressively in the future growth of their churches.

8

A Friar, a King, and a Kingdom

On his way to Aigues-Mortes in 1248, where he would depart on his first crusade, King Louis IX of France, dressed as a pilgrim, stopped at Sens to receive prayers from the Franciscans of France, who were holding a provincial chapter. According to the Franciscan chronicler Salimbene de Adam, who attended the chapter,

> when the king of France had left Paris and arrived at the place of the chapter, all the Friars Minor went out to meet him and receive him with honor. And Brother Rigaud, a Friar Minor, who was a professor at the University of Paris and archbishop of Rouen, went forth dressed in his pontifical robes and hurried along seeking the king and crying out, "Where is the king? Where is the king?" And I followed him, for he was somewhat distracted in making his way alone, with his mitre on his head and his pastoral staff in his hand. He had taken so long in dressing himself that all the other Brothers had already gone out and stationed themselves here and there along the street, and they were standing with expectant faces hoping to catch sight of the approaching king.[1]

The provincial chapter at Sens took place only a few months after Eudes Rigaud's consecration as archbishop. Eudes's encounter there with the French king is the earliest documented meeting between the two men. But was it their first? Could the Franciscan archbishop have been crying, "Where is the king?" in his excitement at the prospect of finally meeting the famous monarch who, in the words of Salimbene, was "an especial benefactor and defender of the Order?" Or was the archbishop eager to see the king because he was already an acquaintance?[2] It may be significant that of the dozens of Franciscans attending the chapter, those privileged to dine at the king's table were the king's three brothers (Robert, count of Artois; Charles, count of Anjou; and Alphonse, count of Poitiers); Eudes de Châteauroux, the cardinal legate; and Archbishop Eudes Rigaud.[3] Neither the minister general nor the provincial minister of the Franciscan order sat with Louis. Can this be taken as evidence, however, that the king was already well acquainted with the Franciscan archbishop? This question is important because of the later close relationship between the two men, which is the subject of this chapter.

In a later section of his chronicle, Salimbene suggested not only that Eudes Rigaud had been a friend of the king but that "the king worked hard to see that he was made archbishop of Rouen."[4] But Salimbene wrote these words at least thirty years after the fact and, as one historian points out, "Salimbene may have confused Rigaud's later intimacy with the king and the period when, as a simple friar, he became archbishop."[5] Nonetheless, it is likely that the king was involved in Eudes's selection for the vacant archiepiscopal see, particularly since in France, the king and chapter traditionally tried to find candidates they could agree on.[6] The king had strong ties to the University of Paris, especially to the Paris friars. As Andrieu-Guitrancourt observes, "the king had at least heard talk about him [Rigaud]; a master as renowned as Rigaud could not have gone unnoticed in the university."[7] In addition, there is every reason to think the king would have taken a personal interest in the selection of an archbishop for Rouen. In 1248, the status of Normandy remained unsettled. Despite the French king's offer to surrender recent conquests in the English-controlled province of Aquitaine in exchange for the English crown's renunciation of all claims to Normandy (which the English had lost in 1204), King Henry III of England refused. Just before leaving on crusade for the Holy Land, the last thing the French king would have wanted was to have an unknown archbishop elected in Rouen, perhaps one with pro-English leanings.

In addition, Louis was undoubtedly aware of the history of bad relations between French monarchs and archbishops of Rouen. During the reign of his grandfather, Philip Augustus, the Norman church had been governed by Archbishop Walter of Coutances (1184–1207), an Englishman by birth, who before being translated to Rouen had been vice-chancellor of England, archdeacon of Oxford, and bishop of Lincoln, and who sympathized with the English in their war with the French.[8] Then, during the 1220s, conflicts had erupted between the royal *bailli* and the servants of Archbishop Théobald of Amiens (1222–29). Matters escalated to the point that the archbishop excommunicated a number of royal officers and placed an interdict on all the king's Norman possessions.[9] When the next archbishop, Maurice (1231–35), failed to get royal approval for an abbess he had appointed, he excommunicated all the nuns who sided with the king. The

king responded by seizing various archiepiscopal properties, and the archbishop placed the entire diocese of Rouen under interdict.[10] In Archbishop
Eudes Clément, the French crown finally had an ally in the Rouen church.
Eudes Clément came from a family of royal *familiares*, and before his episcopal election he had served as a royal clerk, abbot of the royal abbey of
Saint-Denis, dean of the royal foundation of Saint-Martin of Tours, archdeacon of Paris, and even an instructor to Louis IX.[11] As luck would have it,
however, the archbishop died only one year after being installed in Rouen.
Like Eudes Clément, Eudes Rigaud could not have been unknown to the
French king. The Franciscan had spent many years in Paris, making it likely
that he felt some degree of loyalty to the French crown. In addition, he was
a Franciscan, and the king had close ties to the Franciscans in Paris.[12] Finally, Eudes held a reputation for being, in Salimbene's words, "one of the
finest scholars in the world . . . exceedingly adept in disputation and a very
pleasing preacher . . . a holy man, totally devoted to God."[13] Even if the
French king had never met the Franciscan, it is likely that he would have
supported his archiepiscopal candidacy, viewing him as a potentially positive force in the continuing effort to reintegrate the province of Normandy
into the French kingdom.[14]

The *Chronicle of the Twenty-Four Generals of the Friars Minor* reported that
Eudes "was dragged and forced to the archbishopric of Rouen."[15] This may
reflect nothing more than a trope in which a humble Franciscan is reluctant to accept high office. But it is possible that Eudes really did resist accepting the archiepiscopal appointment. There must have still been something startling in 1248 about the notion of a friar minor accepting the
dignity of an archbishopric. By this time, only a few Franciscans had entered the episcopal ranks, and Eudes would have faced opposition from
some fellow friars who worried about how a Franciscan archbishop would
reflect on their order.[16] As with the secular clergy's jealous reaction to the
mendicants' success at the university, there was also the possibility of further
backlash against the mendicants if they began obtaining high ecclesiastical
positions.

The deep devotion of the king to the mendicant orders may help explain
the strong bond he felt with the only Franciscan bishop or archbishop in his
kingdom. Louis trusted and admired those belonging to the mendicant orders. He frequently used the friars in his own government, including appointing them his *enquêteurs* (inspectors) to help rid his government of corruption. The king's devotion to the friars is evident in his patronage of their
convents (including the Dominican and Franciscan convents in Rouen as
well as the convent of the Dominican nuns of Rouen), his frequent visits to
their convents, his enthusiasm for hearing them preach (both Eudes and
Bonaventure frequently preached sermons before the king), and the large
numbers of friars who were part of his retinue on his second crusade.[17] The

king did not merely respect the mendicants from afar but, as Lester K. Little puts it, "associated himself in his religious practices with the new apostolic Christians," whether by rising in the middle of the night to recite matins or by demonstrating Christ-like (and St. Francis–like) humility in washing the feet of friars and the poor.[18] Although Louis IX never joined the lay order of Franciscans, perhaps because he thought doing so would alienate the other orders, it was widely rumored that he was a member of the Third Order, so much so that a painting by Giotto in 1330 depicted the king wearing the Franciscan habit.[19] Perhaps the king's desire to emulate aspects of a friar's life while carrying out his royal duties made him feel a special bond with the Franciscan prelate from Rouen.

Although it is not known how well acquainted the king and Eudes were when Louis left on crusade in 1248, after the king's return to France in 1254 the two men began spending significant amounts of time together. Indeed, Little suggests that Eudes Rigaud was "most likely the closest personal companion Louis ever had."[20] The archbishop made frequent trips to the royal palaces in Saint-Germain-en-Laye, Vernon, Pontoise, Pont-de-l'Arche, Poissy, Fontainebleau, Gisors, Château Gaillard, and Paris. Eudes was called on to officiate at marriage ceremonies involving the royal family. In 1255, for instance, he officiated at the marriage of the king's daughter, Isabelle, to Thibaud of Champagne, the king of Navarre.[21] In 1262, he traveled all the way to Clermont, in the south of France, to officiate at the marriage of the king's eldest son (and the future king), Philip, to Isabelle, daughter of the king of Aragon.[22] Whenever there was a major event in the life of the royal family, Eudes Rigaud seems to have been present. When Blanche of Castille, the king's mother (and regent), died while her son was still in the Holy Land, Eudes attended the funeral, which took place at the Cistercian nunnery of Maubisson, in the diocese of Rouen.[23] On November 8, 1258, Eudes celebrated Mass at Saint-Denis to mark the anniversary of the death of Louis VIII.[24] On August 9, 1260, he attended the baptism of Agnès, daughter of Queen Margaret.[25]

Whenever the king became seriously ill, he called the Norman archbishop to his bedside. On April 20, 1259, for instance, Eudes received a letter from the king "asking us to hasten to him at Fontainebleau without delay as soon as we should see his letter, for he was seriously ill. Ignoring the severity of our own infirmity, we made haste and spent that night at Genainville."[26] Eudes then received word that the king had greatly improved and there was no need to proceed with the trip. Two days later, however, another missive came from the king, "stating that he was ill again, and that he was very much afraid that he was about to die. Having read this, we immediately took our way to him, though not without great travail, hastening along with the aid of horses and a wagon."[27] Convinced that he was lying on his deathbed, the king urgently reached out to the Franciscan prelate, who was only too willing to put aside his own crippling rheumatism to rush to be with Louis. In November 1260, Eudes again received word that the king was ailing and wished to see him. Leaving a synod that was about to begin, the archbishop traveled to the king as quickly as he could, arriving before his equipment and most of his *familia*.[28]

On January 15, 1260, the archbishop learned that sixteen-year-old Prince Louis, the king's beloved eldest son, had died. Eudes immediately departed for Pont-de-l'Arche, where he knew the king would need him. Along the way, he received the following letter from the king:

> Louis, by God's grace king of the Franks, to his beloved and faithful Eudes, archbishop of Rouen, greeting and affection. It has pleased God, Whose Name be blessed above all, that our beloved first-born son, Louis, should depart from this life. Not only bodily affection and the bonds of nature had attached him to our heart by a certain tie of spiritual affection, but also the very nature of his worthy talents and innocence of life had rendered him most dear and lovable to us. Although we have the firmest hope in God for his eternal salvation, not only because of his conduct which was commended by all, but also because of the laudable and faithful end which he had, we earnestly ask and request you in particular to pray to the All-Highest for his soul, and to arrange that, in all the religious and conventual houses of your Province a spiritual offering of Masses and prayers shall be offered for him, for the sake of Divine Mercy and for the love of us. Given at Paris, the Monday after Epiphany.[29]

Eudes desperately wanted to reach Pont-de-l'Arche so he could help comfort the king, but he was once again afflicted by his "old rheumatism" and forced to stop at Beauvais. One can only imagine the archbishop's frustration during the seven days he spent convalescing in Beauvais. On January 26, he finally reached the grief-stricken king.

A popular story from the Minstrel of Reims, written around 1260, describes how Eudes consoled the king after the death of Prince Louis.[30] Although the truth of the story is uncertain, it shows that the affection and intimacy between Louis IX and Eudes Rigaud were well known. According to the story, the Franciscan archbishop tried to comfort the king by citing some words of Scripture, particularly the example of Job. Eudes also told the king a story, or *exemplum*, about a little bird that was captured in a trap in the garden of a peasant. When the peasant informed the little bird that he was going to eat it, the bird warned the peasant, "If you eat me, you will never be satiated by me, because I am a tiny little thing. But if you are willing to let me go, I will teach you three things that you will have a real need for if you wish to put them to use." Once the peasant let the little bird go, the bird instructed him as promised: "That which you hold in your hands, do not throw at your feet; do not believe what you hear; do not stay sad about that which you cannot recover." Realizing that he had been duped, the peasant was furious and vowed that if he ever held the bird again, it would not escape. Angering the peasant even further, the bird bragged that it had a coin in its head as big as a hen's egg and worth at least one hundred pounds. The peasant was unimaginably disappointed at letting such a valuable creature go. But then the little bird began laughing at him, telling him that he had failed to follow all three pieces of advice: he had held the bird in his hands but dropped it to his feet; he had believed what the bird had told him (including the part about the coin); and he had become so sad at losing the bird that he would never be content again. The bird flew away, leaving the peasant in his sadness. Having recounted the story, the archbishop reminded the king that he could not recover his son and had to believe that he was in paradise. According to the popular account, the king then understood the purpose of the story, was comforted, and from that point on, forgot his grief.

In light of the long periods of time that he spent with the king in and around Paris, it is remarkable that Eudes was able to govern the affairs of his archdiocese as actively as he did. Some of the business taken up by the archbishop and the king, however, dealt with Normandy, and it was not uncommon for the king to visit the province. Both financially and politically, Normandy represented one of the French kingdom's most valuable assets, and as the largest single landholder in the baillage of Rouen, the king had good reason to involve himself in Norman affairs. The king and the Franciscan archbishop made several significant financial transactions. In 1262, for instance, the king gave the archbishop his castle at Gaillon in exchange for 4,000 l.t. and several milling houses and fishponds in Rouen and Déville.[31]

Many of the financial transactions between the king and the archbishop reflected the king's religious concerns. In thirteenth-century France, moreover, royal economic and religious interests were often intertwined. In 1255, for instance, the king formally ceded to the archbishop the archdeaconry of Pontoise, which had been a dependent of the French crown. Thereafter, the archbishop (rather than the king) appointed an archdeacon to reside "within the walls" of the archdeaconry and supervise both religious life and the administration of justice.[32] The king's decision to cede control over the archdeaconry probably stemmed from his belief that the souls of Pontoise would be better served by the archbishop than by the crown. (It is also possible that Eudes had gently prodded the king to make this donation.) With the addition of Pontoise, the Norman archbishop greatly enlarged the size and limits of his diocese, which now extended to within twenty kilometers of Paris.[33]

Both the king and the archbishop had a profound interest in supporting mendicant convents and hospitals. In 1256, for instance, at the king's urging, Eudes enlarged the buildings and rents of the struggling hospital in Vernon, in the diocese of Evreux. This improvement was achieved by the transfer of all rents and immovable goods from another hospital that was no longer usable to the hospital in Vernon. To recompense the Rouen chapter for its generosity in this concession, the king agreed to give an annual rent of 50 l.p. (the same amount that had been transferred to Vernon) to the hospital of Les Andelys.[34] In 1261, the archbishop gave the king his manor house at Saint-Matthieu, along with its meadow, garden, and other dependencies, in exchange for being relieved of several annual rents he owed.[35] The king wanted the Saint-Matthieu property so he could establish a convent for religious women, called Emmurées, under the custody of the Order of Preachers.[36] Behind these property transactions between the archbishop and the king was the common goal of supporting fraternal and charitable institutions.

The king's involvement in the Norman church went beyond his financial contributions, however. As the patron of dozens of parish churches, chapels, monastic houses, colleges, and hospitals, Louis selected many of the curates who administered the sacraments and oversaw the life of the Norman church.[37] After the death of an abbot in an abbey under royal patronage, a new abbot could not be elected until the king had given his authorization.[38] Following the election, the new abbot could not be installed until the king had confirmed the election.[39] Finally, there were the abbey's temporals, which the king collected during an abbatial or episcopal vacancy. After the election of an abbot or bishop, the archbishop formally requested that the king release the temporal regalia that he had collected during the vacancy.[40]

Unlike many lay patrons, whose main interest lay in the financial gains received during vacancies, King Louis was genuinely concerned about the spiritual life of his dependent religious institutions. On learning, for example, that several of the canons of Sainte-Marie-la-Ronde-de-Rouen, a college under his patronage, were receiving "fat prebends" (stipends) while not in residence, the king agreed that Eudes should draft a series of reform statutes requiring canons to take up personal residence or forfeit their prebends. In addition, six of the prebends considered inflated were divided into nine smaller prebends with additional funds even left over for the other canons in residence.[41] It is likely that the king learned from Eudes of the problems at the college of Sainte-Marie; the king and archbishop were together in March 1256, around the time Eudes drafted the reform statutes. In 1266, the archbishop approached the king about a problem at the college of Saint-Mellon-de-Pontoise, which, like Sainte-Marie-la-Ronde, was under royal patronage. Saint-Mellon did not have a prebendary to supervise the care of souls in the college. The king agreed that the office of treasurer should be converted into a deanship.[42] In a separate case, the king learned that some poor Norman clergy and religious had been excommunicated for their failure to pay royal levies. The king immediately authorized the archbishop to absolve them and exempt them from the payments. Louis's involvement in the Norman church, unlike that of a typical lay nobleman, often meant deferring to the church in the person of Eudes Rigaud.

There were, of course, occasional moments of tension between the archbishop and the crown. For example, Eudes refused to admit the priest Jean de Bray to the church at Baudemont because he was found to be deficient in letters. That Jean had been presented by the king does not appear to have swayed the archbishop.[43] Disputes between the king and the archbishop sometimes arose over patronage. One such case had to be adjudicated by the archbishop of Sens and several knights and *baillis*.[44] Overall, however, relations between the crown and the Norman church were remarkably smooth during Eudes's archiepiscopate. Louis projected the image of an *enquêteur*-like king, traveling around his kingdom and correcting problems. The king's chief concern, according to his friend and biographer, Jean de Joinville, was "to find out how the common people were governed, and their rights and interests protected."[45] His travels provided the king with first-hand information on local conditions, just as the archbishop's visitations did. Both Louis and Eudes recognized that information was an essential ingredient for effective government. Moral concerns were at the center of both men's vision of good government. Louis's great ordinance of December 1254, promulgated shortly after his return from crusade, was aimed at cleaning up government corruption. It included a ban on royal officers playing games of chance, drinking in taverns, and frequenting prostitutes— some of the same problems Eudes tried to curb among his clergy. Both the king and the archbishop showed a concern for the weakest members of society, above all, the sick and the poor. The king and the Norman archbishop also shared a talent for conciliation and peacemaking.

Although Eudes frequently served as an arbiter in various kinds of disputes, his major achievement as a peacemaker came when he negotiated the Treaty of 1259, which ended more than fifty years of intermittent war between England and France.[46] Holding lands from both the French and English crowns, Eudes paid homage to both monarchs.[47] The archbishop's familiarity with the English king may have been one of the reasons King Louis chose him as the principal French minister to negotiate with the English. It may also have seemed only appropriate that the archbishop of Rouen, the primate of Normandy, be the one to negotiate a treaty to settle the question of the status of Normandy.

Louis IX, fearful that while he was away on crusade Henry III would try to reconquer French lands, had made peace overtures to the English monarch before departing in 1248. The French king's desire to make peace with England intensified after Henry III's alliance with Alphonse X of Castille in 1254. As part of that alliance, Alphonse had renounced all claims to Gascony, thereby strengthening English hands. Continuing civil war in Flanders also raised fears in France about the dangers of a Franco-German war. In addition to these political considerations, there was familial pressure for the French and English kings to make peace, since their wives were sisters.

Henry III had perhaps even greater reason to make peace with the French. A rebellion was occurring in English-controlled Gascony, and the king faced an even more threatening insurrection from his barons at home. Meanwhile, after 1255, the English king was desperate for the money and men that the pope had said would be necessary to install Henry's second son, Edmund, on the Sicilian throne. Henry was broke, his barons refused to help without substantial governmental reforms, and because of the Sicilian affair, the pope was ordering him to make peace with France. If all this was not enough, famine and plague struck the English kingdom in 1258.[48]

The first sign of an improvement in relations between the two monarchs occurred in December 1254, when Henry III, who was in Bordeaux trying to suppress a revolt by Gascon barons, asked Louis for permission to pass through the French kingdom on his way back to England. Louis not only granted his brother-in-law's request but invited him to Paris, where the two monarchs spent several days together, along with the four sisters: Marguerite, queen of France; Eleanor, queen of England; Sanchie, wife of Richard of Cornwall (Henry III's brother); and Béatrice, wife of Charles of Anjou (Louis's brother).[49] Eudes was also present at this meeting. In 1257, Louis's daughter, Marguerite, married Henry's heir, the Duke of Brabant. In that same year, the pope ordered the English king to open negotiations for a treaty with France. Representing the English king in Paris were Peter of Savoy and Simon of Montfort, the earl of Leicester and a close friend of Eudes Rigaud.[50] Eudes negotiated on behalf of Louis IX, although it is unclear where the archbishop stood on the question of how much France would be willing to concede. In his biography of Saint Louis, Joinville makes clear that there was a good deal of criticism of the French king from those who felt he made too many concessions to the English.[51] Representing the French position, it is possible that Eudes was sympathetic to the king's desire to make concessions in exchange for England's renunciation of its former continental territories. Indeed, Eudes may have helped Louis persuade members of the French Parlement to go along with the conditions for a treaty with England. In negotiating with the English, it no doubt helped that Eudes was already well acquainted with Henry III and a friend of two of the principal English ambassadors, Simon of Montfort and the Franciscan Adam Marsh.

An agreement on the terms of the peace treaty was reached in Paris on May 28, 1258. The treaty was sealed by Eudes Rigaud and Archbishop Raoul of Tarentaise. As part of the agreement, Henry surrendered all claims to Normandy, Maine, Anjou, and Poitou. Louis acknowledged Henry's lordship over Gascony, and Henry agreed to become the French king's vassal and one of the peers of France. Louis recognized Henry's claims to an area west of the Auvergne and also agreed to pay the English monarch an annual rent equal to the revenue from the province of Agenais and Quercy. Finally, Louis agreed to pay Henry the cost of maintaining five hundred knights for two years for the Sicilian enterprise.[52] On December 4, 1258, Henry came to the royal gardens in Paris and formally paid homage to the French king. Reflecting the central role he played in negotiating the treaty, Eudes was given the honor of delivering a solemn reading of the treaty before the two kings and a great multitude of prelates and barons.[53]

A short time after the treaty had been sealed, however, disputes arose over its precise stipulations. The arguments appear to have centered on the exact sum Louis owed for the maintenance of five hundred knights, as well as the annual rent owed for the land of the Agenais.[54] In July 1260, Louis sent two emissaries to England—Eudes Rigaud and the Norman lord Jean de Harcourt—to resolve these disputes.[55] While in England, the two men also became involved in an effort to help defend their friend Simon of Montfort, who, at the English king's instigation, was facing a trial in Parliament on charges of rebellion and treason. In the end, a pre-trial investigation cleared Simon of all charges, and Eudes returned to Normandy with Simon's son, Amauri of Montfort, whom he installed with a prebend in the Rouen cathedral.[56]

During the 1260s, Eudes became even more closely tied to the French king by helping plan and preach a new crusade. Although the king did not actually take the cross until March 25, 1267, thereby formally committing himself to go on another crusade, the papacy had been encouraging a new crusade since 1260, when the Mongols appeared to threaten the Latin establishments in the Holy Land.[57] Eudes had done his own part in supporting the crusading cause. As early as September 1260, the archbishop discussed "the matter of the crusaders" with his suffragans.[58] The last statute promulgated at the Norman provincial council in January 1261 ordered all churches to pray once a day in their masses for the Holy Land.[59] Eudes and his suffragans knew that their brethren in the Holy Land and in Constantinople were in grave danger; indeed, only a few months later, the Latin kingdom in Constantinople would fall to the Greeks. In April, Eudes convened a provincial council dedicated to "revealing how the most wicked Tartars had destroyed, and were, from day to day, striving to destroy the Holy Land, and how the pope and king of France willed and ordered that the Holy Land be supported by manpower and by works of mercy."[60] The archbishop opened the council with a sermon on the crisis in the Holy Land. Two letters from the pope were then read, one dealing with "the destruction of the Holy Land" and another that addressed the need to preach a crusade. Eudes had copies of the second papal letter made for each of his suffragans. During this period, Eudes was in direct communication with the Roman curia (the papal see was vacant, and the college of cardinals was overseeing the curia) about the situation in the Near East. The archbishop's *Register* indicates that two members of the archiepiscopal *familia* had gone to the Roman curia "concerning the business of the Tartars."[61]

Rome was trying to arouse interest in the East among the French clergy generally. In 1262, the bishop of Agen, acting as papal legate, presided over a council in Paris that was attended by prelates and church representatives from all over France. Its purpose was to lobby the French clergy to support a new subsidy, a hundredth, for the recovery of Constantinople and the defense of Acre.[62] Pope Urban IV had assigned Eudes Rigaud and Eudes de Lorris, a canon of Beauvais and the future bishop of Bayeux, the task of collecting the new tax. But the prelates attending the council were not receptive to the pleas for new financial assistance, pointing out that they were already so financially burdened by the various levies they had been paying that in many cases they were still in debt. A recent bad harvest followed by high food prices had compounded their financial problems. Furthermore, the prelates noted, no crusade had yet been called. No prince had taken the cross or begun mobilizing for a "general passage overseas." Finally, truces between Saracens and Christians had long been in place, thus rendering a crusade tax unnecessary.

It is not surprising that the Roman curia called on Eudes to help raise a subsidy for the Roman church, since the mendicants frequently served as papal tax collectors during the 1240s.[63] They were known to be effective at certifying receipts, organizing payments, and resolving payment disputes, precisely the kinds of administrative skills that Eudes performed so well. Beginning in the 1250s, the number of friars serving as tax collectors declined, as friars began seeking exemption from this task on the grounds that it conflicted with their commitment to poverty. As the friars had also discovered, serving as tax collector was a thankless job, earning the scorn of the solicited clergy. But in Eudes Rigaud, the Roman curia had found someone with strong ties to the French crown, excellent relations with the French clergy, and a reputation for piety. If anyone could make a case for the importance of the new crusade tax, it was the Franciscan archbishop. Yet as it turned out, even his persuasive powers were not enough to sway the French prelates.[64]

Eudes's interest in crusading issues did not end with his failure in 1262 to persuade the French clergy to accept a new papal levy. On the Sunday before Christmas, 1264, the archbishop of Tyre preached the crusade in the vestibule of the cathedral of Rouen.[65] With the papacy concentrating most of its resources on Sicily and the attempt to overthrow the Hohenstaufens, however, it was virtually impossible to focus on the situation in the Levant. On April 5, 1266, the papal legate convened a Norman provincial council at Vernon to discuss the issue of Sicily.[66] Even after Charles of Anjou's installation as king of Sicily in 1266, the opponents of the papacy and the Angevins remained a threat. And before Charles had had a chance to solidify his power in Sicily, he was setting his sights on reconquering the Byzantine lands.[67] Thus, as Eudes began meeting more regularly with the king and the papal legate, the Franciscan Simon de Brie (a former member of Eudes's *familia* who would later become Pope Martin IV), the Levant was hardly the sole subject of concern.[68]

Although Pope Clement IV had announced plans in the summer of 1266 for a relatively small passage to the Holy Land, what set the general passage of the eighth crusade into motion was King Louis's taking of the cross before a group of barons and prelates gathered in the Sainte Chapelle for the feast of the Annunciation in 1267.[69] In taking the cross, the king was joined by his three sons, Philip, Jean, and Pierre, and a number of nobles, including the countess of Flanders.[70] With this action, King Louis decisively enlarged the scale of the passage.[71] Just two months later, at a ceremony in Paris celebrating the knighting of two of the king's sons, Philip and Robert, Eudes took the cross, along with the king of Navarre, the count of Dreux, and the lord of Harcourt. Before the king of France, the legate, and numerous barons, prelates, and laypeople, Eudes preached a sermon.[72]

On October 17, 1267, the legate convened a council at Rouen to discuss the collection of a papal tithe.[73] The official announcement that a tenth would be collected for the Holy Land came several months later and was made by Eudes on behalf of the papal legate.[74] Although the Norman archbishop continued performing his regular administrative duties (conducting visitations, attending meetings of the Exchequer, holding various church councils), he was increasingly occupied with preparation for the crusade. He attended church councils in other provinces and met with other archbishops and bishops, presumably trying to round up support for the new crusade and the accompanying tithe.[75] He also preached the crusade to the people of his own archdiocese.[76] Shortly before departing on crusade, Eudes made one last visitation to the major religious houses in the archdiocese, where he formally asked and received permission from the clergy and people of the city of Rouen to go on crusade.

On July 2, 1270, Eudes departed from Aigues-Mortes with the king of France and about ten thousand crusaders.[77] The chronicle of Erfurt recorded that the French king, nobles, and army were accompanied by masters of theology, confessors, and many Franciscan and Dominican preachers.[78] Indeed, Franciscans were so closely identified with the eighth crusade that it has been called a Franciscan crusade.[79] Large numbers of friars were not only quick to join the French king in taking the cross but took a leading role in preaching the crusade and finding ways to arouse public support for an enterprise that was met with resistance from both the French clergy and the nobility.[80] Twenty Franciscans died during the crusade passage alone.

The army made its first landfall at Cagliari, on the island of Sardinia, and it was only then that to everyone's surprise, the French king revealed his intention to go to Tunisia, not Palestine or Egypt. Historians continue to debate the motivations behind the king's decision.[81] Louis may have planned to use Tunisia as a base, thinking that he would reach the Holy Land by land rather than sea. He may also have believed that he had a reasonably good chance of converting the emir of Tunisia to Christianity. Tunisia was ruled by the Hafsids, who were generally on friendly terms with the Christian kingdoms and paid an annual tribute to the king of Sicily (then Louis's brother, Charles of Anjou) in exchange for having access to Sicilian grain supplies. At the same time, however, the emir had supported the Hohenstaufen and continued to provide assistance to enemies of Charles, which may have played a role in Louis's decision to invade Tunisia. Arriving in Tunisia in the heat of summer, the French king ordered his army to wait for the armies of his brother Charles.[82] While the crusaders were waiting, dysentery and typhus quickly spread through the encampment. Louis's son, Jean Tristan, died, as well as the papal legate to France, Raoul de Grosparmi, and the king of Navarre. On August 25, after having been sick for three weeks, Louis IX died. It is likely that Eudes Rigaud was with the dying king, perhaps even administering the final sacraments.

Before his death, Louis had named Eudes one of the executors of his will.[83] The king had also asked his son and heir, Philip, to keep the same royal councillors. Soon after the king's death, Philip became gravely ill and, thinking that he too might die, appointed his brother, Pierre d'Alençon, regent of the kingdom until the majority of his son. Philip specifically named Eudes Rigaud to be Pierre's first councillor.[84] With the crusaders still in a heathen land and the new king on the brink of death, almost everything seemed uncertain. Eudes, who by now would have been about seventy years old, was an important symbol of continuity with the long reign of Louis IX. The Franciscan archbishop had been one of Louis's most trusted councillors, and it was only natural that the new king would turn to him at a time of transition. In the end, Philip recovered from his illness and, after signing an accord with the emir of Tunisia, began the voyage back to France. He and his armies first stopped in Sicily, where they left the flesh and entrails of King Louis with Charles of Anjou. They then continued to the Continent,

carrying the sacred bones of the king with them and stopping, perhaps at
Eudes's urging, at the Franciscan convents of Viterbo, Perugia, Assisi, and
Cremona.[85] The cortege finally arrived at Paris on May 21, 1271, and the
following day, the king's relics were buried in a funeral ceremony at Saint-
Denis, in the royal necropolis.

Eudes reentered Rouen on the Sunday of the Trinity, May 31, 1271.[86]
While he had been away, Jean de Noyentelle, archdeacon of Rouen, had
acted as his vicar. A letter from Jean to King Louis dated February 4, 1270,
for instance, shows the archdeacon acting in Eudes's place in confirming
the election of Pierre de Cahors as the new bishop of Evreux.[87] Because the
archbishop stopped keeping his *Register* in 1269, we know much less about
his activities after his return from the crusade. Chronicles and charters
from these years, however, attest to his continued activity in the administration of his diocese. On May 17, 1271, before he had even returned to
Rouen, Eudes issued a letter to King Philip, confirming the election of
Richard de Gauseville as abbot of Sainte-Catherine-du-Mont and requesting
that the king administer the regalia.[88] A chronicle from the abbey of
Trinité-du-Mont indicates that Eudes was received in the abbey's church on
May 31, 1271, the same day he returned to Rouen. In 1272, in a matter that
went before the Parlement, Eudes appealed to the king that when a case involving the patronage of a parish church or monastery was decided against
him, he be able to defend himself through an attorney. The king granted
the archbishop's request "as a special favor . . . although this is contrary to
the custom of the land" (*ex gracie speciali . . . licet hoc sit contra consuetudinem
terre*).[89] Even in the last years of his life, Eudes continued to have a special
relationship with the French crown and to fight for the rights and privileges
of his office.

In 1273, Eudes was one of three prelates commissioned by Pope Gregory
X to begin an inquiry into the canonization of Louis IX.[90] That same year,
the pope asked the Norman archbishop to help with the preparations for
the Second Council of Lyon, which was one of the most largely attended
conciliar assemblies in the Middle Ages.[91] The pope had sent a letter to
dozens of bishops, archbishops, and leaders of monastic orders all over Europe, soliciting reports from them on the issues they thought should be addressed at the council.[92] Charged by the pope with the task of analyzing
these reports was a commission made up of Pierre de Tarentaise (who
would soon become Pope Innocent V); the Dominican archbishop of Lyon,
Paul de Segni; the Franciscan minister general, Bonaventure, Eudes's now
famous former student; and Eudes himself.[93] Significantly, all four members
of the commission were mendicants.

One of the council's goals was to resolve tensions between mendicants
and seculars, and the mendicant organizers of the council spearheaded this
effort. A firm supporter of the mendicants, Pope Gregory X defended the

friars as competent preachers and confessors. Yet he also recognized that in order to pacify the secular clergy, the friars would need to lend greater public support to the ecclesiastical hierarchy and never give the impression that they wished to usurp the authority of local priests.[94] Before the council convened, the pope called on Franciscan and Dominican leaders to draft a proposal for resolving their conflicts with the seculars. The proposal was first reviewed and edited by the four principal organizers of the council, who then submitted it to the pope. By the conciliar decree *Religionum diversitatem*, which reaffirmed a canon from the Fourth Lateran Council, all religious orders founded after 1215 without the explicit approval of the Apostolic See were suppressed. Those orders founded since 1215 that had received papal approval were banned from accepting new members or building new convents. The Franciscans, Dominicans, Carmelites, and Augustinian Friars were protected from the decree. Several of the smaller orders of friars, however, such as the Sack Friars, the Pied Friars, and the Crutched Friars, were suppressed.[95] As Franciscans and Dominicans increasingly occupied bishoprics, archbishoprics, and cardinalates, the nature of the conflict between seculars and mendicants changed. In some ways, less seemed to separate the secular clergy from friars holding powerful offices. An archbishop like Eudes Rigaud was not viewed as a rival by a local parish priest in the way that an ordinary Franciscan preacher was. Unlike the average Franciscan or Dominican preacher or confessor, Eudes probably had a great deal of respect for the importance of traditional ecclesiastical hierarchies. Yet there was no escaping the fact that mendicants were now in positions of real power, and no matter how judicious and nonpartisan they tried to be, they remained committed members of their orders, unlikely to accept new limitations on their own orders' privileges.[96]

Besides defending the status of the mendicants, Gregory X had three main objectives in convening the Second Council of Lyon. He wished to defend the Holy Land, reunite the Latin and Greek churches, and reform the Latin church. Although the pope read a constitution at the first session of the council in which he called for a new crusade, he believed that a crusade would not be successful without first both unifying and purifying Christian society. In other words, the churches of the East and West would have to be united, and the Latin church would have to be purged of its interior "scandals."[97] In 1273, Gregory had sent ambassadors to the Byzantine emperor, Michael Palaeologus. Representatives of the emperor and the Greek clergy attending the council in Lyon carried with them a critical letter from the emperor, in which he recognized the pope's supremacy and promised fidelity to the Roman church. On June 19, the feasts of Saints Peter and Paul, the pope and the assembled clergy, from both East and West, celebrated the Mass, chanting the Epistle, Gospel, and Creed in both Latin and Greek. The Greeks agreed to chant the most controversial article from the Latin Credo

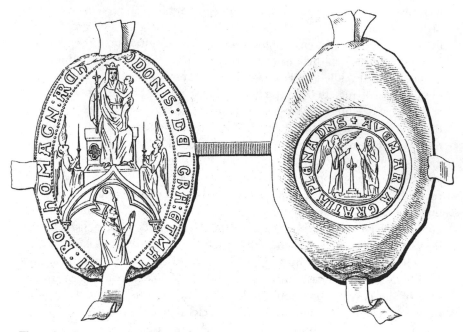

The seal and counterseal of Archbishop Eudes Rigaud

stating that the Holy Spirit proceeds from both the Father and the Son (*qui a patre filioque procedit*), even though they had long maintained that the Holy Spirit proceeded from the Father alone.[98]

The third aim of the council was to reform the church. Constitutions from the council instituted new measures to prevent clerical nonresidence, fight clerical ignorance, and discipline the religious. As much as any of the council's organizers, Eudes was well acquainted with the vices and bad habits of the clergy. He had devoted much of his life to reforming the church, whether as a religious educator in the Franciscan *studium* at Paris or as a parish policeman in Rouen. Eudes had extensive experience with correcting and disciplining the clergy and knew which mechanisms worked and which did not. Indeed, the council at Lyon encapsulated much of his career as a reformer, peacemaker, and crusader.

For the Norman archbishop, surely the most emotional moment of the council, which lasted more than two months, would have been the sudden death of his former student, Bonaventure. Like Eudes, Bonaventure had been a close spiritual adviser to King Louis IX. The king had heard both Franciscans preach dozens of sermons. Eudes and Bonaventure had maintained close ties over the years, especially after Bonaventure became minister general of the Franciscan order. Planning the Council of Lyon afforded the two men an opportunity to work together once again. Then, on July 14, just a few days before the council's final session, Bonaventure died. He was buried at the Franciscan convent in Lyon. Attending his funeral were the pope, all the cardinals, and almost all the prelates from the council, including a large number of mendicants.[99] The Dominican Pierre de Tarentaise delivered a sermon on 2 Samuel 1:26, in which David laments the death of Jonathan, saying, "I am distressed for thee, my brother Jonathan: very pleasant hast thou been unto me: thy love to me was wonderful, passing the love of women."

Just one year later, on July 2, 1276, Eudes died at Gaillon, at about seventy-five years of age. He was buried in the Chapel of the Virgin in the cathedral of Rouen.[100] To his cathedral he bequeathed a gold cross decorated with ninety-seven precious oriental stones and embedded with an alleged piece of the true cross. He also donated a massive bell, which was later called the "Rigaud."[101] In a tradition in Rouen taverns that continues today—and one that surely would have horrified the Franciscan archbishop—Rouennais joke about getting so drunk as to be able to pull the heavy Rigaud bell—"boire à tire-la-Rigaut."[102]

The spirit of the Franciscan archbishop is perhaps best captured by his archiepiscopal seal. Most thirteenth-century episcopal seals depicted the bishop either seated on his episcopal throne or standing, sometimes wearing a mitre, holding a crosier, making the gesture of benediction, or holding a book. Many seals depicted the figure of the bishop on both sides of the seal.[103] In the later thirteenth and early fourteenth centuries, episcopal counterseals tended to focus less on the bishop and more on other figures, such as patron saints. Eudes Rigaud's counterseal is an early indicator of this trend. It represents the Annunciation, showing the Virgin and an angel and, between the two figures, a vase, out of which flows a heraldic lis (lily) with the letters EC for *ecce* and the inscription *Ave Maria, gratia plena, Dominus* ("Hail Mary, full of grace, the Lord [is with thee]").[104] Although some other thirteenth-century bishops were not depicted on their counterseals, the front of Eudes's seal was highly unusual in representing the Virgin Mary, seated, crowned, holding a scepter in her right hand, and holding the infant Jesus on her knees.[105] Angels appear on both sides of her, each one holding a taper and adoring her. Below the Virgin, under a gothic arch, is the tiny figure of an archbishop kneeling, his hands joined in prayer and holding a crosier. Eudes's seal, remarkable for the mid-thirteenth century, expressed the self-effacing humility of Saint Francis and Eudes's king, Saint Louis.

Conclusion

On the feast day of Saint Catherine (November 25), sometime in the 1260s, the famous Franciscan archbishop of Rouen, Eudes Rigaud, returned to the University of Paris, where he had once been a student and a professor.[1] The chancellor and masters of the university had invited him to preach on the occasion when students who had completed the most advanced studies were formally named *baccalarii formati*.[2] In the chapel of the Hospitalers of Saint-Jacques-de-Haut-Pas, the scholars convened for the celebration of the Mass and listened to their distinguished alumnus, Eudes Rigaud, now an old man, give what was essentially a commencement address, on the theme "The Lord chose new wars" (Judges 5:8).[3]

The Franciscan archbishop began by expressing his modesty, comparing his learning to tasteless water and contrasting it with the "savory and sweet" wine-like learning of those who normally preached at the university. Why, he asked, would the brothers be interested in hearing his "old age and tastelessness" (*vestutate et insipiditate*) when they could hear another preacher's more pleasing and refreshing learning? He had "been asked and almost forced by the brothers" to preach, he told them, "so as to lessen your monotony."[4] The excellent learning of other teachers would be even more pleasing and impressive once the brothers experienced Eudes's insipid message.

But in actuality the Franciscan hoped his preaching would be anything but old and tasteless. Indeed, in a sermon meant to rouse the brothers from their spiritual slumber, Eudes called for "war." Invoking the famous phrase from Ecclesiastes, he declared, "This now is not the time for peace." The church of the faithful, he said, must be "a militant church because it is in continual battle, in continual war."[5] The wars Eudes referred to were spiritual wars, and he contrasted them with "the old wars" that God condemned as wicked: wars fought to attain honor, wars fought to acquire or recapture possessions, wars fought out of a desire for revenge (which Eudes viewed as particularly evil), and wars fought in defense of one's life or security (which he considered somewhat more reasonable).[6] Eudes linked these "old wars" with the Old Testament of Cain, Abel, and "the old man," Adam. The "new wars," in contrast, which were introduced by "the new man," Christ, had the effect of revitalizing man and provided the path to the newness and immutability of eternity.[7]

As Eudes told the university community, the world is a battlefield whether one wishes to admit it or not. By recognizing the workings of the devil, the righteous and the saints would be armed for battle. The wicked, however, would not even know that they were in the midst of a war. As a result of their ignorance, they would become the passive victims of the devil. They might naively ask why the Lord would choose wars, "since is He not of peace rather than dissension?" But the Franciscan archbishop reminded his listeners of what Christ said in Matthew 10:37–38: "I have not come to bring peace, but a sword; for I came to set a son against his father, and a daughter against her mother." According to Eudes, there were good reasons for God's choosing new wars. If there were no sinful temptations, humans would invariably become arrogant. The devil's traps, however, encouraged humans to become "humble and erudite."[8] The devil gave humans further reason to believe in God with anxious obedience and enlist in the army of Christ. In using military vocabulary and metaphors to describe the Christian spiritual struggle for redemption, Eudes followed a long Christian tradition. He may also have hoped to channel some of the contemporary crusading fervor toward internal, spiritual discipline.

In his sermon, Eudes warned his listeners against what he regarded as the most dangerous traps laid by the devil: the pleasures of the flesh and the desire for worldly riches. What was exemplary about Saint Catherine, whose feast day was being celebrated, was the way she had overcome these temptations. In the thirteenth century, when increased religious devotion was paid to the Virgin Mary and female saints, it was not surprising, even in the male-centered environment of the University of Paris, that a Franciscan preacher would invoke a female saint as the paragon of a new kind of warfare. The wars Saint Catherine fought were spiritual wars rather than physical ones. Instead of confronting and engaging the adversaries as in a military battle, she fled them, thereby guarding her virginity. "If a totally filthy man were approaching you and were wishing to fight with you, what would you have to do except flee from him, for you would not be able to fight with him without defiling your very self. It is likewise moreover from carnal temptation that it never comes without somewhat defiling a man; it is foul and it mars that which it touches."[9] The best way to resist carnal temptations, in other words, was by avoidance. Eudes's vision of spiritual warfare was thus in some ways a feminized one. Although the University of Paris was a relatively safe haven from carnal temptation, Eudes knew from his experience as archbishop that as soon as graduates left the university, they would be exposed to the real, lascivious world: "Young secular clerics, well dressed and well fed, ought to take note of this when they go to spectacles to see women, and even when they return to their homeland, since many who live chastely in the schools, let go of everything in the quickest moment there."[10]

In addition to sexual temptations, graduates of the university would be exposed to the temptations of worldly riches, which, as the archbishop reminded his listeners, the apostle Paul had called "excrement." "What is more vile than excrement," Eudes asked, "and yet daily those many miserable things are embraced with great desire" by both secular clerics "and even some religious."[11] Concentrating on two themes that reflected his values as a Franciscan, chastity and voluntary poverty, Eudes gave his listeners a sense of the spiritual challenges that awaited them outside the university walls. Fresh from his own experiences on the ecclesiastical battlefields of Normandy, Eudes was deeply aware of the problems posed by clerical indiscipline. He had seen firsthand the results of the devil's snares, and he had returned to the university with a sobering message for the newest troops. A dangerous world awaited them, and in the spirit of Saint Catherine, who faced an even more hostile world, they must hold on for dear life to the spiritual goods that by God's grace they had been given, and flee everything else. Although they were bound to face adversity in the world, they must, like the saintly Catherine, win "new wars" with patience.

In discussions among theologians of the late eleventh and twelfth centuries about the qualities of a good bishop, which often invoked the pseudo-Pauline epistles 1 Timothy and Titus, there were frequent debates over whether monks or secular clerics made better bishops. Some theologians, such as Peter Abelard, maintained that when a monk became a bishop, he lost much of his status as a holy man.[12] Peter Damian agreed, arguing that because of all the worldly preoccupations inherent in a bishop's office, it simply was not possible for a monastic bishop to remain a true monk.[13] Some monks elected to the episcopate refused to accept the office, and some who were persuaded to accept the episcopal dignity later resigned so as to be able to return to the cloister.

In the *Tractatus de moribus et officio episcoporum*, which he addressed to the archbishop of Sens, the Cistercian Bernard of Clairvaux, who himself refused several episcopal positions, maintained that there ought to be some clear distinctions between monastic and episcopal life.[14] Bernard admonished abbots who sought to become bishops or claimed the same privileges as bishops.[15] At the same time, however, he asserted that for a bishop to be a good bishop, whether secular or monastic, he must practice the fundamental monastic virtues, virtues that Bernard believed applied equally to the secular clergy: chastity, charity, and above all humility. Bernard warned prelates that their noble birth, learning, and powerful office made them particularly susceptible to the vices of pride and ambition.[16] Yet Bernard also believed that it was possible for bishops to fulfill their episcopal duties without losing their humility and charity. Being a successful administrator need not diminish a bishop's virtues, especially since it was the bishop's duty to be zealous in pursuing justice and in exercising and protecting the power of the church.[17] Bernard's view represented a departure from the traditional notion that a bishop would be known either for his spirituality or for his skills as an administrator.

Around the same time that Bernard was writing his treatise, Gratian was establishing a new canonical tradition of reconciling the monastic ideal and the episcopal function.[18] Later canonists, such as Johannes Teutonicus and Sinibaldo Fieschi (the future Innocent IV), went much further, arguing that monks could serve as bishops because the active, pastoral life of bishops represented a greater "public usefulness" (*publica utilitas*) than the contemplative life of monks. In stressing the extraordinary importance of the *cura animarum*, Innocent IV even suggested that a pope could exempt a religious bishop from his monastic vows of obedience and poverty (and in extreme cases, even continence) when the salvation of souls was at stake.[19] Thomas Aquinas made a similar kind of argument, rooted in the notion that bishops were of a higher rank (*perfectores*) than the religious (*perfecti*).[20] According to Thomas, a bishop had to be even more perfect than a monk, because in addition to being perfect himself, the bishop was expected to communicate perfection to his people: "The episcopal state presupposes perfection of life . . . but the religious state does not presuppose perfection, but is a way to perfection."[21] Whereas the Franciscan Pierre Jean Olivi suggested that as *perfectores*, all bishops, secular and religious, should ideally live according to strict Franciscan poverty, Thomas argued that the *praelati*'s higher rank meant that they were not bound to observe the obligations of the lower *fratres*.[22]

Biographies of bishops in the later twelfth century increasingly equated piety with administrative ability. As Constance Brittain Bouchard observes, "episcopal spirituality, in becoming identified with administrative ability, grew to be one of a large number of recognized ways to salvation, but a way separate from that of the religious enthusiasts."[23] This shift in how episcopal spirituality was expressed and understood is partly explained by changes taking place in the nature of the episcopate. As ecclesiastical administration grew more complex during the thirteenth century, requiring increasing technical expertise in law and finance, fewer monks were elevated to the episcopate.[24] The thirteenth century also witnessed a decline in the number of bishops who were canonized.[25] But this is not to suggest that the episcopate comprised only technocrats and bureaucrats. There continued to be all kinds of bishops, and many of them cared a great deal about the moral and spiritual health of their dioceses, to say nothing of their own spiritual health.

Shortly after the creation of the Franciscan and Dominican orders, friars began to be elected as bishops and archbishops. The friars had come to embody a new form of personal holiness, opening up the possibility that religious piety need not be expressed through withdrawal from lay society; rather, both Franciscans and Dominicans sought to express piety through a "spirituality of initiative," engaging with the world in the form of preaching and the pastoral ministry.[26] Admittedly, what the friars sought to do was not entirely new, since the canonical movement also sought to achieve a new balance between the active and contemplative life, balancing parish work with community life and individual asceticism. By the mid-thirteenth century, however, it was possible for new forms of evangelical enthusiasm—such as Franciscanism—to be conjoined with the day-to-day details of ecclesiastical administration and institutional power.

Saint Francis had believed that the growing market economy, urbanization, and spread of corruption had eviscerated the cherished religious values of simplicity and poverty. The founder of the minors expressed words of admiration for the unlettered (*idiotae*, which he proudly called the minors in his *Testament*), the obedient, and the poor in society. These were the groups that lacked what he regarded as the three great evils afflicting society: knowledge, power, and wealth.[27] Yet within a few years of Francis's death, some members of his own order had amassed vast expanses of knowledge as university masters, while others served in powerful positions as bishops, papal legates, royal councillors, and even experts on financial matters. As the Franciscan order's identity rapidly changed and was grafted onto the apostolic ministry of the church, becoming clericalized and institutionalized, some felt that the order had compromised its ideals and lost its original inspiration. Seen another way, however, the Franciscan order sought to breathe new life into the church precisely by using the church's existing structures and remaining loyal to the ecclesiastical hierarchy. This was why thirteenth-century popes viewed the Franciscans and Dominicans as promising agents of reform and renewal. The Franciscans contributed to the institutional church in a variety of ways and left a significant imprint on the history of the medieval church; at the same time, the order was changed by the church and its structures (not that the order, even in its infancy, was ever really separate from the church).

As we have seen, for Eudes Rigaud there was no incompatibility between holiness and administration. Rather, administrative ability was a vehicle for achieving the church's goals of reforming and renewing society. The same discipline that was required to perform the *opus dei* and observe an ascetic,

fraternal rule could be called upon to manage a large ecclesiastical bureaucracy, to enact laws, to enforce those laws with systematic visitations of
parishes and monastic houses, to administer justice and finances, and to
keep detailed and orderly records. Eudes displayed enormous energy fighting clerical indiscipline, disorder, and moral inertia. Perhaps because he believed that he would have to answer to God for the conduct of the tens of
thousands under him, Eudes was determined to hold others accountable. It
was, moreover, the Franciscan's piety that fueled his desire for an efficient
bureaucratic system that would unlock the gates to salvation.

Appendix

Perpetual Rents Purchased by Archbishop Eudes Rigaud, 1248–1275

Ref. #	Date	Name	Sale (in *sous tournois*)	Rent (in *sous tournois*)	Rate of return (%)
1	1249	Robert le Tonclier, with consent of wife, Alexandra, on piece of land in Saint-Rémi, Dieppe	30	5	16.6
2	March 1249	Mabilia, with consent of husband, Guibert Leboie, on piece of land in Saint-Rémi, Dieppe	20	2	10
3	December 1249	Guillaume de Fécamp, cleric, on land at Dieppe	30	1	3
4	September 1250	André de Torville, with consent of wife, Emmeline, on masura with building in Dieppe	60	8	13
5	January 1251	Jean Fuarit, with wife's consent	140	4 *mines* of barley	—
6	May 1251	Robert Toupes, with consent of wife, Johanne, on diverse properties in Dieppe	200	40	20
7	May 1251	Robert Toupes, with consent of wife, Johanne, on house in Dieppe	180	26	14

(Appendix—cont.)

Ref. #	Date	Name	Sale (in *sous tournois*)	Rent (in *sous tournois*)	Rate of return (%)
8	1252	Anastasia Waukelin, with consent of daughter, Agnes Potel, on warehouse	10	80	12.5
9	1252	Raoul de Buris, bourgeois of Dieppe	400	40	10
10	1252	Béatrice Dehors Laville, with consent of husband, Guillaume de Hamello, on masura with building in Saint-Rémi, Dieppe	80	10	12.5
11	1252	Guillaume de Puteo Iunior, with consent of wife, on property in Dieppe	120	15	12.5
12	February 1252	Albin de Saukeville on house of Robert de Hotot in Dieppe	50	4	8.5
13	December 1252	Rohaysia and Aelicia Guillebelain (sisters), on masura in Dieppe	20	4	20
14	1253	Jean de Solario of Senlis, with consent of wife, Margueritte, on Gisors mills	10,400 *sous parisis* (13,000 *sous tournois*)	13 muids (or 312 *mines*) of wheat	—
15	1253	Guillaume de Fécamp, cleric, on land at Dieppe	80	10	12.5
16	October 1253	Johanne, wife of Pierre de Cauville from Dieppe, on house in Dieppe	560	55	10
17	August 1255	Cecilia, with consent of husband, Jean Morin, on harbor property in Dieppe	400	40	10
18	August 1255	Cecilia, with consent of husband, Jean Morin, on tenement at Dieppe	140	13	9
19	December 1257	Widow of Pierre Heudoin de Pormor	35	3 *sous* and 2 *corvées*	—
20	1258	Gotins de Beaumes de Dieppe, with consent of wife, Emelie, on manor house in Dieppe	185	20	11

(Appendix—cont.)

Ref. #	Date	Name	Sale (in *sous tournois*)	Rent (in *sous tournois*)	Rate of return (%)
21	1258	Erembert, wife of Gilbert Wasse, on masura	110	20	18
22	June 1258	Cecilia, with consent of husband, Jean Morin, on property by harbor in Dieppe	1,020	103	10
23	September 1258	Cecilia, with consent of husband, Jean Morin, on tenements in Dieppe	770	78	10
24	September 1258	Cecilia, with consent of husband, Jean de Morin, on masura with building in Dieppe	560	50	9
25	November 1258	Michael Clique, bourgeois of Rouen, with consent of wife, Matilde	260	41 *sous* and 5 *capones*	—
26	1260	Roger Gallicus	400	39 *sous* and 2 *capones*	—
27	August 1260	Guibert de Chiéret, of parish La Londe	200	19.5	9.75
28	December 1260	Aelicia de Forneto, widow of Richard, *miles*, on mill at Les Andelys and land in parish of La Fontaine	980	96	10
29	March 1262	Jean de Saneyo	2 *sous parisis*	4 *denarii parisis* (.3 *sous*)	16
30	November 1263	Godefroi Fouquant, with consent of wife, Harsia, on masura in Gaillon	33 *sous parisis*	1 *mine* wheat	—
31	1264	Pierre de Daubeuf, squire and lord of La Fontaine, guarantees rent by totality of his property	900	18 *mines* wheat	—
32	March 1264	Pierre de Daubeuf, squire, on mill in le Vieil Andely	1,800	200	11
33	March 1264	Jean Valegrus and wife, Maria, of parish Saint-Albin de Gaillon	434 *parisis*	40 *parisis*	9
34	October 1266	Raoul de Galod, squire, with consent of wife, Aelicia, on fief in Déville	600	52 *sous* and 4 *sextaria* of wine	—
35	December 1266	Abbot and monks of Gomérifontaine, on lands of the Vexin	2,850	39 *mines* wheat and 70 *sous*	—

(Appendix—cont.)

Ref. #	Date	Name	Sale (in *sous tournois*)	Rent (in *sous tournois*)	Rate of return (%)
36	April 1267	Godefroi Fouquant, of Douvrend parish	520	44 *sous* and 1 hen	—
37	June 1268	Roger Damien, squire, on mill in Les Andelys	360	40	11
38	1270	Johanne, with consent of husband, Raoul	210	20	9.5
39	April 1270	Égide, with consent of wife, Jeanne	30	3	10
40	1272	Égide, with consent of wife, Jeanne	160	16	10
41	1272	Jeanne "dicta Spineto," with consent of husband, Raoul Ruffi, on Dieppe property	210	20	9.5
42	1273	Simon Harene from Déville, with consent of wife, Jeanne	50	5	10
43	1275	Matthieu le Brument, on ferryboat at Dieppe	280	35	12.5
44	April 1275	André le Barier, with consent of wife, Paula, on house at Marioniam	100	13	13

1. Archives départementales Seine-Maritime (ADSM), G870, marked "1002-14886' "' on front; ADSM, G7: 770–71.
2. ADSM, G870, marked "1249' "' on front and back; ADSM, G7: 771.
3. ADSM, G870, marked "1003-14887' "' on front; ADSM, G7: 769.
4. ADSM, G870, marked "996-14880' "' and "997-14881' "' on bottom; ADSM, G7: 771–72.
5. ADSM, G7: 757.
6. ADSM, G870, marked "carta Roberti Toupes' "' on back; ADSM, G7: 754.
7. ADSM, G7: 754–55.
8. ADSM, G1089, marked on front, "14915-1032' "' and "14916-1033' "'; ADSM, G7: 698–99.
9. ADSM, G2034; ADSM, G7:765–66.
10. ADSM, G870, marked "994-14878' "' and "995-14879' "' on bottom; ADSM, G7: 770.
11. ADSM, G870, marked "990-14874" on bottom; ADSM, G7: 772–73.
12. ADSM, G870, marked "993-14877"; ADSM, G7: 766.
13. ADSM, G870, marked "991-14875" and "992-14876" on bottom; ADSM, G7: 768–69.
14. ADSM, G3854, marked "A cotte 2, 1253" on front and top.
15. ADSM, G870, marked on back, "Pour dix sol. de rente Dieppe. Guilliaume du Fecamp 1250"; ADSM, G7: 769.
16. ADSM, G870, marked on front "998-14882 & 999-14883"; ADSM, G7: 758–59.
17. ADSM, G871, marked on bottom, "Robertus"; ADSM, G7: 754.

18. ADSM, G871, marked on bottom, "Robertus"; G7: 750–51.

19. ADSM, G1036, only MS in folder entitled, "1re de la D93"; ADSM, G7: 902.

20. ADSM, G871, marked on front, "1006-14690."

21. ADSM, G871, marked on reverse, "carta de uxor super masura Erebunt."

22. ADSM, G871, dated 1258 on front; ADSM, G7: 752–53.

23. ADSM, G871, marked on reverse, "Cicili di la Vigno 1258"; ADSM, G7: 753.

24. ADSM, G870, marked on bottom, "1000-14884" and "1001-14885."

25. ADSM, G1054, marked on reverse, "Deville plusieurs rentes achetees par O. Rigault a Deville 1258"; ADSM, G7: 703.

26. Th. Bonnin, ed., *Cartulaire de Louviers*, 276–77.

27. ADSM, G1094, marked on bottom, "1034-14921"; ADSM, G7: 908.

28. ADSM, G1036, marked on front, "14929-1047"; G7: 905.

29. ADSM, G7: 700.

30. ADSM, G1025, in envelope titled, "titre de 1263 de presentation du moulin d"Aubervoye au profit d"Odo Rigaud"; ADSM, G7: 898.

31. ADSM, G1036, marked on front, "1048-14930"; ADSM, G7: 905–6.

32. ADSM, G1036, charter from Rouen official, dated 1264, stating that annual rent of 10 l. is on a mill called "molendinum acardi"; in the Vieux Andelys. Contains seal depicting archbishop mitred and seated on episcopal throne. ADSM, G7: 906–7.

33. ADSM, G7: 897.

34. ADSM, G1054, marked on reverse, "de rente vendue a l"archeveque par Raoul de Galod." Also includes smaller charter from the official of Rouen. ADSM, G7: 701–2.

35. ADSM, G7: 932.

36. ADSM, G939, two charters, one from the official of Rouen, and the other from Godefroy. ADSM, G7: 794–95.

37. ADSM, G1036, marked on front, "1031-14914"; ADSM, G7: 907.

38. ADSM, G871, marked on reverse, "vingt sol. de rente Dieppe Joanne d"Espiniy 1270."

39. ADSM, G871, marked on front, "1008-14892." Two charters attached, one small one from the official of Rouen and a larger one from Égide.

40. ADSM, G871, marked on front, "1009-14092."

41. ADSM, G871, marked on front, "1007-14891." Charters both from official of Rouen and Jeanne.

42. ADSM, G2034, two charters from Simon, marked on bottom, "1040-14923." ADSM, G7: 704.

43. ADSM, G7: 757.

44. ADSM, G1054, marked on reverse, "carta super venditione xiii sol. redditus ab andrea le barrier"; ADSM, G7: 705.

Notes

Introduction

1. The original manuscript of Eudes's *Register* is held in the Bibliothèque Nationale de France, ms. lat. 1245. During the seventeenth century, the manuscript belonged to Roger de Gaignières, erudite French collector and governor of the principality of Joinville. In 1701, he bequeathed the manuscript (along with an enormous collection of other documents) to the king's library. The exact dimensions of the manuscript are 221 by 149 mm. There are generally two folio numbers given in the manuscript (a roman numeral in a thirteenth-century hand and an arabic numeral in red in a modern hand), and these do not always correspond with the folio numbering given by Bonnin in his edition of the *Register*. For the purposes of this introduction, all folio numbers given refer to the arabic numerals in the manuscript itself. The organization of the manuscript is a complex subject that deserves further study. Because the manuscript is not entirely chronological (one finds documents from the 1260s inserted into earlier sections that deal with the 1250s), it was probably organized in its present form sometime after 1269.
2. See C. R. Cheney, "Early Norman Monastic Visitations: A Neglected Record," *Journal of Ecclesiastical History* 33, 3 (1982): 412–23. On how revealing the terminology used in episcopal records can be, see Michael Burger, "Sending, Joining, Writing, and Speaking in the Diocesan Administration of Thirteenth-Century Lincoln," *Mediaeval Studies* 55 (1993): 151–82.
3. There were also parallels between Eudes's *Register* and thirteenth-century household rolls of magnates, such as Eleanor of Montfort, sister of the English king Henry III and wife of Simon de Montfort. Her household rolls listed her household's daily expenditures on the right side and the location where the day was spent on the left side. See M. T. Clanchy, *From Memory to Written Record: England, 1066–1307* (Cambridge, Mass.: Harvard University Press, 1979), 71–72. Martha Ballard, the New England midwife studied by Laurel Thatcher Ulrich, used her journal to keep track of the fees owed to her for her services, noting when an account had been settled (often months or even years later). See Ulrich, *A Midwife's Tale: The Life of Martha Ballard, Based on Her Diary, 1785–1812* (New York: Knopf, 1990).
4. On January 18, 1249, the archbishop's secretary received a letter from the priest of Haudricourt dealing with Eudes's visitation of the deanery of Aumale. The secretary indicated receipt of the letter on folio (fol.) 11r of the register, but he then copied the letter on fol. 10v, squeezing it into the upper right-hand corner so that it would be next to the record of the archbishop's visitation of Aumale.

5. A large space was left on fol. 2 between VII kalends of August and VI kalends of August. There is another large gap on the same folio between I kalends of August and IV nones of August. Fol. 62v is almost completely blank, with only three one-line entries and giant spaces between each. The secretary clearly expected to have more to write.

6. See, for instance, fol. 41, where four consecutive entries are crossed out. Eudes ended up staying at Aliermont for several days longer than he had anticipated. On fol. 18r, it is clear that Eudes had intended to visit the priory of Parnes on June 30, 1249, but he did not arrive until July 2. "Visitamus prioratum de Panes" is twice crossed out.

7. The archbishop's secretary numbered two consecutive folios XXXIV but then caught the mistake and changed the second folio to XXXV. Only two pages later, however, he numbered two consecutive folios XXXVIII, a mistake that was never corrected.

8. See, for example, a summary of a bull from Pope Alexander IV: BnF ms. lat. 1245, f. 147.

9. I draw here on Robert F. Berkhofer III, *Day of Reckoning: Power and Accountability in Medieval France* (Philadelphia: University of Pennsylvania Press, 2004). See also Clanchy, *From Memory to Written Record*, 3.

10. Clanchy, *From Memory to Written Record*, 130–45.

11. Raymonde Foreville, "Les statuts synodaux et le renouveau pastoral du XIIIe siècle dans le Midi de la France," in *Le crédo, la morale et l'inquisition* (Toulouse, 1971), 120.

12. The personal interest that bishops and archbishops in the thirteenth century took in the management of their dioceses did not continue, at least in the case of Rouen, into the late Middle Ages. During the fourteenth and fifteenth centuries, the archbishops of Rouen, who during this period tended to originate from outside Normandy, generally delegated tasks to their vicars so they did not have to reside in the province. Late medieval archbishops of Rouen showed little or no interest in examining candidates for benefices, conducting visitations of the archdiocese or province, preaching, or managing the church's temporalities. See Vincent Tabbagh, *Le clergé séculier du diocèse de Rouen à la fin du moyen-âge (1359–1493)* (Paris, 1988), 39, 117.

13. See C. R. Cheney, *Episcopal Visitations of Monasteries in the Thirteenth Century* (Manchester, 1931); Joseph Avril, "Archevêchés, diocèses et paroisses aux XIIe–XIVe siècles: À propos de quelques travaux récents," *Revue d'histoire de l'église de France* 82 (1996): 323–45; on Pisa, see Nicole Bériou, ed., *Les sermons et la visite pastorale de Federico Visconti, archevêque de Pise (1253–1277)* (Rome, 2001); on Germany, see Paul B. Pixton, *The German Episcopacy and the Implementation of the Decrees of the Fourth Lateran Council, 1216–1245: Watchmen on the Tower* (Leiden, 1995).

14. Bernard Delmaire, *Le diocèse d'Arras de 1093 au milieu du XIVe siècle: Recherches sur la vie religieuse dans le nord de la France au moyen âge* (Arras, 1994), 164–65.

15. On the development of the office of the *officialis*, see Paul Fournier, *Les officialités au moyen âge: Étude sur l'organisation, la compétence et la procédure des tribunaux ecclésiastiques ordinaires en France, de 1180 à 1328* (Paris, 1880).

16. Michael Clanchy argues that developments in the English royal government (especially the royal chancery) had a significant influence on ecclesiastical administration, especially since many bishops served in the royal government. Unlike on the Continent, where the first episcopal registers were in the from of a codex, the earliest English episcopal registers were in the same format as royal chancery rolls. In the later thirteenth century, English bishops adopted the codex format for their registers. See Clanchy, *From Memory to Written Record*, 53–54.

17. Indeed, there is no comparable source for pastoral visits in Rouen in the later Middle Ages. For England, many of the surviving registers of thirteenth-century English bishops and archbishops have been published since 1905 by the Canterbury and York Society. See David M. Smith, *Guide to Bishops' Registers of England and Wales: A Survey from the Middle Ages to the Abolition of the Episcopacy in 1646* (London, 1981). More recently, Oxford University Press, under the auspices of the British Academy, has been publishing a multivolume series (now at 28 volumes), directed by David M. Smith, *English Episcopal Acta*, which will include the surviving episcopal *acta* (around ten thousand charters) of every English diocese from roughly the Norman Conquest until the first episcopal registers began being kept in the late twelfth and thirteenth

centuries. For France, the CNRS has begun publishing a multivolume series on French episcopal *acta*.

18. Benoît-Michel Tock, *Une chancellerie épiscopale au XIIe siècle: Le cas d'Arras* (Louvain-la-Neuve, 1991).

19. Clanchy, *From Memory to Written Record*, 55.

20. Robert Brentano, *York Metropolitan Jurisdiction and Papal Judges Delegate (1279–1296)* (Berkeley, 1959), 42.

21. *RER*, xxii–xxiii; David Knowles, *The Religious Orders in England*, 3 vols. (Cambridge, 1948), 1:83–84.

22. Clanchy, *From Memory to Written Record*, 192.

23. Léopold Delisle, "Le clergé normand au XIIIe siècle," *BEC*, 2nd ser., 3 (1846): 479–99. Delisle concluded that the morals of Normandy's regular clergy were far more "pure" than those of the secular clergy.

24. G. G. Coulton, *The Friars and the Dead Weight of Tradition, 1200–1400 A.D.*, vol. 2 of *Five Centuries of Religion* (Cambridge, 1927). See also Coulton's prefaces to both the first and second editions (1906, 1915) of *Ten Medieval Studies*, where he responds to the criticisms of Abbot Gasquet.

25. Coulton even wrote a novel, *Friar's Lantern* (London, 1906), in which two modern Englishmen suddenly find themselves living in the very unpleasant world of the fourteenth century. The Franciscan archbishop in the novel bears a strong resemblance to Eudes Rigaud.

26. Pierre Andrieu-Guitrancourt, *L'archevêque Eudes Rigaud et la vie de l'église au XIIIe siècle d'après le "Regestrum Visitationum"* (Paris, 1938).

27. Christopher Cheney has an extensive discussion of Eudes in his *Episcopal Visitations*. On Eudes's travels and his *familia*, see Oscar G. Darlington, "The Travels of Odo Rigaud, Archbishop of Rouen (1248–1275)" (Ph.D. diss., 1940). In his magisterial *Western Society and the Church in the Middle Ages* (Harmondsworth, U.K., 1970), R. W. Southern devotes several pages (190–93) to the career of Eudes Rigaud. For a short biography of Eudes Rigaud and his contemporary Franciscan bishops, see Williell R. Thomson, *Friars in the Cathedral: The First Franciscan Bishops, 1226–1261* (Toronto, 1975). Penelope Johnson uses Eudes's *Register* for what it reveals about female monastic life in the thirteenth century. See Johnson, *Equal in Monastic Profession: Religious Women in Medieval France* (Chicago, 1991). Most recently, on the impact of Eudes's visitations over time on specific religious houses and parishes, see Phyllis E. Pobst, "Visitation of Religious and Clergy by Archbishop Eudes Rigaud of Rouen," in *Religion, Text, and Society in Medieval Spain and Northern Europe: Essays in Honor of J. N. Hillgarth*, ed. Thomas E. Burman, Mark D. Meyerson, and Leah Shopkow, 223–49 (Toronto, 2002).

28. This notion of the division of power comes from Herbert Grundmann, "Sacerdotium-Regnum-Studium: Zur Wertung des Wissenschaft im 13. Jahrhundert," *Archiv für Kulturgeschichte* 34 (1952): 5–21.

29. *The Chronicle of Salimbene de Adam*, trans. Joseph L. Baird, Giuseppe Baglivi, and John Robert Kane (Binghamton, N.Y., 1986), 440–41; Salimbene de Adam, *Chronica*, ed. Giuseppe Scalia, 2 vols. (Turnholt, 1998), 2:655–56. Even if the story is accurate (and there is reason to doubt some of what Salimbene wrote), Eudes's words might rather be the expression of a Franciscan still somewhat horrified in 1254 by the size of his archiepiscopal income, one of the largest in the French kingdom. If the Italian bishop had viewed Eudes as merely a grandee, he likely would not have offered to pay his expenses.

30. Thomson, *Friars in the Cathedral*, 160–61.

31. Salimbene de Adam, *Chronicle*, 440–41.

32. Bernard of Bessa, *Liber de laudibus beati Francisci*, in *Analecta Franciscana* 3 (1897), 674: "Fuit enim post eum [Jean de la Rochelle] venerabilis pater frater Odo Rigaldi genere clarus, sed clarior moribus, magister in theologia, similiter deinde Rothomagensis ecclesiae archipraesul, famosissimus praedicator."

33. Ibid., 74: "Qui tractus et coactus ad curiam, vita et doctrina ut prius in ordine, sic excellenter in regimine fulsit, ut forma praesulum censeretur."

34. Other Franciscan bishops, such as John Pecham, were said to have resisted accepting their episcopal offices.
35. Southern, *Western Society and the Church*, 190, 193. Southern's description of Eudes's "firm but not unreasonable" governance could hardly be more different than the corrupt and scandalous medieval world Coulton found laid bare in the pages of Eudes's *Register*.
36. See J. Leclercq, "Disciplina," in *Dictionnaire de spiritualité* 3 (1957): cols. 1291–1302; H.-I. Marrou, " 'Doctrina' et 'Disciplina' dans la langue des pères de l'église," *Bulletin du Cange* 9 (1934): 5–25.
37. There are also parallels with developments in Flemish comital administration during the later thirteenth century, with the rise of the office of general receiver, the first central bureaucratic office in Flanders. Ellen Kittell has studied how ad hoc actions of a Flemish count's household became the routine administrative functions of an appointed bureaucrat. See Kittell, *From Ad Hoc to Routine: A Case Study in Medieval Bureaucracy* (Philadelphia, 1991).
38. Marion Gibbs and Jane Lang suggest that there was a link between a university background and a reforming episcopate. See Gibbs and Lang, *Bishops and Reform, 1215–1272* (London, 1934).

1. The Formation of a Reformer at the Franciscan *Studium* in Paris

1. Jacques Le Goff, *Intellectuals in the Middle Ages*, trans. Teresa Lavender Fagan (Oxford, 1993), 117. See also Jean Dunbabin, "Jacques Le Goff and the Intellectuals," in *The Work of Jacques Le Goff and the Challenges of Medieval History*, ed. M. Rubin (Woodbridge, Suffolk, U.K., 1997), 157–67.
2. Nicole Bériou, *L'avènement des maîtres de la parole: Le prédication à Paris au XIIIe siècle*, 2 vols. (Paris, 1998); David d'Avray, *The Preaching of Friars: Sermons Diffused from Paris before 1300* (Oxford, 1985).
3. Michèle M. Mulchahey, *"First the bow is bent in study": Dominican Education before 1350* (Toronto, 1998). On the relationship between Franciscan education in the universities and in provincial study houses, see Bert Roest, *A History of Franciscan Education (c. 1210–1517)* (Leiden, 2000).
4. Alain Boureau, *Théologie, science et censure au XIIIe siècle: Le cas de Jean Peckham* (Paris, 1999); Jacques Verger, *L'essor des universités au XIIIe siècle* (Paris, 1997); John Baldwin, *Masters, Princes, and Merchants: The Social Views of Peter the Chanter and His Circle*, 2 vols. (Princeton, 1970); Louis-Jacques Bataillon, "Intermédiaires entre les traités de morale pratique et les sermons: Les Distinctiones bibliques alphabétiques," in *La prédication au XIIIe siècle en France et Italie* (Aldershot, Hampshire, U.K., 1993); R. Avi-Yonah, "Career Trends of Parisian Masters of Theology, 1200–1320," *History of Universities* 6 (1987): 47–64; Robert Bartlett, *Trial by Fire and Water: The Medieval Judicial Ordeal* (Oxford, 1986); Ian Wei, "The Self-Image of the Masters of Theology at the University of Paris in the Late Thirteenth and Early Fourteenth Centuries," *Journal of Ecclesiastical History* 46, 3 (1995): 398–431.
5. Two of Eudes Rigaud's archiepiscopal predecessors at Rouen, Robert Poulain and Pierre de Colmieu, had, like him, been university masters of theology, as had recent bishops of Bayeux, Sées, and Coutances. See Thomson, *Friars in the Cathedral*, 79.
6. Avi-Yonah, "Career Trends," 61. This figure includes all thirteenth-century masters of theology at the University of Paris (not just mendicant masters). It does not include the masters who left the university to become secular administrators.
7. For a list of all extant manuscripts of Eudes's *Sentences* commentary, see P. Glorieux, *Répertoire des maîtres en théologie de Paris au XIIIe siècle*, 2 vols. (Paris, 1934); Victorin Doucet, "Maîtres Franciscains de Paris," *AFH* 27 (1934): 541–42; F. M. Henquinet, "Les manuscrits et l'influence des écrits théologiques d'Eudes Rigaud, O.F.M.," *Recherches de théologie ancienne et médiévale* 11 (October 1939): 324–50. For a list of extant manuscripts of Rigaud's "disputed questions," see Leonardo Sileo, *Teoria della scienzia teologica: Quaestio de scientia theologiae di Odo Rigaldi e altri testi inediti (1230–1250)*, vol. 1 (Rome, 1984), 18 n. 15.

8. Sileo, *Teoria della scienza teologica*; F. M. Fresneda, "La ciencia humana de Jesucristo según Odón Rigaldo," *Recherches de théologie ancienne et médiévale* 62 (1995): 157–81; Fresneda, "La plenitud de gracia en Jesucristo según Odón Rigaldo," *Carthaginensia* 4, 5 (1988): 45–77; The best treatment of Eudes's theology is in Odon Lottin, *Psychologie et morale aux XII et XIIIe siècles*, 6 vols. in 8 (Louvain, 1942–60).

9. J.-B. Schneyer, *Repertorium der Lateinischen Sermones des Mittelalters für die Zeit von 1150–1350*, 11 vols. (Münster-Westfalen, 1969–90), 6 (1975): 93–107; 9 (1980): 210–25. All the following sermons bear the rubric *fratris rigaldi* or *frater rigaudus*. BM Arras, ms. lat. 759 (691) f. 112rb (RLS VI, No. 77), 120va (RLS VI, No. 82), 228vb (RLS VI, No. 178); BnF, ms. lat. 16502, f. 157ra (RLS IX, No. 267). On the Arras manuscript, see Ch.-V. Langlois, "Sermons parisiens de la première moitié du XIIIe s., contenus dans le ms. 691 de la bibliothèque d'Arras," *Journal des savants* 14 (1916): 488–94, 548–59. Schneyer's attribution of six of the sermons in the Arras manuscript (RLS VI, Nos. 175, 180, 183, 190, 197, 198) to Eudes Rigaud has been questioned; a number of the sermons bear the rubric *collatio prioris provincialis*, making it likely that they were preached by Humbert de Romans, the Dominican provincial of France. See Bériou, *L'avènement des maîtres*, 2:657–58 and n. 3; Simon Tugwell, "Humbert of Romans' Material for Preachers," in *De ore Domini: Preacher and Word in the Middle Ages*, ed. Th. Amos, E. A. Green, and B. M. Kienzle (Kalamazoo, Mich., 1989), 105–17; M.-P. Toutain, "Sept sermons en quête d'auteur" (Master's thesis, Paris IV, 1997). The Paris manuscript is discussed in detail in Jacques Foviaux, "Les sermons donnés à Laon," *Recherches Augustiniennes* 20 (1985): 203–56, and Bériou, *L'avènement des maîtres*, 2:674–75, 694. As Bériou has indicated, another version of Eudes's Saint Nicolas sermon found in the Paris ms. is in Bruxelles BR.II.1142, f. 134ra (RLS VII, No. 158).

10. Several of these "disputed questions" have been published: Basilio Pergamo, ed., "Il desiderio innato del soprannaturale nelle questioni inedite di Oddone Rigaldo, O.F.M., Arivesco de Rouen (†1275)" *Studi francescani* 7, 4 (1935): 414–46; 8, 1 (1936): 76–108; Odon Lottin, "Une question disputée d'Odon Rigaud sur le libre arbitre," *Revue Thomiste* 36 (1931): 886–95; A. van Dijk, ed., "Quaestiones quaedam scholasticae de officio divino et cantu ecclesiastico," *Ephemerides liturgicae* 56 (1942): 20–43; Sileo, *Teoria della scienza teologica*, vol. 2. For a list of the chapter headings for Eudes's "disputed questions" contained in BM: Toulouse, ms. lat. 737, see J. Barbet, "Note sur le ms. 737 de la Bibliothèque Municipale de Toulouse, Quaestiones disputatae," *Bulletin d'information de l'Institut de Recherche et d'Histoire des Textes* 5 (1957): 7–51.

11. In particular, Sileo points to the way in which three of Eudes's *quaestiones disputatae* (*De modo essendi Dei in creatures*, *De existentia rerum in Deo*, and *De voluntate Dei*) grew out of his commentary on dist. 35–48 of book I of Lombard's *Sententiae*. See Leonardo Sileo, "Dalla *lectio* alla *disputatio*: Le questioni *De modo essendi Dei in creaturis*, *De existentia rerum in Deo* e *De voluntate Dei* di Odo Rigaldi," in *Editori di Quaracchi: 100 anni dopo bilancio e prospettive: Atti del colloquio internazionale, Roma 29–30 Maggio 1995*, ed. Alvaro Cacciotti and Barbara Faes de Mottoni (Rome, 1997), 109–31.

12. In arguing for a multitude of divine ideas (very much an Augustinian, Neoplatonic notion that echoes the Platonic forms), Eudes joined Richard Rufus (who made precisely this argument around 1236) but challenged the consensus of most contemporary theologians, including Alexander of Hales, who later in life became an extreme unitarian. Rejecting the notion that it would somehow reduce God's majesty if God were to know and have an idea corresponding to every different created individual directly, Eudes instead argued that it was a divine and noble attribute for God to know every single creature and material object directly. See Rega Wood, "Distinct Ideas and Perfect Solicitude: Alexander of Hales, Richard Rufus, and Odo Rigaldus," *Franciscan Studies* 53 (1993): 7–46.

13. Although the teaching of some of the newly translated books of Aristotle on natural philosophy was officially forbidden at the University of Paris, it is clear that this prohibition was not heeded.

14. André Tuilier, "La renaissance de l'aristotélisme universitaire à Paris au XIIIe siècle," *Mélanges de la Bibliothèque de la Sorbonne* 1 (1980): 7–21.

15. Bernard G. Dod, "Aristoteles latinus," in *The Cambridge History of Later Medieval Philosophy: From the Rediscovery of Aristotle to the Disintegration of Scholasticism, 1100–1600*, ed. Norman Kretzmann, Anthony Kenny, and Jan Pinborg (1982; reprint, Cambridge, 1989), 71–72.

16. Beryl Smalley, *The Gospels in the Schools, c. 1100–c. 1280* (London, 1985), 182–83.

17. Christian Trottman, *Théologie et noétique au XIIIe siècle: À la recherché d'un statut* (Paris, 1999), 49.

18. F. van Steenberghen, *The Philosophical Movement in the Thirteenth Century* (Edinburgh, 1955), 38–55. One example of Eudes's Neoplatonic-Aristotelian synthesis: Eudes made various philosophical arguments for the immortality of the soul while also using Aristotle's theory of abstraction. See J. Obi Oguejiofor, *The Arguments for the Immortality of the Soul in the First Half of the Thirteenth Century* (Leuven, 1995), 315.

19. *Chronica XXIV generalium ordinis minorum*, in *Analecta Franciscana* 3 (1897): 220; R. Ménindès, "Eudes Rigaud, Frère Mineur," *Revue d'histoire Franciscaine* 8 (1931): 166–67.

20. V. Doucet, "Alessandro di Hales," *Enciclopedia Cattolica* 1 (1948): 784–87; R. M. Huber, "Alexander of Hales, O.F.M. (ca. 1170–1245): His Life and Influence on Medieval Scholasticism," *Franciscan Studies* 26, 4 (1945): 353–65.

21. Roest, *History of Franciscan Education*, 14.

22. Verger, *L'essor des universités*, 76–77.

23. On the university curriculum, see P. Glorieux, "L'enseignement au moyen âge: Techniques et méthodes en usage à la faculté de théologie de Paris, au XIIIe siècle," *Archives d'histoire doctrinale et littéraire du moyen âge* 43 (1968): 65–186.

24. van Steenberghen, *La philosophie au XIIIe siècle*, 145–46. It was Alexander of Hales who helped make the *Sentences* the standard theological textbook of his day, but his commentary on the *Sentences* dates from his years as a secular master.

25. Marcia Colish, "From the Sentence Collection to the *Sentence* Commentary and the *Summa*: Parisian Scholastic Theology, 1130–1215," in *Manuels, programmes de cours et techniques d'enseignement dans les universités médiévales: Actes du colloque international de Louvain-la-Neuve, 9–11 septembre 1993*, ed. Jacqueline Hamesse (Louvain-la-Neuve, 1994), 9–12.

26. There are far fewer extant manuscripts of *Sentences* commentaries by most of Eudes's contemporary Franciscans, including Guillaume de Meliton, Eudes de Rosny, Gauthier de Bruges, John Peckham, Guillaume de la Mare, Matthieu d'Aquasparta, and Guillaume de Falguières. On the other hand, the Dominican Pierre de Tarentaise's commentary on the *Sentences* seems to have been much more popular than Eudes Rigaud's, since there are over fifty extant manuscripts. See note 7 above.

27. Lottin, *Problèmes de psychologie*, vol. 1 of *Psychologie et morale aux XIIe et XIIIe siècles*, 173–74; Lottin, *Problèmes de morale*, vol. 3 of *Psychologie et morale aux XIIe et XIIIe siècles*, 592–94, 684–735. See also Leonardo Sileo, "Rigaud," in *Dictionnaire de spiritualité* 13 (1988): cols. 670–73.

28. B. Pergamo has found a reference in book 2 of Eudes's commentary on the *Sentences* to the 1241 condemnation of the errors of "Vescovo di Parigi." In fact, Eudes was referring to Etienne de Venizy, who was a sententiary bachelor at the University of Paris from 1240 to 1242. Errors contained in Etienne's commentary on the *Sentences* were condemned in 1241 by the bishop of Paris and the masters of theology. Thus we can date Eudes's book 2 to late 1241 or later. See Pergamo, "Il desiderio innato del soprannaturale," 444.

29. In *Quo elongati*, published on September 28, 1230, Gregory IX confirmed Saint Francis's wish that the rule never be glossed, although the papal bull itself represented a kind of gloss on the rule. When, in 1241, the Chapter of Diffinitors requested that each province submit an *expositio* on the rule, a group of learned Franciscans in England pleaded with the minister general to respect Saint Francis's wish and leave the rule untouched. See Rosalind Brooke, *Early Franciscan Government: Elias to Bonaventure* (Cambridge, 1959), 205.

30. *Expositio quatuor magistrorum super regulam fratrum minorum, 1241–1242*, ed. P. L. Oliger (Rome, 1950), 124: "Novam autem expositionem vel glosaturam contra regulam non astruimus, sicut a quibusdam intentionis purae damnatoribus et zelum suum in animarum suarum periculum et fratrum scandalum pervertentibus praedicatur." Some

modern historians have argued that the four masters did indeed change certain elements of the Rule of 1223. L. C. Landini, for instance, shows that the *expositio* incorporated elements from several papal bulls dealing with the constitution of the Franciscan order. See Landini, *The Causes of the Clericalization of the Order of Friars Minor, 1209–1260, in the Light of the Early Franciscan Sources* (Chicago, 1968), 77–80.

31. Alexander of Hales and Jean de la Rochelle had been two of the fiercest opponents of Brother Elias, and their *expositio* came in the wake of legislation passed in 1239 at the general chapter meeting in Rome that placed limits on the power of the minister general and granted provincial chapters the right to appoint ministers. See Brooke, *Early Franciscan Government*, 205–22; Jacques Dalarun, *François d'Assise ou le pouvoir en question: Principes et modalités du gouvernement dans l'ordre des Frères mineurs* (Paris, 1999), 90–95.

32. Malcolm Lambert, *Franciscan Poverty: The Doctrine of the Absolute Poverty of Christ and the Apostles in the Franciscan Order, 1210–1323* (Saint Bonaventure, N.Y., 1998), 83.

33. *Expositio quatuor magistrorum*, 136.

34. On *Quo elongati*, see Landini, *Causes of the Clericalization*, 60–61.

35. It has been shown that Jean de la Rochelle and Alexander of Hales held regent-master chairs in the Franciscan *studium* at the same time. See Jacques-Guy Bougerol, *Introduction à Saint Bonaventure* (Paris, 1988), 37–42.

36. Jacques-Guy Bougerol, "A propos des condamnations parisiennes de 1241 et 1244," *AFH* 80:3–4; (1987): 464–65.

37. Kilian Lynch shows that three manuscripts have been misattributed as Eudes Rigaud's fourth book on the *Sentences*. See Lynch, "The Alleged Fourth Book on the Sentences of Odo Rigaud and Related Documents," *Franciscan Studies* 9, 11 (1949): 87–145.

38. Salimbene de Adam, *Chronicle*, 441.

39. Odo Rigaldi, "Quaestio de scientia theologiae," pars I, quaest. 1, par. 35, in Sileo, *Teoria della scienza teologica*, 2:18: "Ad illud quod obicitur quod 'scientia parum aut nihil valet ad virtutem',—potest dici quod illud verbum intelligitur de scientiis quae sunt pure speculativae; theologia autem non est pure speculativa, immo practica."

40. I draw on a summary of Aquinas's quodlibetal debate given by Wei, "Self-Image of the Masters," 409–10. Wei also summarizes Henry of Ghent's response to the same question in 1276, which followed Aquinas's quite closely.

41. Bériou, *L'avènement des maîtres*, 41 n. 124.

42. Ibid., 44.

43. Peter the Chanter may have been alluding here to a problem that was often denounced in sermons, namely, that clerics with career ambitions were known to prolong their academic studies, with the result that the care of their congregations was turned over to incompetent clerics.

44. On the various new preaching tools, such as the collections of *distinctiones* for preachers, *postillae*, model sermons, and *summae* on vices and virtues, see Bériou, *L'avènement des maîtres*, 178–86.

45. Bériou, *L'avènement des maîtres*, 38–39.

46. Baldwin, *Master, Princes, and Merchants*, 1:315–43.

47. Joseph Avril, ed., *Les statuts synodaux des anciennes provinces de Bordeaux, Auch, Sens et Rouen (fin XIIIe siècle)*, vol. 5 of *Les statuts synodaux français du XIIIe siècle*, ed. Odette Pontal and Joseph Avril (Paris, 2001), 183–87. Avril demonstrates the extent to which the canons of councils in this period derived from earlier councils. The Rouen council of 1231 was particularly influential as one of the principal reforming councils of the early thirteenth century.

48. Smalley, *Gospels in the Schools*, 117–18.

49. Peter the Chanter, *Summa de sacramentis et animae consiliis*, chap. 14, par. 248, ed. Jean-Albert Dugauquier (Louvain, 1963), vol. 3: 2a, p. 252.

50. Ibid., chap. 22, par. 260, pp. 269–272; chap. 24, par. 266, pp. 281–82.

51. John Baldwin's classic study exposed the extent to which Peter the Chanter and his circle were connected to the realities of their time (from issues faced by merchants to those involved in royal finances) and influenced those realities. See Baldwin, *Master, Princes, and Merchants*.

52. Richard C. Trexler, *The Christian at Prayer* (Binghamton, N.Y., 1987). As Trexler has shown, the "De penitentia et partibus eius," a section of which dealt with prayer ("De oratione et speciebus illius"), was part of a later version of the *Verbum abbreviatum*.

53. Trexler, *Christian at Prayer*, 47–48.

54. Peter the Chanter, *Summa de sacramentis*, chap. 38, par. 293, vol. 3: 2a, pp. 326–28, to take just one example.

55. Ibid., par. 207, pp. 157–59; par. 342, pp. 421–25. It is worth noting that Eudes regularly collected procurations at the religious houses he visited.

56. Bériou, *L'avènement des maîtres*, 71.

57. In the following discussion of the role of sermons in the mendicant *studia*, I draw on J.-G. Bougerol, "Les sermons dans les 'studia' des mendiants," in *Le scuole degli ordini mendicanti (secoli XIII–XIV)* (Todi, 1978), 251–80, which also briefly discusses Eudes's sermon contained in BnF, ms. lat. 16502, fol. 157ra (RLS IX, No. 267).

58. See d'Avray, *Preaching of the Friars*, 7–8, 10–11, 180–203, 242–43, 255.

59. Bériou, *L'avènement des maîtres*, 166–69. Bériou gives the example of the Franciscan Guibert de Tournai, who was asked by Pope Alexander IV to compile a collection of model sermons from those he preached at the university and rework them for a non-university audience.

60. R. H. Rouse and M. A. Rouse, "Biblical Distinctions in the Thirteenth Century," *Archives d'histoire doctrinale et littéraire du moyen âge* 49 (1974): 27–37.

61. "Consummatum est" is part of the description of the Passion according to Saint John 19:30, read on Good Friday. The passage is also recited in the votive mass for the Passion of Our Lord, which can be celebrated on Fridays.

62. BM: Arras, ms. lat. 691 (759), fol. 112rb: "Et ipsum karissimi qui est auctor fidei et consummator rogemus ut eadem misericordia qua natus est pro nobis et passus det virtutem verbo suo ut penetret ad corda nostra sermo suus et notabile illud exemplum."

63. Bougerol, "Les sermons dans les 'studia,'" 261.

64. The friars of course were not alone in denouncing the three vices. A collection of sermons preached in and around Paris in 1210–20 contains a number of sermons that take up this same theme. See Bériou, *L'avènement des maîtres*, 63.

65. It was not unusual for secular students to attend sermons preached by friars, but some secular masters discouraged the practice precisely because they feared they would lose their students to the friars. See Bériou, *L'avènement des maîtres*, 123–24. On mendicant recruitment at the university, see J. Verger, "Studia et universités," in *Le scuole degli ordini mendicanti (secoli XIII–XIV)* (Todi, 1978), 173–204; L. Beaumont-Maillet, *Le grand couvent des Cordeliers de Paris: Étude historique et archéologique du XIIIe siècle à nos jours* (Paris, 1975); M. M. Davy, *Les sermons universitaires parisiens de 1230–1231* (Paris, 1931), 108–9.

66. BnF, ms. lat. 16502, fol. 157: "Sepe predicatum est vobis facere penitentiam et relinquere vanitatem mundi et intrare religionem."

67. BnF, ms. lat. 16502, fol. 157: "Quidam enim ab oriente, id est in principio iuventutis, veniunt ad deum et intrant religionem, alii ab occidente, sic ut illi qui iam cum sunt in decrepita etate et occasu vite veniunt tunc ad religionem."

68. BnF, ms. lat. 16502, fol. 157: "Ostense sunt etiam vobis miserie et cure et angustie seculi que artant suos amatores et possessores, que debent satis revocare nos ab amore ipsorum, immo etiam ad contemptum eorum provocare."

69. BnF, ms. lat. 16502, fol. 157: "Et si hec non sufficiunt ad commendationem religionis et contemptum terrenorum, proponimus vobis in exemplum beatos confessores Augustinum, Ieronimum, beatum Nicholaum et beatum Martinum, sanctos heremitas et monachos. Omnes isti contemptum seculi nobis predicant et commendant verbis, operibus et exemplis, vitam religionis quam omnes isti confessi sunt."

70. BnF, ms. lat. 16502, fol. 157: "Ipsi econtrario nobis proponunt antiquos patres Abraham, Moysem, et Job, et alios qui divites fuerunt in seculo, quibus tamen meliores non sumus et tamen ipsi religionem non intraverunt. ad quid ergo tota die predicamus ordinem et paupertatem et huiusmodi?"

71. BnF, ms. lat. 16502, fol. 157: "Karissimi nondum venerat Christum, nec erat adhuc evangelium, nec tunc adhuc audierant 'beati pauperes' etc. nec dum adhuc audierant verbum illud de ore Domino: 'si vis perfectus esse vade et vende omnia etc. . . . ' "

72. BnF, ms. lat. 16502, fol. 157: "Credo quod si hoc audissent, libenter aquievissent huic consilio."

73. BnF, ms. lat. 16502 fol. 157: "Karissimi, rogemus ipsum filium Dei qui paupertatem eligit, ut ea que nos retrahunt ab ipso ipse amoneat, et dicat aquiloni: 'Da.' Et austero: 'Noli prohibere.' Et dicat quilibet 'Pater noster.'" Eudes has the aquilo, or northern wind, signify the tribulations of the present life through which God recalls us from loving temporal things. The auster, or southern wind, signifies the carnal pleasures that take many people away from God and his service. Eudes's protheme is based on Isaiah 43:5–6.

74. BnF, ms. lat. 16502, fol. 157: "Omnes isti contemptum seculi nobis predicant et commendant verbis, operibus et exemplis, vitam religionis quam omnes isti confessi sunt, preter quamque [cancell] beatum Nicholaum de quo non legitur scriptum quod ipse fuerit monacus, nec votum religionis fecisse, et hunc vocavit dominus ad populi sui conservationem et gubernationem sic manere qui nihilominus religionis vitam satis tempestive duxit."

75. BnF, ms. lat. 16502, fol. 157v: "Ipse habundaret in diviciis ex hereditate parentum, et nobilis genere, nobilior fuit sanctitate et moribus, hoc est vere nobilitas, nec maculam posuit in gloria sua. . . ."

76. BnF, ms. lat. 16502, fol. 157vb: "Karissimi, si nolumus esse beati pauperes, saltem simus sicut iste dives beatus fuit, ut simus sine macula, sicut iste fuit."

77. Jussi Hanska, *"And the Rich Man also died; and He was buried in Hell": The Social Ethos in Mendicant Sermons* (Helsinki, 1997), 79 and n. 59. Hanska draws on part II, bk. II, I.3, T.3, SIII, QIII ("De ornatu corporis," c. 1) of the *Summa theologica* of Alexander of Hales. As Hanska shows, mendicant attitudes toward wealth are most evident in commentaries on the parable of Lazarus in the Gospel according to Luke. Whereas the early church fathers used the parable to draw a link between wealth and sin, some thirteenth-century university friars questioned the connection.

78. Hanska, *Rich Man*, 30–31, discusses the *Commentarius in evangelium Lucae*, c. 18, where Bonaventure refers to the Old Testament patriarchs as the virtuous rich.

79. BM: Arras, ms. lat. 691 (759), fol. 112: "Unde Dominus illam predicationem audiri fecit verbo, postea fecit exemplo, ut insufficiens predicacio per verbum redderetur sufficiens per exemplum."

80. Bériou, *L'avènement des maîtres*, 35–36.

81. BM: Arras, ms. lat. 691 (759), fol. 113v: "Primo est suggestio, postea titillacio in delectacione, deinde est consensus ad peccatum, postea peccati perpetracio et egressio in opus." Eudes draws here on a long tradition that went back to Augustine of Hippo, who, in his commentary on the Sermon on the Mount, suggested that there were three ways in which a sin was committed: "suggestione, delectatione, et consensione." See *PL*, vol. 34, col. 1246.

82. BM: Arras, ms. lat. 691 (759), fol. 113v–114: "Prima consummacio est excellencie et hec est in consilio, item est consummacio sufficience, et perseverancie et hec due sunt in precepto, set quarta consummacio est glorie."

83. BM: Arras, ms. lat. 691 (759), fol. 122r: "Karissimi illi qui dant aliis exemplum in malum patres sunt eorum in malum et ideo dicitur in libro Sapientie: ex iniquis enim omnes filii qui nascuntur etc . . . [testes sunt nequitiae adversus parentes in interrogatione sua]" (Wisdom of Solomon 4:6).

84. Bériou, *L'avènement des maîtres*, 321–23.

85. BM: Arras, ms. lat. 691 (759), fol. 122r: "Et Bernardus dicit quod bona consciencia est necessaria coram Deo et bonum exemplum coram homine." I have not been able to locate the citation Eudes attributes to Saint Bernard in the *Patrologia latina* database.

86. BnF, ms. lat. 16502, fol. 157v: "Quadruplicem maculam legimus quam lex detestabatur, sicut patet in Levitico, scilicet maculam in domo, maculam in vestimento, maculam in oblatione, et [maculam] in offerente, quia nullus maculam habens debebat offere sacrificia Domino. Per maculam domus intelligitur macula familie proprie, per maculam in vestimento intelligitur macula in conversatione, macula in oblatione dicitur macula in opere, nam per oblationem intelligitur opus quod Deo offertur. Persona offerens dicitur voluntas hominis que dicitur offere Domino." Eudes is referring to a passage in Leviticus dealing with laws regarding leprosy, which was viewed as a form of impurity.

87. This is not to suggest that theologians could not be innovative in their lectures on the *Sentences*. Bougerol has argued that Eudes's distinction 26 on book 3 of the *Sentences* was the first elaboration of a theology of hope. Eudes maintained that hope is not just a part of faith, as other theologians had suggested, but rather should be included alongside the triad of theological virtues. See Jacques-Guy Bougerol, *La théologie de l'espérance aux XIIe et XIIIe siècles*, 2 vols. (Paris, 1985), 1:214–39.

88. Like the sermon manuscripts we possess, the manuscripts of Eudes's disputed questions represent a written version, undoubtedly different from the live, oral version. The written versions of the disputed questions show no signs of having been hurried. It is unclear to what degree Eudes himself was responsible for them. See Sileo, *Teoria della scienza teologica*, 1:55–56.

89. See Trottman, *Théologie et noétique*, 28–49.

90. Odo Rigaldi, *Quaestio de scientia theologiae*, pars I, quaest. 2, par. 50–60, in Sileo, *Teoria della scienza teologica*, 2:24–28.

91. Odo Rigaldi, *Quaestio de scientia theologiae*, pars I, quaest. 1, par. 20, in Sileo, *Teoria della scienza teologica*, 2:11.

92. Trottman, *Théologie et noétique*, 43.

93. Odo Rigaldi, *Quaestio de scientia theologiae*, pars I, quaest. 1, par. 7, in Sileo, *Teoria della scienza teologica*, 2:7–8, where Eudes responds to bk. 2, chap. 4, of Aristotle's *Ethica ad Nicomachum*. See *The Greek Commentaries on the Nicomachean Ethics of Aristotle in the Latin Translation of Robert Grosseteste, Bishop of Lincoln (†1253)*, ed. H. P. F. Mercken (Leiden, 1973), 209: "Ad virtutes autem scire quidem parum aut nihil potest. . . . Sed multi haec quidem non operantur. Ad rationem autem confugientes existimant philosophari et sic fore studiosi, simile aliquid facientes laborantibus qui medicos audiunt quidem studiose, faciunt autem nihil eorum quae praecepta sunt. Quemadmodum igitur neque illi bene habebunt corpus ita curati, neque isti animam ita philosophantes." In an earlier passage in the *Ethics*, however, Aristotle had written: "Quoniam igitur praesens negotium non contemplationis gratia est quemadmodum alia (non enim ut sciamus quid est virtus scrutamur sed ut boni efficiamur, quia nullum utique esset proficuum eius), necessarium est scrutari ea quae circa operationes, qualiter operandum est eas." See bk. 2, chap. 2, 1103b26–30, 200. It is unclear whether Eudes could already have had access to Robert Grosseteste's direct translation of the *Nicomachean Ethics* from Greek to Latin, which Robert completed around 1246. See Mercken's introduction to *Greek Commentaries*, 32–45.

94. Odo Rigaldi, *Quaestio de scientia theologiae*, pars 1, quaest. 1, par. 35, in Sileo, *Teoria della scienza teologica*, 2:18.

95. Odo Rigaldi, *Quaestio de scientia theologiae*, pars 1, quaest. 1, par. 35, in Sileo, *Teoria della scienza teologica*, 2:18.

96. Bériou, *L'avènement des maîtres*, 47.

97. Ibid., 44.

98. Pergamo, "Il desiderio innato del sopranaturale."

99. Odo Rigaldi, "Quaestiones quaedam scholasticae de officio divino et cantu ecclesiastico," ed. van Dijk, 36–37.

100. Ibid., 41–43: "Quarto quaeritur utrum liceat cantare Deo cum organis et instrumentis." Eudes is most likely not referring to an organ here, since there was no organ in Notre Dame of Paris before the fourteenth century. *Organum* could refer to any sort of contrivance or device and in this case probably denoted a type of polyphonic sacred song. Although no musical instruments (other than the organ) were used in Notre Dame before the sixteenth century, Eudes may have been considering (as Thomas Aquinas did) whether instruments should have a role in liturgical music. Friars in the thirteenth century (especially the Dominicans) tended to be quite conservative about liturgical music. This seems to have been the case with Eudes Rigaud. See Craig Wright, *Music and Ceremony at Notre Dame of Paris, 500–1550* (Cambridge, 1989), 143–44, 343–46.

101. Odo Rigaldi, "Quaestiones quaedam scholasticae de officio divino et cantu ecclesiastico," ed. van Dijk, 26–28.

102. Ibid., 39.

103. *RV*, 106–7.
104. See the works of Lottin, *Psychologie et morale*, especially vol. 1, *Problèmes de psychologie*, 151–73.
105. BM: Toulouse, ms. lat. 737, fol. 233v.
106. BM: Toulouse, ms. lat. 737, fol. 235v: "Deinde queritur si omnibus hominibus in hac vita est usus liberi arbitrii quia videtur quod non sit in pueris quia nec videntur habere usum rationis nec voluntatis."
107. See Plato, *Protagoras*, 352B–353A, trans. C. C. W. Taylor (Oxford, 1991), 46–47. Again, Eudes may have been drawing on book 7 of the *Nicomachean Ethics*, where Aristotle challenged the Socratic argument about moral weakness and posited that it is possible for a man to know what is right and yet do what is wrong. See Jonathan Lear, *Aristotle: The Desire to Understand* (Cambridge, 1988), 174–86.
108. The position Eudes was arguing against came to be known as the *propositio magistralis* in the late 1270s. It was espoused by Giles of Rome, who was censured for his views by Stephen Tempier, the bishop of Paris. Tempier appointed a commission of Parisian theologians to study the orthodoxy of Giles's positions. The commissioners initially sided with Tempier on the question of whether the will can act contrary to a "dictate" of right reason but later changed their minds, supporting Giles on this point. See S. D. Dumont, "Time, Contradiction, and Freedom of the Will," *Documenti e studi sulla tradizione filosofica medievale* 3, 2 (1992): 577–79.
109. Lottin, *Problèmes de psychologie*, 163.
110. Ibid., 86–87.
111. John W. Baldwin, "'Studium et Regnum': The Penetration of University Personnel into French and English Administration at the Turn of the Twelfth and Thirteenth Centuries," *Revue des études Islamiques* 44 (1976): 199–215. See also John W. Baldwin, "Masters at Paris from 1179 to 1215: A Social Perspective," in *Renaissance and Renewal in the Twelfth Century*, ed. Robert L. Benson and Giles Constable (Cambridge, 1982), 138–72.

2. Itinerant Archbishop, Itinerant *Familia*

1. Andrieu-Guitrancourt, *L'archevêque Eudes Rigaud*, 13.
2. Ibid., 13 n. 2.
3. Bernard of Bessa, *Liber de laudibus beati Francisci*, 74: "venerabilis pater frater Odo Rigaldi genere clarus. . . ." See Andrieu-Guitrancourt, *L'archevêque Eudes Rigaud*, 16–18.
4. *RER*, 42; *RV*, 39. It is unclear whether Eudes played any role in Marie's election. The Paraclete adopted canons from the Council of Rouen of 1231, including canons that made the nunnery subject to episcopal supervision. Eudes Rigaud may have had some influence in the adoption of these canons, which run counter to the liberties the Paraclete had earlier enjoyed. See John Benton, "The Paraclete and the Council of Rouen of 1231," in *Culture, Power, and Personality in Medieval France*, edited by Thomas N. Bisson (London, 1991), 411–16.
5. For Adam de Vernolio, see *RER*, 606; *RV*, 532. See also Vincent Tabbagh, *Fasti Ecclesiae Gallicanae: Répertoire prosopographique des évêques, dignitaires et chanoines de France de 1200 à 1500*, vol. 2, *Diocèse de Rouen* (Turnhout, 1998), 148; Ménindès, "Eudes Rigaud," 163–64.
6. *RER*, 460; *RV*, 405. Ménindès, "Eudes Rigaud," 164–65.
7. Eudes refers to Peter as *germanus noster*. In one instance in the *Register*, Peter served as a witness. See *RER*, 246; *RV*, 224.
8. For Eudes's visits to Courquetaine, see *RER*, 357, 527, 685; *RV*, 313, 462, 595. See also Andrieu-Guitrancourt, *L'archevêque Eudes Rigaud*, 10–13.
9. *RER*, 542; *RV*, 476.
10. It is possible, of course, that Pierre Rigaud was quite a bit younger than Eudes and that this was not Pierre's first marriage.
11. *RER*, 541–42, 606, 646; *RV*, 475, 531, 563, 668, 669, 670. It was not uncommon for bishops to have relatives in their cathedral's chapter, and it is likely that Eudes's nephews received their prebends through their uncle's influence.

12. Andrieu-Guitrancourt, *L'archevêque Eudes Rigaud*, 33.

13. The papal registers contain no record of the pope's confirmation of Eudes Rigaud's election, although it is almost certain that the pope would have confirmed the election. Eudes's archiepiscopal consecration took place in March 1248 before Innocent IV in Lyon.

14. Luke Wadding, *Annales Minorum*, ed. Jospehi Mariae Fonseca, vol. 3 (Quaracchi, 1931), 183–84.

15. The earliest reference I have been able to find to the oft-repeated story about Eudes's election at Rouen is in Jean-François Pommeraye, *Histoire des archevesques de Rouen* (Rouen, 1667), 475. The story bears a striking resemblance to the way the Roman Breviary described the election of Saint Nicolas. See Andrieu-Guitrancourt, *L'archevêque Eudes Rigaud*, 36 and n. 1.

16. According to this story, Eudes de Sully, who was bishop of Paris (and brother of Henri de Sully, the archbishop of Bourges who had recently died), was determined that a Cistercian succeed his brother as archbishop of Bourges. Eudes de Sully wrote the names of three Cistercian abbots on ballots and placed them on the altar in the cathedral at Bourges. After celebrating the Mass, he randomly chose a ballot, which turned out to be the one with Guillaume's name on it. The Cistercian showed great reluctance in accepting the dignity but did so after being ordered to by the pope and the Cistercian general. Guillaume was canonized in 1218. See *GC*, 10:1509–10.

17. Adolphe Chéruel, ed., *Normanniae nova chronica . . .* (Caen, 1851), 22.

18. In 1245, the pope had quashed the election of Magister Odo of Saint-Denis, a canon of the Rouen chapter, citing an irregularity in the voting procedure. The pope instead named Eudes Clément, former abbot of Saint-Denis, dean of Saint-Martin of Tours, and royal familiar. Konrad Eubel, ed., *Hierarchia Catholica medii aevi* (2nd ed., Regensburg, 1913), 425 n. 5; Élie Berger, ed., *Les registres d'Innocent IV*, 4 vols. (Paris, 1844–[1920]), no. 1187.

19. Salimbene de Adam, *Chronicle*, 441; Salimbene de Adam, *Chronica*, 2:656.

20. Episcopal elections in Normandy were frequently contested. Indeed, in each of the four previous archiepiscopal elections in Rouen (in 1222, 1231, 1235, and 1245), there had been more than one candidate. There were more contested episcopal elections in Normandy during the reign of Louis IX (10 out of 29) than in any other province in France. When a chapter could not agree on a candidate, the king (or pope) frequently intervened by supporting a particular candidate, including, at times, a candidate not previously considered by the chapter. See Fernando Alberto Picó, "The Bishops of France in the Reign of Louis IX (1226–1270)" (Ph.D. diss., Johns Hopkins University, 1970), 11–16, 90; Pascal Montaubin, "Les chapitres cathédraux séculiers de Normandie et la centralisation pontificale au XIIIe siècle," in *Chapitres et cathédrales en Normandie*, ed. Sylvette Lemagnen and Philippe Manneville (Caen, 1997), 259. More generally on electoral procedures, see Hélène Millet, *Les chanoines du chapitre de Laon, 1272–1412* (Paris, 1982), 263–65.

21. Picó, "Bishops of France," 9–10.

22. On Eudes Clément, see John W. Baldwin, *The Government of Philip Augustus: Foundations of French Royal Power in the Middle Ages* (Berkeley, 1986), 119, 306.

23. According to Eudes's polyptych, there were 7,639 parishioners in the city of Rouen. But this figure did not account for the poor, the unattached, the religious, or the Jewish population. Mollat estimates the city's population at 30,000–40,000. See Michel Mollat and François J. Gay, *Histoire de Rouen* (Toulouse, 1979), 78–79.

24. Mollat and Gay, *Histoire de Rouen*, 80–82.

25. Lindy Grant, *Architecture and Society in Normandy, 1120–1270* (New Haven, 2005), 222.

26. Much of the cathedral must have been rebuilt by 1237, when a large consecration ceremony took place there for the new archbishop of Rouen, Pierre de Colmieu. Ibid., 125.

27. Chéruel, *Normanniae nova chronica*, 22–23.

28. Pobst notes that Eudes did not demand a procuration from Saint-Ouen during his visitation, which followed the fire by only a few weeks. However, during Eudes's fifteen recorded visitations of the abbey over the course of twenty-one years, he never once de-

manded a procuration. Saint-Ouen was unusual in being one of the few Benedictine abbeys to be exempt from paying procurations. At other monastic houses where Eudes did not spend the night but visited, he still demanded a procuration. Pobst, "Visitation of Religious and Clergy," 229.

29. The Norman chronicle records a fire during the night of Easter 1251 that destroyed the house of the vice-presbyter of Rouen. Chéruel, *Normanniae nova chronica*, 23.

30. *RER*, 61, 72, 80, 239, 523, 526; *RV*, 55, 63–64, 71, 218, 459, 461.

31. Grant, *Architecture and Society*, 8.

32. Economic, political, and religious connections continued between Normandy and England, which from 1066 until 1204 had repeatedly been united and separated. Norman ecclesiastical institutions continued to hold property in England. Much of the aristocracy in both England and Normandy was, as Robert Bartlett puts it, a "cross-channel aristocracy," holding estates in both realms. Although vulnerable to periods of political separation, these aristocrats proved surprisingly resilient and continued to treat Normandy and England as "one extended theatre of action." See Bartlett, *England under the Norman and Angevin Kings, 1075–1225* (Oxford, 2000), 11–28.

33. During the 1250s, the export of wine to England stopped almost completely, owing to competition from Gascony. See Mollat and Gay, *Histoire de Rouen*, 82.

34. Ibid., 81–82.

35. Tabbagh, *Diocèse de Rouen*, 6.

36. Grant, *Architecture and Society*, 10–11.

37. Darlington, "Travels of Odo Rigaud," 74.

38. Michael Burger, "Officiales and the Familiae of the Bishop of Lincoln, 1258–1299," *Journal of Medieval History* 16, 1 (1990): 39–53. I have found a few cases in Eudes's *Register* where the archbishop's official, probably the most powerful member of the *familia*, is listed last. I find it difficult to imagine, however, that the archbishop (or his *clericus*) would have failed to record the official's presence in a witness list.

39. They included Guillaume de Premery, a *panetarius*, or baker (*RV*, 217, 311); Pierre de Fresne, *noster servientus* (*RV*, 217); Henri de Mucegros, *noster servientus* (*RV*, 156); Gaufridus, *boticularius*, or herbalist (*RV*, 217); and Philippe, *servientus curie Rothomagensis* (*RV*, 264). On the number in Eudes's entourage, I draw on Darlington, "Travels of Odo Rigaud," 34–41. Tabbagh suggests that during the later Middle Ages, the archbishop of Rouen's entourage numbered around fifteen. See Tabbagh, *Le clergé séculier*, 49–51.

40. The English translation of Salimbene's *Chronicle* mistranslates a passage, referring to Eudes as "Brother Rigaud of Mantua." The Latin text is "Largas expensas fecit Mantue fratri Rigaldo et toti familie sue, cum transisset per eum eundo ad curiam." Salimbene then describes "frater Regaldus ex Ordine fratrum Minorum et Rotomagensis archiepiscopus et unus de maioribus clericis de mundo." I do not believe Salimbene was referring to a certain "Brother Rigaud of Mantua" but rather was describing Eudes's stopover in Mantua on February 16–17, 1254 (according to Eudes's *Register*), en route to Rome. See Salimbene de Adam, *Chronicle*, 440–41; Salimbene de Adam, *Chronica*, 2:655–56.

41. Canon 3 of the Third Lateran Council (1179) limited archbishops' entourages to forty or fifty horses or other mounts, cardinals to twenty or twenty-five mounts, bishops to twenty or thirty, archdeacons to five or seven, and deans and their delegates to two. Canon 33 of the Fourth Lateran Council reaffirmed these limits. See Norman P. Tanner, ed., *Decrees of the Ecumenical Councils*, vol. 1 (London, 1990), 213, 250.

42. Eudes was definitely accompanied on his trip to Rome by two Franciscans, Walter and Hardouin; two canons from Rouen, Magister Pierre d'Aumale and Magister Robert; and the dean of the Rouen chapter, Guy of Bourbon.

43. They included Simon de Montpensier, Jean de Neuilly-en-Thelle, Pierre d'Aumale, Jean de Jumièges, Richard de Sap, Etienne de Sens, Guillaume de Flavacourt, Pierre d'Ons, Richard de Salmonville, Etienne de Lorris, Radulph de Cotevrart, and Guillaume de Saâne. It was not unusual for bishops in secular cathedrals (and all the Norman cathedrals except Sées had chapters of secular canons) to use cathedral canons in the administration of the diocese. In Limoges, the bishop referred to the canons as *clerici nostri* or *ministri nostri*. The archdeacon was himself often a member of the cathedral

chapter. See Jean Becquet, ed., *Actes des évêques de Limoges: Des origines à 1197* (Paris, 1999), 9–11.

44. Hélène Millet, *I canonici al servizio dello stato in Europa, secoli XIII–XVI* (Modena, 1992), 40.

45. As bishops began spending more time away from their cathedral cities, deans replaced them as the immediate heads of cathedrals. Although in various situations, such as the alienation of church property, Eudes needed his chapter's authorization, it was customary by the thirteenth century for the Rouen chapter to function as a separate corporation with the dean presiding. See Millet, *Les chanoines du chapitre cathédral*, 44; Kathleen Edwards, *The English Secular Cathedrals in the Middle Ages*, 2nd ed. (New York, 1967), 98–99, 106.

46. Joseph Avril, "La participation du chapitre cathédral au governement du diocèse," in *Le monde des chanoines (XI–XIVe siècles)*, Cahiers de Fanjeaux, no. 24 (Toulouse, 1989), 47–50.

47. On the social background of canons in Norman cathedral chapters during the ducal period, see David S. Spear, "Membership in the Norman Cathedral Chapters During the Ducal Period: Some Preliminary Findings," *Medieval Prosopography* 5, 1 (1984): 1–18.

48. This figure is based on those known to have been canons in the Rouen cathedral in 1260 and known to have obtained at minimum the master's of arts. See Tabbagh, *Diocèse de Rouen*. In comparison, slightly fewer than half the canons of Laon during the thirteenth century carried the title *magister*. See Millet, *Les chanoines du chapitre cathédral*, 88.

49. Montaubin, "Les chapitres cathédraux séculiers," 259–65, 271–72; Grant, *Architecture and Society*, 26–27. As Montaubin has shown, many of the Norman cathedral canons who were Italian or who had worked at the papal curia (which, combined, never represented more than about 10% of an entire chapter) received their prebends through apostolic collation. It was papal provisions, in other words, that brought foreign canons to Rouen. Pierre de Colmieu, who had been chaplain to Gregory IX before becoming archbishop of Rouen, brought a number of Italians to the chapters of Rouen and Bayeux, including Arnulf of Capua (Pope Gregory's nephew) and Gregory of Naples, who would become bishop of Bayeux in 1274. Pierre also introduced some Norman clergy, such as Guillaume de Saâne, to the papal curia. In Laon, there were many Italian canons in the thirteenth century. See Millet, *Les chanoines du chapitre cathédral*, 62–64.

50. Christopher R. Cheney, *English Bishops' Chanceries, 1100–1250* (Manchester, 1950), 8–9; Andrieu-Guitrancourt, *L'archevêque Eudes Rigaud*, 284–85. Cheney makes this argument with reference to bishops' use of archdeacons and canons as episcopal officials, but the argument can be extended. Eudes used beneficed canons as his personal secretary, official, and regular members of his *familia*.

51. *RV*, 742–44.

52. Similarly, during the ducal period, a number of Rouen canons were appointed archdeacons, and five Rouen archdeacons became bishops or archbishops. See David S. Spear, "Les archidiacres de Rouen au cours de la période ducale," *Annales de Normandie* 34 (1984): 33.

53. In 1281, Jean was elected cardinal.

54. For bibliographical notices on Rouen canons, see Tabbagh, *Diocèse de Rouen*.

55. On the archdeacon in the thirteenth century as a rival of the bishop, see A. Amanieu, "Archdiacre," in *Dictionnaire de droit canonique*, 1 (1935): cols. 962–79; also Robert Génestal, "La patrimonialité de l'archidiaconat dans la province ecclésiastique de Rouen," in *Mélanges Paul Fournier* (Paris, 1929), 285–91. On archdeacons in England, see A. H. Thompson, *The English Clergy and Their Organization in the Later Middle Ages* (Oxford, 1947), 60–62.

56. *RER*, 71; *RV*, 61.

57. Similarly, on September 9, 1250, Guillaume de Saâne, archdeacon of Eu, represented the archbishop in visiting the monastery belonging to Tiron at Longues in the diocese of Bayeux. *RER*, 108; *RV*, 93–94.

58. There are occasional references in the *Register* to earlier visitations by archdeacons. See, for instance, a reference to a visitation of the Maîson-Dieu at Chaumont by the archdeacon of the French Vexin: *RER*, 183, *RV*, 167. Eudes learns that the archdeacon of the Norman Vexin had visited three or four churches in the deanery of Ecouis and had re-

ceived procurations in each: *RER*, 52; *RV*, 45–46. Eudes also hears about disciplinary actions taken by the archdeacon of the Grand-Caux in the deanery of Fauville, *RER*, 153–54; *RV*, 136–37.

59. *RER*, 16, 42, 85, 127, 135, 203, 250, 283, 295, 429 (Eudes represented by Adam Rigaud and Master Jean de Neuilly-en-Thelle), 568; *RV*, 13, 38, 75, 112, 120, 190, 228, 252, 263, 379, 499.

60. It may have been that archdeacons in Rouen needed the archbishop's authority to accept a priest's resignation, especially since in most cases the priest was essentially being forced by the archbishop to give up his church. It is curious that even when Eudes is present for a priest's resignation of his church, the archbishop has the archdeacon accept the resignation rather than doing so himself. Eudes also seems to have preferred to have the archdeacon of Eu accept a priest's resignation even when the church was located outside the archdeaconry of Eu. For example, the archdeacon of Eu accepted the resignation of a priest named Guillaume, who had been rector of the church in Héricourt. But Héricourt was in the archdeaconry of the Grand-Caux, and its archdeacon, a certain Reginald (probably Reginald de Bullis, later archdeacon of the Petit-Caux), was even present for the resignation ceremony. In another case, Eudes had the archdeacon of Eu deprive a priest named Roger of his church in Bourgtheroulde, located in the greater archdeaconry of Rouen. See *RER*, 170, 179; *RV*, 154, 164; Jean Laporte and Charles de Beaurepaire, eds., *Dictionnaire topographique du département de Seine-Maritime*, 2 vols. (Paris, 1984), 2:509.

61. For one instance of many, *RV*, 662–63.

62. See William C. Jordan, *Louis IX and the Challenge of the Crusade: A Study in Rulership* (Princeton, 1979), 35–64; for Philip IV, see Joseph R. Strayer, *The Reign of Philip the Fair* (Princeton, 1980). At least in the fourteenth century, the metropolitan *officialis* of Rouen received 160 *livres tournois* as remuneration, a handsome sum. See Tabbagh, *Le clergé séculier*, 78.

63. When Eudes visited the leprosary for women at La Salle-aux-Puelles on March 17, 1249, for instance, he found that the nuns who ran the leprosary did not hold chapter twice a week as the archdeacon had ordered. See *RER*, 38; *RV*, 34.

64. The Rouen official's consistory court had a staff of around thirty, including a promoter (public prosecutor), a master of wills, an examiner of witnesses, a collector, and two guards of the registers of excommunicates. Unlike some dioceses that had more than one *officialis* for the bishop, the archbishop of Rouen had only one, although the exempt abbeys of Montivilliers and Fécamp also had *officiales*. Once the archbishop organized the vicariate of Pontoise in 1255, the archbishop's vicar began performing the function of the *officialis* for that region. Tabbagh, *Diocèse de Rouen*, 8. The trend during the thirteenth century seems to have been for bishops' officials to leave their bishops' *familiae*, at least in the physical sense. Under bishops Gravesend and Sutton (1258–99), for example, the *officialis* was no longer physically a member of the bishop's *familia*. See Burger, "Officiales and the Familiae," 39–40. On the jurisdiction exercised by the bishop's official, see Charles H. Haskins, "Formulary of the Officialité of Rouen," in *Mélanges Paul Fournier* (Paris, 1929), 359–62. On the origins of the office of the official in the diocese of Beauvais, see Olivier Guyotjeannin, "Juridiction gracieuse ecclésiastique et naissance de l'officialité à Beauvais (1175–1220)," in *À propos des actes d'évêques: Hommage à Lucie Fossier*, ed. Michel Parisse (Nancy, 1991), 295–310.

65. Before being called an *officialis*, the bishop's delegate was called his *vicarius* or *ministerialis*. Beauvais was one of the first dioceses to have an *officialis*, the first recorded mention being in 1179. The first recorded mention of the *officialis* of the archbishop of Rouen occurred in 1192. However, it was only around 1213–14 that the *officialis* began to exert gracious jurisdiction and act as an agent of episcopal justice. See Guyotjeannin, "Juridiction gracieuse ecclésiastique"; for Rouen, see Tabbagh, *Diocèse de Rouen*, 8; for Angers, see Joseph Avril, *Le gouvernement des évêques et la vie religieuse dans le diocèse d'Angers, 1148–1240* (Paris, 1984), 623–27.

66. Delmaire, *Le diocèse d'Arras*, 177–87; Anne Lefebvre-Teillard, *Les officialités à la veille du concile de Trente* (Paris, 1973), 26.

67. Tabbagh, *Le clergé séculier*, 78.

68. The jurisdiction of archdeacons and deans in Angers grew during the thirteenth century as they increasingly exercised their own justice, separate from the bishop's, and, like the bishop, delegated the office of judge to their own *officiales*. The archdeacons in Rouen, in contrast, did not have their own *officiales*. See Avril, *Le gouvernement des évêques*, 635–40.

69. Haskins, "Formulary of the Officialité of Rouen," 359–62. There are seven thirteenth-century forms in the name of the official of Rouen at the back of a manuscript of Geoffrey de Trano's *Summa*: BnF ms. lat. 18224, fol. 282r–283v.

70. *RER*, 231; *RV*, 210.

71. *RV*, 525: "in aula nostra minori Rothomagensi"; *RV*, 485: "in mediocri camera nostra manerii nostri Rothomagensis"; *RV*, 475: "in aula nostri maiori." On Eudes's Rouen manor, see Léon Alfred Jouen, *Comptes, devis et inventaires du manoir archiépiscopal de Rouen* (Paris, 1908), xx–xxiii. On medieval bishops' palaces in northern and central Italy, see Maureen C. Miller, *The Bishop's Palace: Architecture and Authority in Medieval Italy* (Ithaca, 2000).

72. *RER*, 712; *RV*, 619–20.

73. When Evrard disappeared from the *Register* after March 1259, John seems to be the only secretary Eudes had, except for the occasional mention of another name.

74. Some of Eudes's charters were copied in "secretary" cursive, a quicker and messier script that was characterized by clubbed ascenders (as opposed to the gracefully looped and forked ascenders in English documentary script). Almost all of the *Register*, however, and a large number of Eudes's charters were copied using the English documentary script. Jean de Morgneval is also referred to in the *Register* as *magister*. On scripts, see M. P. Brown, *A Guide to Western Historical Scripts from Antiquity to 1600* (London, 1990), 92–95.

75. Auguste Longnon, ed., *Pouillés de la province de Rouen* (Paris, 1903).

76. *RER*, 594; *RV*, 520.

77. *RV*, 733–34.

78. Brothers Walter, Harduin, and Adam appear most frequently. Walter served in the *familia* for thirteen years, Harduin for nine years, and Adam for sixteen years. Both Walter and Harduin accompanied the archbishop to Rome in 1254.

79. J. H. Srawley, "Grosseteste's Administration of the Diocese of Lincoln," in *Robert Grosseteste: Scholar and Bishop*, ed. D. A. Callus (Oxford, 1955), 147–48.

80. Cheney, *Episcopal Visitation*, 64–72.

81. Salimbene de Adam, *Chronicle*, 441; Salimbene, *Chronica*, 2:656.

82. In addition to his frequent visits to the Franciscan convent in Rouen, Eudes visited the Franciscan convents in Paris, Lyon, Soissons, Pontoise, Vernon, and Mantes-sur-Seine, as well as the female house of Longchamp, just outside Paris, which had recently been founded by Isabelle of France, sister of Louis IX. The *Register* mentions forty-two visits by Eudes to Franciscan houses.

83. Oscar Darlington, Sydney Brown (*RER*, 726 n. 6), and Théodore Bonnin (*RV*, 631 n. 1) all thought that the Franciscan "frater Adam" was Eudes's nephew. In an article in 1931, however, R. Ménindès argued that Adam was Eudes's own brother, pointing out that the "frater Adam" who joined Eudes's entourage in 1252 could not have been the son of Pierre Rigaud, whose marriage Eudes celebrated in 1263. See Ménindès, "Eudes Rigaud, Frère Mineur," 162 n. 1. Andrieu-Guitrancourt, in *L'archevêque Eudes Rigaud*, also correctly identified Adam as Eudes's brother. There are two references in the *Register* to Adam as "frater Adam, meus frater." See *RV*, 580, 670. The confusion about "frater Adam" stems from the fact that Eudes had two nephews, both named Adam (Adam Rigaud and Adam de Vereuil).

84. *RER*, 531; *RV*, 466–67.

85. *RER*, 382–83; *RV*, 336.

86. *RER*, 726; *RV*, 631.

87. *RER*, 705; *RV*, 612.

88. *RER*, 730; *RV*, 635.

89. *RER*, 382; *RV*, 335.

90. *RER*, 382; *RV*, 335.

91. *RER*, 382; *RV*, 335.
92. *RER*, 404; *RV*, 355.
93. Travel by boat or horse was not mutually exclusive, since horses were taken on boats. Even archdeacons appear to have conducted their visitations by horseback. Eudes refers to the archdeacons in the diocese of Sées, who were buying their horses and keeping them as their own. See *RER*, 91; *RV*, 80–81.
94. *RER*, 149–50, 180, 182, 206, 391, 604; *RV*, 132, 165–66, 167, 192, 345, 529. Andrieu-Guitrancourt, *L'archevêque Eudes Rigaud*, 374.
95. Darlington, "Travels of Odo Rigaud," 76–80.
96. *RER*, 195; *RV*, 178. On Eudes's trip to Rome, see Yves Renouard, "Routes, étapes et vitesses de marche de France à Rome au XIIIe et au XIVe siècles d'après les itinéraires d'Eudes Rigaud (1254) et de Barthélemy Bonis (1350)," in *Studi in onore di Amintore Fanfani nel venticinquennio di cattedra universitaria*, vol. 3 (Milan, 1962), 404–28.
97. Many of the routes Eudes followed were formerly Roman roads. Quite a few modern highways follow roughly the same routes.
98. Thomson, *Friars in the Cathedral*, 93–101.
99. Salimbene de Adam, *Chronicle*, 440–41; Salimbene de Adam, *Chronica*, 2:655–56.
100. Salimbene is contradictory in his attitude toward wealth and power. Quite often, he seems to want to boast to his readers just how many powerful figures he knew personally, leading Rosalind Brooke to write that Salimbene's "standards were not those of a true friar minor." In other places in his chronicle, however, Salimbene denounces those he regards as worldly and unspiritual, the very traits he at times seems to embody. Thus, the tensions and seeming contradictions in his descriptions of Eudes Rigaud may reveal more about Salimbene than about Eudes. See Brooke, *Early Franciscan Government*, 49.
101. Salimbene de Adam, *Chronicle*, 440; Salimbene de Adam, *Chronica*, 2:655.
102. Thomson, *Friars in the Cathedral*, 101–5. Although Eudes was the only Franciscan bishop in the French kingdom, at least nineteen (and possibly as many as twenty-six) Franciscans occupied episcopal seats in Italy before 1261. See Thomson, *Friars in the Cathedral*, 93.
103. *RER*, 198 n. 4; *RV*, 186 n. 5.
104. Darlington, "Travels of Odo Rigaud," 74–82.
105. *RER*, 689; *RV*, 599; Grant, *Architecture and Society*, 36.
106. *RER*, 417; *RV*, 366.
107. *RER*, 460; *RV*, 404.
108. *RER*, 530; *RV*, 466.
109. Darlington, "Travels of Odo Rigaud," 43–44. I use Darlington's figures for the number of nights Eudes spent at his manor houses. A table of these figures can be found in "Travels of Odo Rigaud," 70.
110. Vincent Tabbagh, "Le temporel des archevêques de Rouen aux derniers siècles du moyen-âge," *Journal of Medieval History* 6, 2 (1980): 214. See Annie Renoux, "Palais princiers, royaux et épiscopaux normanno-angevins (Xe–XIIIe siècles)," in *Cavalieri alla conquista del sud: Studi sull'Italia normanna in memoria di Léon-Robert Ménager*, ed. Errico Cuozzo and Jean-Marie Martin (Rome, 1998), 53. For comparison with English episcopal see palaces, see Michael Thompson, *Medieval Bishops' Houses in England and Wales* (Aldershot, U.K., 1998), 29–70. Most episcopal palaces were two-storied buildings with one hall on the ground floor and another hall and chamber on the second floor. A two-story chapel was either attached to the palace or freestanding, with the chapel itself usually on the second floor and a crypt or undercroft below. Some bishops' palaces were directly linked to the cathedral, as was the case in Paris in the late twelfth century. The second-floor hall and chamber of Eudes de Sully's palace connected to the southern side of the cathedral of Notre Dame.
111. Marie Casset, "Les résidences rurales et semi-rurales des archevêques et évêques normands au moyen âge" (Diss., Université du Maine, 1999), 220–21. It was fairly common both in England and on the Continent for a bishop's manor houses to be quite similar to his see palace. See Thompson, *Medieval Bishops' Houses*, 126–54.
112. Tabbagh, "Le temporel des archevêques," 214.

113. Casset, "Les résidences rurales," 240.
114. *RV*, 404 n. 1. It was common for French bishops to have manor houses in Paris and for English bishops to have residences in London. See Thompson, *Medieval Bishops' Houses*, 71–83.
115. On the archiepiscopal manor at Aliermont, see Abbé Cochet, "Le manoir des archevêques de Rouen sur l'Alihermont," *Revue de Rouen et de Normandie*, n.s., 3 (1849): 57–66. Eudes purchased Pinterville in 1260 from "Petrus de Meullanto, scancius domini regis Francie, et Ligardis eius uxor." He purchased Gaillon from King Louis in 1263. See *RV*, 394 n. 1; Th. Bonnin, ed., *Cartulaire de Louviers: Documents historiques originaux du Xe au XVIIIe siècle*, vol. 1 (Evreux-Paris, 1870), 286–87; Darlington, "Travels of Odo Rigaud," 49–50. There is no evidence that Eudes owned a residence in Maretot. Beginning in 1260 and continuing through 1269, however, Eudes frequented a residence there, spending a total of 121 nights. See Darlington, "Travels of Odo Rigaud," 53–54.
116. *RV*, 766–73.
117. The king stayed at the archbishop's manor house at Déville, as well as the château at Gaillon, which the king had sold to Eudes only shortly before. Eudes does not seem to have been able to accommodate the king in Aliermont; the king stayed in nearby Arques. See *RER*, 305, 306, 576; *RV*, 272, 505. The queen stayed at Eudes's residences in Rouen and Fresne. *RER*, 306; *RV*, 273. The archbishop of Tyre stayed at the archiepiscopal residence in Rouen. *RER*, 576; *RV*, 505. Eudes's manor house at Pinterville housed the papal legate and the bishop of Evreux. *RER*, 576; *RV*, 506.
118. Casset, "Les résidences rurales," 40–60, 299.

3. A Metropolitan's Contested Jurisdiction

1. Some primateships encompassed multiple metopolitanates. Lyon claimed to be the primate of the provinces of Rouen, Tours, and Sens, but this was contested by the metropolitans of both Rouen and Sens. The metropolitans of Rouen considered themselves the primates of Normandy. See Jean-François Lemarignier, Jean Gaudemet, and Guillaume Mollat, *Institutions ecclésiastiques*, vol. 3 of *Histoire des institutions françaises au moyen âge*, ed. Ferdinand Lot and Robert Fawtier (Paris, 1962), 161.
2. A. Amanieu, "Archevêque," *Dictionnaire de droit canonique* 1 (1935): cols. 927–34; Andrieu-Guitrancourt, *L'archevêque Eudes Rigaud*, 113–14.
3. F. C. Bouuaert, "Métropolitain," *Dictionnaire de droit canonique* 6 (1957): cols. 875–77.
4. Robert Benson, *The Bishop-Elect: A Study in Medieval Ecclesiastical Office* (Princeton, 1968), 167–89.
5. *CR*, 2:80.
6. See Kenneth Pennington, *Popes and Bishops: The Papal Monarchy in the Twelfth and Thirteenth Centuries* (Philadelphia, 1984).
7. Ibid., 192.
8. I. S. Robinson, "'Periculosus homo': Pope Gregory VII and Episcopal Authority," 103–31, quoted in Pennington, *Popes and Bishops*, 6 n. 12. Robinson was describing the bishops of the eleventh century, but as Pennington argues, this view of the church persisted and was just as prominent in the thirteenth century.
9. Louis Boisset, *Un concile provincial au treizième siècle: Vienne 1289, église locale et société* (Paris, 1973), 33. Boisset counts ninety known provincial councils in France for the thirteenth century.
10. *RER*, 140; *RV*, 125.
11. *RER*, 140, 408; *RV*, 125, 358.
12. *RER*, 97, 108, 344, 425, 443, 486, 496, 526, 551, 608, 632, 636, 675; *RV*, 85, 93, 303, 375, 389, 427, 436, 461, 483, 533, 552, 556, 586.
13. *RER*, 249; *RV*, 226.
14. *RER*, 472; *RV*, 414, where Eudes mediates a dispute between the bishop of Evreux and his cathedral chapter; *RER*, 276–77; *RV*, 248, where Eudes tries to resolve a dispute between the bishop of Coutances and his cathedral chapter by appointing arbiters.

15. *RER*, 456; *RV*, 399–400.
16. *RER*, 171, 381, 383, 708, 713; *RV*, 156, 334, 337, 616, 620.
17. *RER*, 77; *RV*, 69.
18. *RER*, 87, 683–84; *RV*, 77, 593–94.
19. *RER*, 91–92; *RV*, 80–82, where Eudes visits the cathedral chapter of Sées in the presence of the bishop of Sées. Following the visitation, Eudes sends the bishop a formal letter of complaint about the chapter's abuses.
20. *RER*, 78; *RV*, 70.
21. *RER*, 79; *RV*, 71.
22. *RER*, 424; *RV*, 374.
23. *RER*, 110, 260, 420; *RV*, 94, 233, 371.
24. *RER*, 92–93; *RV*, 81–82.
25. *RER*, 83; *RV*, 74.
26. *RER*, 140; *RV*, 125. The *Register's* use of *nos* can at times be confusing. Eudes regularly uses "we" to refer to the office of the archbishop (in other words, he would be speaking for himself and all those in his staff who represented his office). At other times, however, he uses "we" to refer to himself in the company of others. In this case, it appears that Eudes is using "we" in the former sense.
27. *Sexti decretal*, lib. III, titulus XX, in *Corpus iuris canonici*, ed. E. A. Friedberg and A. L. Richter, vol. 2 (Leipzig, 1881), 1056–59.
28. Although this papal bull dealt specifically with a dispute between the archbishop of Reims and his suffragans, it came to have universal force. However, whereas in *Romana Ecclesia* Innocent IV had stipulated that an archbishop could visit his province only after having visited "*omnia loca ecclesiastica*" of his own diocese, the pope had subsequently lessened the requirements in the case of the archbishop of Rouen, requiring him to visit only "*loca magis famosa suae diocesis.*" See Berger, *Les registres d'Innocent IV*, vol. 3, no. 7550, p. 419.
29. See Chapter 2, n. 41, for limits on episcopal entourages. See Joseph Avril, "L'encadrement diocésain et l'organisation paroissiale," in *Le troisième concile de Latran (1179): Sa place dans l'histoire*, ed. Jean Longère (Paris, 1982), 55–57.
30. *Sexti decretal*, lib. III, titulus XX, in *Corpus iuris canonici*, 2:1057.
31. Lemarignier et al., *Institutions ecclésiastiques*, 375–79.
32. At the priory of Nogent-en-Bray, which had a population of four monks, Eudes collected a procuration of more than 12 l.t. At Etouteville, a cell dependent on Cluny with only two monks, the archbishop collected more than 11 l. as procuration.
33. Procuration amounts were probably calculated based on the cost of feeding the archbishop's entourage and the amount a monastic house had paid as procuration in the past. The procuration collected at a particular religious house varied quite a bit from year to year. As far as I have been able to tell, these variations do not correlate with fluctuations in the house's economic health or population. Rather, during certain years, such as 1254, the procurations tended to be quite a bit lower, whereas during other years (1262), they tended to be consistently high, most likely owing to either fluctuations in the value of currency or changes in the size of Eudes's entourage.
34. AD: Seine-Maritime, G. 1123; *RV*, 742.
35. *RV*, 743.
36. F. M. Powicke and C. R. Cheney, eds., *Councils and Synods II*, 2 vols. (Oxford, 1964), 1:447–48; *Annales monastici*, ed. Henry Richards Luard, 4 vols. (London, 1825–91), 3:151, 181.
37. *Annales monastici*, 3:185.
38. *RER*, 145; *RV*, 129.
39. *RER*, 146–47; *RV*, 130–31. See also Pope Innocent IV's bull of 1254, summarizing the suffragans' position on this point, *RV*, 750. Also see Andrieu-Guitrancourt, *L'archevêque Eudes Rigaud*, 127–28. Andrieu-Guitrancourt notes that the Norman bishops were invoking as canonical custom an Anglo-Norman provincial custom whereby the grand seneschal could visit only once every three years.
40. *RER*, 146; *RV*, 130.
41. Andrieu-Guitrancourt, *L'archevêque Eudes Rigaud*, 78–79.

42. *RER,* 142–44; *RV,* 127–29. On the Sées case, see Andrieu-Guitrancourt, *L'archevêque Eudes Rigaud,* 227–28.

43. Jean Gaudemet, "Un règlement pour l'administration de la justice d'église dans la province de Reims au XIIIe siècle: La constitution 'Romana Ecclesia,'" in *Administration et droit: Actes des Journées de la Société internationale d'histoire du droit, tenues à Rennes, les 26, 27, 28 mai 1994,* ed. François Burdeau (Paris, 1996), 29–39.

44. *RV,* 749.

45. *RER,* 147; *RV,* 131.

46. *RV,* 751.

47. *RER,* 147; *RV,* 131.

48. *RV,* 751.

49. Normandy had a custom whereby anyone remaining excommunicate for forty days was captured and detained by the *bailli* of the king by mandate of the diocesan and made to be absolved. See Andrieu-Guitrancourt, *L'archevêque Eudes Rigaud,* 79.

50. *RV,* 750; Andrieu-Guitrancourt, *L'archevêque Eudes Rigaud,* 80–81.

51. *RER,* 192–93; *RV,* 175.

52. On September 29–30, 1252, a reconciliation was attempted at Lisieux. On October 9, 1253, another attempt was made at a meeting at Pont-Audemer.

53. After spending seven years in Lyon because of the threat posed by Frederick II, Innocent IV returned to Rome in October 1253. The pope died on December 7, 1254, only a few months after Eudes's visit.

54. *RV,* 754. In a separate bull of the same year (AD: Seine-Maritime, G. 1150), the pope ruled that if the archbishop needed to interrupt a provincial visitation for a reasonable cause, he could recommence the visitation of the same diocese after receiving the consent of the bishop.

55. Andrieu-Guitrancourt, *L'archevêque Eudes Rigaud,* 125.

56. *RER,* 326; *RV,* 288.

57. *RV,* 749–50.

58. The text of this accord can be found in *CR,* 1:148–49. The original charter is in AD: Seine-Maritime, G. 1151, marked on reverse, "composition faicte entre l'Archevesque de Rouen et les Eveques de Bayeux, Lisieux et Coutance, 1256."

59. AD: Seine-Maritime, G. 1152.

60. Ibid. Two charters from the bishop of Bayeux's official which deal with the accord have survived. One is marked on the reverse, "littera ratificationis compositum fuit . . . 1256." The other charter has illegible markings on its reverse and begins, "Reverendo in Christo patri Odo Dei gratia Rothomagensis archiepiscopus, officialis Baiocensis, salutem patri ac domino debitam ac devotam."

61. *CR,* 1:148–49. See Andrieu-Guitrancourt, *L'archevêque Eudes Rigaud,* 87–88.

62. *CR,* 1:148–49.

63. In his letter to the pope, Eudes claimed never to have asserted the right to maintain permanent archiepiscopal courts in the dioceses of the province, but his suffragans argued that he was already in the practice of doing so.

64. Decima L. Douie, *Archbishop Pecham* (Oxford, 1952); Jeremiah Smith, *The Attitude of John Pecham toward Monastic Houses under His Jurisdiction* (Washington, D.C., 1949), 34–45.

65. *RER,* 670 and n. 7; *RV,* 581–82.

66. It is unclear whether Eudes meant that he did not like the way the canons at Coutances chanted or that the canons did not use modulation in saying the offices.

67. *RER,* 123; *RV,* 106–7.

68. Cheney, *Episcopal Visitations;* Boisset, *Concile provincial;* Brentano, *York Metropolitan Jurisdiction,* 1–13.

69. For an example of this view and Andrieu-Guitrancourt's critique of it, see Andrieu-Guitrancourt, *L'archevêque Eudes Rigaud,* 92 n. 3; also Bouuaert, "Métropolitain," 875: "L'influence croissante du Pontife romain y produisit une sensible réduction de leurs pouvoirs."

70. Cheney, *Episcopal Visitations,* 23–35.

71. *CR,* 2:381–82.

72. At his first provincial council in 1252, Eudes appointed a group of "proved and honest men" (*viri providi et honesti*) as the province's investigators (*inquisitores*). Most of these investigators were deans and rectors. At each of the next three councils, however, Eudes found the investigators to have been negligent in performing their duties and appointed a new group, until finally, in 1261, he made archdeacons from each diocese the official investigators. The appointment of provincial *inquisitores* was in accordance with canon 8 of the Fourth Lateran Council. On King Louis IX's use of *enquêteurs*, see Jordan, *Louis IX*.
73. Jouen, *Comptes, devis et inventaires*, 140.

4. Fixing Broken Windows

1. Lucien Musset, "Monachisme d'époque franque et monachisme d'époque ducale en Normandie: Le problème de la continuité," in *Aspects du monachisme en Normandie (IVe–XVIIIe siècles)*, ed. Musset (Paris, 1982), 55–74.
2. See Cassandra Potts, *Monastic Revival and Regional Identity in Early Normandy* (Woodbridge, Suffolk, U.K., 1997).
3. The movements of both the Cistercians and the regular canons developed somewhat later in Normandy than in the Île de France, Beauvaisis, the Loire valley, or even Britain. Likewise, the Gregorian reforms were implemented later in Normandy than other parts of northern France, probably because of resistance from the ducal power, which did not wish to see an increase in the papacy's involvement in the Norman church. See Mathieu Arnoux, ed., *Des clercs au service de la réforme: Études et documents sur les chanoines réguliers de la province de Rouen* (Turnhout, 2000), 7–8.
4. Ibid., 23. The Premonstratensians were also an unusually strong presence in Normandy. Eudes collected procurations at ten different Premonstratensian houses.
5. Ibid., 92–95.
6. Ibid., 105.
7. At the priory of Sainte-Barbe-en-Auge, for instance, there were generally between thirty-two and forty resident canons and about thirty-six canons living outside the priory. Ibid., 175.
8. Ibid., 183.
9. Ibid., 130.
10. Ibid., 183. Eudes frequently complained about regular canons living alone in dependencies near the parishes they served, although he also at times accepted this arrangement as a necessity. See his visitation of Sainte-Barbe-en-Auge, *RER*, 215; *RV*, 199.
11. Arnoux, *Des clercs au service*, 184.
12. Ibid., 127–29.
13. Ibid., 172.
14. Pixton, *German Episcopacy*, xiv. The phrase "watchmen on the tower" was used by Archbishop Dietrich II of Trier (1212–42) while reforming his cathedral chapter following the Fourth Lateran Council. The prophet Ezekiel claimed to have been appointed "a watchman for the House of Israel" (Ezekiel 3:17, 33:7). I am indebted to Professor Pixton for informing me of the origins of this phrase.
15. Knowles, *Religious Orders*, 1:3.
16. *PL*, vol. 11, no. 281; Ursmer Berlière, "Innocent III et la réorganisation des monastères Bénédictins," *Revue Bénédictine* 32 (1920), 39–41.
17. As early as the twelfth century, the Benedictines in certain provinces, such as Reims, were holding chapter general meetings. In 1210, Benedictine abbots in the province of Rouen established annual chapter meetings. Pope Innocent III approved the Norman Benedictines' plan but insisted that the decisions of the chapter meetings be sent to Rome every four years for papal approval. The only record of a Benedictine chapter meeting in the province of Normandy under Eudes Rigaud's archiepiscopate was on May 15, 1263, in Lisieux. See Ursmer Berlière, "Les chapitres généraux de l'ordre de S. Benoît avant le IVe concile de Latran," *Revue Bénédictine* 8 (1891): 264; *Revue Bénédictine* 19 (1902): 386, 394.

18. In provinces that had not customarily held general chapter meetings (and very few provinces had), it was recommended that two Cistercian abbots (presumably familiar with the way general chapter meetings were run within their own order) be selected to help two Benedictine abbots preside over the meetings. See Berlière, "Les chapitres généraux," *Revue Bénédictine* 8 (1891): 264; Tanner, *Decrees of the Ecumenical Councils*, 1:240–41.

19. Knowles, *Religious Orders*, 79–85. There is evidence that Benedictine capitular visitations were being conducted in Normandy during Eudes Rigaud's archiepiscopate. According to the *Register*, the archbishop went to the Benedictine priory of Saint-Thomas (dependent on Saint-Victor-en-Caux), where William, the former abbot of Saint-Victor-en-Caux, was staying. Eudes had heard unpleasant rumors "from the visitor of his order" about the former abbot. See *RER*, 466; *RV*, 410. At the Benedictine abbey of Saint-Wandrille, Eudes found that the "visitors of their Order" had punished a certain monk for speaking evil words in chapter. Eudes left the Benedictine visitors' ordinance in place. See *RER*, 589; *RV*, 516. The order of Augustinian canons and congregation of Tiron also dispatched their own visitors. See *RER*, 465, 666; *RV*, 409, 578–79.

20. Cheney, *Episcopal Visitation*, 19–21.

21. Lemarignier, *Institutions ecclésiastiques*, 237.

22. In 1246–47, Innocent IV dispatched his legate, Eudes de Châteauroux, to visit and reform certain French monastic houses. See Lemarignier, *Institutions ecclésiastiques*, 242.

23. See *RER*, 266, 361; *RV*, 240, 316–17. The bishop also confirmed the ordination of the religious performed by the abbot. See Jacques Hourlier, *L'âge classique, 1140–1378: Les religieux*, vol. 10 of *Histoire du droit et des institutions de l'église en occident*, ed. Gabriel Le Bras (Paris, 1974), 459–61; Tabbagh, *Le clergé*, 121.

24. Already in the eleventh century, there were more synods being convened in the province of Normandy than in comparable provinces in England and France. See Raymonde Foreville, "The Synod of the Province of Rouen in the Eleventh and Twelfth Centuries," trans. Geoffrey Martin, in *Church and Government in the Middle Ages*, ed. C. N. L. Brooke, D. E. Luscombe, G. H. Martin, and Dorothy Owens (Cambridge, 1976), 35–36.

25. Cheney, *Episcopal Visitations*, 22.

26. See, for example, the Rouen Councils of 1223 and 1231: J. D. Mansi, ed., *Sacrorum conciliorum nova et amplissima collectio*, 54 vols. (Paris, 1901–27), 22:1197–1200, 23:213–22.

27. AD: Seine-Maritime, G7: 448–51.

28. The papal statutes are contained in the original, thirteenth-century manuscript of the archbishop's Register, BnF, ms. lat. 1245, ff. 121v–122v. See *RER*, 737–46; *RV*, 643–48.

29. R. N. Sauvage, *Histoire et développement économique d'un monastère normand au moyen âge: L'abbaye de Saint-Martin de Troarn au diocèse de Bayeux des origines au seizième siècle* (Caen, 1911), 97. The abbot of Saint-Ouen, for instance, was able to get a dispensation from Pope Alexander IV, relaxing the rule of silence (in the Benedictine Rule). The pope asked the Norman archbishop to "moderate" the rule of silence if, as the abbot claimed, it posed a danger to some monks' weak souls. See Giovanni Giacinto Sbaraglia, ed., *Bullarium Franciscanum*, 4 vols., (Rome, 1759–1804; reprint, Assisi, 1984), vol. 2, no. 316, p. 208.

30. Twenty-eight parishes in the archdiocese of Rouen belonged to Fécamp and sixteen belonged to Montivilliers and were therefore exempt from episcopal jurisdiction. See Charles de Beaurepaire and J. J. Vernier, *Inventaire-sommaire des Archives départementales antérieures à 1790, Seine-Inférieure, Archives Ecclésiastiques—Série G*, 7 vols. in 9, vol. 1 (Paris, 1868), 4. On monastic privileges of exemption more generally, see Hourlier, *L'âge classique*, 442–48.

31. The Cistercian nunneries he visited were Bival, Bondeville, and Saint-Aubin. Eudes never conducted visitations at any of Normandy's male Cistercian houses, although he did collect procurations.

32. Eudes ordained as many as 228 Cistercian monks and consecrated 18 Cistercian abbesses during his archiepiscopate. See Bernard Lucet, "Les ordinations chez les Cisterciens: Témoignage d'Eudes Rigaud pour la Normandie," *Analecta Sacri Ordinis Cisterciensis* 10 (1954): 289. Eudes was not the only bishop or archbishop to exercise his right to con-

firm abbatial elections. Oliver Sutton, bishop of Lincoln, quashed as many abbatial elections as he confirmed. Like Sutton, Eudes often quashed an election on procedural grounds, thereby depriving the monastery of the power to elect, but then went on to name the same candidate himself. See Rosalind Hill, "Bishop Sutton and the Institution of Heads of Religious Houses in the Diocese of Lincoln," *English Historical Review* 58 (1943): 324–50.

33. See Lemarignier, *Institutions ecclésiastiques*, 117–22. On a bishop's right to visit dependent priories, see Martin Heale, *The Dependent Priories of Medieval English Monasteries* (Woodbridge, Suffolk, U.K., 2004), 73–83.

34. See *RER*, 102; *RV*, 89. At Rocher-de-Mortain in Avranches, Eudes conducted full visitations. See *RER*, 95, 272, 521–22; *RV*, 83, 245, 458. At the exempt Premonstratensian house of Île Dieu, Eudes sought to conduct a visitation until he was shown two letters, one of them from the pope, confirming the house's exemption from episcopal visitation. He continued to collect a procuration, however. See *RER*, 268–69; *RV*, 243.

35. See *RER*, 635; *RV*, 555.

36. For common monastic complaints of bishops and archbishops, see Hourlier, *L'âge classique*, 465–66.

37. *RER*, 90; *RV*, 80.

38. *RER*, 258; *RV*, 234.

39. In the last record of Saint-Martin-de-Bellême in the archbishop's *Register*, Eudes merely collected a procuration. See *RER*, 422; *RV*, 375.

40. Baldwin, *Masters, Princes, and Merchants*, 1:70.

41. *RER*, 10, 635; *RV*, 7, 554–55.

42. Quoted in Coulton, *Friars*, 249.

43. Quoted in Brentano, *York Metropolitan Jurisdiction*, 1. The debate over monastic exemption from episcopal control only intensified during later decades. For one example of how it played out in the early fourteenth century, see William Chester Jordan, *Unceasing Strife, Unending Fear: Jacques de Thérines and the Freedom of the Church in the Age of the Last Capetians* (Princeton, 2005).

44. In 1242, Innocent IV had issued a bull in response to an appeal by Pierre de Colmieu, who complained that he was refused procurations while conducting provincial visitations. The pope supported the archbishop and threatened houses that were disobedient with ecclesiastical censure. AD: Seine-Maritime, G. 1144, a paper copy (marked "12" on the front) of the bull from Innocent IV to the archbishop of Rouen, dated XIII kalends, the first year of Innocent's pontificate.

45. Cheney, *Episcopal Visitations*, 100–101.

46. This incident is reported in the *Register* in the entry for June 22, 1252. See *RER*, 159; *RV*, 141.

47. AD: Seine-Maritime, G. 1755, a bull of Pope Innocent IV, addressed to the official of Paris, dated Assisi, the eleventh year of the pope's pontificate, 13 kalends of June. The ms. is marked on the reverse, "Bulle contre le prieuré de Gisors."

48. On September 17, 1253 (*RER*, 184; *RV*, 168), Eudes ordered the prior of Gisors to appear before the feast of Saint Remy "to answer whether he would be willing to admit us for the purpose of investigating his priory with reference to the observance there of the Statutes of Pope Gregory, as the Lord Pope has commanded." Eudes seems to be referring to Innocent IV's reaffirmation in 1253 of Gregory IX's statutes on the reform of Benedictine monks, but as Eudes knew, the priory of Gisors was exempt from episcopal jurisdiction. Then, on February 5, 1255 (*RER*, 223; *RV*, 205), Eudes issued a verbal warning to the prior of Gisors "to receive us at his priory both for visitation and procuration." On October 26, 1255 (*RER*, 249–50; *RV*, 227), Eudes conducted a full visitation of the priory, apparently without opposition, and collected a procuration. This visitation appears to be the only one he ever conducted there, however. At every one of his ten subsequent stops at the priory, he received a procuration without conducting a visitation.

49. AD: Seine-Maritime, G. 1755, contains two relevant mss., one marked on its reverse, "Compromis touchant le droit de visiter un prieuré de Gisors, ordre de Marmoutier, pretendu par l'Archev. 1257." The other is marked on the reverse, "Sentence arbitrale qui

exempte le prieuré de Gisors ordre Marmoutier de la visite de l'arch. et l'oblige a luy payer procuration."

50. JoAnn Kay McNamara, *Sisters in Arms: Catholic Nuns through Two Millennia* (Cambridge, Mass., 1996), 265.

51. *RER*, 331; *RV*, 293.

52. *RER*, 401; *RV*, 353.

53. At his visitation the following year, Eudes cited a bull of Innocent III, which reportedly declared that the abbey of Montivilliers was subject to the archbishop of Rouen just as any non-exempt house was subject to its diocesan. There is no record of this papal bull. It is clear, however, that Eudes was aware of another bull, in which Innocent had granted the abbey of Montivilliers and its abbess various special privileges. See *RER*, 434–36; *RV*, 383–84.

54. *RER*, 59; *RV*, 54.

55. *RER*, 612; *RV*, 536.

56. Eudes possessed a charter from 1224, which was an agreement between the priory of Sainte-Gauburge and Thibault d'Amiens, then the archbishop of Rouen, granting the archbishop and his successors the right of visitation every three years and a procuration not to exceed forty shillings (the small size of this sum appears to have been a concession to the priory). Despite this charter, however, the priory successfully resisted the archbishop's attempted visitations. See *RER*, 89, 421–22; *RV*, 78, 372.

57. Cheney has calculated forty-seven cases involving monasteries, forty-seven involving regular canons, and one involving a nunnery. See Cheney, *Episcopal Visitations*, 154.

58. *RER*, 332; *RV*, 293–94.

59. The statutes of synods and general chapters sometimes included specific provisions forbidding monastics to conspire to keep silent about known crimes. A thirteenth-century abbot at the abbey of Evesham admitted making a pact with his brethren to conceal their former abbot's crimes from a visiting bishop. See G. G. Coulton, "The Interpretation of Visitation Documents," *English Historical Review* 29, 113 (1914): 37; Cheney, *Episcopal Visitations*, 86–92.

60. Cheney, *Episcopal Visitations*, 89.

61. Matthew Paris, *English History*, trans. J. A. Giles, vol. 2 (London, 1853), 434–35.

62. Avril, *Le gouvernement des évêques*, 790 n. 31.

63. This was also true of secular cathedral chapters. When a much-hated papal legate made a visitation of the cathedral chapter of Rouen in 1227, the chapter complained that its legal and spiritual head was the archbishop, Théobald, to whom it looked for protection from the oppressive legate. See Richard Kay, "Romanus and Rouen: A Papal Legate's Tainted Visitation in 1227," *Annales de Normandie* 51, 2 (2001): 111–18.

64. *RER*, 77; *RV*, 69. Finding the prior of Saint-Pierre absent for his visitation on January 27, 1266, Eudes noted that he had forewarned the prior of his visitation. See *RER*, 612; *RV*, 536.

65. *RER*, 66 n. 85.

66. Although sermons appear to have been a regular part of episcopal visitations of monasteries, none of Eudes's visitation sermons has survived. For a study of such episcopal visitation sermons, see Bériou, *Les sermons et la visite pastorale*.

67. See, for example, Eudes's visitation of the cathedral chapter of Evreux, *RER*, 81, 215; *RV*, 72, 199.

68. *RER*, 96; *RV*, 84. The preliminary questions that Eudes asked appear to reflect the issues that most interested him. Among his hundreds of visitations recorded in the *Register*, for instance, we never hear him asking monks whether they had round-pointed shoes, as the Benedictine Rule required. Yet this was one of the standard questions that Robert Grosseteste posed during his monastic visitations. For the visitation articles of Robert Grosseteste, see Coulton, *Friars*, 478–70.

69. When recording a verbal warning, Eudes often made a note to himself that this was the second or third time he had had to issue a warning. At the abbey of Jumièges, for instance, on December 6, 1257, "we warned the abbot in full chapter for the second time to place monks in those priories where there have been monks within thirty years; this

was the second warning." *RER*, 330; *RV*, 292–93. Visiting the chapter of Gournay, on February 16, 1250, Eudes found Firmin, a priest, to be publicly known for drunkenness. "We ordered Firmin to be removed from office altogether, inasmuch as we had warned him last year [October 16, 1248] and he had not reformed." *RER*, 75–76; *RV*, 67. On sanctions against monastics in canon law, see Hourlier, *L'âge classique*, 237–41.

70. Medieval canonists defined *infamia* (ill fame) in a variety of ways. In his *Summa* on the *Decretum*, Rufinus defined *infamia* as "nothing other than the diminution or consumption of reputation" (*infamia nihil est aliud quam diminutio vel consumptio famae*). Others defined it as the substitution of "opinion" for "reputation." But others, such as Johannes Faventinus, pointed out that *infamia* was hardly just an opinion but rather represented the wholesale "discoloring," "wounding," or "corruption" of someone's name. See Peter Landau, *Die Entstehung des kanonischen Infamiebegriffs von Gratian bis zur Glossa Ordinaria* (Cologne, 1966), 3–10.

71. In cases where he wanted to conduct a formal inquiry, he usually left behind a member of his archiepiscopal entourage.

72. There have been several earlier attempts at summarizing the state of the Norman clergy on the basis of Eudes's *Register*. See Delisle, "Le clergé Normand," 479–99; Charles Richard, "Le clergé de Normandie au XIIIe siècle d'après le Journal des visites pastorales d'Eudes Rigaud," *Revue de Rouen et de Normandie* 30 (March–June 1848), 155–72, 216–27, 268–74, 343–61.

73. On the vow of chastity in canon law, see Hourlier, *L'âge classique*, 226–29.

74. *RER*, 300; *RV*, 268.

75. Eudes tried to avoid letting cases involving defamed clerics go to court. If a defamed cleric pleaded innocent, Eudes generally allowed him to find a certain number of compurgators (often seven), who put up surety and attested to his innocence. Defamed clerics who were unable to clear themselves with compurgation were forced to resign their benefices without further appeal. See *RV*, 649–74. Also see Mary Mansfield, *The Humiliation of Sinners: Public Penance in Thirteenth-Century France* (Ithaca, 1995), 120–21.

76. During a visitation of the Benedictine monastery of Saint-Georges-de-Boscherville, Eudes learned of a monk named Lawrence who was defamed of incontinence with a woman he had been seeing for fourteen years. One wonders whether the other monks had just learned about this illicit relationship or whether it was during this visitation that the archbishop first learned of the matter. If the other monks had known about the relationship for some time, it is quite possible that it provoked no real scandal. Yet Eudes ordered the abbot "to conduct a thorough investigation and to do what seemed best, so that scandal and the occasion of scandal might be removed." *RER*, 399–400; *RV*, 352.

77. Cheney, *Episcopal Visitations*, 83–84.

78. *RER*, 424; *RV*, 374.

79. *RER*, 309; *RV*, 275.

80. Smith, *Attitude of John Pecham*, 119–21.

81. One common complaint monastic communities made against their superiors was that they were being denied their pittances, or portions of extra food and drink. In the archbishop, religious communities had an advocate with the power to ensure that they received the pittances they were owed. See *RER*, 506; *RV*, 444. At the abbey of Eu, the kitchener refused to perform his duties because the abbot had taken away his horse, even though, as Eudes noted, the abbot had offered him another horse. See *RER*, 54; *RV*, 48.

82. *RER*, 226–27; *RV*, 207. For an example of monks not on speaking terms, see Eudes's visitation of the abbey of Aumale, *RER*, 251–52; *RV*, 229.

83. *RER*, 252; *RV*, 229.

84. See, for example, the case of William the Englishman, whom Eudes removed from Aumale and had transferred to Jumièges. See *RER*, 386; *RV*, 339. A transfer was not necessarily a permanent solution, of course, since a rebellious monk might cause just as many problems in a different house.

85. *RER*, 691; *RV*, 600.

86. *RER*, 629; *RV*, 550.

87. *RER*, 218, 457, 490–91; *RV*, 201–2, 401, 431. The origin of the monastic custom of keeping individual, locked coffers is unclear. There is no reference to coffers in Gregory IX's statutes on the reform of the Benedictines, and although Eudes never prohibited nuns or monks from keeping coffers, it is clear that he disapproved of the practice. From his perspective, coffers and the vice of personal property represented a particularly serious problem in nunneries, although some male houses also appear to have kept personal coffers. At the nunnery of Montivilliers, he learned that when the abbess had asked the nuns to turn over their keys, some had refused for several days while they removed the hidden property they did not wish the abbess to see. See *RER*, 491; *RV*, 431. The Franciscan archbishop of Canterbury, John Pecham, was equally disturbed by the problem of personal property in monasteries. See John R. H. Moorman, *Church Life in England in the Thirteenth Century* (Cambridge, 1955), 341 n. 2.
88. *RER*, 93, 260; *RV*, 82, 260–61.
89. *RER*, 386; *RV*, 339–40. This practice contradicted the monastic reform statutes of Gregory IX, which strictly forbade that monies be given to monks or lay brothers for clothing or footwear. See *RER*, 740; *RV*, 645.
90. *RER*, 446; *RV*, 391.
91. *RER*, 373, 591; *RV*, 326–27, 517–18. See Susan M. Carroll-Clark, "Bad Habits: Clothing and Textile References in the Register of Eudes Rigaud, Archbishop of Rouen," in *Medieval Clothing and Textiles*, vol. 1, ed. Robin Netherton and Gale R. Owen-Crocker (Woodbridge, Suffolk, U.K., 2005), 83–84.
92. *RER*, 591; *RV*, 517–18. For the statutes of Gregory IX, see *RER*, 739–40; *RV*, 644. Andrieu-Guitrancourt suggests that gilded belts were a distinctive sign of a prostitute or woman of bad repute and, therefore, forbidden for religious women. See Andrieu-Guitrancourt, *L'archevêque Eudes Rigaud*, 388.
93. Ibid., 384–88.
94. At the nunnery of Villarceaux, some nuns placed saffron on their veils, curled their hair and let it grow below the ears, used silver metaled belts, and wore animal skins. Eudes also objected to nuns who wore their hair in braids or curls. See *RER*, 50, 647; *RV*, 44, 564. Although the archbishop was particularly concerned about the problem of decadent dress among the female religious, he also objected when he found monks with cloaks made of cat and fox fur, as he did at the priory of Pré. See *RER*, 39; *RV*, 34–35. See also Carroll-Clark, "Bad Habits," 88–89.
95. On cloture of monastics in canon law, see Hourlier, *L'âge classique*, 214–21.
96. Smith, *Attitude of John Pecham*, 31.
97. *RER*, 151; *RV*, 133–34. At Saint-Martin-de-Pontoise, Eudes ordered that a porter keep laypeople out of the cloister "in as polite a manner as possible." See *RER*, 120; *RV*, 105.
98. *RER*, 131; 116–17.
99. *RER*, 566; *RV*, 497.
100. *RER*, 395; *RV*, 348.
101. *RER*, 515; *RV*, 452–53.
102. *RER*, 512; *RV*, 451.
103. In addition to having lay servants, some monastic houses accepted lay boarders. In the diocese of Canterbury, for instance, some nunneries accepted laywomen as boarders in an effort to bring in additional income. The archbishop of Canterbury expressed concern about the threat lay boarders posed to religious discipline. See Smith, *Attitude of John Pecham*, 103.
104. *RER*, 227; *RV*, 208.
105. *RER*, 344; *RV*, 303.
106. *RER*, 48–49, 93, 207, 300, 399–400, 470–71; *RV*, 43–44, 82, 193, 268, 352, 412. For a detailed analysis comparing sexual misbehavior in Norman houses of nuns and monks, see Johnson, *Equal in Monastic Profession*, 112–30.
107. *RER*, 301; *RV*, 268–69.
108. *RER*, 373; *RV*, 326.
109. Arnoux, *Des clercs au service*, 184.
110. One wonders whether the large naves of many Norman monasteries were built that way

to accommodate laypeople. It was not uncommon for the nave of a monastic church to function as a parish church while the choir served as the church of the conventual priory. See Grant, *Architecture and Society*, 20.

111. At Saint-Ouen-de-Rouen, Eudes found that "the Divine Service of the community was greatly disturbed because of the parish which was in their monastery. They agreed that another church, reserved for the parish, would be built near the abbey." See *RER*, 631; *RV*, 551–52. Eudes ordered the priors of Saint-Léonard and the nearby hospital not to permit parishioners of the town to come to them to hear Mass but to send them to their own parish church. See *RER*, 444; *RV*, 390.

112. *RER*, 411; *RV*, 361. Eudes frequently expressed his disapproval of allowing laypeople to stand in the choirs of monastic churches during services.

113. *RER*, 155, 492, 538; *RV*, 137, 432, 472. Given the height of the rood screens, the laity standing in the nave of an abbey's church might not have been able to see into the choir much at all. See discussion in Grant, *Architecture and Society*, 224.

114. *RER*, 46; *RV*, 41.

115. *RER*, 315; *RV*, 280.

116. In the first half of the thirteenth century, 160 new hospitals were founded in England. In the fourteenth and fifteenth centuries, 360 hospitals were endowed in the province of Reims and 250 hospitals were founded in the province of Sens. For England, see Carole Rawcliffe, *Medicine for the Soul: The Life, Death, and Resurrection of an English Medieval Hospital, St. Giles's, Norwich, c. 1249–1550* (Stroud, 1999), 1.

117. *RER*, 740; *RV*, 644–45.

118. Rawcliffe, *Medicine for the Soul*, 4.

119. François-Olivier Touati, *Maladie et société au moyen âge: La lèpre, les lépreux et les léproseries dans la province ecclésiastique de Sens jusqu'au milieu du XIVe siècle* (Brussels, 1998), 659–78.

120. Ibid., 668.

121. These included the leprosaries of Bellencombre, Gournay, Mont-aux-Malades-de-Rouen, Saint-Aubin, la Salle-aux-Puelle at Quevilly, and the hospitals of Saint Thomas at Caen, Chaumont, Gournay, Les Andelys, Neufchâtel-en-Bray, Pontoise, la Madeleine-de-Rouen, and Saultchevreuil.

122. Touati, *Maladie et société*, 700.

123. In addition to Guibert de Tournai and Jacques de Vitry, Touati gives the examples of the Dominican, Humbert of Romans, and the secular cardinal legate, Eudes de Châteauroux, all of whom preached in leprosaries or about those afflicted with leprosy. See Touati, *Maladie et société*, 694–700.

124. Touati, *Maladie et société*, 697–98.

125. For a few of the many examples, see *RER*, 54, 75, 99, 115–17, 127; *RV*, 48, 66, 86–87, 101–2, 111–12.

126. See, for instance, his injunction at the abbey of Sainte-Catherine that a physician and suitable servant for the infirmary be procured. *RER*, 489; *RV*, 430.

127. Miri Rubin, *Charity and Community in Medieval Cambridge* (Cambridge, 1987), 150–53.

128. *RER*, 211; *RV*, 195. Even the large abbey of Saint-Ouen-de-Rouen was found to be without an infirmary. See *RER*, 220; *RV*, 202–3.

129. See various examples in diocesan legislation in Odette Pontal, ed., *Les statuts de Paris et le synodal de l'Ouest (XIIIe siècle)*, vol. 1 of *Les statuts synodaux français*, ed. Pontal and Avril.

130. *RER*, 127; *RV*, 111.

131. *RER*, 415; *RV*, 364.

132. *RER*, 285; *RV*, 255.

133. *RER*, 221; *RV*, 203. Eudes also wanted the Divine Offices read to nuns in the infirmary at Saint-Amand. See *RER*, 322; *RV*, 285.

134. This was at the Hôtel-Dieu at Rouen. See *RER*, 645; *RV*, 563.

135. Arnoux, *Des clercs au service*, 119–26, 186–87.

136. *RER*, 585; *RV*, 513.

137. At the Hôtel-Dieu at Pontoise, for instance, Eudes found that the brothers, while dressed in religious habit, "had no definite rule, nor did they follow the observances of

any order, nor did they make any profession." The sisters, on the other hand, lived according to the Rule of Saint Augustine, even though they did not possess a copy of the rule. See *RER*, 545, 580–81; *RV*, 478, 510.

138. *RER*, 364; *RV*, 319.

139. *RER*, 183–84, n. 23 and 25; *RV*, 167–68.

140. Touati, *Maladie et société*, 663–64.

141. Ibid., 691–94. Touati suggests that during the later Middle Ages, lepers were increasingly viewed as social outcasts rather than holy figures. Even during the thirteenth century, however, one finds ambivalent and seemingly contradictory attitudes toward lepers (and, for that matter, others afflicted with illness or poverty), who were simultaneously admired as holy figures and persecuted as outcasts.

142. *RER*, 410; *RV*, 361.

143. *RER*, 471; *RV*, 413.

144. See Eudes's ordinance for the leper hospital of Salle-aux-Puelles, drawn up on March 17, 1251. See *RER*, 115–17; *RV*, 101–2.

145. Christopher Cheney came to the same general conclusion, although I have defined my categories somewhat differently. Cheney assumed that every one of the archbishop's injunctions recorded in the *Register* reflected an actual transgression. I have instead counted the number of times the *Register* mentions either an infraction or an injunction. I've also been careful in the way that I have counted (and defined) the total number of visitations for each year. See Cheney, *Episcopal Visitations*, 156–67.

146. *RER*, 635; *RV*, 555.

147. For a useful discussion of the interpretative problems posed by the *Register*'s data, see Carolyn P. Schriber, "Eudes Rigaud and the Monasteries of Normandy," *Locus* 6, 1 (1993): 53–71.

148. *RER*, 613–14; *RV*, 537.

149. There was certainly a long tradition of ecclesiastical councils republishing laws that had ceased to be relevant.

150. *RER*, 64; *RV*, 58.

151. Edwin N. Gorsuch, "Mismanagement and Ecclesiastical Visitation of English Monasteries in the Early Fourteenth Century," *Traditio* 28 (1972): 473–82.

152. I draw here on Berkhofer's work on how monasteries used new written tools, particularly in the twelfth century, to manage their patrimonies more effectively. Berkhofer points out that there were parallels in medieval royal and monastic administration, particularly the use of written instruments. This argument applies equally well to developments in episcopal administration in the late twelfth and thirteenth centuries. See Berkhofer, *Day of Reckoning*.

153. On the different monastic officers, see Hourlier, *L'âge classique*, 331–43.

154. *RER*, 251; *RV*, 228. The role of this monastic supervisor seems similar to that of the *circator* in earlier Cluniac houses. See Scott Bruce, "Lurking with Spiritual Intent: A Note on the Origin and Functions of the Monastic Roundsman (*Circator*)," *Revue Bénédictine* 109 (1999): 75–89.

155. Stéphanie Lavacry, "L'archevêque Eudes Rigaud et les abbayes et prieurés normands" (Master's thesis, University of Rouen, 1998), 114–16. The violation of fasts is the second most commonly mentioned infraction, with 284 references, or roughly 30% of all infractions mentioned. Together the eating of meat and the violation of fasts make up 70% of all infractions listed in the *Register*.

156. The complexity of the rules about meat eating may explain why they were so often violated. The statutes of Gregory IX reaffirmed the provision in the Benedictine Rule allowing sick monks or lay brothers to eat meat in the infirmary. What tended to happen, however, was that healthy monks who were "visiting" the sick in the infirmary partook of meat dishes. Monks were also generally permitted to eat meat when they were invited to the abbot's table. At some priories, such as Bures, the monks argued that their abbot had the right to grant them a dispensation on the matter of meat eating. See *RER*, 384; *RV*, 338. See Knowles, *Religious Orders*, 18; Moorman, *Church Life*, 335–37.

157. *RER*, 268; *RV*, 241.

158. On May 6, 1258, Eudes warned the monks of Saint-Sulpice-Près-l'Aigle that they would be punished if they continued to eat meat freely. Only two days later, however, on May 8, finding that the two monks of the priory of Rai ate meat, Eudes decided to leave the matter to their consciences. See *RER*, 348–49; *RV*, 306. The statutes of Gregory IX prescribed regular discipline for anyone who ate meat in violation of the rule. After the third offense, the monk was to fast the following Wednesday and Friday on bread and water. If the offense became habitual, he was to receive grave censure. An abbot who persisted in eating meat after being warned by the local bishop or visitor could be deprived of his office. See *RER*, 740; *RV*, 644.

159. During Eudes's six visitations of Saint-Ouen-de-Rouen between 1264 and 1268, he specifically recorded finding the abbey good in its spirituals while bad in its temporals. See *RER*, 563, 599, 630–31, 675, 703, 733–34; *RV*, 494–95, 525, 551–52, 585, 611, 638.

160. On monastic management of temporalities, see Hourlier, *L'âge classique*, 299–310.

161. Joel Kaye, *Economy and Nature in the Fourteenth Century: Money, Market Exchange, and the Emergence of Scientific Thought* (Cambridge, 1998), 130–31.

162. *RER*, 216; *RV*, 200.

163. *RER*, 286; *RV*, 255.

164. *RER*, 60; *RV*, 55.

165. *RER*, 149, 208, 216, 249, 255, 411, 463; *RV*, 132, 194, 200, 227, 232, 361, 407.

166. *RER*, 127, 359–60, 390, 573; *RV*, 111, 315–16, 344, 503. One of the recurring themes in the Parisian statutes of Eudes de Sully (repeated in other synodal legislation, including in the diocese of Angers) was that altar cloths and chalices be kept clean and that the real presence of Christ in the Eucharist be treated with the greatest respect and devotion. See Pontal, *Les statuts de Paris*, nos. 16, 21, 22, pp. 58, 60; Avril, *Le gouvernement des évêques*, 742.

167. *RER*, 360; *RV*, 316.

168. *RER*, 62; *RV*, 57.

169. *RER*, 274; *RV*, 246.

170. Louis Duval-Arnould, ed., "Trois sermons synodaux de la collection attribué à Jean de la Rochelle," *AFH* 70 (1977): 60–71.

171. For the text of canon 19 of the Fourth Lateran Council, see Tanner, *Decrees of the Ecumenical Councils*, vol. 1, 244.

172. Geneviève Nortier, *Les bibliothèques médiévales des abbayes Bénédictines de Normandie* (Paris, 1971).

173. *RER*, 44, 77; *RV*, 40, 70.

174. *RER*, 266; *RV*, 240.

175. *RER*, 446; *RV*, 391.

176. *RER*, 565, 620; *RV*, 496, 543. Synods appear to have been a popular time for books to be copied. Eudes encouraged the priory of Ouville, for instance, to have an ordinal copied at an upcoming synod: *RER*, 593; *RV*, 519.

177. *RER*, 565; *RV*, 497. On rebinding, see *RER*, 390, 463; *RV*, 344, 407.

178. *RER*, 727; *RV*, 632.

179. *RER*, 625–26; *RV*, 547.

180. *RER*, 257; *RV*, 233–34.

181. *RER*, 462; *RV*, 407.

182. *RER*, 569; *RV*, 500.

183. Bonaventure, *Major Life*, part I, chap. 2, in Marion A. Habig, ed., *St. Francis of Assisi: Writings and Early Biographies* (Chicago, 1983), 640–46; Thomas of Celano, *First Life*, book 1, chaps. 8, 9, in Habig, *St. Francis of Assisi*, 243–47.

184. *RER*, 573; *RV*, 503.

185. *RER*, 579; *RV*, 508.

186. *RER*, 166; *RV*, 147.

187. *RER*, 604, 651; *RV*, 529, 567.

188. There are various explanations for this supposed decline. One is that the extraordinary popularity of the mendicant orders diverted lay donations away from traditional recipients, such as Benedictine houses. Another argument is that Benedictine monasteries were especially hard hit by rising inflation because much of their income was depen-

dent on fixed rents. Benedictine monasteries had difficulty adapting to the new economy, which was based in the towns.

189. These rural domains were primarily clustered southeast of Rouen but also included some domains as far away as Sancy (near Soissons), Vaux-les-Moines (east of the Meuse River), Rots (near Caen), and Wanchy and Les Ifs (east of Dieppe). See Henri Dubois, Denise Angers, and Catherine Bébéar, eds., *Un censier normand du XIIIe siècle: Le Livre des Jurés de l'abbaye Saint-Ouen de Rouen* (Paris, 2001), vii.

190. *GC*, 11:147. See also a discussion of Saint-Ouen in Pobst, "Visitation of Religious and Clergy," 229–34.

191. *RER*, 130; *RV*, 115–16.

192. *RER*, 219–21; *RV*, 202–3.

193. *RER*, 296; *RV*, 264–65.

194. Although the pope granted the abbot the right to wear a miter in 1255, the costs associated with this legal campaign still appear to have been afflicting the financial health of the abbey in 1263. In general, however, Saint-Ouen was one of the wealthiest abbeys in France. In 1338, its gross annual revenue was more than 10,500 l. See Dubois et al., *Un censier normand*, vii.

195. Eudes frequently complained not only that various priories were not fully staffed but that they were impoverished because abbots retained priory funds.

196. *RER*, 222, 416; *RV*, 204, 364. Normally, Eudes expected these individual audits to be performed monthly, but when a monastic house faced serious financial trouble, he requested that they be conducted even more frequently. In 1255, the kitchener of Saint-Ouen, for instance, was expected to conduct weekly or at least bimonthly audits. By 1260, Eudes wanted the kitchener, granarian, infirmarian, and other officers of Saint-Ouen to conduct audits daily.

197. *RV*, 645; *RER*, 741. In his Benedictine reform statutes of 1253, Innocent IV insisted that all rents of an abbey be set down in writing and that income that was not fixed be estimated. One copy of all accounts was to be kept by the abbot and a second one by the convent. See R. H. Snape, *English Monastic Finances in the Later Middle Ages* (Cambridge, 1926), 132–33.

198. Snape, *English Monastic Finances*, 37.

199. Ibid., 46–50.

200. Ibid., 52. Prelates such as John Pecham and Eudes Rigaud opposed the decentralized obedientiary system. See Smith, *Attitude of John Pecham*, 83.

201. Snape, *English Monastic Finances*, 66.

202. *RER*, 186; *RV*, 169.

203. *RER*, 209; *RV*, 194.

204. *RER*, 357; *RV*, 314. Eudes showed a greater willingness to employ a secular cleric to manage the finances of nunneries than of monasteries. This may have been because nunneries tended to have more serious financial problems. Nunneries generally were larger in population; they had the added financial burden of having to hire a male cleric for their sacramental needs; and most important, they tended to be much more poorly endowed than the average male monastery. Eudes may have had doubts about the competency of a female monastic superior to manage finances and thus saw a need for hiring a procurator or provost (which of course presented yet another financial burden). Even at the male Benedictine monastery of Saint-Victor-en-Caux, Eudes found that secular clerics were employed as the monastery's kitchener and granarian, and he ordered the abbot to fill these offices with monks of the community. See *RER*, 362; *RV*, 317. On the differences between male and female houses, see Johnson, *Equal in Monastic Profession*; William C. Jordan, "The Cistercian Nunnery of La Cour Notre-Dame de Michery: A House That Failed," *Revue Bénédictine* 95 (1985): 311–20.

205. *RER*, 357; *RV*, 314.

206. During the first half of the thirteenth century, various papal decretals and canons from church councils insisted that monastic superiors seek the consent of their chapters before raising loans or alienating monastic properties. On the conventual chapter, see Hourlier, *L'âge classique*, 347–54; Snape, *English Monastic Finances*, 55–57.

207. Beginning with Innocent III, popes encouraged monasteries to involve more members of their communities in important decisions rather than leave them to the abbot's sole control. Of course, the Rule of Saint Benedict had itself placed certain checks on the abbot's power, and there had long been a tradition of appointing coadjutors for abbeys in which the abbot was incompetent or lazy. Nonetheless, there appears to have been a shift during the thirteenth century toward greater involvement of monastics in Benedictine abbeys. Archbishop John Pecham approached these issues much as Eudes did, sometimes convening a council of the elder members of a monastery when he had doubts about the competency of a monastic superior. See Smith, *Attitude of John Pecham*, 80–82. On the obedience (and limits of obedience) owed to a monastic superior in canon law, see Hourlier, *L'âge classique*, 224–26, 315–30.

208. On monastic debt, see Lemarignier, *Institutions ecclésiastiques*, 235–37.

209. Donald Matthew, *The Norman Monasteries and Their English Possessions* (London, 1962), 66.

210. Ibid., 67–69.

211. Ibid., 73–74.

212. Ibid., 74, 77.

213. Ibid., 75.

214. Ibid., 78–81.

215. *RER*, 341; *RV*, 301.

216. The priory normally received 100 l. in revenue from England. See *RER*, 76, 568; *RV*, 67, 499.

217. *RER*, 61; *RV*, 55.

218. *RER*, 247; *RV*, 224.

219. *RER*, 414; *RV*, 363.

220. Lavacry, "L'archevêque Eudes Rigaud." According to Lavacry, the *Register* refers to a shortage of meat twice, wheat thirteen times, oats thirty-three times, and wine thirty-eight times.

221. Lucien Musset, "Essai sur les vignobles des monastères normands (Xe–XIIIe siècles)," *Cahiers Léopold Delisle*, special issue (1978): 231–44.

222. *RER*, 361; *RV*, 316.

223. *RER*, 223–24; *RV*, 205.

224. Cheney, *Episcopal Visitations*, 172.

225. Ibid., 171–74; Snape, *English Monastic Finances*, 178–81.

226. Cheney concluded that smaller monasteries tended to be more indebted than larger houses. He also found that for the average monk, debt made up 30% of his revenue, whereas for the average nun, debt represented only 15% of revenue.

227. Even when the ordinary income is provided for a particular house, it might be recorded for only one or two of Eudes's many visitations. Nor can one assume that a monastery's ordinary income was constant. Consider the nunnery of Saint-Saëns, which in 1251 had an ordinary income of 140 l., in 1253, 100 l., in 1257, 270 l., and in 1260, 450 l. The ordinary income of Sainte-Catherine-du-Mont ranged from 1,000 to 2,000 l.; at Saint-Martin-de-Pontoise, from 1,000 to 1,875 l.; and at Saint-Georges-de-Boscherville, from 1,100 to 1,500 l.

228. When the *Register* does provide a monastery's ordinary income, it also provides what the monastery owed and was owed in extraordinary debentures and incomes.

229. *RER*, 362–63; *RV*, 318.

230. For fourteenth-century examples, see William Chester Jordan, *Two Fourteenth-Century Fiscal Accounts of the Benedictine Abbey of Saint-Pierre-le-Vif of Sens*, vol. 1 of *Fra spazio e tempo: Studi in onore di Luigi de Rosa*, ed. Ilaria Zilli (Naples, 1995).

231. Some Norman monasteries were also borrowing from Jews. In 1250, the abbey of Saint-Pierre-des-Préaux owed a certain Jew 400 l., although it was not owed at interest and the abbey believed that it might be cleared of the debt. In 1266, the female priory of Villarceaux owed 100 l., 20 l. of which was owed at interest to Jews and Cahorsins (Christian usurers) of Mantes. *RER*, 66, 658; *RV*, 59, 572.

232. In 1261, Saint-Ouen owed 1,800 l. at interest; in 1263, 1,000 l. out of its total debt of

4,000 l. was at interest; in 1267, 500 out of 4,812 l. was owed at interest; in 1268, 1,170 out of 5,104 l. was owed at interest; and in 1269, 1,500 out of 5,000 l. was owed at interest.

233. This is not to suggest that Eudes had only a basic understanding of economics. The way he managed his own archiepiscopal finances shows that he recognized the importance of long-term investments, even at the expense of incurring debt (see chapter 7).

234. *RER*, 516–17, 565; *RV*, 453, 496–97.

235. *RER*, 620; *RV*, 543.

236. *RER*, 701, 728; *RV*, 609, 633. The sale of woodlands appears to have been a common means of raising capital in order to pay off debts. The Cistercian nuns at Saint-Saens reduced their debts by selling 350 l. worth of woodlands, as did the monks from the priory of Beaulieu, who received 400 l. from the sale of woods and the tithes of Préaux.

237. *RER*, 516; *RV*, 453. In another entry, Eudes again makes reference to "the many goods, donated and willed to the monastery by the faithful," with which rents were being purchased. *RER*, 620; *RV*, 543.

238. Johnson, *Equal in Monastic Profession*, 215; Lemarignier, *Institutions ecclésiastiques*, 236.

239. Alain Sadourny has found that Norman monasteries actually bought relatively few rents in the thirteenth century, especially compared with cathedral chapters. It was significant when a monastery was able to buy one or two rents during an entire decade. During the thirteenth century, Saint-Ouen-de-Rouen spent 49 l. on rents, Saint-Amand spent 176 l., and the hospital of Mont-aux-Malades spent 249 l. See Sadourny, "Les rentes à Rouen au XIIIe siècle," *Annales de Normandie* 21 (June 1971): 99–108.

240. Robert Génestal, *Le rôle des monastères comme établissements de crédit en Normandie du XI à la fin du XIIIe siècle* (Paris, 1901), 181–203. The average rent was worth 10% of its sale price, and most rents were quite small, usually worth less than 5 l. annually. Innocent IV opposed new rents, calling them usurious, but as Génestal shows, new rents were very common.

241. *RER*, 338; *RV*, 298. On monastic houses investing in, selling, and renting tithes, see Delmaire, *Le diocèse d'Arras*, 122–33.

242. Génestal, *Le rôle des monastères*, 162. As discussed earlier, in the later 1260s Eudes mentions finding monasteries in satisfactory temporal states much more frequently.

243. Jordan, "Two Fourteenth-Century Fiscal Accounts."

244. *RER*, 345; *RV*, 304.

245. *RER*, 468; *RV*, 411.

246. *RER*, 545–46; *RV*, 478.

247. *RER*, 500; *RV*, 440.

248. *RER*, 347; *RV*, 305.

249. *RER*, 325; *RV*, 287. Eudes also instructed the bishop of Sées that "in all places where there used to be monks but are none now, he should strive to bring the number up to the former total, and wherever the number has been reduced, he should see that the old number is restored." *RER*, 261; *RV*, 236.

250. Arnoux, *Des clercs au service*, 174–75, 177–78, 182.

251. According to the *Register*'s statistics on monastic population, the vast majority of Norman priories in the thirteenth century had fewer than ten monastics and almost no priories had more than twenty. Most Norman abbeys had populations of twenty to forty monastics, and few had fewer than ten or more than fifty. Female abbeys tended to be larger than male abbeys, and several female abbeys in Normandy had more than fifty resident nuns. Using the *Register*, Penelope Johnson calculates that the average Norman nunnery housed thirty-five nuns whereas the average male house held only twenty-three monks. See Johnson, *Equal in Monastic Profession*, 173. Snape found that the average income per head of monks in the diocese of Rouen was 63 l., compared with 24 l. for nuns. In the other Norman dioceses, the average income per head of monks was 62 l., compared with 14 l. for nuns. See Snape, *English Monastic Finances*, 150.

252. *RER*, 48–50; *RV*, 43–45.

253. *RER*, 384; *RV*, 338.

254. Joseph H. Lynch, *Simoniacal Entry into Religious Life from 1000 to 1260: A Social, Eco-*

nomic, and Legal Study (Columbus, Ohio, 1976). As Lynch shows, it was only in the twelfth century that theologians and canonists began to question whether entry dowries constituted a form of simony. Gratian devoted a *questio* in his *Decretum* to the issue. Whereas some twelfth-century decretists and theologians criticized monastic entry dowries and called them simoniacal, others maintained that they were technically not simoniacal so long as they were given freely. Even Peter the Chanter, who in general criticized entry dowries, suggested that it was acceptable for a monastic house to demand some money for a new brother if the house was otherwise truly too poor to support him. By the thirteenth century, although many monastic entrants continued to offer gifts to their religious house, it was far less common for religious houses to demand outright payments from recruits. Eudes Rigaud even reported learning of a monk who, perhaps wracked with guilt, gave up his habit after voluntarily admitting in full chapter that he had entered his order through simony. See *RER*, 710; *RV*, 617; Lynch, *Simoniacal Entry*, 214–15.

255. For canon 30 of the Rouen synod of 1214, see Pontal, *Les statuts de Paris.*
256. As Lynch and Johnson suggest, the focus of thirteenth-century legislation dealing with simoniacal entry into religious houses (in contrast to the twelfth century) was on female houses. Lynch, *Simoniacal Entry*, 194–95; Johnson, *Equal in Monastic Profession*, 24–26.
257. *RER*, 478; *RV*, 419.
258. Nor did Eudes look kindly on some nunneries' practice of schooling children as a source of revenue. See Johnson, *Equal in Monastic Profession*, 220; *RER*, 369, 471; *RV*, 324, 412.
259. *RER*, 411; *RV*, 361; Lynch, *Simoniacal Entry*, 220–21.
260. *GC*, 11:148; *RER*, 512 n. 27; *RV*, 451.
261. *RER*, 63; *RV*, 57. The archbishop's prohibition against granting new pensions was not heeded, however. On January 28, 1255, Eudes found that the abbey had granted three new pensions to lawyers and that the chapter seal was "freely employed in conferring benefices and pensions." He ordered that the seal of the chapter be applied to no document until after great deliberation. *RER*, 220–21; *RV*, 202–3.
262. *RER*, 563; *RV*, 495. During a subsequent visitation, Eudes was told that the abbot was extravagant in his consumption of food and wines, that he invited nephews to live at the expense of the monastery, and that he frequently rode outside Normandy with a large and sumptuous retinue. See *RER*, 631; *RV*, 551. The foodstuffs for the abbot's guests were supposed to come out of a separate fund assigned to the abbot, not from the community kitchen.
263. *RER*, 274; *RV*, 246. For other examples of monastic superiors supporting relatives at schools, see *RER*, 202, 335, 343; *RV*, 189, 296, 302.
264. Moorman, *Church Life*, 266–67.
265. Snape, *English Monastic Finances*, 99–101.
266. *RER*, 393; *RV*, 345.
267. See, for instance, *RER*, 337. Eudes visited Gasny every year between 1249 and 1269 except for 1251, 1257, and 1260.
268. These examples are taken from the case of Benvenuto Scotivoli, bishop of Osimo, whose visitation in 1273 of the monastery of San Fiorenzo d'Osimo provoked litigation. See Philippe Jansen, "Benvenuto Scotivoli, évêque d'Osimo (1264–1282), prelat combatif ou saint réformateur?" in *Les prelats, l'église et la société, XIe–Xve siècles: Hommage à Bernard Guillemain*, ed. Françoise Bériac (Bordeaux, 1994), 49–57.

5. Shepherding the Shepherds

1. Henri de Vézelay, archdeacon of the Hiemois, noted in his register the names of parishioners who failed to come to church. See Léopold Delisle, "Visites pastorales de Maître Henri de Vézelai, archidiacre d'Hiémois (1267–1268)," *Bibliothèque de l'École des Chartes* 54 (1893): 463. Andrew Finch uses the fourteenth-century register of the officiality of

Cerisy-la Forêt to argue that the Norman church was deeply engaged in policing the laity's religious and sexual lives. See Finch, "The Disciplining of the Laity in Late Medieval Normandy," *French History* 10, 2 (1996): 163–81.

2. Simon Townley, "Unbeneficed Clergy in the Thirteenth Century: Two English Dioceses," in *Studies in Clergy and Ministry in Medieval England*, ed. David M. Smith (York, 1991), 38–64.

3. On clerical examinations in England, see John Shinners and William J. Dohar, eds., *Pastors and the Care of Souls in Medieval England* (Notre Dame, Ind., 1998), 55–70. Like Eudes Rigaud, Robert Grosseteste, bishop of Lincoln, took his right of presentation to the *cura animarum* seriously. See Leonard Boyle, "Robert Grosseteste and the Pastoral Care," in *Pastoral Care, Clerical Education, and Canon Law, 1200–1400* (London, 1981), 1:13–16.

4. On the ordination of Cistercian monks, see Lucet, "Les ordinations chez les Cisterciens," 290.

5. The *Register* records that Eudes performed three or four ordination ceremonies each year but does not describe the archbishop's role at these ceremonies. It may be revealing, however, that Eudes was rarely at the location for an ordination ceremony more than one day even though preordination scrutinies generally went on for several days before the ceremony itself. On ordination ceremonies more generally, see Shinners and Dohar, *Pastors and the Care of Souls*, 49–55.

6. Numerous examples can be found in the original manuscript of the *Register*, BnF, ms. lat. 1245, ff. 124v–137r.

7. There is scholarly debate about the reasons for the disproportionate amount of lay patronage in Normandy. Some scholars point to the Viking invasions of Normandy, which destroyed the ecclesiastical organization of Neustria, requiring new endowments from new patrons, the rebuilding of churches, and the reestablishment of cures. Marcel Baudot counters this argument by noting that the areas of Normandy with the strongest Scandinavian immigration did not end up with the highest percentages of lay patronage. See Baudot, "Observations sur le patronage des églises en Normandie," in *Recueil d'études normandes en hommage au docteur Jean Fournée: Cahiers Léopold Delisle, no. exceptionnel 1978* (Nogent-sur-Marne, 1979), 43, 48.

8. Baudot, "Observations sur le patronage," 45–46. Guy Devailly gives a similar figure of 37.6% for Normandy's lay patronage. See Devailly, "Les patronats d'église en Normandie aux XIIIe et XIVe siècles," in *Recueil d'études en hommage à Lucien Musset, no. 23 of Cahiers des Annales de Normandie* (Caen, 1990), 354. According to Tabbagh, lay patronage was as high as 45% in Normandy and even 60% in certain deaneries in Caux. See Tabbagh, *Le clergé séculier du diocèse de Rouen*, 5.

9. According to Devailly, only four patrons in the entire province held patronage over more than ten churches. See Devailly, "Les patronats d'église," 354–55.

10. Baudot gives the following figures for episcopal patronage in the Norman province: Bayeux, 3.5%; Avranches, 13%; Lisieux, 10%; Rouen, 6%; Coutances, 6%; Sées, 4%; and Evreux, 4%. See Baudot, "Observations sur le patronage," 45. Devailly provides similar figures. He calculates that the archbishop of Rouen held patronage in 139 churches (out of a total of 1,506 churches), which amounts to 7.2%. See Devailly, "Les patronats d'église," 358–59. Nadine-Josette Chaline calculates the highest percentage of episcopal patronage (13%), but even this figure is well below that of comparable dioceses in other provinces. See Chaline, *Le diocèse de Rouen–Le Havre* (Paris, 1976), 37. Also see Olivier Guyotjeannin, *Episcopus et comes: Affirmation et déclin de la seigneurie épiscopale au nord du royaume de France (Beauvais-Noyon, Xe–XIIIe siècle)* (Geneva, 1987), 229–30.

11. Norman communities of regular canons were patrons of a large number of parishes. The Augustinian priory of Sainte-Barbe-en-Auge, for instance, had patronage of some thirty parish churches. Indeed, in some cases, as many parishes were under the patronage of Augustinian canons as Benedictines. See Arnoux, *Des clercs au service*, 8, 96. Initially, the Cistercians had been vehemently opposed to the idea of having patronage of parish churches. Lucet, "Les ordinations chez les Cisterciens," 290. For background on monastic possession of churches and tithes, see Hourlier, *L'âge classique*, 461–64.

12. Guy Devailly, ed., *Le diocèse de Bourges* (Paris, 1973), 54.

13. *RER*, 406; *RV*, 357.

14. Henri Dubois, "Patronage et revenu ecclésiastique en Normandie au XIIIe siècle," in *Papauté, monachisme et théories politiques: Études d'histoire médiévale offertes à Marcel Pacaut*, vol. 2, *Les églises locales*, ed. P. Guichard, M.-T. Lorcin, J.-M. Poisson, and M. Rubellin (Lyon, 1994), 461–71.

15. Génestal, "La patrimonialité de l'archidiaconat," 286–91; Guillaume Bessin, ed., *Concilia Rotomagensis provinciae*, 2 vols. (Rouen, 1717), 2:22.

16. The thirteenth-century "polyptychum Rothomagensis diocesis" has been published in *HF*, 23:228–329. The original manuscript is in the BnF, ms. lat. 11052. On two thirteenth-century polyptychs from the diocese of Coutances, see H. Dubois, "La hiérarchie des paroisses dans le diocèse de Coutances au moyen âge," in *Villages et villageois au moyen âge* (Paris, 1992).

17. The number of parishioners seems to represent only the heads of households. On the polyptych, see Longnon, *Les pouillés de la province de Rouen*.

18. *RV*, 649–74.

19. Raoul, rector of the church of Saint-Albin de Sarquels, was ill-famed of incontinence in both 1260 and 1262; he was forced to resign after the second occurrence. According to the polyptych, the archbishop was the patron of the church. See *HF*, 23:280; *RV*, 661–62, 665–66.

20. See G. Mollat, "Bénéfices ecclésiastiques en occident: Le régime de droit commun, des origines au Concordat de Vienne (1448)," *Dictionnaire de droit canonique*, 2 (1937): cols. 406–49.

21. There were some instances of a lay patron donating his church to a monastery or bishop. In a charter dated August 1260, for instance, Clément de Senooz and his wife, Alice, a bourgeois couple from Rouen, surrendered to Archbishop Eudes Rigaud their right of patronage over a chapel in the Rouen cathedral which had been endowed by Jean de Senooz, Clément's brother, with a sum of 300 l.t. The charter was confirmed by the official of Rouen. It is located in AD: Seine-Maritime, G. 1211, marked on reverse, "chapelle a notre dame de rouen 1260." Whenever the right of patronage was transferred, the ordinary had to authorize the transfer, receiving a procuration for doing so. Eudes complained to the monks at Eu that they had not yet paid him the procuration he was owed for authorizing their appropriation of some churches. See *RER*, 340; *RV*, 300.

22. I take this figure from Devailly, whose calculations were based on the polyptych. See Devailly, "Les patronats d'église," 358–59.

23. *RER*, 171; *RV*, 154.

24. When a church had more than one patron, the normal procedure was for the two patrons to take turns presenting a candidate for the benefice. The parish of "Houlebec," for instance, in the deanery of Bourg-Therouard (the greater archdeaconry of Rouen), had two patrons: "Ricardus, presbiter, Symon de Houlebec, patroni alternatim." See "Polyptychum Rotomagensis Diocesis," *HF*, 23:235.

25. The charter describing this agreement, dated February 27, 1250, is published as no. 478 in *CN*, 80.

26. The polyptych indicates that the archbishop had earlier been the patron of the church of Watervilla but that during Eudes Rigaud's archiepiscopate, patronage was lost to the king "in assisiis Novi Castri." See "Polyptychum Rotomagensis Diocesiis," *HF*, 23:268. Some cases of contested patronage were decided by courts, and others were decided by arbitrators appointed by both parties. A dispute in 1252–53 between Eudes Rigaud and a certain Galterus over the right of patronage for the church of Saint-Pierre-de-Tocqueville was decided by Guillaume de Saâne, treasurer of Rouen, and Regnaud de Bullis, archdeacon of the Petit-Caux. AD: Seine-Maritime, G. 1702, an arbitrational sentence, ms. marked on reverse, "pour le patronage de Torqueville." Another ms. dated Déville, on the Sunday before the Purification of the Virgin, 1252, is from "Galterus de altero armiger."

27. According to Cheney, thirteenth-century bishops and archbishops were generally more insistent than their predecessors had been about a patron's obligation to present a candidate to the ecclesiastical ordinary. See C. R. Cheney, *English Synodalia of the Thirteenth Century*, 2nd ed. (Oxford, 1941), 38–39.

28. Different councils established different statutory periods, ranging from three months to six months. The custom in Normandy was six months, as evidenced by the *Très ancien coutumier de Normandie*, in Ernest-Joseph Tardif, ed., *Coutumiers de Normandie: Textes critiques*, 2 vols., 1:75; and *Summa de legibus*, in Tardif, *Coutumiers de Normandie*, 2:33.

29. "Polyptychum Rotomagensis diocesis," *HF*, 23:238. The archbishop appears to have been very careful in calculating the precise time that elapsed between a church's vacancy and the presentation of a candidate by its patron. See *RER*, 382–83; *RV*, 336.

30. After the death of Almauricus, the prior of Beaulieu once again presented a candidate for the parish of Haye-Routot. It is noteworthy, though, that a dispute over the patronage of the parish arose between the prior and a knight, Johannes Martel, ending in a judgment for the prior at the assize of Pont-Audemer. The dispute may have been the result of confusion stemming from the archbishop's having acted some years before as patron during the church's protracted vacancy.

31. *RER*, 11; *RV*, 8.

32. *RER*, 535; *RV*, 469–70. This case was more complex because there was an ongoing dispute between the abbot of Saint-Josse and Richard of Mesnil-David, a lay lord of the town, over who possessed the right of presentation. According to the polyptych, when the church was next vacant, the dispute was re-ignited and this time settled in a secular court, where the judgment was in favor of Guillaume Torel, a lord of the town. See "Polyptychum," *HF*, 23:269.

33. Eudes was almost always present for the institution of clerics presented to him and personally inspected nearly every candidate for a benefice in his diocese. Only occasionally did he have the official of Rouen or Jean de Noyentelle, archdeacon of Rouen and his vicar, confer a benefice in his place. After a clerical candidate had been canonically presented by the patron and instituted by the bishop or archbishop, he was symbolically invested with the benefice with a hat, ring, or staff. (Eudes also used hats to symbolically divest a curate of his benefice.) At the investiture ceremony, the cleric promised the bishop or archbishop that he would fulfill his priestly duties with justice, obedience, and fidelity. The rector was finally installed in his new church by the local archdeacon. See Mollat, "Bénéfices ecclésiastiques," 406–49.

34. Lemarignier, *Institutions ecclésiastiques*, 206.

35. *RER*, 262; *RV*, 237.

36. *RER*, 398; *RV*, 351. The candidate whom the king presented to the archbishop for the church at Baudemont was the priest John of Bray.

37. In their edition of the *Register*, O'Sullivan and Brown render the church "Amécourt," but the newest edition of the *Dictionnaire topographique du département de Seine-Maritime*, ed. Laporte and de Beaurepaire, 1:8, lists the name as "Ancourt." In the thirteenth-century polyptych, the church was listed as "Aenort."

38. *RER*, 191–92; *RV*, 173–74.

39. *RER*, 450–51; *RV*, 395–96.

40. For more, see Pierre Aubry, *La musique et les musiciens d'église en Normandie au 13e siècle d'après le Journal des visites pastorales d'Odon Rigaud* (Paris, 1906), 12.

41. *RER*, 451; *RV*, 396.

42. The *Register* describes only a handful of the dozens of candidates Eudes examined.

43. Hugh of Wells, bishop of Lincoln (1209–35), examined 1,958 men instituted to benefices in his diocese and refused to admit only 101 (roughly 5%) on the grounds of illiteracy. Of the 101, only 4 were already ordained priests. See Shinners and Dohar, eds., *Pastors and the Care of Souls*, 35.

44. Heinrich Denifle and Emile Chatelain, *Chartularium Universitatis Parisiensis* (Paris, 1889), 1:458–59, 476–78, 482–83, 584–85.

45. Charter no. 428 in Denifle, *Chartularium Universitatis Parisiensis*, 482–83, is a confirmation by King Louis IX of the rents and tithes purchased by Guillaume de Saâne to sustain the school in Paris.

46. Ibid., 584.

47. Ibid., 585.

48. Ibid., 584–85.

49. Olga Dobiache-Rojdestvensky, *La vie paroissiale en France au XIIIe siècle d'après les actes épis-copaux* (Paris, 1911), 77–98.
50. In his own greater archdeaconry, Eudes conducted only one visitation of the deaneries of Bourgtheroulde, Cailly, Perriers, Pont-Audemer, and Rouen. He conducted multiple visitations of the chapters at Gournay, Les Andelys, and Saint-Mellon-de-Pontoise.
51. *RV*, 743.
52. For the discussion that follows, see Carroll-Clark, "Bad Habits," 83–103. Carroll-Clark calculates that 20% of the records in Eudes's *Register* refer to clothing or textiles.
53. Carroll-Clark points to the crucial distinction between the *cappa clausa*, the long, closed gown with no sleeves, and the *tabardo*, which was shorter, had sleeves, and was usually worn open in front. On clerical dress in the thirteenth century, especially conciliar legislation, see Louis Trichet, *Le costume du clergé: Ses origines et son évolution en France d'après les réglements de l'église* (Paris, 1986), 59–72. The statutes on clerical dress from the synods of Paris and the synod of the west can be found in Pontal, *Les statuts de Paris*, no. 22, 32, pp. 60, 158–60. The Fourth Lateran Council treated the issue in canon 16.
54. Clerical dress was a major concern of thirteenth-century bishops of Angers as well. See Avril, *Le gouvernement des évêques*, 680–81.
55. *RER*, 204; *RV*, 191. In the diocese of Angers, priests were permitted to wear short capes or another layer of clothing when it rained. See the synods of Saint Luc in 1264 and 1265, in Joseph Avril, ed., *Les statuts synodaux angevine de la seconde moitié du XIIIe siècle*, vol. 3 of *Les statuts synodaux français du XIIIe siècle*, ed. Odette Pontal and Joseph Avril (Paris, 1988), 86, 100.
56. The *Register* indicates that Eudes wore pontificals while celebrating mass on Sundays and feast days, but it is not clear whether he ordinarily wore episcopal robes or the Franciscan habit during the week. The fourteenth-century Franciscan bishop of Toulouse, Saint Louis, continued to wear his Franciscan habit rather than the episcopal robes. See M. R. Toynbee, *Saint Louis of Toulouse and the Process of Canonisation in the Fourteenth Century* (Manchester, 1929), 110.
57. Duval-Arnould, "Trois sermons synodaux," 55.
58. *RER*, 377; *RV*, 330.
59. Eudes's predecessor at Rouen, Pierre de Colmieu, had been equally concerned with clerical dress. In a synodal statute he threatened that any priest found wearing a military tunic (*tabard*) or long robe (*garnarch*) without a closed cape would have it taken away from him and given to a leper or poor person. See Odette Pontal, ed., *Les statuts de 1230 à 1260*, vol. 2 of *Les statuts synodaux français du XIIIe siècle*, ed. Odette Pontal and Joseph Avril (Paris, 1983), no. 22, p. 134.
60. Quoted in Lecoy de la Marche, *La chaire française au moyen âge* (Paris, 1886).
61. Shinners and Dohar, *Pastors and the Care of Souls*, 22–23. On John Stratford, see Roy Martin Haines, *Archbishop John Stratford: Political Revolutionary and Champion of the Liberties of the English Church, ca. 1275/80–1348* (Toronto, 1986).
62. A medieval chronicle reported that in 1256 Eudes performed a reconciliation ceremony at the church of Saint-Trinité-du-Mont after one priest killed another with a blow to the head during a fight. Chéruel, *Normanniae nova chronica*, 24.
63. *RER*, 24; *RV*, 21.
64. These calculations are based on the thirteenth-century polyptych's list of the number of churches in each deanery. The visitations can be found in *RER*, 31, 21–22; *RV*, 26–28, 18.
65. See *RER*, 21; *RV*, 18.
66. There is one case in which Robertus, rector of the church of "Regalis Campus," was forced to swear an oath before the archbishop that if he were caught drinking excessively again, he would resign his benefice. See *RV*, 668. But almost every actual resignation was the result of a priest being found unchaste. For the law regarding clerical drunkenness, see Gregory IX, *Decretales*, c. III, tit. 1, c. 14, in *Corpus iuris canonici*, 1:452–53.
67. *RER*, 377; *RV*, 329. There is only one case of heresy in the *Register*, involving a certain Jean Morel, whom Eudes warned, excommunicated, and detained for a long period in the archiepiscopal prison. After refusing to retract his heretical assertions, Morel was condemned for heresy by the archbishop.

68. *RER*, 429–30; *RV*, 379.
69. The Paris statute prohibiting priests from playing games of chance and attending spectacles was incorporated into the Fourth Lateran Council in canon 16. Eudes found priests playing dice, chess, a game called knucklebones, and quoits, a game comparable to horseshoes. For the Paris statute, see Pontal, *Les statuts de Paris*, 74. For the Fourth Lateran Council, see Tanner, *Decrees of the Ecumenical Councils*, 1:243.
70. *RER*, 27, 30, 31, 34; *RV*, 22, 26, 27, 30.
71. *RER*, 24; *RV*, 20.
72. Lemarignier, *Institutions ecclésiastiques*, 211.
73. *RER*, 32; *RV*, 28.
74. *RER*, 52; *RV*, 46.
75. *RER*, 27, 22; *RV*, 23, 18.
76. Canon 14 of the Third Lateran Council and canon 29 of the Fourth Lateran Council prohibited pluralism. See Tanner, *Decrees of the Ecumenical Councils*, 1:218, 248–49.
77. Lemarignier, *Institutions ecclésiastiques*, 206.
78. *RV*, 734, 735, 742, 746.
79. *RER*, 288; *RV*, 257.
80. *RER*, 204; *RV*, 190.
81. *RER*, 572; *RV*, 502. Eudes clearly held the legal right to deprive a rector of his benefice for nonresidence. See Gregory IX, *Decretales*, c. III, tit. IV, c. 6, 11, 12, in *Corpus iuris canonici*, 1:461–63.
82. See canon 14 of the Fourth Lateran Council, which dealt with punishing clerical incontinence. See Tanner, *Decrees of the Ecumenical Councils*, 1:242.
83. In the following discussion, I draw on John W. Baldwin, "A Campaign to Reduce Clerical Celibacy at the Turn of the Twelfth and Thirteenth Centuries," in *Études d'histoire du droit canonique: Dédiées à Gabriel Le Bras*, vol. 2 (Paris, 1965), 1041–53.
84. James A. Brundage, "Playing by the Rules: Sexual Behaviour and Legal Norms in Medieval Europe," in *Desire and Discipline: Sex and Sexuality in the Premodern West*, ed. Jaqueline Murray and Konrad Eisenbichler (Toronto, 1996), 25; James A. Brundage, "Proof in Canonical Criminal Law," *Continuity and Change* 11, 3 (1996): 331.
85. James Brundage points out that these changes in criminal procedure were the result of not only the church's campaigns against heresy and usury, as has often been argued, but also the church's attempt to wage a more effective battle against clerical concubinage. See Brundage, "Playing by the Rules," 28.
86. Ibid., 29. Brundage has aptly called Innocent's ruling a "judicial bombshell" and a significant restriction in individuals' rights of due process. There was, of course, much discussion among canonists about what exactly differentiated *notorium* and *fama*.
87. For the archdeaconry of Eu, for instance, Eudes found that at the deanery of Bures, 33% of the priests were defamed of incontinence; at Longueville, 25%; at Aumale, 23%; at Foucarmont, 26%; and at Neufchatel, 9%.
88. For examples of such letters, see *RV*, 649–74.
89. There are instances in which Eudes could have stripped a priest of his benefice but did not, even though the priest was found ill-famed of incontinence for a second or third time, despite repeated warnings. Eudes showed mercy on an ill-famed canon at the chapter of Saint-Mellon, for instance, who, when given a choice between resigning his benefice or facing judicial proceedings, pleaded in tears with the archbishop. Eudes permitted the canon to exchange his church for another one elsewhere. In another case, Eudes pardoned an incontinent priest because he was suffering from an unnamed infirmity. See *RER*, 543, 505; *RV*, 477; 444.
90. I draw on the discussion about this priest in Pobst, "Visitation of Religious and Clergy," 244.
91. The fines ranged from 10 to 30 l. It is not clear why in some cases Eudes demanded fines whereas in other cases he deprived the priests of their benefices.
92. Fournier, *Les officialités au moyen âge*, 263–66.
93. *RER*, 376; *RV*, 328. On how Guillaume de Beaumont, bishop of Angers, dealt with this problem, see Avril, *Le gouvernement des évêques*, 683.

94. On the various ways French synodal legislation turned the children of priests into undesirables, see Kathryn Ann Taglia, " 'On Account of Scandal . . . ': Priests, Their Children, and the Ecclesiastical Demand for Celibacy," *Florilegium* 14 (1995–96): 57–70.

95. *RER*, 29; *RV*, 25.

96. *RER*, 30; *RV*, 25–26.

97. Around 1239, Robert Grosseteste, bishop of Lincoln, promulgated a statute that imposed solemn and public denunciation on any layman who knowingly gave lodging to a cleric's concubine. Prelates were looking to the laity for help in holding the secular clergy to the law. See Shinners and Dohar, *Pastors and the Care of Souls*, 93.

98. Sbaraglia, *Bullarium Franciscanum*, vol. 2, no. 473, pp. 326–28.

99. Pontal, *Les statuts de 1230 à 1260*, no. 24, p. 136.

100. On the career of Federico Visconti, see most recently Bériou, *Les sermons et la visite pastorale*; Alexander Murray, "Archbishop and Mendicants in Thirteenth-Century Pisa," in *Stellung und Wirksamkeit der Bettelorden in der städtischen Gesellschaft*, ed. Kaspar Elm (Berlin, 1981), 19–75.

101. We have already observed that as archbishop Eudes took special interest in the learning (or lack thereof) of candidates for the priesthood. He also frequently inquired at monastic houses about the contents of their libraries.

102. Murray, "Archbishop and Mendicants," 29–31.

103. See chapter 1 as well as the discussion in Lottin, *Problèmes de psychologie*, vol. 1 of *Psychologie et morale*, 87.

104. Murray, "Archbishop and Mendicants," 57.

105. Ibid., 50–51.

106. Bériou, *Les sermons et la visite pastorale*, 239.

107. Eudes de Sully was so concerned that priests remain clean during the celebration of the Mass that one of his statutes enjoined every priest to keep a handkerchief (*manutergium*) next to the altar to use to wipe his mouth or nose, if necessary. Some synodal statutes stipulated that cloths stained by the consecrated wine automatically took on the value of relics and ought to be treated as such. Priests were ordered to use the best-quality wine and bread for the Eucharist. Much of the synodal legislation in the thirteenth century grew out of not only the influential Parisian statutes of Eudes de Sully but the sacramental theology of Peter the Chanter and his disciples. See Pontal, *Les statuts de Paris*, no. 79, p. 82; Avril, *Le gouvernement des évêques*, 701–3.

108. Murray, "Archbishop and Mendicants," 47–49.

109. Ibid., 54.

110. Ibid.

111. Ibid., 56.

112. Ibid., 54.

113. Bériou, *Les sermons et la visite pastorale*, 241; Murray, "Archbishop and Mendicants," 23.

114. Bériou, *Les sermons et la visite pastorale*, 234.

115. Ibid.

116. Pontal, *Les statuts de 1230 à 1260*, no. 21, p. 134.

117. Ibid., no. 18, p. 134.

118. For example, a statute in Eudes's provincial councils insisted that a certain number of monastics be maintained in all abbeys and priories and that no monk ever be allowed to dwell in a priory by himself. This statute, which Eudes enforced during his visitations, was a repetition of one of Gregory IX's statutes on the reformation of Benedictine monks. See *RER*, 407; *RV*, 357.

119. Pontal, *Les statuts de Paris*, lxvi, lxxiv–lxxv. As Pontal indicates, conciliar legislation was also influenced by papal reforms, canon law, monastic reforms (such as statutes passed by the Cistercian order), and academic discussions in the universities.

120. Pontal, *Les statuts de Paris*, lv. More generally on synodal legislation in Rouen, see Avril, *Les statuts synodaux des anciennes provinces de Bordeaux, Auch, Sens et Rouen*, vol. 5 of *Les statuts synodaux français*, ed. Pontal and Avril, 183–89.

121. Pontal, *Les statuts de Paris*, lvi, lx.

122. Canon 6 of the Fourth Lateran Council. See Tanner, *Decrees of the Ecumenical Councils*, 236–37.

123. Andrieu-Guitrancourt, "L'œuvre conciliaire d'Eudes Rigaud," *Revue historique de droit français et étranger* 15 (1936): 827–29. For a list of thirteenth-century Norman synodal statutes, see André Artonne, L. Guizard, and Odette Pontal, eds., *Répertoire des statuts synodaux des diocèses de l'ancienne France* (Paris, 1963), 214, 378–79. From 1223 to 1350, there were twenty-five provincial councils in the Norman province, nine of them under Eudes Rigaud. During roughly the same period, Reims held forty-six provincial councils and Sens held forty. Joseph Avril, ed., *Les conciles de la province de Tours* (Paris, 1987), 52 n. 5.

124. It is unlikely that the archdeacon of Rouen felt that Eudes was usurping his rights as ordinary of the archdeaconry. As discussed in chapter 2, Eudes made a practice of employing the archdeacon of Rouen in his archiepisopal *familia*, fostering a sense of loyalty and cooperation between the two prelates.

125. According to the *Register*, Eudes presided over twenty-five synods for the greater archdeaconry of Rouen. He was absent for three additional synods, because of illness or business in Paris. During his absences, the synods were run by members of his archiepiscopal *familia*.

126. See, for instance, Eudes's admonitions to the deans of Envermeu and Bures to hold monthly synods. *RER*, 375–77; *RV*, 328–29. It is not clear how regularly these synods of deaneries met, but occasional references to them in the *Register* indicate that they were being held. The deanery of Foucarmont, for instance, had held a recent synod when Eudes visited in January 1259. See *RER*, 378; *RV*, 330–31.

127. I have counted eighty synods and councils in the *Register*. The archbishop was absent from six of them because of illness or other business and was represented by members of his *familia*. The number of synods Eudes celebrated personally is almost certainly higher than seventy-four. The *Register* usually indicates that Eudes celebrated the synod for the archdeaconry of Rouen on Monday, the greater synod for the parish priests of the diocese on Tuesday, and a synod for the deans of the diocese on Wednesday. But occasionally, the *Register* lists only the "holy synod of Rouen," even though Eudes was in Rouen for more than one day and was in all probability celebrating the other synods as well. See also Tabbagh, *Diocèse de Rouen*, 6.

128. There are eight extant sets of statutes from councils and synods over which Eudes presided: the provincial councils of August 1257 (*RER*, 322–26; *RV*, 286–89), January 1260 (*RER*, 405–9; *RV*, 356–58), January 1261 (*RER*, 440–43; *RV*, 387–89), January 1263 (*RER*, 549–51; *RV*, 481–83), and 1267 (Bessin, *Concilia Rotomagensis*, 1:150); the synods of the deans of Rouen, October 1254 (*RER*, 203–4; *RV*, 190–91) and 1267 (Rouen, BM: ms. Y. 223A, f. 36v; Bessin, *Concilia Rotomagensis*, 2:83; Pommeraye, *Sanctae Rotomagensis ecclesiae concilia*, 259); and the synod of the archdeaconry of Pontoise, 1258 (*RER*, 368; *RV*, 323). Both Bessin and Pommeraye date the 1267 synod of the deans as 1275. Avril (*Les statuts synodaux des anciennes provinces*, 190) dates these same statutes as 1248. I date them as 1267, however, because the manuscript in the Rouen municipal library (ms. Y.223A, f. 36v), containing the statutes from 1335 of Archbishop Pierre Roger, states that the statutes come from a council held in 1267: "Anno domini 1267 fuerant ista precepta data a domino et patre nostre Odone archiepiscopo Rothomagensi." It is possible, of course, that Eudes held another synod in 1275 (the year he died), in which he republished the statutes from his 1267 synod.

129. Eudes either notes in his *Register* that he was in Rouen for several days before the synod or specifically refers to having conducted preliminary business for the synod with his suffragans one or two days beforehand. In this sense, the Rouen synods were like the Fourth Lateran Council, where the seventy canons were drafted before the actual celebration of the council. See Richard Kay, "Mansi and Rouen: A Critique of the Conciliar Collections," in *Councils and Clerical Culture in the Medieval West* (Aldershot, Hampshire, U.K., 1997), 157–85.

130. Pontal suggests that a diocesanal synod was different from other councils in the bishop's almost exclusive deliberative and legislative power. The bishop functioned as the prin-

cipal legislator in a synod much the way a pope did in a general council. See Pontal, *Les statuts de Paris*, xxvi, lxi.

131. Gregory IX, *Decretales*, c. iii, tit. 10, c. 4, in *Corpus iuris canonici*; Cheney, *English Synodalia*, 9–10.

132. *RER*, 203–4; *RV*, 190–91.

133. The constitution dealing with procurations was contained in *Romana Ecclesia*, which was part of one of the collections promulgated by the Council of Lyon of 1245. See Mansi, *Sacrorum conciliorum nova*, 23:668. Canon 33 of the Fourth Lateran Council also sought to curb excessive or unfair collections of procurations during visitations. See Tanner, *Decrees of the Ecumenical Councils*, 249–50.

134. The statutes for the provincial council at Pont-Audemer on September 9, 1257, are repeated at the councils on January 29, 1260; January 26, 1261; and January 29, 1264. By the provincial council of 1261, several new statutes had been added. One ordered that a special mass be celebrated for every deceased Norman bishop and archbishop. Another statute decreed that Psalm 78 be sung at the daily mass to pray for the brethren living in the Holy Land and in Constantinople. As Jean Longère shows, local synodal statutes could incorporate legislation that originated at the University of Paris, yet another example of the university's influence in local ecclesiastical administration. But reforming ideas could also spread from province to province through personal connections. See Longère, "Les évêques et l'administration du sacrement de pénitence au XIIIe siècle: Les cas réservés," in *Papauté, monachisme et théories politiques*, vol. 2, *Les églises locales* (Lyon, 1994), 537–50. On the Rouennais council of 1231 held by Archbishop Maurice, see Monique Cuillieron, "Un concile de réformation: Le concile Rouennais de 1231," *Revue historique de droit français et étranger* 61, 3 (1983): 345–69.

135. Raymonde Foreville shows that sixteen out of Guillaume's eighteen statutes published in 1279 came from Eudes's 1257 council. Foreville thus ascribes great importance to Eudes's 1257 council. See Foreville, "La réception des conciles généraux dans l'église et la province de Rouen au XIIIe siècle," in *Gouvernement et vie de l'église au moyen-âge* (London, 1979), 251–52.

136. André Artonne, "L'influence du Décret de Gratien sur les statuts synodaux," *Studia Gratiana* 2 (1954): 645–47; Pontal, *Les statuts de Paris*, lxi; Boisset, *Concile provincial*, 36–37.

137. C. R. Cheney, "Statute-Making in the English Church in the Thirteenth Century," in *Monumenta Iuris Canonici: Proceedings of the Second International Congress of Medieval Canon Law*, vol. 1 (Vatican, 1965), 409–10.

138. Cheney, *English Synodalia*, 47; Pommeraye, *Sanctae Rotomagensis ecclesiae concilia*, 252.

139. Andrieu-Guitrancourt, "L'œuvre conciliaire," 828.

140. Avril, *Les statuts synodaux des anciennes provinces*, 189.

141. *RER*, 203–4; *RV*, 190–91. As noted earlier in the chapter, it was not uncommon for a patron to present to the bishop or archbishop a candidate for a cure of souls who was not yet ordained. Such candidates were often able to receive their benefices simply by promising the bishop that they would soon receive priestly ordination. See Avril, *Le gouvernement des évêques*, 656.

142. Nicole Bériou, "La prédication synodale au XIIIe siècle d'après l'exemple cambrésien," in *Le clerc séculier au moyen âge*, 229–47 (Paris, 1993).

143. Duval-Arnould, "Trois sermons synodaux," *AFH* 69 (1976): 336–400. The sermons are found in BnF ms. lat. 18188. The third sermon carries the rubric "sermo in synodo Rothomagensi," making it almost certain that it was not preached by Jean de la Rochelle, who died in 1245 as regent master of the Franciscan *studium* in Paris and never held episcopal office. Eudes Rigaud, however, celebrated dozens of synods in Rouen and was closely associated with Jean de la Rochelle, with whom he had studied at Paris. Thus it would not be surprising to find some sermons belonging to Eudes in a manuscript collection containing the sermons of Jean. Duval-Arnould believes that the third synodal sermon can be dated 1250, pointing to what he believes is a reference in the sermon to the seventh crusade and the capture of King Louis in April 1250: "et haec debet esse oratio nostrorum sacerdotum his diebus in tribulatione Ecclesiae et captivatione militum utra mare" (Duval-Arnould, "Trois sermons synodaux," *AFH* 70 [1977]:

67). Having calculated the distance and speed for a boat to travel from Damietta to Aigues-Mortes and then for a horse to travel from Aigues-Mortes to Rouen, Duval-Arnould argues that by the time of the synod at Rouen on May 24, 1250, Eudes would almost certainly have known about the capture of King Louis six weeks earlier, not yet having received news of the king's release only some two weeks earlier. Duval-Arnould also points to the three sermons' similarities in both style and content.

144. Eudes suggested that the clergy's responsibility to teach through preaching sermons was signified in the Bible in the sounds of temple priests' trumpets and the bells attached to Aaron's priestly garment, heard as he entered and exited the sanctuary. See Duval-Arnould, "Trois sermons synodaux," *AFH* 70 (1977): 63–64.

145. Ibid., 60.

146. Ibid., 57 nn. 113–14. Eudes showed a persistent interest in the image of the *stabularius*. He also refers to it in the third synodal sermon (Duval-Arnould, "Trois sermons synodaux," *AFH* 70 (1977): 63), as well as in one of the sermons he preached at the University of Paris before becoming archbishop. BM: Arras ms. 691 (759), f.114ra: "Karissimmi, si rex diceret alicui: elige tibi quod vis officium in domo mea, fatuus esset qui eligeret esse stabularius regis . . . immo si sapiens esset quis potius eligeret fieri camerarius vel senscallus [*sic*]. Sic stulta electione quidam consilia volunt dimittere et precepta quocumque modo servare. Fastidiunt quod perfectius est et tepide implent que imperfectionis sunt."

147. Duval-Arnould, "Trois sermons synodaux," *AFH* 70 (1977): 36. All translations from these sermons are my own.

148. Ibid.

149. I summarize and paraphrase much of the sermon here. It is the first of Duval-Arnould's "Trois sermons synodaux," *AFH* 70 (1977): 36–52.

150. Ibid., 38.

151. Ibid., 46.

152. Ibid., 44.

153. Ibid., 47.

154. This is the third of Duval-Arnould's "Trois sermons synodaux," *AFH* 70 (1977): 60–71.

155. Ibid., 67.

156. Ibid., 64.

157. Ibid., 66–67, from Jerome, *Commentarii in Aggaeum prophetam ad Paulam et Eustochium*, 2, 12, in *PL* 25: col. 1406B.

158. Cheney, *English Synodalia*, 39.

6. An Ecclesiastical Administrator of Justice

1. Robert Génestal, *Le privilegium fori en France du Décret de Gratien à la fin du XIVe siècle* (Paris, 1924), 61. The *privilegium fori* was an established principle, dating back to Constantine, that prohibited secular judges from hearing cases involving clerics. On the *officialis*, see Edouard Fournier, *Les origines du vicaire général* (Paris, 1922); Lefebvre-Teillard, *Les officialités*, 25–29.

2. In some regions, defendants considered to have partial ecclesiastical privileges would have their cases heard in an ecclesiastical court only if they made such a request. In other regions, cases were heard in ecclesiastical courts only on appeal. See Génestal, *Le privilegium fori*, 58–59; Fournier, *Les officialités au moyen âge*, x–xvii.

3. Tardif, *Coutumiers de Normandie*. In the introduction to both volumes of *Coutumiers*, Tardif discusses the various versions of the *Très ancien coutumier* (including the Old French versions) and the *Summa de legibus*. Whereas Tardif dates the first treatise of the *Très ancien coutumier* to 1199–1200, that is, before the Capetian conquest, Paul Viollet argues that it was compiled a bit later, c. 1203–4. See Viollet, "Les Coutumiers de Normandie," *Histoire littéraire de la France* 33 (1906): 43–65.

4. Léopold Delisle, ed., *Recueil de jugements de l'échiquier de Normandie* (Paris, 1864), 185–86.

5. Tardif, *Coutumiers de Normandie*, 1:2.

6. Delisle, *Recueil de jugements de l'échiquier*, 186.

7. Tardif, *Coutumiers de Normandie*, 1:83–84.

8. Ibid., 1:5–6. See also Jean Yver, "Le 'Très ancien coutumier' de Normandie, miroir de la léglisation ducale? Contribution à l'étude de l'ordre public normand à la fin du XIIe siècle," *Revue d'histoire du droit* 39, 3 (1971): 333–74.

9. Baldwin, *Government of Philip Augustus*, 321–23.

10. The right of advowson was a recognized part of twelfth-century Norman customary law and was reaffirmed in Philip II's inquest of 1205. See Tardif, *Coutumiers de Normandie*, 1:23, 75; Baldwin, *Government of Philip Augustus*, 318–19.

11. Tardif, *Coutumiers de Normandie*, 1:23.

12. Ibid., 77–78. On the function of the *bailli* as the personification of the royal tribunal in the mid-thirteenth century, see R. de Fréville, "Étude sur l'organisation judiciare en Normandie aux XIIe et XIIIe siècles," *Nouvelle revue historique de droit français et étranger* 36 (1912): 681–736.

13. If the panel was unable to determine the proprietary question of right, it still ruled on the question of possession.

14. Tardif, *Coutumiers de Normandie*, 1:75, 2:33.

15. See, for instance, the case involving Richard of Grainville, a knight, and the squires Hugh and John of Grainville, over the patronage of the church of Grainville. *RER*, 525–26; *RV*, 460. The polyptych confirms that Eudes ruled in favor of Richard. "Polyptychum Rotomagensis Diocesis," *HF*, 23:310.

16. *RER*, 171; *RV*, 154. Pierre d'Aumale and Etienne de Lorris, both canons in the Rouen chapter, were members of Eudes's *familia*. Guillaume was treasurer of the Rouen chapter, Reginald was archdeacon of the Petit-Caux, Simon was archdeacon of Eu, and Hugh of Auvergne and Gilles of Picardy were both Rouen canons. According to the polyptych, the archbishop was the patron of Touqueville, the church in question. "Polyptychum Rotomagensis Diocesis," *HF*, 23:302.

17. Ralph V. Turner, "Richard Lionheart and the Episcopate in His French Domains," *French Historical Studies* 21, 4 (1998): 517–42.

18. Baldwin, *Government of Philip Augustus*, 306–11. See also John Baldwin, "Philip Augustus and the Norman Church," *French Historical Studies* 6, 1 (1969): 1–30. As Baldwin points out, an additional factor that almost certainly influenced Philip's policy toward the French church in 1200 was the interdict that the pope had placed on the kingdom.

19. Baldwin, *Government of Philip Augustus*, 309–11.

20. As Baldwin writes, "The king was eager to display a beneficent side before 1204, but he became intent upon vindicating his traditional rights afterwards. From being a beguiling seducer, Philip became a stern master." Ibid., 328.

21. *RER*, 324 and nn. 25–27; *RV*, 287. These statutes, first promulgated in the provincial council of Rouen of 1231 in canons 28, 23, and 26, were again promulgated at the provincial council of 1257 and were repeated in subsequent Norman provincial councils during the 1260s. See Pontal, *Les statuts de 1230 à 1260*. There was some protective immunity for *baillis* against excommunication, namely, a Norman custom stipulating that a bishop needed the king's permission in order to excommunicate a royal official or a lord. This protection lasted only two weeks, however. See Baldwin, *Government of Philip Augustus*, 324.

22. *RV*, 741.

23. *RER*, 160; *RV*, 142.

24. Blanche, not wishing to make any concession that would be prejudicial to the absent king, granted the church the right to detain the prisoners for only two years, by which time she believed her son would have returned from the crusade. If he returned before two years' time, the prisoners could be kept by the church for up to two months following his return.

25. Tardif, *Coutumiers de Normandie*, 2:69.

26. *RER*, 288–89; *RV*, 257–58.

27. Pierre Adolphe Chéruel, *Histoire de Rouen pendant l'époque communale, 1150–1382*, vol. 1 (Rouen, 1843), 160.

28. Ibid., 1:160–61.
29. Tardif, *Coutumiers de Normandie*, 1:69, 2:195–96; Baldwin, *Government of Philip Augustus*, 325–26.
30. In some provinces, the archbishop presided over two separate courts, one that served the province and another that served his own diocese. In Normandy, however, there appears to have been one court that dealt with cases for both the province and diocese. See Lefebvre-Teillard, *Les officialités*, 31–33.
31. *RER*, 577; *RV*, 506–7.
32. *RER*, 443; *RV*, 389.
33. See, for instance, *RER*, 250, 253, 332; *RV*, 228, 230, 294.
34. *RER*, 168; *RV*, 151.
35. *RER*, 84–85; *RV*, 74–75. Although the archbishop's permanent court was in Rouen, where the official who directed most legal business was stationed, legal proceedings could occur at any time or place of the archbishop's choosing. André de St-Léonard, for example, was summoned to make his pledge to the archbishop at Bonport, a Cistercian abbey where Eudes happened to be staying.
36. Jean Yver, *Les contrats dans le très ancien droit normand (XIe–XIIIe siècles)* (Caen, 1926), 135–39. The *Summa de legibus* defined pledges as persons who obliged themselves to pay or do someone else's debt. See Tardif, *Coutumiers de Normandie*, 2: 148–53.
37. *RV*, 779–80.
38. *RV*, 780.
39. *RER*, 286; *RV*, 256; Yver, *Les contrats*, 44–48; Tardif, *Coutumiers de Normandie*, 2:180.
40. Joseph R. Strayer, *The Administration of Normandy under Saint Louis* (Cambridge, Mass., 1932), 27–30. Contrary to Strayer, Paul Fournier argues that the power of ecclesiastical courts actually grew during the thirteenth century. See Fournier, *Les officialités au moyen âge*, x–xiv.
41. Strayer, *Administration of Normandy*, 27.
42. Ibid., 28.
43. There are actually two separate papal bulls from Alexander IV dated Anagni, II Kalends February, 1259. The first dealt with lay crusaders charged with serious crimes, and the second dealt with bigamous clergy, widowed clergy, and married clergy. Both bulls are in *RV*, 759.
44. *CR*, 1:150; Lemarignier, *Institutions ecclésiastiques*, 265–67.
45. Strayer, *Administration of Normandy*, 97.
46. Ibid., 28.
47. Ibid., 29.
48. Jean de Joinville, *Life of Saint Louis*, in *Chronicles of the Crusades*, trans. M. R. B. Shaw (Baltimore, 1963), 177–78.
49. See William Chester Jordan, "Archbishop Eudes Rigaud and the Jews of Normandy, 1248–1275," in *Friars and Jews in the Middle Ages and Renaissance*, ed. Steven J. McMichael and Susan E. Myers (Leiden, 2004), 39–52.
50. *RER*, 618; *RV*, 541. A similar event likely occurred on June 22, 1253, when, according to the *Register*, the archbishop preached a sermon to a gathering of Rouennais citizens and clergy at the same location, the Mare-du-Parc. The occasion was the formal condemnation of Jean Marel for heresy. As the *Register* indicates, Jean had long been detained in the archiepiscopal prison. It is likely that following Eudes's written and verbal condemnation, Jean was turned over to the *bailli* and publicly burned. See *RV*, 160 n. 2.
51. There are at least thirty-four chronicle accounts of the Pastoureaux attacks of 1251. See Malcolm Barber, "The Crusade of the Shepherds in 1251," in *Proceedings of the Tenth Annual Meeting of the Western Society for French History, 14–16 October 1982, Winnipeg, Manitoba, Canada*, ed. John F. Sweets (Lawrence, Kan., 1984); Jordan, *Louis IX*, 113–15.
52. *E Chronico sancti Laudi Rotomagensis*, in *HF*, 23:396; *E Chronico sanctae Catharinae de Monte Rotomagi*, in *HF*, 23:401–2; Chéruel, *Normanniae nova chronica*, 23–24.
53. Matthew Paris, *English History*, 453.
54. *RER*, 141; *RV*, 127 n. 1; Andrieu-Guitrancourt, *L'archevêque Eudes Rigaud*, 321–22.

55. *Omnis utriusque sexus* is canon 21 of the Fourth Lateran Council. See Tanner, *Decrees of the Ecumenical Councils*, 1:245.

56. *RER,* 626; *RV,* 548. Eudes decided that a priest could confess to a neighboring priest so long as the atoning priest saw a penitentiary within two weeks of his confession.

57. *RER,* 424; *RV,* 374.

58. This is one of Mary Mansfield's central arguments in *The Humiliation of Sinners: Public Penance in Thirteenth-Century France* (Ithaca, 1995). Mansfield often cites examples from Eudes's *Register.*

59. Mansfield has calculated that Eudes spent twenty-one Ash Wednesdays and sixteen of twenty-one Maundy Thursdays at Rouen. In a number of cases, his *Register* specifically reports that he performed the Lenten expulsion and reconciliation ceremonies. See Mansfield, *Humiliation of Sinners,* 97 n. 16.

60. Mansfield contrasts these nonsolemn forms of public penance with the solemn Lenten rite of expelling and reconciling sinners at the cathedral. Although medieval theologians drew this distinction between solemn and nonsolemn public penance, in practice the lines were often not clear.

61. *RER,* 179; *RV,* 164.

62. *RER,* 372; *RV,* 325–26.

63. *RER,* 558; *RV,* 490.

64. Mansfield, *Humiliation of Sinners,* 125. In addition to forcing penitents to go on pilgrimages as public penance, Eudes conducted his own pilgrimages to the sites of holy relics, quite often setting off after being stricken with serious illness. On October 31, 1252, for instance, only a few weeks after being extremely sick, Eudes made a pilgrimage to Saint-Thibault-aux-Bois to pray to the saint protector of those sick with fevers. Immediately after Easter in 1260, he traveled all the way to the south of France to visit the relics of Saint Gilles in an abbey near Nîmes. Along the way he visited the relics at Notre-Dame-le-Puy and Saint-Léonard-de-Corbigny. He also made a pilgrimage by foot to Chartres, accompanied by the bishop of Auxerre. See Richard, "Le clergé de Normandie"; see also *RER,* 417, 460; *RV,* 366–67, 404.

65. Mansfield, *Humiliation of Sinners,* 127.

66. *RER,* 27–29; *RV,* 23–24.

67. Mansfield, *Humiliation of Sinners,* 17.

68. My description of the ritual of Saint Romain is drawn from Thomas P. Campbell, "Cathedral Chapter and Town Council: Cooperative Ceremony and Drama in Medieval Rouen," *Comparative Drama* 27, 1 (1993): 100–113; Amable Floquet, *Histoire de privilège de Saint Romain,* 2 vols. (Rouen, 1883).

69. On these judicial procedures, see Robert E. Rodes, Jr., *Ecclesiastical Administration in Medieval England: The Anglo-Saxons to the Reformation* (Notre Dame, Ind., 1977), 90–98, 143–45.

70. *RER,* 578; *RV,* 507.

71. Ibid.; Mansfield, *Humiliation of Sinners,* 111–12.

72. The church claimed legal jurisdiction over the servants of clerics.

73. *RER,* 287; *RV,* 256. Eudes first questioned Pierre on May 12, 1256, but did not hear the confessions of Matthieu and Renaud until August 5.

74. Denifle, *Chartularium,* 1:304–5, 336, 340–41; Michel-Marie Dufeil, *Guillaume de Saint-Amour et la polémique universitaire parisienne, 1250–1259* (Paris, 1972); Andrieu-Guitrancourt, *L'archevêque Eudes Rigaud,* 401–2.

75. My discussion of the Noyon case draws on Erika J. Laquer, "Ritual, Literacy, and Documentary Evidence: Archbishop Eudes Rigaud and the Relics of St. Eloi," *Francia* 13 (1985): 625–37; and Olivier Guyotjeannin, "Les reliques de Saint Éloi à Noyon: Procès et enquêtes du milieu du XIIIe siècle," *Revue Mabillon* n.s. 1 (1990): 57–110. Guyotjeannin includes a transcription of the legal proceedings (copied by a monk in the 1260s). The text of the compromise for the Noyon case can be found in *RV,* 342.

76. A little more than ten years after the settlement, the dispute between the cathedral chapter and monastery re-ignited, and it continued to resurface for several centuries. See Laquer, "Ritual," 634.

77. *RER*, 408–9; *RV*, 359.
78. *RER*, 487 and n. 3; *RV*, 427.
79. *GC*, 11:69.

7. A Franciscan Money Manager

1. The first Franciscan bishop, Agnello, bishop of Fez, was raised to the episcopate some-time between 1226 and 1232. See Thomson, *Friars in the Cathedral*, 27. Thomson suggests that the very concept of a Franciscan bishop or archbishop was a contradiction in terms. There may be some significance to the fact that the first Dominican cardinal, Hugues de Saint-Cher, antedated the first Franciscan cardinal, Bonaventure, by some thirty years. Yet there appears to have been fairly little opposition within the Franciscan order to having friars enter the episcopacy, perhaps in part owing to the Franciscans' rapid clericalization. See Landini, *Causes of the Clericalization.*
2. *Regula non bullata*, trans. Paul Schwartz and Paul Lachance, in *The Birth of a Movement: A Study of the First Rule of St. Francis*, ed. David Flood and Thaddée Matura (Chicago, 1975), 73.
3. Ibid., 76–77.
4. Example cited in David Burr, *The Spiritual Franciscans: From Protest to Persecution in the Century after Saint Francis* (University Park, Pa., 2001), 5.
5. See Kaye, *Economy and Nature*, 130–31 and n. 53. Kaye is reluctant to argue for the case of Franciscan exceptionalism in economic theory, particularly since, as he points out, there were plenty of non-Franciscan thinkers who made similar arguments about the principles of economics.
6. 2 Celano 148, in Habig, *St. Francis of Assisi*, 481–82.
7. Salimbene de Adam, *Chronica*, 1:480; see also Robert Brentano, *Two Churches: England and Italy in the Thirteenth Century* (Princeton, 1968), 184–88. Displaying one's humility by showing reluctance to accept high ecclesiastical office had a long tradition in the church (predating the Franciscan order) and was something of a trope in medieval hagiography and other forms of literature. Like other Franciscans who built on this tradition, John Pecham, archbishop of Canterbury, stressed that it was incumbent on a friar minor to decline an episcopal office when it was offered unless the pope essentially forced him to accept it.
8. Salimbene de Adam, *Chronica*, 1:494; Salimbene de Adam, *Chronicle*, 322.
9. For examples of thirteenth-century bishops in Britain who resigned their sees in order to become friars, see Robert N. Swanson, "Mendicant Bishops in the British Isles in the Thirteenth and Early Fourteenth Centuries," in *Dal pulpito alla cattedra: I vescovi degli ordini mendicanti nel '200 e nel primo '300* (Spoleto, 2000), 309–10.
10. See Paul Remy Oliger, *Les évêques réguliers: Recherche sur leur condition juridique depuis les origines du monachisme jusqu'à la fin du moyen-âge* (Paris, 1958).
11. *Magna vita Sancti Hugonis*, ed. Decima L. Douie and Hugh Farmer (London, 1961).
12. Angelo Clareno, "Historia septem tribulationum ordinis minorum," ed. F. Ehrle, in *Archiv für Litteratur und Kirchengeschichte des Mittelalters* 2 (1886): 267–68.
13. Ibid., 271.
14. I draw here on Michael F. Cusato, "Hermitage or Marketplace? The Search for an Authentic Franciscan Locus in the World," *Spirit and Life* 10 (2000): 1–30.
15. John Pecham, *Tractatus pauperis*, in *Quaestio disputata de privilegio Martini papae IV* (Quaracchi, 1925), 79–88; Boureau, *Théologie, science et censure*, 181. Although the secular clergy had not taken a vow of chastity, it was of course a violation of canon law for a cleric to engage in sexual activity.
16. See Boureau, *Théologie, science et censure*, 182.
17. David Burr, *Olivi and Franciscan Poverty: The Origins of the Usus Pauper Controversy* (Philadelphia, 1989), 93–94. This argument of Olivi's was condemned as a serious error by a commission, and in 1283 Olivi modified his position, saying that Franciscan bishops were not held to *usus pauper* more stringently than nonbishops if it would hinder their performance of their episcopal duties.

18. Before 1302, only twenty-five mendicants (ten of whom were Franciscan) were promoted to the episcopate in France (roughly 3% of all French bishops), and most were promoted at the end of the thirteenth century. During this same period, about the same number of Benedictines and Cistercians were promoted to the episcopate, so it was not until the late thirteenth and fourteenth centuries that friars began to outnumber other regulars in episcopal offices. See Jacques Paul, "Les religieux mendiants évêques en France au XIIIe siècle," in *Dal pulpito alla cattedra*, 255–56.

19. Dorothy Sutcliffe, "The Financial Condition of the See of Canterbury, 1279–1292," *Speculum* 10, 1 (1935): 53–68.

20. *Registrum epistolarum fratris Johannis Peckham, archiepiscopi cantuariensis*, ed. C. T. Martin, (reprint, Wiesbaden, 1965), 1:lix–lx.

21. Ibid., 1:lx. This was reported by Rodolfo da Tossignano in his *Historia seraphicae religionis*.

22. Decima L. Douie, *Archbishop Pecham* (Oxford, 1952), 47–48.

23. Smith, *Attitude of John Pecham*, 142–51.

24. *Registrum epistolarum*, 1:17–23, a letter from the archbishop to Pope Nicholas III, dated July 11, 1279, in which he asks the pope for a loan of 5,000 marks from the money collected for the crusade to help pay his outstanding loan of 4,000 marks. See also R. W. Kaeuper, *Bankers to the Crown: The Riccardi of Lucca and Edward I* (Princeton, 1973), 25–27.

25. *Registrum epistolarum*, 1:18; Sutcliffe, "Financial Condition," 55.

26. *Registrum epistolarum*, 1:21–23; Sutcliffe, "Financial Condition," 58.

27. *Registrum epistolarum*, 1:21–23.

28. Jacques-Guy Bougerol, ed., *Saint Bonaventure: Sermones de tempore* (Paris, 1990), 153–54.

29. It is noteworthy that Eudes never referred to Benedictine or Cistercian nuns as *sororum nostrarum*, nor did he even refer to Franciscan males as *fratrorum nostrorum*. It is particularly curious that Eudes would have felt such a bond with these nuns since many Franciscan men felt quite ambivalent about Franciscan nuns and their place within the order. See Lezlie Knox, "Audacious Nuns: Institutionalizing the Franciscan Order of Saint Clare," *Church History* 69, 1 (2000): 41–62. On the abbey at Longchamp, see Sean Field, *Isabelle of France: Capetian Sanctity and Franciscan Identity in the Thirteenth Century* (Notre Dame, Ind., forthcoming 2006).

30. Eudes's *Register* indicates that he frequently wore pontificals while celebrating Mass (even while celebrating Mass in a Franciscan convent). It is possible that at other times the archbishop wore his Franciscan habit, but unlike some friar-bishops, he was not averse to appearing in episcopal robes. See *RER*, 497–98; *RV*, 438.

31. *RER*, 48–50, 384; *RV*, 43–45, 338.

32. Several dozen original charters are contained in the departmental archives of the Seine-Maritime (Rouen) under the G series (secular clergy). A cartulary (AD: Seine Maritime, G7) compiled c. 1372 by the archbishop of Rouen, Pierre d'Alençon, contains many copies of charters and *acta* from the archiepiscopate of Eudes Rigaud, some of which are not extant in the original.

33. The archdioceses of Bourges and Tours both had average annual net revenues of 3,000 l.t., and Reims had an average annual revenue of 6,000 l.t. Michèle Bordeaux, *Aspects économiques de la vie de l'église aux XIVe et XVe siècles* (Paris, 1969), 341. See also Tabbagh, "Le temporel des archevêques," 206; Jean Gaudemet, *Le gouvernement de l'église à l'époque classique*, Part 2: *Le gouvernement local* (Paris, 1979), 149–50. The figures just given, which admittedly permit only a rough sense of episcopal incomes, were calculated by multiplying the average tithes each bishopric paid by a factor of ten. Although Rouen was the wealthiest diocese in France in the later thirteenth century, several English dioceses had net annual revenues that surpassed those of Rouen. For example, episcopal vacancy receipts collected by King Henry III from the diocese of Winchester in the twenty months from December 25, 1260, to August 14, 1262, amounted to £6,216 sterling, or 14,918 l.t. over a twelve-month period. See Margaret Howell, *Regalian Right in Medieval England* (London, 1962), 239.

34. Tabbagh, "Le temporel des archevêques," 204. On how thirteenth-century bishops managed their patrimonies generally, see Gaudemet, *Le gouvernement de l'église*, 141–50.

35. *RV*, 744–45. The merchants were from Florence, Sienna, and Pari, a town just south of Sienna. The lenders' names were listed as Giardino Zamponi, Raynaldo Raynerii, Arnigo Abadingi, Philipo Rodulphi, Turclo (the brother of Raynaldo), Engiffredo de Garmannis, and Jacobo Bosoli.

36. *RV*, 744.

37. Eudes and his *familia* remained at the papal curia in Lyon for sixteen days.

38. *HF*, 23:739; Jordan, *Louis IX*, 89. During the thirteenth century, French kings found various ways to capitalize on the wealth of the Norman church, including through the collection of regalia during episcopal vacancies. In 1231, for instance, the French crown used 1,300 l. of the regalia it collected from the vacant see of Rouen in defense of the Avranchin. See Strayer, *Administration of Normandy*, 45–46 and n. 2; Gerard J. Campbell, "Temporal and Spiritual Regalia during the Reigns of Saint Louis and Philip III," *Traditio* 20 (1964): 351–84; *HF*, 24:296.

39. By the thirteenth century, the church permitted such penalties on the loss arising (*damnum emergens*) from late payments of loans. The argument was that such damages were not usurious because, unlike interest on a loan, they were unexpected: the lender had no intention of collecting more than the principal, and damages merely compensated him for losses he suffered and served as a deterrent against late payment. See Baldwin, *Masters, Princes, and Merchants*, 1:283–84; John T. Noonan, *The Scholastic Analysis of Usury* (Cambridge, Mass., 1957), 107–9.

40. *RV*, 782.

41. *RV*, 766–67.

42. By 1257, Eudes was still leasing Dieppe to the same two individuals, but the value of the lease had fallen slightly, from 3,740 l. to 3,600 l.

43. In 1255 and again in 1258, Eudes leased his manor houses at Aliermont and Croixdalle with all the rights pertaining to them, such as tithes, tile works, and forests, for 1,000 l. per year. See *RV*, 770–73. In 1261, Eudes leased the town of Fresne (including any wheat collected from the granary and whatever he owned at Pormor) for an annual rent of 700 l. See *RV*, 773. In 1262, he leased sixty-four acres of arable land at Douvendrel and fifty-three acres of woodland at Hupy to Master Jean de Flainville, a canon of Rouen. The canon rendered homage to the archbishop and promised to pay an annual rent of 40 l. on the land. AD: Seine Maritime, G939, marked on bottom, "978-14862." Eudes leased Louviers for 900 l. in 1252, for 950 l. in 1256; and for 1,000 l. in 1259. *RV*, 768–69.

44. AD: Seine Maritime, G1054, marked on reverse, "Déville plusieurs rentes acheptees par O. Rigault a Déville 1258."

45. AD: Seine Maritime, G948, marked on reverse, "littere quitationis . . . super doce Emeline de Humenillo."

46. AD: Seine Maritime, G7:760.

47. For the sale of a part of the garden at Alizay, which the archbishop bought from Anes, wife of Martin "the forester," see AD: Seine Maritime, G1095, marked on reverse, "acquisition d'une portion de jardin a Alizy 1261"; for the "pecia" (piece) of the vineyard at Gaillon, which Eudes purchased from Pierre de Chapelle and his wife, Petroville, in 1264, see G7:893; for the hovel in Dieppe, which Eudes bought from Johanne de Barrière and her husband, Richard de Belleville, see G7:767.

48. Tabbagh, "Le temporel des archevêques," 205.

49. For instance, Gilbert Maquerel sold Eudes a pecia of land called "Le tuterel" for 60 s. which adjoined land already belonging to the archbishopric on one side and a certain Jean on the other side. AD: Seine Maritime, G7:896.

50. Guillaume de Salmonville, a canon of Rouen, held the mill at Angreville as part of his prebend. In order to rent the mill to Eudes Rigaud in 1252, Guillaume had to get confirmation from the Rouen chapter. AD: Seine Maritime, G947, a charter from Guillaume, is marked on the reverse, "carta molendiny de Angrevilla." A charter from the chapter of Rouen confirming the sale is marked on the reverse, "confirmant la chapitre de Rouen tous le droit qu'il . . . sur le moulin d'Angreville à l'Archeveque." A third charter is a confirmation by the dean of Lisieux, Jean de St. Evroul, with the incipit "Universis presentes litteras inspecturi magister Johannes de Sancto Ebrulfo Decanus."

51. Gérard Sivéry, *L'économie du royaume de France au siècle de Saint Louis* (Lille, 1984), 90.
52. Bonnin, *Cartulaire de Louviers*, 1:278–79; *CN*, charter no. 654, pp. 132–33. Later that year, Eudes gave the French crown the manor house of Saint-Matthieu, located on the south bank of the Seine across from Rouen and previously occupied by the Dominicans of the city, in exchange for the rights of high justice in Pinterville, the repurchase of a rent in Pinterville, and the cancellation of the annual rent that the archbishop owed the king on the ponds in Martinville. AD: Seine Maritime, G1089–90; Tabbagh, "Le temporel des archevêques," 204.
53. Bonnin, *Cartulaire de Louviers*, 1:289–91. This is a charter dated July 12–13, 1262, at Nevers, from Eudes Rigaud, stating the terms of an exchange with the king of France. The archbishop had received the consent of the Rouen chapter for the transaction. There is also a charter from Louis IX, approving and confirming the exchange. See Bonnin, *Cartulaire de Louviers*, 1:291–293.
54. Tabbagh, "Le temporel des archevêques," 204. The figures for Eudes's investments and those of his predecessors are derived from the collection of charters in the fourteenth-century cartulary of Pierre d'Alençon. Although it is possible that the difference between the purchases of Eudes and his predecessors is merely a matter of better documentation for the later period (as incorporated into the cartulary), the records still suggest that Eudes's successors invested far less than he did.
55. Tabbagh, "Le temporel des archevêques," 206.
56. Perpetual rents were also a favorite form of investment of the Rouen cathedral chapter. Alain Sadourny argues that the Rouen chapter was the main buyer of rents in the archdiocese during the thirteenth century. He makes no reference, however, to the archbishop's purchase of rents, which, according to my archival findings, outnumbered those of the Rouen chapter from 1248 until 1275. See Sadourny, "Les rentes à Rouen," 99–108.
57. AD: Seine Maritime, G3854, marked on top "A cotte 2, 1253."
58. AD: Seine Maritime, G7:932; Tabbagh, "Le temporel des archevêques," 206.
59. On perpetual rents, see Pierre Petot, "La constitution de rente aux XIIe et XIIIe siècles dans les pays coutumiers," in *Mélanges*, ed. A. Boutaric et al. (Dijon, 1928); M. de Tribolet, "La rente urbaine à Genève au XIIIe siècle," *BEC* 133 (1975): 5–20; Sadourny, "Les rentes à Rouen." On the evolution of perpetual rents in France during the fourteenth to sixteenth centuries, see Bernard Schnapper, *Les rentes au XVIe siècle: Histoire d'un instrument de crédit* (Paris, 1957), 46.
60. Most of the rents Eudes purchased came from urban bourgeois families. They presumably used the income to make other investments or pay off debts.
61. Studying the rents purchased by the chapter of Rouen and Norman monasteries during the thirteenth century, Sadourny and Génestal both observe "une grande stabilité" in the rates of return. Of the Rouen chapter's rents, for instance, 75% carried a return of 9 to 11%. See Sadourny, "Les rentes à Rouen," 101; Génestal, *Le rôle des monastères*, 199.
62. AD: Seine Maritime, G870, marked "991-14875" and "992-14876" on bottom; AD: Seine Maritime, G7:768–69. Tabbagh, "Le temporel des archevêques," 205.
63. Tabbagh, "Le temporel des archevêques," 205–6.
64. Eudes bought the house from Richard, abbot of Saint-Taurin, in January 1261. The abbey of Saint-Taurin owed an annual rent of 8 l. 13 s. to the dean and chapter of Rouen. By buying the house, Eudes agreed to pay the annual rent to the Rouen chapter. See Bonnin, *Cartulaire de Louviers*, 1:285–86.
65. AD: Seine Maritime, G7:994–1000. Tabbagh, "Le temporel des archevêques," 205. Eudes had purchased the rights of justice in Dieppe from Nicolas in 1251 in exchange for a rent of 25 l.t. on the watermill in Dieppe. Within two years, however, Eudes sold the rent he owed.
66. Sadourny, "Les rentes à Rouen," 101; Petot, "La constitution de rente," 71–73.
67. Bernard Schnapper, "Les rentes chez les théologiens et les canonistes du XIIIe au XVI siècle," *Études d'histoire du droit canonique* 2 (1965): 969. Schnapper concluded that in the thirteenth century, perpetual rents on property were generally accepted as legal.

68. Odd Inge Langholm, *Economics in the Medieval Schools: Wealth, Exchange, Value, Money, and Usury According to the Paris Theological Tradition, 1200–1350* (Leiden, 1992), 364–65.
69. Schnapper, "Les rentes chez les théologiens," 969–71.
70. Bernard of Auvergne and other theologians disagreed with Henry on this point. Bernard argued that a rent contract involved the right to collect money (*ius percipiendi pecuniam*), which was different from the money itself. It was this right, according to Bernard, that could be bought and sold. See Langholm, *Economics in the Medieval Schools*, 298.
71. Innocent IV made this pronouncement not as pope but as a canonist (Sinibaldo de'Fieschi).
72. Langholm, *Economics in the Medieval Schools*, 307.
73. Schnapper, *Les rentes au XVIe siècle*, 67–72. The customary of Orléans also fixed the maximum rate of return on rents at 10%. During the sixteenth century, the Parlement lowered the maximum rate to 8.33% and finally to 6.66%.
74. Sbaraglia, *Bullarium Franciscanum*, 3:404–17; Duncan Nimmo, *Reform and Division in the Medieval Franciscan Order: From Saint Francis to the Foundation of the Capuchins* (Rome, 1987), 58.
75. Nimmo, *Reform and Division*, 61–66.
76. For an example of the kind of form the pope used, see Michel Andrieu, ed., "Le pontifical romain du XIIe siècle," in *Le pontifical romain au moyen-âge*, vol. 1 (Vatican, 1938), 290–91.
77. Luke 12:42.
78. Bonaventure disagreed with Gerard of Abbeville (the secular master at Paris who joined Guillaume de Saint-Amour in his attacks on the mendicants) and those who argued that the church lacked dominium. See Virpi Mäkinen, *Property Rights in the Late Medieval Discussion on Franciscan Poverty* (Leuven, 2001), 79.
79. Ibid., 84–85.
80. Bonaventure, *Apologia pauperum*, trans. J. de Vinck (Paterson, N.J., 1966), 4:159–63. See also Mäkinen, *Property Rights*, 91 and n. 90. Bonaventure was rumored to have been appointed by the pope to the archbishopric of York in 1265 but resigned the promotion in fear of the English. If this story is true, the Franciscan's moderate position on the necessity and usefulness of ecclesiastical revenues would have made him a more likely candidate for the episcopate in the eyes of the pope. See *Annales monastici*, ed. Luard, 4:184.
81. This was precisely the suggestion of Pierre Tort, a member of the Third Order of Saint Francis and an accused heretic in the south of France, who was arrested and confessed (c. 1322) to harboring fugitive Spiritual Franciscans and beguins in his home. In his replies to the inquisitors' questions, Tort explained that he believed Franciscan bishops should appoint secular officials to oversee their bishoprics' temporalities, thereby freeing them to concentrate on prayer, preaching, and the administration of the sacraments. See Burr, *Spiritual Franciscans*, 222–23.

8. A Friar, a King, and a Kingdom

1. Salimbene de Adam, *Chronicle*, 212; Salimbene, *Chronica*, 1:335.
2. Andrieu-Guitrancourt, *L'archevêque Eudes Rigaud*, 407.
3. Salimbene de Adam, *Chronicle*, 214; Salimbene, *Chronica*, 1:338.
4. Salimbene de Adam, *Chronicle*, 441; Salimbene, *Chronica*, 2:656.
5. Darlington, "Travels of Odo Rigaud," 10.
6. Although there is no direct evidence, it is possible that Louis IX had employed Eudes Rigaud as an *enquêteur* in 1247. A large percentage of the *enquêteurs* were mendicants. See Ch. Petit-Dutaillis, "Querimoniae Normannorum," in *Essays in Medieval History Presented to Thomas Frederick Tout*, ed. A. G. Little and F. M. Powicke (Manchester, 1925), 105.
7. Andrieu-Guitrancourt, *L'archevêque Eudes Rigaud*, 405.
8. On Philip Augustus's relations with the Norman church, see Baldwin, "Philip Augustus."

9. Gerard J. Campbell, "The Attitude of the Monarchy toward the Use of Ecclesiastical Censures in the Reign of Saint Louis," *Speculum* 35, 4 (1960): 538–39.

10. "E chronico Rothomagensi," in *HF*, 23:332–34; Darlington, "Travels of Odo Rigaud," 6–8; Campbell, "Attitude of the Monarchy," 539–40.

11. Baldwin, *Government of Philip Augustus*, 119, 222, 306.

12. Lester K. Little, "Saint Louis' Involvement with the Friars," *Church History* 33, 2 (1964): 125–48.

13. Salimbene de Adam, *Chronicle*, 441; Salimbene, *Chronica*, 2:656.

14. It was no accident that so many of the thirteenth-century leaders of the Norman church were also members of the royal court: Eudes de Lorris (master of the Norman Exchequer, royal chaplain, and bishop of Bayeux), Jean de la Cour (master of the Norman Exchequer and bishop of Evreux), Jean d'Evreux (chancellor and bishop of Evreux), Eudes Rigaud, and Guillaume de Flavacourt (chancellor of the count of la Manche and later archbishop of Rouen).

15. *Chronica XXIV generalium ordinis minorum*, 220.

16. See Thomson, *Friars in the Cathedral.*

17. Little, "Saint Louis' Involvement."

18. Ibid., 128–29, 131.

19. Jacques Le Goff, *Saint Louis* (Paris, 1996), 331–32 and n. 3.

20. Little, "Saint Louis' Involvement," 132.

21. *RER*, 233; *RV*, 212.

22. *RER*, 495–96; *RV*, 435–36. This marriage was dictated by the Treaty of Corbeil. Louis IX was eager to have as many barons, prelates, and knights attend the wedding as possible and therefore temporarily suspended the Parlement so its members could make the trip to Clermont. The wedding was almost called off when Louis IX learned that the king of Aragon had just concluded a marriage between his heir, Pedro, and Constance, the daughter of Manfred, who had usurped the throne of Sicily and had been excommunicated by Rome. Upset by the prospect of having an ally who was an enemy of the papacy, Louis made the king of Aragon promise not to give any aid to Manfred. Eudes Rigaud was one of twenty-two witnesses who sealed this agreement. See Louis Carolus-Barré, *Le procès de canonisation de Saint Louis (1272–1297): Essai de reconstitution* (Rome, 1994), 142.

23. *RER*, 167; *RV*, 150.

24. *RER*, 368; *RV*, 322.

25. *RER*, 419; *RV*, 370.

26. *RER*, 382; *RV*, 335.

27. Ibid.

28. *RER*, 427; *RV*, 377.

29. *RER*, 404; *RV*, 355.

30. The relevant story is cited in the original medieval French by Andrieu-Guitrancourt, *L'archevêque Eudes Rigaud*, 423–24; also see *HF*, 22:325–36. The translation is my own. For an English translation of the Minstrel of Reims, see "The Chronicle of Reims," trans. E. Stone, *Washington University Publications in Social Sciences* 10 (1939). The Dominican Vincent of Beauvais also helped the king cope with the loss of his son in a *consolatio*. See Peter von Moos, "Die Trostschrift des Vincenz von Beauvais für Ludwig IX: Vorstudie zur Motiv und Geistesgeschichte der *consolatio*," in *Mittellateinisches Jahrbuch* 4 (1967): 173–218.

31. The actual act of exchange did not take place until July 1262, but the dean and chapter of Rouen granted their approval as early as March 21, 1262. See *CN*, 143 (nos. 682, 685, 686).

32. The archdeacon heard all simple complaints of the bourgeois and served as the justice of first instance except in cases of heresy, fraud, sacrilege, usury, and simony, which were heard by the archiepiscopal court (the archbishop or his official).

33. Andrieu-Guitrancourt, *L'archevêque Eudes Rigaud*, 364.

34. Eudes Rigaud's letter of November 29, 1256, concerning the hospitals at Vernon and Les

Andelys can be found in *CN*, 106; *LTC*, 2:335–36; Jules Joseph Vernier, ed., *Recueil de facsimilés de chartes normandes . . .* (Rouen, 1919), 29–30.

35. For charters relating to the exchange between Eudes and Louis for the Saint-Matthieu property, see *CN*, 138–39; for the charter recording the king's subsequent donation of the property to the Emmurées, see *CN*, 151–52.

36. The history behind the Saint-Matthieu property is a complex one. Several years earlier, it was in the hands of the Dominicans, until Eudes Rigaud bought it. Then Eudes gave it to the king, who used it to endow a convent for female religious under the habit and order of Saint Dominic.

37. See Campbell, "Temporal and Spiritual Regalia." See also Jean Gaudemet, *La collation par le roi de France des bénéfices vacants en régale* (Paris, 1935).

38. While King Louis was away on his first crusade, Norman abbeys sought such permission from Blanche of Castille, who was acting as regent. See, for instance, a letter from the prior of Saint-Ouen, on August 11, 1251, asking Blanche's permission to proceed with the election of a new abbot after the death of Abbot Hugo. *LTC*, 3:141.

39. On November 2–3, 1254, Eudes wrote to Louis, asking him to confirm the election of Geoffroi de Noitot as abbot of Saint-Wandrille. See *CN*, 92.

40. Among many cases, see Eudes's request to Blanche of Castille on January 20, 1251, that she release the temporals for the abbey of Jumièges following its election of Robert d'Estelant as its new abbot. The abbey of Jumièges also sent its own request to the queen. See *LTC*, 3:116.

41. *LTC*, 3:289–91. Again, on September 30, 1257, when a canon from the college of Sainte-Marie-la-Ronde died, Eudes used the opportunity to split the canon's prebend of 107 l.t. per year into two prebends, one worth 50 l. and another worth 90 l. See *LTC*, 3:377–78.

42. Eudes's letter to the treasurer of Saint-Mellon can be found in *CR*, 2:224–25; Eudes's letter to the king, concerning Saint-Mellon, is in *LTC*, 4:178; Eudes's charter on converting the treasurer into the dean is found in *LTC*, 4:178.

43. *RER*, 398; *RV*, 351.

44. This was a dispute in 1256 over the right of patronage of the church of Guinvevilla. See *CN*, 98.

45. Joinville, *Life of Saint Louis*, 341.

46. Eudes also served as an arbiter in a dispute between the crowns of France and Aragon over Montpellier, which almost led to armed conflict. In 1256, the Norman archbishop was called to arbitrate in the struggle between the mendicants and seculars at the University of Paris. See Jean Richard, *Saint Louis: Roi d'une France féodale, soutien de la terre sainte* (Paris, 1983), 359.

47. Soon after being consecrated archbishop, Eudes went to England and formally paid homage to King Henry III. See *RER*, 41; *RV*, 37.

48. Michel Gavrilovitch, *Étude sur le traité de Paris de 1259* (Paris, 1899), 11–20.

49. Le Goff, *Saint Louis*, 258.

50. Simon was married to Henry's sister, Eleanor, and moved back and forth between France and England during this period. During the 1240s, he administered the duchy of Gascony on behalf of the English king. But the earl's relations with Henry fluctuated widely during the 1240s and 1250s. Simon was one of the baronial leaders who demanded reform in June 1258 at the "Mad Parliament" at Oxford, where he helped draft the Provisions of Oxford, which limited the powers of the English king.

51. Joinville, *Life of Saint Louis*, 334.

52. Gavrilovitch, *Étude sur le traité*, 24.

53. Ibid., 37. See I. J. Sanders, "The Texts of the Peace of Paris, 1259," *English Historical Review* 66, 258 (1951): 81–97.

54. See Gavrilovitch, *Étude sur le traité*, 57–59.

55. Ibid., 60–61. The issue of how much Louis owed for five hundred knights was not resolved until 1264.

56. F. M. Powicke, "The Archbishop of Rouen, John de Harcourt, and Simon de Montfort in 1260," *English Historical Review* 51, 201 (1936): 108–13; J. R. Maddicott, *Simon de Montfort*

(Cambridge, 1994), 197-99. In July of 1260 Simon in turn helped Eudes by sealing a charter that restored the archbishop's rights to the manor at Bentworth, which had been seized by the earl's bailiffs of Odiham.

57. The principal threat to the Christian establishments in the Levant was not the Mongols but the Mamluks under Baybars, sultan of Cairo. His armies conquered Christian fortresses in Caesarea, Arsuf, Safed, Jaffa, and Antioch. By 1266, it looked as though the Christian states in the East were not going to survive and the Mongols began to seem like potential allies in the common struggle against Baybars. See Richard, *Saint Louis*, 483–530.

58. This was likely the issue of crusaders who redeemed their crusading vow for cash. See *RER*, 425 and n. 7; *RV*, 375.

59. See *RER*, 443 and n. 26; *RV*, 389. The prayers included Psalm 78, "O God, the heathens are come into my inheritance."

60. *RER*, 453; *RV*, 398.

61. *RER*, 463; *RV*, 407.

62. See papal letter of June 20, 1262, from Urban IV to Baldwin II: Sbaraglia, *Bullarium Franciscanum*, vol. 2, no. 37, p. 448. The imposition of a hundredth over a five-year period would effectively have reinstated the crusading tax imposed in 1245 at the First Council of Lyon.

63. Maier, *Preaching the Crusades*, 131–34.

64. There continued to be discussions about new papal levies. On August 24, 1264, Eudes attended a council in Paris, at which the papal legate, Simon de Brie, proposed a three years' tithe to assist the Roman church in its attempt to help Charles of Anjou in Sicily. See *RER*, 564; *RV*, 495.

65. In 1261, the pope had asked Gilles de Saumur, archbishop of Tyre, to remain in France as papal legate and not to return to the East. The pope was convinced that the archbishop could be of greatest help to Christians in the East by impressing on the French king and clergy the dangers that existed there and the need for additional funds. Gilles had served as the keeper of King Louis's seal during the king's stay in the East. See Jean Richard, *The Crusades, c. 1071–c. 1291*, trans. Jean Birrell (Cambridge, 1999), 507–8.

66. *RER*, 617; *RV*, 540.

67. Jean Dunbabin, *Charles I of Anjou: Power, Kingship, and State-Making in Thirteenth-Century Europe* (London, 1998), 134–36.

68. See *RER*, 576, 598, 617, 678–79, 696, 724, 730; *RV*, 506, 524, 540, 589, 604, 629, 635. In January 1268, Simon de Brie was succeeded as papal legate to France by Raoul de Grosparmi, the former bishop of Evreux and member of Eudes's *familia*. It certainly helped cement Eudes's relations with the papacy that during most of the 1260s, the papal legate to France was someone with strong connections to Normandy.

69. In September 1266, Louis IX had secretly informed the pope of his intention to take the cross, and as a result, the pope had abandoned his own project in order to help plan the "general passage." Until 1266 and Charles of Anjou's victory at Benevento, Louis had not been able to seriously consider a new crusade, for Charles had drained France of many fighting men in his struggle to capture the kingdom of Sicily. See Joseph Strayer, "The Crusades of Louis IX," in *Medieval Statecraft and the Perspectives of History: Essays by Joseph R. Strayer* (Princeton, 1971), 181–83.

70. *RER*, 658; *RV*, 573. Eudes was present at this ceremony.

71. Richard, *Crusades*, 424.

72. *RER*, 669; *RV*, 580. About fifty men were knighted at this ceremony, including Eudes's brother, Pierre Rigaud.

73. *RER*, 678–79; *RV*, 589.

74. The archbishop of Bourges was supposed to make this announcement, but because he was sick, Eudes was asked to fill in. See *LTC*, 4:254–55.

75. Eudes attended councils in Cambrai and Bourges. He also met with the archbishops of Lund, Bourges, and Tours and the bishops of Auxerre, Beauvais, and Lübeck. See *RER*, 680, 684–85, 696, 726; *RV*, 591, 595, 604, 631.

76. *RER*, 687, 724; *RV*, 597, 629.
77. Strayer, "Crusades of Louis IX," 189.
78. "Monumenta Erphesfurtensia," ed. O. Holder-Egger, in *Scriptores rerum Germanicarum* (Hannover, 1899), 682.
79. André Callebaut, "La deuxième croisade de S. Louis et les Franciscains (1267–70)," *La France Franciscaine* 5 (1922): 282–88.
80. Several years before Louis took the cross, the papacy enlisted Dominicans and Franciscans to lobby for public support for a crusade. Once the French king took the cross, the leading friars preached crusading sermons, and the Dominican Humbert de Romans even wrote a manual on how to preach the crusade. See Maier, *Preaching the Crusades*; André Callebaut, "Les provinciaux de la province de France au XIIIe siècle," *AFH* 10 (1917): 333–34.
81. Strayer argues that Louis already intended to attack Tunisia in late 1268 or early 1269 but kept it a secret. The choice of Tunisia, according to Strayer, stemmed from Charles of Anjou's troubles with the emir, Muhammad I, who continued to support Charles's enemies. See Strayer, "Crusades of Louis IX," 185–88. For different hypotheses concerning Louis's interest in Tunisia, see Richard, *Crusades*, 428–31.
82. For Charles's role in the Tunisian expedition, see Dunbabin, *Charles I*, 194–97.
83. *LTC*, 4:469.
84. Callebaut, "Les provinciaux," 284; Bonnin, *Cartulaire de Louviers*, 1:328–29. As in the reign of Louis IX, a disproportionate number of councillors appointed by Philip came from Normandy. They included Eudes Rigaud, the bishop of Bayeux, the bishop of Evreux, the *bailli* of Rouen (Julien de Peronne), and two archdeacons of Bayeux (Henri de Vezelai and Jean de Troyes).
85. Callebaut, "La deuxième croisade," 288.
86. "E chronico Rothomagensi," in *HF*, 23:341.
87. *CN*, 177.
88. *CN*, 187.
89. Arthur Beugnot, ed., *Les olim ou registres des arrêts rendus par la cour du roi* (Paris, 1839), 1:918.
90. Callebaut, "Les provinciaux," 338.
91. Five hundred bishops, sixty abbots, and more than a thousand prelates or procurators attended the Second Council of Lyon. See Carolus-Barré, "Les pères du IIe Concile de Lyon (1274): Esquisses prosopographiques," in *1274: Année charnière*, 377–78.
92. Only three of these reports—of Bruno von Holstein (bishop of Olmütz), Humbert de Romans, and Guibert de Tournai—have survived. See Jacques-Guy Bougerol, "Le rôle de Saint Bonaventure," in *1274: Année charnière*, 428.
93. *Chronica XXIV generalium ordinis minorum*, 353.
94. Some of the more newly instituted mendicant orders were suppressed at the Second Council of Lyon. This both placated seculars opposed to mendicants and lent greater legitimacy to the major orders such as the Franciscans and Dominicans. See Gratien de Paris, *Histoire de la fondation et de l'évolution de l'Ordre des frères mineurs au XIIIe siècle* (Gembloux, 1928), 322–25.
95. C. H. Lawrence, *The Friars: The Impact of the Early Mendicant Movement on Western Society* (London, 1994), 59, 93, 158–59.
96. In 1256, when the conflicts between the seculars and mendicants were at their peak at the University of Paris, Eudes Rigaud was called on to arbitrate. Although a former regent master of the Franciscan *studium*, Eudes apparently had a reputation for fairness.
97. Jacques Le Goff, "Le dossier des mendiants," in *1274: Année charnière*, 211–12.
98. The doctrinal conflict over the *filioque* continued to be debated at the Council of Florence in 1439. See Jaroslav Pelikan, *The Spirit of Eastern Christendom, (600–1700)*, vol. 2 of *The Christian Tradition: A History of the Development of Doctrine* (Chicago, 1974), 183–98, 275–78.
99. The Franciscans and Dominicans had both held chapters general in Lyon during the 1274 council, most likely because there were so many members already in Lyon. See Carolus-Barré, "Les pères," 381.

100. Andrieu-Guitrancourt, *L'archevêque Eudes Rigaud*, 438.

101. Pommeraye, *Histoire des archevesques*, 587; Andrieu-Guitrancourt, *L'archevêque Eudes Rigaud*, 439.

102. When I mentioned to an elderly Rouen innkeeper that I was studying the career of Archbishop Eudes Rigaud, he grinned and said, "Boire à tire-la-Rigaut," making a swigging gesture.

103. This was true of the seal of Jourdain du Hommet, bishop of Lisieux (1202–18) and the 1298 seal of Pierre de Beneis, bishop of Bayeux. See Germain Demay, ed., *Inventaire des sceaux de la Normandie* (Paris, 1881), nos. 2217 and 2187, pp. 236, 241. It was only during the late twelfth and early thirteenth centuries that the reverse sides of seals began to be decorated as well. The first counterseal in Rouen appeared around 1209. See Robert-Henri Bautier, "Apparition, diffusion et évolution typologique du sceau épiscopal au moyen âge," in *Die Diplomatik der Bischofsurkunde vor 1250*, ed. Christoph Haidacher and Werner Köfler (Innsbruck, 1995), 236.

104. Although Eudes's counterseal was somewhat atypical, the bishop of Coutances, Jean d'Essey (1251–76), had a very similar counterseal representing the Annunciation. See Demay, *Inventaire des sceaux*, no. 2204, p. 236.

105. The 1265 counterseal of Raoul de Grosparmi, bishop of Evreux, also represented the Virgin Mary holding the infant Jesus, but the front of the seal (unlike Eudes's) was quite traditional, showing the bishop standing, mitred, crosiered, and making a benediction. See Demay, *Inventaire des sceaux*, no. 2217, p. 240. Interestingly, the seal of the *officialis* of Rouen during Eudes's archiepiscopate is quite traditional, showing the figure of the archbishop seated, wearing a mitre, holding a crosier, and performing a benediction. Unlike episcopal seals, which varied from bishop to bishop, the seals of the *officiales* remained largely unchanged. Indeed, the same image that appeared on the Rouen official's seal in 1272 was used in 1308, 1410, and 1513. See Demay, *Inventaire des sceaux*, nos. 2299–2302, p. 251.

Conclusion

1. On the dating of the sermon, see Jacques-Guy Bougerol, "Un sermon inédit d'Eudes Rigaud," *Archives d'histoire doctrinale et littéraire du moyen âge* 62 (1995): 345–46. Based on the chronological order of other sermons found in this Vatican library manuscript, Bougerol argues that Eudes most likely delivered the sermon in 1265 or 1266. I see no reason why Eudes could not also have preached the sermon in 1261 or 1267, however, when he was also in Paris. The sermons in the manuscript would still be in chronological order.

2. Saint Catherine's feast day was the special feast day for scholars from the "Gallic nation." The University of Paris was divided into four nations: Gallic, Norman, Picardian, and English.

3. If Eudes indeed delivered this sermon on Saturday, November 25, 1266, as Bougerol believes, it would have been in the chapel of the Hospitalers of Saint-Jacques-de-Haut-Pas, as the *Register* indicates. See Bougerol, "Un sermon inédit," 346.

4. Ibid., 349.

5. Ibid., 350.

6. Ibid., 351–52.

7. Ibid., 352–55.

8. Ibid., 355.

9. Ibid., 357.

10. Ibid.

11. Ibid.

12. Constance Brittain Bouchard, *Spirituality and Administration: The Role of the Bishop in Twelfth-Century Auxerre* (Cambridge, Mass., 1979), 71.

13. Ibid.

14. *Bernard of Clairvaux on Baptism and the Office of Bishops*, trans. Pauline Matarasso (Kalamazoo, Mich., 2004).

15. Bouchard, *Spirituality and Administration*, 77–82.
16. Martha G. Newman, "Contemplative Virtues and the Active Life of Prelates," in *Bernard of Clairvaux on Baptism*, 30.
17. Bouchard, *Spirituality and Administration*, 66–67.
18. Diego Quaglioni, "Riflessi ecclesiologici e canonistici dell'ascesa dei frati alle cattedre vescovili," in *Dal pulpito alla cattedra* (Spoleto, 2000), 357–58.
19. Ibid., 359–63, 368.
20. Ibid., 370–75. There were certainly dissenting views during the thirteenth century. Unlike those who saw the religious and episcopal professions as reconcilable, the canonist (and later cardinal) Hostiensis did not accept the proposition that the episcopate was inherently superior to the religious life. In his *Summa aurea*, he argued that the religious and secular professions were distinct and that strict observance of a fraternal or monastic rule was not compatible with the life of a bishop. See ibid., 365–66.
21. Thomas Aquinas, *The Pastoral and Religious Lives*, ed. Jordan Aumann, vol. 47 of *Summa theologiae* (Cambridge, 1973), 2a, 2ae, q. 185, I, pp. 62–63; Gaudemet, *Le gouvernement de l'église*, 50–51.
22. Quaglioni, "Riflessi ecclesiologici," 370–75.
23. Bouchard, *Spirituality and Administration*, 144.
24. This explanation is not entirely satisfactory since monks were often careful managers of their monastic patrimonies and were steeped in a culture of discipline and accountability.
25. Bouchard, *Spirituality and Administration*, 74–75.
26. The phrase "spirituality of initiative" is used by Jacques Le Goff in *Saint Francis of Assisi*, trans. Christine Rhone (London, 2004), 103.
27. Le Goff, *Saint Francis*, 75.

Bibliography

Manuscripts

AD: Seine-Maritime
   G: 007, 870, 871, 939, 947, 948, 1025, 1036, 1054, 1089, 1094, 1095, 1144, 1151, 1152, 1211, 1702, 1755, 2034, 3658, 3854.
Arras, BM: ms. lat. 691 (759), f. 112rb, f. 120va, 228vb, 250rb, 260rb
BnF: ms. lat. 1245
   ms. lat. 11052
   ms. lat. 16502, f. 157ra
   ms. lat. 18224, f. 282r-283r
Rouen, BM: ms. Y. 223A
Toulouse, BM: ms. lat. 737, f. 167ra

Printed Sources

Andrieu, Michel, ed. "Le pontifical romain du XIIe siècle." In *Le pontifical romain au moyen-âge.* Vol. 1. Vatican: Biblioteca Apostolica Vaticana, 1938.

Angelo Clareno. "Historia septem tribulationum ordinis minorum." Edited by F. Ehrle. *Archiv für Litteratur und Kirchengeschichte des Mittelalters* 2 (1886).

Annales monastici. Edited by Henry Richards Luard. 4 vols. London: Longman, Green, Longman, Roberts, and Green, 1825–91.

Becquet, Jean, ed. *Actes des évêques de Limoges: Des origines à 1197.* Paris: CNRS Éditions, 1999.

Berger, Élie, ed. *Les registres d'Innocent IV.* 4 vols. Paris: E. Thorin, 1884–[1920].

Bernard of Bessa. *Liber de laudibus beati Francisci. Analecta Franciscana* 3 (1897): 666–92.

Bernard of Clairvaux on Baptism and the Office of Bishops. Translated by Pauline Matarasso. Kalamazoo, Mich.: Cistercian Publications, 2004.

Bessin, Guillaume, ed. *Concilia Rotomagensis provinciae.* 2 vols. Rouen: Franciscum Vaultier, 1717.

Beugnot, Arthur, ed. *Les olim ou registres des arrêts rendus par la cour du roi.* 3 vols. Paris: Imprimerie royale, 1839–48.

Bonaventure. *Apologia pauperum.* Translated by J. de Vinck. Vol. 4 of *The Works of Bonaventure.* Paterson, N.J.: St. Anthony Guild Press, 1966.

Bonnin, Th., ed. *Cartulaire de Louviers: Documents historiques originaux du Xe au XVIIIe siècle.* 4 vols. Evreux-Paris: A. Hèrissey, 1870–78.

Bougerol, Jacques-Guy, ed. *Saint Bonaventure: Sermones de tempore.* Paris: Éditions Franciscaines, 1990.

——. "Un sermon inédit d'Eudes Rigaud." *Archives d'histoire doctrinale et littéraire du moyen âge* 62 (1995): 343–58.

Bouquet, M., et al., eds. *Recueil des historiens des Gaules et de la France.* 24 vols. Paris: Aux dépens des librairies, 1738–1904.

Chéruel, Adolphe, ed. *Normanniae nova chronica ab anno Christi CCCCLXXIII ad annum MCCCLXXVIII et tribus chronicis mss. Sancti Laudi, Sancti Catharinae et majoris ecclesiae Rotomagensium collecta.* Caen: Bibliopolam a Hardel, 1851.

Chronica XXIV generalium ordinis minorum. Analecta Franciscana 3 (1887): 1–575.

Corpus iuris canonici. Edited by Emil Albert Friedberg and Aemilius Ludwig Richter. 2 vols. Leipzig: Bernhard Tauchnitz, 1879–81.

Delisle, Léopold, ed.. *Cartulaire normand de Philippe-Auguste, Louis VIII, Saint-Louis, et Philippe le Hardi.* Caen, 1882. Reprint, Geneva: Mégariotis, 1978.

——. *Recueil de jugements de l'échiquier de Normandie.* Paris: Imperiale, 1864.

——. "Visites pastorales de Maître Henri de Vézelai, archidicacre d'Hiémois (1267–1268)." *Bibliothèque de l'École des Chartes* 54 (1893): 457–67.

Demay, Germain, ed. *Inventaire des sceaux de la Normandie.* Paris: Imprimerie Nationale, 1881.

Denifle, Heinrich, and Emile Chatelain, eds. *Chartularium Universitatis Parisiensis.* 4 vols. Paris: ex typis fratrum Delalain, 1889–97.

Dubois, Henri, Denise Angers, and Catherine Bébéar, eds. *Un censier normand du XIIIe siècle: Le Livre des jurés de l'abbaye Saint-Ouen de Rouen.* Paris: CNRS, 2001.

Duval-Arnould, Louis, ed. "Trois sermons synodaux de la collection attribué à Jean de la Rochelle." *Archivum Franciscanum Historicum* 69 (1976): 336–400; 70 (1977): 35–71.

Eubel, Konrad, et al., eds. *Hierarchia Catholica medii aevi.* 6 vols. 2nd ed. Regensburg: Monasterii, Sumptibus Librariae Regensbergianae, 1913–67.

Expositio quatuor magistrorum super regulam fratrum minorum, 1241–1242. Edited by P. L. Oliger. Rome: Edizioni di storiz e letteratura, 1950.

Gallia christiana in provincias ecclesiasticas distributa. 16 vols. Paris: Ex Typographia Regia, 1715–1865.

Habig, Marion A., ed. *St. Francis of Assisi: Writings and Early Biographies.* Chicago: Franciscan Herald Press, 1983.

Jean de Joinville. *The Life of Saint Louis.* In *Chronicles of the Crusades,* translated by M. R. B. Shaw. Baltimore: Penguin Books, 1963.

Layettes du trésor des chartes. Edited by A. Teulet, J. de Laborde, E. Berger, and H. F. Delaborde. 5 vols. Paris: H. Plon, 1863–1909.

Longnon, Auguste, ed. *Pouillés de la province de Rouen.* Paris: Imprimerie Nationale, 1903.

Lottin, Odon. "Une question disputée d'Odon Rigaud sur le libre arbitre." *Revue Thomiste* 36 (1931): 886–95.

Magna vita Sancti Hugonis. Edited by Decima L. Douie and Hugh Farmer. London: Nelson, 1961.

Mansi, Johannes Dominicus, ed. *Sacrorum conciliorum nova et amplissima collectio.* 54 vols. Paris: H. Welter, 1901–27.

Matthew Paris. *English History.* Translated by J. A. Giles. 3 vols. London: H. G. Bohn, 1852–54.

Mercken, H. P., ed. *The Greek Commentaries on the Nicomachean Ethics of Aristotle in the Latin Translation of Robert Grosseteste, Bishop of Lincoln (†1253).* Leiden: Brill, 1973.

Minstrel of Reims. "The Chronicle of Reims." Translated by E. Stone. *Washington University Publications in Social Sciences* 10 (1939).

"Monumenta Erphesfurtensia." Edited by O. Holder-Egger. In *Scriptores rerum Germanicarum.* Hannover: Impensis bibliopolii Hahniani, 1899.

Pecham, John. *Tractatus pauperis.* In *Quaestio disputata de privilegio Martini papae IV.* Quaracchi: Typographia Collejii S. Bonaventurae, 1925.

Pergamo, Basilio, ed. "Il desiderio innato del soprannaturale nelle questioni inedite di Oddone Rigaldo, O.F.M., Arcivesco di Rouen (†1275)." *Studi francescani* 7, no. 4 (1935): 414–46; 8, no. 1 (1936): 76–108.

Peter the Chanter. *Summa de sacramentis et animae consiliis.* Edited by Jean-Albert Dugauquier. 4 vols. Louvain: Editions Nauwelaerts, 1957–67.

Plato. *Protagoras.* Translated by C. C. W. Taylor. Rev. ed. Oxford: Clarendon Press, 1991.

Pommeraye, Jean-François, ed. *Sanctae Rotomagensis ecclesiae concilia.* Rouen: Impensis & Typis Bonaventurae Le Brun, 1677.

Pontal, Odette, and Joseph Avril, eds. *Les statuts synodaux français du XIIIe siècle.* 5 vols. Paris: Bibliothèque Nationale, 1971–[2001].

Powicke, F. M., and C. R. Cheney, eds. *Councils and Synods.* 2 vols. Oxford: Clarendon Press, 1964.

Regestrum visitationum archiepiscopi Rothomagensis. Edited by Th. Bonnin. Rouen: A. Le Brument, 1852.

The Register of Eudes of Rouen. Translated by Sydney M. Brown. Edited by Jeremiah F. O'-Sullivan. New York: Columbia University Press, 1964.

Registrum epistolarum fratris Johannis Peckham, archiepiscopi cantuariensis. Edited by C. T. Martin. 3 vols. Reprint, Wiesbaden: Kraus, 1965.

Regula non bullata. Translated by Paul Schwartz and Paul Lachance. In *The Birth of a Movement: A Study of the First Rule of St. Francis.* Edited by David Flood and Thaddée Matura. Chicago: Franciscan Herald Press, 1975.

The Rule of St. Benedict. Translated by Anthony C. Meisel and M. L. del Mastro. Garden City, N.Y.: Image Books, 1975.

Salimbene de Adam. *Chronica.* Edited by Giuseppe Scalia. 2 vols. Turnhout: Brepols, 1998.

———. *The Chronicle of Salimbene de Adam.* Translated by Joseph L. Baird, Giuseppe Baglivi, and John Robert Kane. Binghamton, N.Y.: Medieval and Renaissance Texts and Studies, 1986.

Sbaraglia, Giovanni Giacinto, ed. *Bullarium Franciscanum Romanorum Pontificum.* 4 vols. Rome, 1759–1804. Reprint, Assisi, 1984.

Shinners, John, and William J. Dohar, eds. *Pastors and the Care of Souls in Medieval England.* Notre Dame, Ind.: University of Notre Dame Press, 1998.

Sileo, Leonardo. *Teoria della scienza teologica: Quaestio de scientia theologiae di Odo Rigaldi e altri testi inediti (1230–1250).* 2 vols. Rome: Pontificium Athenaeum Antonianum, 1984.

Smith, David M., ed. *English Episcopal Acta.* 28 vols. London: Published for the British Academy by Oxford University Press, 1980–.

Tanner, Norman P., ed. *Decrees of the Ecumenical Councils.* 2 vols. London: Sheed and Ward, 1990.

Tardif, Ernest-Joseph. *Coutumiers de Normandie: Textes critiques.* 2 vols. 1881–1903. Reprint, Geneva: Slatkine, 1977.

Thomas Aquinas. *The Pastoral and Religious Lives.* Trans. Jordan Aumann. Vol. 47 of the *Summa theologiae.* Cambridge: Blackfriars, 1973.

van Dijk, A., ed. "Quaestiones quaedam scholasticae de officio divino et cantu ecclesiastico." *Ephemerides liturgicae* 56 (1942): 20–43.

Vernier, Jules Joseph, ed. *Recueil de fac-similés de chartes normandes publiés à l'occasion du cinquantenaire de sa fondation (1869–1919) par la société de l'histoire de Normandie.* Rouen: A. Lestringant, 1919.

Wadding, Luke. *Annales Minorum.* Edited by Jospehi Mariae Fonseca. 28 vols. Quaracchi, 1931–41.

Secondary Sources

Amanieu, A. "Archdiacre." *Dictionnaire de droit canonique* 1 (1935): cols. 948–1004.

———. "Archevêque," *Dictionnaire de droit canonique* 1 (1935): cols. 927–34.

Andrieu-Guitrancourt, Pierre. *L'archevêque Eudes Rigaud et la vie de l'église au XIIIe siècle d'après le "Regestrum Visitationum."* Paris: Librairie du Recueil Sirey, 1938.

———. "L'œuvre conciliaire d'Eudes Rigaud." *Revue historique de droit français et étranger* 15 (1936): 827–29.

Arnoux, Mathieu. *Des clercs au service de la réforme: Études et documents sur les chanoines réguliers de la province de Rouen.* Turnhout: Brepols, 2000.

Artonne, André. "L'influence du Décret de Gratien sur les statuts synodaux." *Studia Gratiana* 2 (1954): 643–56.

Artonne, André, L. Guizard, and O. Pontal. *Répertoire des statuts synodaux des diocèses de l'ancienne France.* Paris: CNRS, 1963.

Aubry, Pierre. *La musique et les musiciens d'église en Normandie au 13e siècle d'après le Journal des visites pastorales d'Odon Rigaud.* Paris: H. Champion, 1906.

Avi-Yonah, Reuven. "Career Trends of Parisian Masters of Theology, 1200–1320." *History of Universities* 6 (1987): 47–64.

Avril, Joseph. "Archevêchés, diocèses et paroisses aux XIIe–XIVe siècles: À propos de quelques travaux récents." *Revue d'histoire de l'église de France* 82 (1996): 323–45.

———. *Les conciles de la province de Tours.* Paris: CNRS, 1987.

———. "L'encadrement diocésain et l'organisation paroissiale." In *Le troisième concile de Latran (1179): Sa place dans l'histoire,* edited by Jean Longère, 53–74. Paris: Études Augustiniennes, 1982.

———. *Le gouvernement des évêques et la vie religieuse dans le diocèse d'Angers, 1148–1240.* Paris: Cerf, 1984.

———. "La participation du chapitre cathédral au gouvernement du diocèse." In *Le monde des chanoines (XI–XIVe siècles).* Cahiers de Fanjeaux, no. 24, 41–63. Toulouse: Privat, 1989.

Baldwin, John W. "A Campaign to Reduce Clerical Celibacy at the Turn of the Twelfth and Thirteenth Centuries." In *Études d'histoire du droit canonique: Dédiées à Gabriel Le Bras,* 2 vols. 2:1041–53. Paris: Sirey, 1965.

———. *The Government of Philip Augustus: Foundations of French Royal Power in the Middle Ages.* Berkeley: University of California Press, 1986.

———. *Masters, Princes, and Merchants: The Social Views of Peter the Chanter and His Circle.* 2 vols. Princeton: Princeton University Press, 1970.

———. "Masters at Paris from 1179 to 1215: A Social Perspective." In *Renaissance and Renewal in the Twelfth Century,* edited by Robert L. Benson and Giles Constable. Cambridge, Mass.: Harvard University Press, 1982.

———. "Philip Augustus and the Norman Church." *French Historical Studies* 6, no. 1 (1969): 1–30.

———. "'Studium et Regnum': The Penetration of University Personnel into French and English Administration at the Turn of the Twelfth and Thirteenth Centuries." *Revue des études Islamiques* 44 (1976): 199–215.

Barber, Malcolm. "The Crusade of the Shepherds in 1251." In *Proceedings of the Tenth Annual Meeting of the Western Society for French History, 14–16 October 1982, Winnipeg, Manitoba, Canada,* edited by John F. Sweets, 1–23. Lawrence: University of Kansas, 1984.

Barbet, J. "Note sur le ms. 737 de la Bibliothèque Municipale de Toulouse, Quaestiones disputatae." *Bulletin d'information de l'Institut de Recherche et d'Histoire des Textes* 5 (1957): 7–51.

Bartlett, Robert. *England under the Norman and Angevin Kings, 1075–1225.* Oxford: Clarendon Press, 2000.

———. *Trial by Fire and Water: The Medieval Judicial Ordeal.* Oxford: Clarendon Press, 1986.

Bataillon, Louis-Jacques. *La prédication au XIIIe siècle en France et Italie.* Aldershot, Hampshire, U.K.: Variorum, 1993.

Baudot, Marcel. "Observations sur le patronage des églises en Normandie." In *Recueil d'études normandes en hommage au docteur Jean Fournée: Cahiers Léopold Delisle, no. exceptionnel 1978,* 43–49. Nogent-sur-Marne: Société Parisienne d'Histoire et d'Archéologie Normandes, 1979.

Bautier, Robert-Henri. "Apparition, diffusion et évolution typologique du sceau épiscopal au moyen âge." In *Die Diplomatik der Bischofsurkunde vor 1250,* edited by Christoph Haidacher and Werner Köfler, 225–41. Innsbruck: Tiroler Landesarchiv, 1995.

Beaumont-Maillet, L. *Le grand couvent des Cordeliers de Paris: Étude historique et archéologique du XIIIe siècle à nos jours.* Paris: H. Champion, 1975.

Benson, Robert. *The Bishop-Elect: A Study in Medieval Ecclesiastical Office.* Princeton: Princeton University Press, 1968.

Benton, J. "The Paraclete and the Council of Rouen of 1231." In *Culture, Power, and Personality in Medieval France,* edited by Thomas N. Bisson, 411–16. London: Hambledon Press, 1991.

Bériou, Nicole. *L'avènement des maîtres de la parole: La prédication à Paris au XIIIe siècle.* 2 vols. Paris: Institut d'Études Augustiniennes, 1998.

———. "La prédication synodale au XIIIe siècle d'après l'exemple cambrésien." In *Le clerc séculier au moyen âge: XXIIe congrès de la S.H.M.E.S. (Amiens, juin 1991),* 229–47. Paris: Publications de la Sorbonne, 1993.

———, ed. *Les sermons et la visite pastorale de Federico Visconti, archevêque de Pise (1253–1277).* Paris: École Française de Rome, 2001.

Berkhofer, Robert E., III. *Day of Reckoning: Power and Accountability in Medieval France.* Philadelphia: University of Pennsylvania Press, 2004.

Berlière, Ursmer. "Les chapitres généraux de l'ordre de S. Benoît avant le IVe concile de Latran." *Revue Bénédictine* 8 (1891): 255–64; 19 (1902): 38–75, 268–78, 374–411.

———. "Innocent III et la réorganisation des monastères Bénédictins." *Revue Bénédictine* 32 (1920): 22–42, 145–59.

Boisset, Louis. *Un concile provincial au treizième siècle, Vienne 1289, église locale et société.* Paris: Beauchesne, 1973.

Bordeaux, Michèle. *Aspects économiques de la vie de l'église aux XIVe et XVe siècles.* Paris: Librairie général de droit et de jurisprudence, 1969.

Bouchard, Constance Brittain. *Spirituality and Administration: The Role of the Bishop in Twelfth-Century Auxerre.* Cambridge, Mass.: Medieval Academy of America, 1979.

Bougerol, Jacques-Guy. "À propos des condamnations parisiennes de 1241 et 1244." *Archivum Franciscanum Historicum* 80, nos. 3–4 (1987): 462–66.

——. *Introduction à Saint Bonaventure.* Paris: Librairie Philosophique J. Vrin, 1988.

——. "Le rôle de Saint Bonaventure au concile de Lyon." In *1274: Année charnière, mutations et continuités; Actes du colloque international, Lyon-Paris, 30 septembre–5 octobre, 1974,* 425–33. Paris: CNRS, 1977.

——. "Les sermons dans les 'studia' des mendiants." In *Le scuole degli ordini mendicanti (secoli XIII–XIV),* 251–80. Todi: Presso l'Accademia tudertina, 1978.

——. *La théologie de l'espérance aux XIIe et XIIIe siècles.* 2 vols. Paris: Études Augustiniennes, 1985.

Boureau, Alain. *Théologie, science et censure au XIIIe siècle: Le cas de Jean Peckham.* Paris: Les Belles Lettres, 1999.

Bouuaert, F. Claeys. "Métropolitain." *Dictionnaire de droit canonique* 6 (1957): 875–77.

Boyle, Leonard E. "Robert Grosseteste and the Pastoral Care." In *Pastoral Care, Clerical Education, and Canon Law, 1200–1400,* 3–51. London: Variorum Reprints, 1981.

Brentano, Robert. *Two Churches: England and Italy in the Thirteenth Century.* Princeton: Princeton University Press, 1968.

——. *York Metropolitan Jurisdiction and Papal Judges Delegate (1279–1296).* Berkeley: University of California Press, 1959.

Brooke, Rosalind. *Early Franciscan Government: Elias to Bonaventure.* Cambridge: Cambridge University Press, 1959.

Brown, Michelle P. *A Guide to Western Historical Scripts from Antiquity to 1600.* London: British Library, 1990.

Bruce, Scott. "Lurking with Spiritual Intent: A Note on the Origin and Functions of the Monastic Roundsman (*Circator*)." *Revue Bénédictine* 109 (1999): 75–89.

Brundage, James. "Playing by the Rules: Sexual Behaviour and Legal Norms in Medieval Europe." In *Desire and Discipline: Sex and Sexuality in the Premodern West,* edited by Jaqueline Murray and Konrad Eisenbichler, 23–41. Toronto: University of Toronto Press, 1996.

——. "Proof in Canonical Criminal Law." *Continuity and Change* 11, no. 3 (1996): 329–39.

Burger, Michael. "Officiales and the Familiae of the Bishop of Lincoln, 1258–1299." *Journal of Medieval History* 16, no. 1 (1990): 39–53.

——. "Sending, Joining, Writing, and Speaking in the Diocesan Administration of Thirteenth-Century Lincoln." *Mediaeval Studies* 55 (1993): 151–82.

Burr, David. *Olivi and Franciscan Poverty: The Origins of the Usus Pauper Controversy.* Philadelphia: University of Pennsylvania Press, 1989.

——. *The Spiritual Franciscans: From Protest to Persecution in the Century after Saint Francis.* University Park: Pennsylvania State University Press, 2001.

Callebaut, André. "La deuxième croisade de S. Louis et les Franciscains." *La France Franciscaine* 5 (1922): 282–88.

——. "Les provinciaux de la province de France au XIIIe siècle." *Archivum Franciscanum Historicum* 10 (1917): 289–356.

Campbell, Gerard J. "The Attitude of the Monarchy toward the Use of Ecclesiastical Censures in the Reign of Saint Louis." *Speculum* 35, no. 4 (1960): 535–55.

——. "Temporal and Spiritual Regalia during the Reigns of St. Louis and Philip III." *Traditio* 20 (1964): 351–84.

Campbell, Thomas P. "Cathedral Chapter and Town Council: Cooperative Ceremony and Drama in Medieval Rouen." *Comparative Drama.* 27, no. 1 (1993): 100–113.

Carolus-Barré, Louis. "Les pères du IIe Concile de Lyon (1274): Esquisses prosopographiques." In *1274: Année charnière. Actes du colloque international, Lyon-Paris, 30 septembre–5 octobre, 1974,* 377–423. Paris: CNRS, 1977.

——. *Le procès de canonisation de Saint Louis (1272–1297): Essai de reconstitution.* Rome: École Française de Rome, 1994.

Carolus-Barré, Louis, and Jean-Charles Payen. "Le dit du concile de Lyon (ms. Zagreb MR92)." In *1274: Année charnière: Actes du colloque international, Lyon-Paris, 30 septembre–5 octobre, 1974,* 917–66. Paris: CNRS, 1977.

Carroll-Clark, Susan M. "Bad Habits: Clothing and Textile References in the Register of Eudes Rigaud, Archbishop of Rouen." In *Medieval Clothing and Textiles,* 2 vols., edited by Robin Netherton and Gale R. Owen-Crocker, 1:83–103. Woodbridge, Suffolk, U.K.: Boydell Press, 2005.

Casset, Marie. "Les résidences rurales et semi-rurales des archevêques et évêques normands au moyen âge." Dissertation, Université du Maine, 1999.

Chaline, Nadine-Josette. *Le diocèse de Rouen-Le Havre.* Paris: Éditions Beauchesne, 1976.

Cheney, Christopher R. "Early Norman Monastic Visitations: A Neglected Record." *Journal of Ecclesiastical History* 33, no. 3 (1982): 412–23.

——. *English Bishops' Chanceries, 1100–1250.* Manchester: Manchester University Press, 1950.

——. *English Synodalia of the Thirteenth Century.* 2nd ed. Oxford: Oxford University Press, 1941.

——. *Episcopal Visitations of Monasteries in the Thirteenth Century.* Manchester: Manchester University Press, 1931.

——. "Statute-Making in the English Church in the Thirteenth Century." In *Monumenta Iuris Canonici: Proceedings of the Second International Congress of Medieval Canon Law,* 1:399–414. Vatican: S. Congregatio de Seminariis et Studiorum Universitatibus, 1965.

Chéruel, Pierre Adolphe. *Histoire de Rouen pendant l'époque communale, 1150–1382.* 2 vols. Rouen: N. Periaux, 1843–44.

Clanchy, M. T. *From Memory to Written Record: England, 1066–1307.* Cambridge, Mass.: Harvard University Press, 1979.

Cochet, (Abbé). "Le manoir des archevêques de Rouen sur l'Alihermont." *Revue de Rouen et de Normandie* n.s. 3 (1849): 57–66.

Colish, Marcia. "From the Sentence Collection to the *Sentence* Commentary and the *Summa*: Parisian Scholastic Theology, 1130–1215." In *Manuels, programmes de cours et techniques d'enseignement dans les universités médiévales: Actes du colloque international de Louvain-la-Neuve, 9–11 septembre 1993,* edited by Jacqueline Hamesse, 9–29. Louvain-la-Neuve: Institut d'Études Médiévales de l'Université Catholique de Louvain, 1994.

Coulton, G. G. *The Friars and the Dead Weight of Tradition, 1200–1400 A.D.* Vol. 2 of *Five Centuries of Religion.* Cambridge: Cambridge University Press, 1927.

——. *Friar's Lantern.* London: J. Clarke, 1906.

——. "The Interpretation of Visitation Documents." *English Historical Review* 29, no. 113 (1914): 16–40.

——. *Ten Medieval Studies.* Cambridge: The University Press, 1930.

Cuillieron, Monique. "Un concile de réformation: Le concile rouennais de 1231." *Revue historique de droit français et étranger* 61, no. 3 (1983): 345–69.

Cusato, Michael F. "Hermitage or Marketplace? The Search for an Authentic Franciscan Locus in the World." *Spirit and Life* 10 (2000): 1–30.

Dalarun, Jacques. *François d'Assise ou le pouvoir en question: Principes et modalités du gouvernement dans l'ordre des Frères mineurs.* Paris: DeBoeck Université, 1999.

Darlington, Oscar G. "The Travels of Odo Rigaud, Archbishop of Rouen (1248–1275)." Ph.D. dissertation, University of Pennsylvania, Philadelphia, 1940.

d'Avray, David. *The Preaching of Friars: Sermons Diffused from Paris before 1300.* Oxford: Oxford University Press, 1985.

Davy, M. M. *Les sermons universitaires parisiens de 1230–1231.* Paris: J. Vrin, 1931.

de Beaurepaire, Charles, and J. J. Vernier. *Inventaire-sommaire des Archives départementales antérieures à 1790, Seine-Inférieure, Archives Ecclésiastiques—Série G.* 7 vols. in 9. Paris: Imprimerie et librairie administratives de P. Dupont, 1868–1912.

de Fréville, R. "Étude sur l'organisation judiciare en Normandie aux XIIe et XIIIe siècles." *Nouvelle revue historique de droit français et étranger* 36 (1912): 681–736.

de la Marche, Lecoy. *La chaire française au moyen âge.* Paris: Renouard, 1886.

Delisle, Léopold. "Le clergé normand au XIIIe siècle." *Bibliothèque de l'École des Chartes,* 2nd ser., 3 (1846): 479–99.

Delmaire, Bernard. *Le diocèse d'Arras de 1093 au milieu du XIVe siècle: Recherches sur la vie religieuse dans le nord de la France au moyen âge.* Arras: Commission départementale d'histoire et d'archéologie du Pas-de-Calais, 1994.

de Tribolet, M. "La rente urbaine à Genève au XIIIe siècle." *Bibliothèque de l'École des Chartes* 133 (1975): 5–20.

Devailly, Guy. "Les patronats d'église en Normandie aux XIIIe et XIVe siècles." In *Recueil d'études en hommage à Lucien Musset.* Cahiers des Annales de Normandie, no. 23, 351–59. Caen: Annales de Normandie, 1990.

Devailly, Guy, ed. *Le diocèse de Bourges.* Paris: Letouzey and Ané, 1973.

Dobiache-Rojdestvensky, Olga. *La vie paroissiale en France au XIIIe siècle d'après les actes épiscopaux.* Paris: A. Picard, 1911.

Dod, Bernard G. "Aristoteles latinus." In *The Cambridge History of Later Medieval Philosophy: From the Rediscovery of Aristotle to the Disintegration of Scholasticism, 1100–1600,* edited by Norman Kretzmann, Anthony Kenny, and Jan Pinborg, 45–79. 1982. Reprint, Cambridge: Cambridge University Press, 1989.

Doucet, Victorin. "Alessandro di Hales." *Enciclopedia Cattolica* 1 (1948): 784–87.

——. "Maîtres Franciscains de Paris." *Archivum Franciscanum Historicum* 27 (1934): 531–64.

Douie, Decima L. *Archbishop Pecham.* Oxford: Clarendon Press, 1952.

Dubois, Henri. "La hiérarchie des paroisses dans le diocèse de Coutances au moyen âge." In *Villages et villageois au moyen âge.* Société des historiens médiévistes de l'enseignement supérieur public, 21e Congrès, Caen, juin 1990. Paris: Publications de la Sorbonne, 1992.

——. "Patronage et revenu ecclésiastique en Normandie au XIIIe siècle." In *Papauté, monachisme et théories politiques: Études d'histoire médiévale offertes à Marcel Pacaut.* Vol. 2, *Les églises locales,* edited by P. Guichard, M.-T. Lorcin, J.-M. Poisson, and M.

Rubellin, 461–71. Lyon: Centre interuniversitaire d'histoire et d'archéologie médiévales, Presses universitaires de Lyon, 1994.

Dufeil, Michel-Marie. *Guillaume de Saint-Amour et la polémique universitaire parisienne, 1250–1259.* Paris: A. & J. Picard, 1972.

Dumont, S. D. "Time, Contradiction, and Freedom of the Will." *Documenti e studi sulla tradizione filosofica medievale* 3, no. 2 (1992): 561–97.

Dunbabin, Jean. *Charles I of Anjou: Power, Kingship, and State-Making in Thirteenth-Century Europe.* London: Longman, 1998.

——. "Jacques Le Goff and the Intellectuals." In *The Work of Jacques of Le Goff and the Challenges of Medieval History*, edited by Miri Rubin, 157–67. Woodbridge, Suffolk, U.K.: Boydell Press, 1997.

Edwards, Kathleen. *The English Secular Cathedrals in the Middle Ages: A Constitutional Study with Special Reference to the Fourteenth Century.* 2nd ed. New York: Barnes & Noble, 1967.

Finch, Andrew. "The Disciplining of the Laity in Late Medieval Normandy." *French History* 10, no. 2 (1996): 163–81.

Floquet, Amable. *Histoire de privilège de Saint Romain.* 2 vols. Rouen: Le Grand, 1883.

Foreville, Raymonde. "La réception des conciles généraux dans l'église et la province de Rouen au XIIIe siècle." In *Gouvernement et vie de l'église au moyen-âge*, 243–53. London: Variorum Reprints, 1979.

——. "Les statuts synodaux et le renouveau pastoral du XIIIe siècle dans le Midi de la France." In *Le crédo, la morale et l'inquisition*, 119–50. Cahiers de Fanjeaux, no. 6. Toulouse: Privat, 1971.

——. "The Synod of the Province of Rouen in the Eleventh and Twelfth Centuries." Translated by Geoffrey Martin. In *Church and Government in the Middle Ages: Essays Presented to C. R. Cheney on His Seventieth Birthday*, edited by C. N. L. Brooke, D. E. Luscombe, G. H. Martin, and Dorothy Owens, 19–39. Cambridge: Cambridge University Press, 1976.

Fournier, Edouard. *Les origines du vicaire général.* Paris: A. Picard, 1922.

Fournier, Paul. *Les officialités au moyen âge: Étude sur l'organisation, la compétence et la procédure des tribunaux ecclésiastiques ordinaires en France, de 1180 à 1328.* Paris: E. Plon, 1880.

Foviaux, Jacques. "Les sermons donnés à Laon, en 1242, par le Chanoine Jacques de Troyes, futur Urbain IV." *Recherches Augustiniennes* 20 (1985): 203–56.

Fresneda, F. M. "La ciencia humana de Jesucristo según Odón Rigaldo." *Recherches de théologie ancienne et médiévale* 62 (1995): 157–81.

——. "La plenitud de gracia en Jusucristo según Odón Rigaldo." *Carthaginensia: Revista semestral de estudiose investigación* 4, no. 5 (1988): 45–77.

Gaudemet, Jean. *La collation par le roi de France des bénéfices vacants en régale.* Paris: Leroux, 1935.

——. *Le gouvernement de l'église à l'époque classique.* Part 2: *Le gouvernement local.* Vol. 8 of *Histoire du droit et des institutions de l'église en occident.* Edited by Gabriel Le Bras and Jean Gaudemet. Paris: Éditions Cujas, 1979.

——. "Un règlement pour l'administration de la justice d'église dans la province de Reims au XIIIe siècle: La constitution 'Romana Ecclesia.' " In *Administration et droit: Actes des Journées de la Société internationale d'histoire du droit, tenues à Rennes, les 26, 27, 28 mai 1994*, edited by François Burdeau, 29–39. Paris: L.G.D.J., 1996.

Gavrilovitch, Michel. *Étude sur le traité de Paris de 1259.* Bibliothèque de l'École des Hautes Études, no. 125. Paris: Librairie Emile Bouillon, 1899.

Génestal, Robert. "La patrimonialité de l'archidiaconat dans la province ecclésiastique de Rouen." In *Mélanges Paul Fournier*, 285–91. Paris: Recueil Sirey, 1929.

———. *Le privilegium fori en France du Décret de Gratien à la fin du XIVe siècle*. Bibliothèque de l'École des Hautes Études, Science Religieuses, vol. 35. Paris, 1924.

———. *Le rôle des monastères comme établissements de crédit en Normandie du XIe à la fin du XIIIe siècle*. Paris: Rousseau, 1901.

Gibbs, Marion, and Jane Lang. *Bishops and Reform, 1215–1272*. London: Oxford University Press, 1934.

Glorieux, P. "L'enseignement au moyen âge: Techniques et méthodes en usage à la faculté de théologie de Paris, au XIIIe siècle." *Archives d'histoire doctrinale et littéraire du moyen âge* 43 (1968): 65–186.

———. *Répertoire des maîtres en théologie de Paris au XIIIe siècle*. 2 vols. Paris: J. Vrin, 1934.

Gorsuch, Edwin N. "Mismanagement and Ecclesiastical Visitation of English Monasteries in the Early Fourteenth Century." *Traditio* 28 (1972): 473–82.

Grant, Lindy. *Architecture and Society in Normandy, 1120–1270*. New Haven: Yale University Press, 2005.

Gratien de Paris. *Histoire de la fondation et de l'évolution de l'Ordre des frères mineurs au XIIIe siècle*. Gembloux: Duculot, 1928.

Grundmann, Herbert. "Sacerdotium-Regnum-Studium: Zur Wertung des Wissenschaft im 13. Jahrhundert." *Archiv für Kulturgeschichte* 34 (1952): 5–21.

Guyotjeannin, Olivier. *Episcopus et comes: Affirmation et declin de la seigneurie épiscopale au nord du royaume de France (Beauvais-Noyon, Xe–XIIIe siècle)*. Geneva: Librairie Droz, 1987.

———. "Juridiction gracieuse ecclésiastique et naissance de l'officialité à Beauvais (1175–1220)." In *À propos des actes d'évêques: Hommage à Lucie Fossier*, edited by Michel Parisse, 295–310. Nancy: Presses Universitaires de Nancy, 1991.

———. "Les reliques de Saint Éloi à Noyon: Procès et enquêtes du milieu du XIIIe siècle." *Revue Mabillon* n.s. 1 (1990): 57–110.

Haines, Roy Martin. *Archbishop John Stratford: Political Revolutionary and Champion of the Liberties of the English Church, ca. 1275/80–1348*. Toronto: University of Toronto Press, 1986.

Hanska, Jussi. *"And the Rich Man also died; and He was buried in Hell": The Social Ethos in Mendicant Sermons*. Helsinki: Suomen Historiallinen Seura, 1997.

Haskins, Charles Homer. "Formulary of the Officialité of Rouen." In *Mélanges Paul Fournier*, 359–62. Paris: Recueil Sirey, 1929.

Heale, Martin. *The Dependent Priories of Medieval English Monasteries*. Woodbridge, Suffolk, U.K.: Boydell Press, 2004.

Henquinet, F. M. "Les manuscrits et l'influence des écrits théologiques d'Eudes Rigaud, O.F.M." *Recherches de théologie ancienne et médiévale* 11 (October 1939): 324–50.

Hill, Rosalind. "Bishop Sutton and the Institution of Heads of Religious Houses in the Diocese of Lincoln." *English Historical Review* 58 (1943): 324–50.

Hourlier, Jacques. *L'âge classique, 1140–1378: Les religieux*. Vol. 10 of *Histoire du droit et des institutions de l'église en occident*, edited by Gabriel Le Bras. Paris: Éditions Cujas, 1974.

Howell, Margaret. *Regalian Right in Medieval England*. London: Athlone Press, 1962.

Huber, R. M. "Alexander of Hales, O.F.M. (ca. 1170–1245): His Life and Influence on Medieval Scholasticism." *Franciscan Studies* 26, no. 4 (1945): 353–65.

Jansen, Philippe. ''Benvenuto Scotivoli, évêque d'Osimo (1264–1282), prélat combatif ou saint réformateur?" In *Les prélats, l'église et la société, XIe–XVe siècles: Hommage à Bernard Guillemain,* edited by Françoise Bériac, 49–57. Bordeaux: Université Michel de Montaigne, CROCEMC, 1994.

Johnson, Penelope. *Equal in Monastic Profession: Religious Women in Medieval France.* Chicago: University of Chicago Press, 1991.

Jordan, William Chester. "Archbishop Eudes Rigaud and the Jews of Normandy, 1248–1275." In *Friars and Jews in the Middle Ages and Renaissance,* edited by Steven J. McMichael and Susan E. Myers, 39–52. Leiden: Brill, 2004.

——. "The Cistercian Nunnery of La Cour Notre-Dame de Michery: A House That Failed." *Revue Bénédictine* 95 (1985): 311–20.

——. *Louis IX and the Challenge of the Crusade: A Study in Rulership.* Princeton: Princeton University Press, 1979.

——. *Two Fourteenth-Century Fiscal Accounts of the Benedictine Abbey of Saint-Pierre-le-Vif of Sens.* Vol. 1 of *Fra spazio e tempo: Studi in onore di Luigi de Rosa,* edited by Ilaria Zilli, 535–44. Naples: Edizioni Scientifiche Italiane, 1995.

——. *Unceasing Strife, Unending Fear: Jacques de Thérines and the Freedom of the Church in the Age of the Last Capetians.* Princeton: Princeton University Press, 2005.

Jouen, Léon Alfred. *Comptes, devis et inventaires du manoir archiépiscopal de Rouen.* Paris: Rover, A. Picard, 1908.

Kaeuper, R. W. *Bankers to the Crown: The Riccardi of Lucca and Edward I.* Princeton: Princeton University Press, 1973.

Kay, Richard. "Mansi and Rouen: A Critique of the Conciliar Collections." In *Councils and Clerical Culture in the Medieval West,* 157–85. Aldershot, Hampshire, U.K.: Variorum, 1997.

——. "Romanus and Rouen: A Papal Legate's Tainted Visitation in 1227." *Annales de Normandie* 5, no. 2 (2001): 111–18.

Kaye, Joel. *Economy and Nature in the Fourteenth Century: Money, Market Exchange, and the Emergence of Scientific Thought.* Cambridge: Cambridge University Press, 1998.

Kittell, Ellen E. *From Ad Hoc to Routine: A Case Study in Medieval Bureaucracy.* Philadelphia: University of Pennsylvania Press, 1991.

Knowles, David. *The Religious Orders in England.* 3 vols. Cambridge: Cambridge University Press, 1948.

Knox, Lezlie. "Audacious Nuns: Institutionalizing the Franciscan Order of Saint Clare." *Church History* 69, 1 (2000): 41–62.

Lambert, Malcolm D. *Franciscan Poverty: The Doctrine of the Absolute Poverty of Christ and the Apostles in the Franciscan Order, 1210–1323.* Saint Bonaventure, N.Y.: Franciscan Institute, St. Bonaventure University, 1998.

Landau, Peter. *Die Entstehung des kanonischen Infamiebegriffs von Gratian bis zur Glossa Ordinaria.* Cologne: Böhlau-Verlag, 1966.

Landini, L. C. *The Causes of the Clericalization of the Order of Friars Minor, 1209–1260, in the Light of the Early Franciscan Sources.* Chicago: Pontifical Universitas Gregoriana, Facultas Historiae Ecclesiasticae, 1968.

Langholm, Odd Inge. *Economics in the Medieval Schools: Wealth, Exchange, Value, Money, and Usury According to the Paris Theological Tradition, 1200–1350.* Leiden: Brill, 1992.

Langlois, Ch.-V. "Sermons parisiens de la première moitié du XIIIe s., contenus dans le ms. 691 de la bibliothèque d'Arras." *Journal des savants* 14 (1916): 488–94, 548–59.

Laporte, Jean, and Charles de Beaurepaire, eds. *Dictionnaire topographique du département de Seine-Maritime.* 2 vols. Paris: Bibliothèque Nationale, 1982–84.

Laquer, Erika J. "Ritual, Literacy, and Documentary Evidence: Archbishop Eudes Rigaud and the Relics of St. Eloi." *Francia* 13 (1985): 625–37.

Lavacry, Stéphanie. "L'archevêque Eudes Rigaud et les abbayes et prieurés normands." Master's thesis, University of Rouen, 1998.

Lawrence, C. H. *The Friars: The Impact of the Early Mendicant Movement on Western Society.* London: Longman, 1994.

Lear, Jonathan. *Aristotle: The Desire to Understand.* Cambridge: Cambridge University Press, 1988.

Leclercq, Jean. "Disciplina." *Dictionnaire de spiritualité* 3 (1957): cols. 1291–1302.

Lefebvre-Teillard, Anne. *Les officialités à la veille du concile de Trente.* Paris: R. Pichon et R. Durand-Auzias, 1973.

Le Goff, Jacques. "Le dossier des mendiants." In *1274: Année charnière: Actes du colloque international, Lyon-Paris, 30 septembre–5 octobre, 1974,* 211–22. Paris, CNRS, 1977.

———. *Intellectuals in the Middle Ages.* Translated by Teresa Lavender Fagan. Oxford: Blackwell, 1993.

———. *Saint Francis of Assisi.* Translated by Christine Rhone. London: Routledge, 2004.

———. *Saint Louis.* Paris: Gallimard, 1996.

Lemarignier, Jean-François, Jean Gaudemet, and Guillaume Mollat. *Institutions ecclésiastiques.* Vol. 3 of *Histoires des institutions françaises au moyen âge.* Edited by Ferdinand Lot and Robert Fawtier. Paris: Presses Universitaires de France, 1962.

Little, Lester K. "Saint Louis' Involvement with the Friars." *Church History* 33, no. 2 (1964): 125–48.

Longère, Jean. "Les évêques et l'administration du sacrement de pénitence au XIIIe siècle: Les cas réservés." In *Papauté, monachisme et théories politiques,* vol. 2, *Les églises locales,* 537–50. Lyon: Centre interuniversitaire d'histoire et d'archéologie médiévales, Presses universitaires de Lyon, 1994.

Lottin, Odon. *Psychologie et morale aux XII et XIIIe siècles.* 6 vols. in 8. Louvain: Abbaye du Mont César, 1942–60.

Lucet, Bernard. "Les ordinations chez les Cisterciens: Témoignage d'Eudes Rigaud pour la Normandie." *Analecta Sacri Ordinis Cisterciensis* 10 (1954): 268–301.

Lynch, Joseph H. *Simoniacal Entry into Religious Life from 1000 to 1260: A Social, Economic, and Legal Study.* Columbus: Ohio State University Press, 1976.

Lynch, Kilian F. "The Alleged Fourth Book on the Sentences of Odo Rigaud and Related Documents." *Franciscan Studies* 9, no. 11 (1949): 87–145.

Maddicott, J. R. *Simon de Montfort.* Cambridge: Cambridge University Press, 1994.

Maier, Christoph T. *Preaching the Crusades: Mendicant Friars and the Cross in the Thirteenth Century.* Cambridge: Cambridge University Press, 1994.

Mäkinen, Virpi. *Property Rights in the Late Medieval Discussion on Franciscan Poverty.* Leuven: Peeters, 2001.

Mansfield, Mary. *The Humiliation of Sinners: Public Penance in Thirteenth-Century France.* Ithaca: Cornell University Press, 1995.

Marrou, H.-I. "'Doctrina' et 'Disciplina' dans la langue des pères de l'église." *Bulletin du Cange* 9 (1934): 5–25.

Matthew, Donald. *The Norman Monasteries and Their English Possessions.* London: Oxford University Press, 1962.

McNamara, JoAnn Kay. *Sisters in Arms: Catholic Nuns through Two Millennia.* Cambridge, Mass.: Harvard University Press, 1996.

Ménindès, R. "Eudes Rigaud, Frère Mineur." *Revue d'histoire Franciscaine* 8 (1931): 157–78.

Miller, Maureen C. *The Bishop's Palace: Architecture and Authority in Medieval Italy.* Ithaca: Cornell University Press, 2000.

Millet, Hélène. *I canonici al servizio della stato in Europa, secoli XIII–XVI.* Modena, 1992.

———. *Les chanoines du chapitre cathédral de Laon, 1272–1412.* Paris: École Française de Rome, 1982.

Mollat, G. "Bénéfices ecclésiastiques en occident: Le régime de droit commun, des origines au Concordat de Vienne (1448)." *Dictionnaire de droit canonique* 2 (1937): cols. 406–49.

Mollat, Michel, and François J. Gay. *Histoire de Rouen.* Toulouse: Privat, 1979.

Montaubin, Pascal. "Les chapitres cathédraux séculiers de Normandie et la centralisation pontificale au XIIIe siècle." In *Chapitres et cathédrales en Normandie,* edited by Sylvette Lemagnen and Philippe Manneville, 253–72. Caen: Musée de Normandie, 1997.

Moorman, John R. H. *Church Life in England in the Thirteenth Century.* Cambridge: University Press, 1955.

Mulchahey, M. Michèle. *"First the bow is bent in study": Dominican Education before 1350.* Toronto: Pontifical Institute of Mediaeval Studies, 1998.

Murray, Alexander. "Archbishop and Mendicants in Thirteenth-Century Pisa." In *Stellung und Wirksamkeit der Bettelorden in der städtischen Gesellschaft,* edited by Kaspar Elm, 19–75. Berlin: Duncker and Humblot, 1981.

Musset, Lucien. "Essai sur les vignobles des monastères normands (Xe–XIIIe siècles)." *Cahiers Léopold Delisle,* special issue (1978): 231–44.

———. "Monachisme d'époque franque et monachisme d'époque ducale en Normandie: Le problème de la continuité." In *Aspects du monachisme en Normandie (IVe–XVIIIe siècles): Actes du colloque scientifique de "l'Année des Abbayes Normandes," Caen, 18–20 octobre 1979,* edited by Lucien Musset, 55–74. Paris: Librairie Philosophique J. Vrin, 1982.

Nimmo, Duncan. *Reform and Division in the Medieval Franciscan Order: From Saint Francis to the Foundation of the Capuchins.* Rome: Capuchin Historical Institute, 1987.

Noonan, John T. *The Scholastic Analysis of Usury.* Cambridge, Mass.: Harvard University Press, 1957.

Nortier, Geneviève. *Les bibliothèques médiévales des abbayes Bénédictines de Normandie.* Paris: Lethielleux, 1971.

Oguejiofor, J. Obi. *The Arguments for the Immortality of the Soul in the First Half of the Thirteenth Century.* Leuven: Peeters, 1995.

Oliger, Paul Remy. *Les évêques réguliers: Recherche sur leur condition juridique depuis les origines du monachisme jusqu'à la fin du moyen-âge.* Paris: Deselée de Brouwer, 1958.

Paul, Jacques. "Les religieux mendiants évêques en France au XIIIe siècle." In *Dal pulpito alla cattedra: I vescovi degli ordini mendicanti nel '200 e nel primo '300; Atti del XXVII Convegno internazionale, Assisi, 14–16 ottobre 1999.* Spoleto, Centro italiano di studi sull'alto Medioevo, 2000.

Pelikan, Jaroslav. *The Christian Tradition: A History of the Development of Doctrine.* 5 vols. Chicago: University of Chicago Press, 1971–83.

Pennington, Kenneth. *Pope and Bishops: The Papal Monarchy in the Twelfth and Thirteenth Centuries.* Philadelphia: University of Pennsylvania Press, 1984.

Petit-Dutaillis, Charles. "Querimoniae Normannorum." In *Essays in Medieval History Presented to Thomas Frederick Tout,* edited by A. G. Little and F. M. Powicke, 99–118. Manchester, 1925.

Petot, Pierre. "La constitution de rente aux XIIe et XIIIe siècles dans les pays coutumiers." In *Mélanges,* edited by A. Boutaric, Georges Auguste Albert Connes, Pierre Petot, and Louis Stouff, 59–81. Dijon: A. Picard, 1928.

Picó, Fernando. "The Bishops of France in the Reign of Louis IX (1226–1270)." Ph.D. dissertation, Johns Hopkins University, 1970.

Pixton, Paul B. *The German Episcopacy and the Implementation of the Decrees of the Fourth Lateran Council, 1216–1245: Watchmen on the Tower.* Leiden: Brill, 1995.

Pobst, Phyllis E. "Visitation of Religious and Clergy by Archbishop Eudes Rigaud of Rouen." In *Religion, Text, and Society in Medieval Spain and Northern Europe: Essays in Honor of J. N. Hillgarth,* edited by Thomas E. Burman, Mark D. Meyerson, and Leah Shopkow, 223–49. Toronto: Pontifical Institute of Mediaeval Studies, 2002.

Pommeraye, Jean-François. *Histoire des archevesques de Rouen.* Rouen: Laurens Maurry, 1667.

Potts, Cassandra. *Monastic Revival and Regional Identity in Early Normandy.* Woodbridge, Suffolk, U.K.: Boydell Press, 1997.

Powicke, F. M. "The Archbishop of Rouen, John de Harcourt, and Simon de Montfort in 1260." *English Historical Review* 51, no. 201 (1936): 108–13.

Quaglioni, Diego. "Riflessi ecclesiologici e canonistici dell'ascesa dei frati alle cattedre vescovili." In *Dal pulpito alla cattedra: I vescovi degli ordini mendicanti nel '200 e nel primo '300; Atti del XXVII Convegno internazionale, Assisi, 14–16 ottobre 1999.* Spoleto, Centro italiano di studi sull'alto Medioevo, 2000.

Rawcliffe, Carole. *Medicine for the Soul: The Life, Death, and Resurrection of an English Medieval Hospital, St. Giles's, Norwich, c. 1249–1550.* Stroud: Sutton, 1999.

Renouard, Yves. "Routes, étapes et vitesses de marche de France à Rome au XIIIe et au XIVe siècles d'après les itinéraires d'Eudes Rigaud (1254) et de Barthélemy Bonis (1350)." In *Studi in onore di Amintore Fanfani nel venticinquennio di cattedra universitaria,* 6 vols. 3:404–28. Milan, 1962.

Renoux, Annie. "Palais princiers, royaux et épiscopaux normanno-angevins (Xe–XIIIe siècles)." In *Cavalieri alla conquista del sud: Studi sull'Italia normanna in memoria di Léon-Robert Ménager,* edited by Errico Cuozzo and Jean-Marie Martin, 23–56. Rome: Editori Laterza, 1998.

Richard, Charles. "Le clergé de Normandie au XIIIe siècle d'après le Journal des visites pastorales d'Eudes Rigaud." *Revue de Rouen et de Normandie* 30 (March–June 1848): 155–72, 216–27, 268–74, 343–61.

Richard, Jean. *The Crusades, c. 1071–c. 1291.* Translated by Jean Birrell. Cambridge: Cambridge University Press, 1999.

——. *Saint Louis: Roi d'une France féodale, soutien de la terre sainte.* Paris: Fayard, 1983.

Rodes, Robert E., Jr. *Ecclesiastical Administration in Medieval England: The Anglo-Saxons to the Reformation.* Notre Dame, Ind.: University of Notre Dame Press, 1977.

Roest, Bert. *A History of Franciscan Education (c. 1210–1517).* Leiden: Brill, 2000.

Rouse, R. H., and M. A. Rouse. "Biblical Distinctions in the Thirteenth Century." *Archives d'histoire doctrinale et littéraire du moyen âge* 49 (1974): 27–37.

Rubin, Miri. *Charity and Community in Medieval Cambridge.* Cambridge: Cambridge University Press, 1987.

Sadourny, Alain. "Les rentes à Rouen au XIIIe siècle." *Annales de Normandie* 21, no. 2 (1971): 99–108.

Sanders, I. J. "The Texts of the Peace of Paris, 1259." *English Historical Review* 66, 258 (1951): 81–97.

Sauvage, R. N. *Histoire et développement économique d'un monastère normand au moyen âge: L'abbaye de Saint-Martin de Troarn au diocèse de Bayeux des origines au seizième siècle.* Caen, 1911.

Schnapper, Bernard. *Les rentes au XVIe siècle: Histoire d'un instrument de crédit.* Paris: SEVPEN, 1957.

——. "Les rentes chez les théologiens et les canonistes du XIIIe au XVIe siècle." *Études d'histoire du droit canonique* 2 (1965): 965–95.

Schneyer, J.-B. *Repertorium der lateinischen Sermones des Mittelalters für die Zeit von 1150–1350.* 11 vols. Münster-Westfalen: Aschendorffsche Verlagsbuchhandlung, 1969–90.

Schriber, Carolyn. "Eudes Rigaud and the Monasteries of Normandy." *Locus* 6, no. 1 (1993): 53–71.

Sileo, Leonardo. "Dalla *lectio* alla *disputatio.* Le questioni *De modo essendi Dei in creaturis, De existentia rerum in Deo* e *De voluntate Dei* di Odo Rigaldi." In *Editori di Quaracchi: 100 anni dopo bilancio e prospettive: Atti del colloquio internazionale, Roma 29–30 maggio 1995,* edited by Alvaro Cacciotti and Barbara Faes de Mottoni, 109–31. Rome: Edizioni Antonianum, 1997.

——. "Rigaud." *Dictionnaire de spiritualité* 13 (1988): cols. 670–74.

Sivéry, Gérard. *L'économie du royaume de France au siècle de Saint Louis.* Lille: Presses Universitaires de Lille, 1984.

Smalley, Beryl. *The Gospels in the Schools, c. 1100–c. 1280.* London: Hambledon Press, 1985.

Smith, David M. *Guide to Bishops' Registers of England and Wales: A Survey from the Middle Ages to the Abolition of Episcopacy in 1646.* London: Offices of the Royal Historical Society, University College, 1981.

Smith, Jeremiah J. *The Attitude of John Pecham toward Monastic Houses under His Jurisdiction.* Washington, D.C.: Catholic University of America Press, 1949.

Snape, R. H. *English Monastic Finances in the Later Middle Ages.* Cambridge: University Press, 1926.

Southern, R. W. *Western Society and the Church in the Middle Ages.* Harmondsworth, U.K.: Penguin Books, 1970.

Spear, David S. "Les archidiacres de Rouen au cours de la période ducale." *Annales de Normandie* 34 (1984): 15–50.

——. "Membership in the Norman Cathedral Chapters during the Ducal Period: Some Preliminary Findings." *Medieval Prosopography* 5, no. 1 (1984): 1–18.

Steenberghen, F. van. *The Philosophical Movement in the Thirteenth Century.* Edinburgh: Nelson, 1955.

Srawley, J. H. "Grosseteste's Administration of the Diocese of Lincoln." In *Robert Grosseteste: Scholar and Bishop,* edited by D. A. Callus, 146–77. Oxford: Clarendon Press, 1955.

Strayer, Joseph Reese. *The Administration of Normandy under Saint Louis.* Cambridge, Mass.: Mediaeval Academy of America, 1932.

——. "The Crusades of Louis IX." In *Medieval Statecraft and the Perspectives of History: Essays by Joseph R. Strayer,* 159–92. Princeton: Princeton University Press, 1971.

——. *The Reign of Philip the Fair.* Princeton: Princeton University Press, 1980.

Sutcliffe, Dorothy. "The Financial Condition of the See of Canterbury, 1279–1292." *Speculum* 10, no. 1 (1935): 53–68.

Swanson, Robert N. "Mendicant Bishops in the British Isles in the Thirteenth and Early Fourteenth Centuries." In *Dal pulpito alla cattedra: I vescovi degli ordini mendicanti nel '200 e nel primo '300; Atti del XXVII Convegno internazionale, Assisi, 14–16 ottobre 1999.* Spoleto, Centro italiano di studi sull'alto Medioevo, 2000.

Tabbagh, Vincent. *Le clergé séculier du diocèse de Rouen à la fin du moyen-âge (1359–1493).* Paris: Université de Paris-IV, 1988.

——. *Fasti Ecclesiae Gallicanae: Répertoire prosopographique des évêques, dignitaires et chanoines de France de 1200 à 1500.* Vol. 2, *Diocèse de Rouen.* Turnhout: Brepols, 1998.

——. "Le temporel des archevêques de Rouen aux derniers siècles du moyen-âge." *Journal of Medieval History* 6, no. 2 (1980): 199–218.

Taglia, Kathryn Ann. "'On Account of Scandal . . .': Priests, Their Children, and the Ecclesiastical Demand for Celibacy." *Florilegium* 14 (1995–96): 57–70.

Thompson, A. Hamilton. *The English Clergy and Their Organization in the Later Middle Ages.* Oxford: Clarendon Press, 1947.

Thompson, Michael. *Medieval Bishops' Houses in England and Wales.* Aldershot, Hampshire, U.K.: Ashgate, 1998.

Thomson, Williell R. *Friars in the Cathedral: The First Franciscan Bishops, 1226–1261.* Toronto: Pontifical Institute of Mediaeval Studies, 1975.

Tock, Benoît-Michel. *Une chancellerie épiscopale au XIIe siècle: Le cas d'Arras.* Louvain-la-Neuve: Institut d'études médiévales de l'Université Catholique de Louvain, 1991.

Touati, François-Olivier. *Maladie et société au moyen âge: La lèpre, les lépreux et les léproseries dans la province ecclésiastique de Sens jusqu'au milieu du XIVe siècle.* Brussels: De Boeck, 1998.

Toutain, M.-P. "Sept sermons en quête d'auteur." Master's thesis, Paris IV, 1997.

Townley, Simon. "Unbeneficed Clergy in the Thirteenth Century: Two English Dioceses." In *Studies in Clergy and Ministry in Medieval England,* edited by David M. Smith, 38–64. York: Borthwick Institute of Historical Research, University of York, 1991.

Toynbee, M. R. *S. Louis of Toulouse and the Process of Canonisation in the Fourteenth Century.* Manchester: University Press, 1929.

Trexler, Richard C. *The Christian at Prayer: An Illustrated Prayer Manual Attributed to Peter the Chanter (d. 1197).* Binghamton, N.Y.: Medieval and Renaissance Texts and Studies, 1987.

Trichet, Louis. *Le costume du clergé: Ses origines et son évolution en France d'après les règlements de l'église.* Paris: Cerf, 1986.

Trottmann, Christian. *Théologie et noétique au XIIIe siècle: À la recherche d'un statut.* Paris: Librairie Philosophique J. Vrin, 1999.

Tugwell, Simon. "Humbert de Romans' Material for Preachers." In *De ore Domini: Preacher and Word in the Middle Ages,* edited by Th. Amos, E. A. Green, and B. M. Kienzle, 105–17. Kalamazoo, Mich.: Medieval Institute Publications, 1989.

Tuilier, André. "La renaissance de l'aristotélisme universitaire à Paris au XIIIe siècle." *Mélanges de la Bibliothèque de la Sorbonne* 1 (1980): 7–21.

Turner, Ralph V. "Richard Lionheart and the Episcopate in His French Domains." *French Historical Studies* 21, no. 4 (1998): 517–42.

Ulrich, Laurel Thatcher. *A Midwife's Tale: The Life of Martha Ballard, Based on Her Diary, 1785–1812.* New York: Knopf, 1990.

Verger, Jacques. *L'essor des universités au XIIIe siècle.* Paris: Cerf, 1997.

——. "Studia et universités." In *Le scuole degli ordini mendicanti (secoli XIII–XIV),* 173–204. Centro di Studi sulla Spiritualità Medievale. Todi: Presso Accademia Tudertina, 1978.

Viollet, Paul. "Les Coutumiers de Normandie." *Histoire littéraire de la France* 33 (1906): 43–65.

von Moos, Peter. "Die Trostschrift des Vincenz von Beauvais für Ludwig IX: Vorstudie zur Motiv und Geistesgeschichte der *consolatio.*" *Mittellateinisches Jahrbuch* 4 (1967): 173–218.

Wei, Ian. "The Self-Image of the Masters of Theology at the University of Paris in the

Late Thirteenth and Early Fourteenth Centuries." *Journal of Ecclesiastical History* 46, no. 3 (1995): 398–431.

Wood, Rega. "Distinct Ideas and Perfect Solicitude: Alexander of Hales, Richard Rufus, and Odo Rigaldus." *Franciscan Studies* 53 (1993): 7–46.

Wright, Craig. *Music and Ceremony at Notre Dame of Paris, 500–1550*. Cambridge: Cambridge University Press, 1989.

Yver, Jean. *Les contrats dans le très ancien droit normand (XIe–XIIIe siècles)*. Caen: Domfront, 1926.

——. "Le 'Très ancien coutumier' de Normandie, miroir de la législation ducale? Contribution à l'étude de l'ordre public normand à la fin du XIIe siècle." *Revue d'histoire du droit* 39, no. 3 (1971): 333–74.

Index

abbots. *See* monasteries, superiors of
Abelard, Peter, 176
Adam de Verneuil, 30
Adam of Eynsham, *Life of Saint Hugh of Lincoln*, 146
administration, 4, 13, 36, 37, 63, 79, 177–179; royal, 5, 10, 11, 38, 106, 237n14. *See also* finances
advowson. *See* presentation, right of (advowson)
Agen, bishop of, 167
Albertus Magnus, 16, 27
Alexander III, 106, 131–132
Alexander IV, 115, 119, 136
Alexander of Hales, 15, 16, 17, 22, 23, 191n12, 193n31; *Summa*, 17
Aliermont, 46, 47, 48, 139
Almauricus, 108
Almenèches, nunnery of, 53–54, 76
Alphonse X of Castille, 165
Alphonse, count of Poitiers, 158
Amauri of Montfort, 166
Amaury de Muzy, 30
Amiens, cathedral of, 140
André de St-Léonard, 135
Andrieu-Guitrancourt, Pierre, 6, 158
Angers, 202n68; diocese of, 73; synod of, 112
Anglo-French Treaty of 1259, 164–166
Anglo-French wars, 94
Angreville, 150–151
appellate jurisdiction. *See* jurisdiction
archbishop(s), 5, 49, 50, 58, 62, 130
archdeacon(s), 29, 52, 57, 123, 125; and ER, 5, 9, 36–39, 105; visitations by, 63, 64, 86, 112

Aristotle, 13, 14, 15, 21, 197n107; *Nicomachean Ethics*, 26
Arnoux, Mathieu, 66
Auffay, priory of, 90
Augustine, St., 15, 22, 155
Augustine, St., Rule of, 76, 81
Augustinians, 65, 171; and bishops, 69; and ER, 73, 89, 97–98, 99–100; ordination of, 105; and patronage, 106; and secular clergy, 66
Aumale, abbey of, 78, 97
Avranches, 33; bishop of, 52, 53, 56–57, 60

bailli(s): authority of, 131, 132, 133, 134, 136; and ER, 141; rotation of, 38; and Rouen archbishops, 158
Barrier, Guillaume le, 152
Baudemont, church at, 164
Bayeux, 33, 61; bishop of, 52, 56–57, 60, 62
Beaulieu, priory of, 89, 93, 95, 108
Beaumont-le-Roger, priory of, 98–99
Beauvais, 201n65; archdeacon of, 142; cathedral of, 140; diocese of, 106
Bellencombre, châtelain of, 100
Benedict XII, 55–56
Benedict, St., Rule of, 8, 76, 79, 217n207
Benedictines, 65, 66, 67–68, 79, 90, 99, 100
benefice(s), 104; of ER's canons, 36; and nonresidence, 115–116; and patronage, 106, 107, 108, 109–110, 111, 112; Peter the Chanter on, 19; in polyptych/census book, 107; reversion of, 124; suspension of, 114, 117–118, 119, 125, 141. *See also* finances
Bériou, Nicole, 12
Bernard of Bessa, 7